GRITS

*Christina
McCall-Newman*

GRITS

An Intimate Portrait of
The Liberal Party

MACMILLAN OF CANADA
A Division of Gage Publishing Limited
Toronto, Canada

Macmillan of Canada
A Division of Gage Publishing Limited

Canadian Cataloguing in Publication Data

McCall-Newman, Christina,. date
  Grits

Bibliography: p.
Includes index.
ISBN -7715-9573-5

1. Liberal Party of Canada.   I. Title.

JL197.L5M32   324.27106   C82-095057-2

Printed in the United States of America

CONTENTS

This book is for
STEPHEN HUGH ELLIOTT CLARKSON
It is dedicated with love and admiration

FOREWORD

Lord knows the Liberals should have been ready for the election of 1979 when it was finally called on March 26 that year. They had been preparing for it for more than eighteen months — talking tactics, revising strategies, recruiting candidates, raising funds — and using all the wiles at their command to make sure the odds were in their favour.

When they got right down to the moment, though, the old hands among the Grits were full of foreboding. Since 1921, the Liberals had been out of office federally in Canada for only two protracted periods, from 1930 to 1935, and from 1957 to 1963, when the Conservatives had managed to wrest power from their grasp. But this time their popularity in the country was so seriously eroded that political analysts were predicting the election could mark the end not just of the Trudeau régime but of the Liberal era.

Provincially, the party held only the government of Prince Edward Island, a situation made more dismaying by the fact that when the 1970s began six out of the ten provinces had boasted Liberal administrations. Federally, the Grits were still in possession of all the advantages that more than half a century of only rarely interrupted power had bequeathed them: the smoothest patronage system this side of Suez, the organizational savvy, the media-manipulation techniques, the governmental managerial experience, and above all the deep collective confidence that great and continuing success endows. But they were burdened also with great disadvantages: bad economic times throughout the Western world which had seen the value of the Canadian dollar fall towards record lows over the previous eighteen months and inflation and unemployment continue to rise; regional conflicts shaking the historic French-English entente on which their power had been based for more than eighty years; a weak, demoralized cabinet; a swollen, confused bureaucracy; and a controversial leader in Prime Minister Pierre Elliott Trudeau.

Certainly the perils ahead were clear in the minds of the six men who would have the greatest effect on the electorate's perceptions of the Liberal Party in the fight to come: Trudeau himself; Keith Davey and Marc Lalonde, his campaign co-chairmen; James Coutts, his principal secretary and political alter ego; Michael Pitfield, the secretary of his cabinet; and John Turner, his former minister of finance and continuing rival for the party's leadership and loyalty.

To anyone who knew their personal histories, they made a distinctly odd sextet: six disparate men whose ambitions were bound to the same beleaguered institution. For nearly two years they had been arguing fiercely about the timing and probable outcome of this election, and at the precise hour, 8:30 in the evening, when the decision to go to the country was made official at last, all six men were suffering from the accumulated tensions of that protracted build-up; Trudeau walking up the winding driveway of Rideau Hall in Ottawa on his way to inform the Governor General of his decision to go to the country; Pitfield waiting inside to conduct the official ceremony involved; Davey listening distractedly to the proceedings in the Senate's Red Chamber downtown; Coutts in the Prime Minister's Office in the Parliament Buildings standing by the phone to hear the word from Rideau Hall so that he could inform the party's House Leader that the time had come to dissolve Parliament; Lalonde preparing to set in motion the Quebec electoral machine; and Turner, the prince in exile in Toronto, countering the complaints of party dissidents (*If only you were the leader, John, we wouldn't be in this mess*) with evasions of his own (*I'm not sure anybody could turn this one around*).

One of the most dramatic periods in the Liberal Party's long, turbulent history was drawing to a close. And another was about to begin.

PART ONE

KEITH DAVEY AND THE POLITICS OF JOY
The Liberal Party, 1957–1965

KEITH DAVEY WAS RESTLESS in the Senate chamber only partly because he was anxious to get on with directing the election campaign that could officially begin as soon as the ceremonial exchange taking place at Rideau Hall was over. The truth was that the Senate's business usually bored him, however important the occasion. He had always seen himself as a dynamite guy who liked to be at the centre of the action, and despite his predilection for putting the best face on every situation, he had difficulty pretending the Senate was a centre of anything but political payoffs, no matter how hard the other men enclosed in its warm red womb might try to kid themselves.

Still, he loved having the title Senator and he used it constantly in his daily life. "I'm Senator Davey," he would say to young secretaries and small children and they would gaze back at him round-eyed with respect. Headwaiters in expensive restaurants would leap to greet him when he came in for lunch, calling him "Senator" repeatedly as they tendered their leatherbound menu cards, and Davey would look suitably self-effacing and at the same time pleased.

He loved the title and he even professed to love his fellow senators, taking time to talk to even the most intransigent bores among them when they knocked on the door of his corner office in the Senate wing of the Parliament Buildings. He spent most mornings when he was in Ottawa in that room, three or four days a week, perhaps forty weeks a year, making free phone calls on the government line to his contacts around the country. A big, hefty, handsome man, he looked like an old football player gone to flesh. He had a habit of running a comb through his silvery hair and then brushing off the shoulders of his chalk-striped, navy-blue suit with the breast-pocket handkerchief chosen to match one of the colours in his tie. "Sharp," Davey would say to people whose clothes he admired, "Boy, you look sharp," and sharp was what he always tried to look himself.

For nearly twenty years he had been a familiar figure in the corridors of the Centre Block, moving purposefully up and down the marble staircases and echoing halls, talking non-stop to whoever was with him — a backbencher, a journalist, a Liberal organizer from out of town — mixing new gossip, old anecdotes, quick jokes, and good-natured greetings to other people in passage into a marvellous effluence of hot talk that seemed to eddy in his wake like the exhaust from a fifties Ford.

Davey had been a senator for thirteen years and a Liberal for more than thirty. As co-chairman of the Liberal campaign committee, he was still a dominant figure in federal politics, despite the grumblings heard among Liberals in the last few anxious months about his intellectual weaknesses and his obsolescent campaign techniques. He had reached the pinnacle of his career during the previous federal campaign in 1974 when he engineered for his leader a majority victory in an election whose outcome had been so far from certain that Davey spent the duration suffering from a nervous eczema that turned his large pale hands into rough red paws, a condition that cleared only when he had absorbed the importance of his triumph several weeks after it occurred. Even then, when his life as a political organizer was at its zenith, and his party was hitting new highs in the opinion polls, he had figured it couldn't last. He had been in politics long enough to realize that polls can change almost overnight, unmanageable crises can occur, huge victories can turn into sour defeats, and this year, next year, maybe the year after, another man could wear his laurels as the power behind the PM. Now in March of 1979, five years after that great victory, he knew that in the eyes of many Liberals, particularly those in the restless generation behind him, he was old-guard and, what's worse, old-fashioned. Jim Coutts, the Prime Minister's principal secretary and Davey's former protégé, had more suasion in the party these days than he did. Coutts was the Grit with the smarts, a phrase the Liberals were fond of using in the late seventies, a couple of years after it had become current in New York.

All the same, Davey's favour was still curried in Ottawa, his opinions were sought and his actions assayed by people concerned with the vagaries of politics, from cabinet ministers toiling in their departmental offices to commissionaires gossiping at the

Senate's east door. His power was the power of access. When he
spoke, the Prime Minister was said to listen. Out in the country,
in boardrooms, editorial offices, and riding association meeting-
halls, his name was invoked constantly as a shorthand term for
inside-influence-within-the-Liberal-ascendancy.

It was an essential part of Keith Davey's manner that he dis-
paraged his considerable success while clearly enjoying its mani-
festations, saying over and over again that he was "really just an
ordinary guy who had been lucky". Thirty-five years earlier, when
he was a boy in Toronto, his high school friends had called him
"Beef", and described him as a "kid with personality", which
meant he was not particularly brainy or athletic, but a boy whose
popularity depended on the fact that he was just like everybody
else only more so — high-spirited, good-natured, energetic, and
above all loyal, a boy unfailingly supportive of his friends and
scornful of his enemies. These qualities of heart and mind had
motivated him ever since and were seen — by people who under-
estimated his shrewdness and overestimated his charm — as the
secret of his success.

The election of 1979 that was about to begin was meant to be
Keith Davey's last campaign, the fifth he had run for the Liberal
Party and, in many ways, the most difficult. He had been tuning
the party machine in English Canada for this fight for nearly two
years, and during all the months of hard work, all the sixteen-
hour days devoted to the party's business, all the exhausting
hours of pretending optimism while feeling dismay, he had been
aching to get this election over and won. He was fifty-two years
old and far from rich. He knew very well how precarious was the
position of the political organizer. "You're only as good as your
last campaign" was a favourite among his many aphorisms. And
for this campaign the omens were alarming. The editorialists in
every medium had become increasingly shrill in their condemna-
tion of the Liberal government's management of the country over
the previous five years. The public opinion polls, which Davey
believed in as implicitly as he had in the United Church Sunday-
school texts he had memorized as a child, were showing the Liberals neck-and-neck with the Conservatives in terms of electoral
support. Once the huge Liberal lead in Quebec had been set aside,

the party was trailing badly in English Canada. The party's candidates were fractious and had been venting their fears on Davey
for months. In keeping with the code he lived by, the Senator was
obliged to assure them repeatedly that the election was winnable
and that the party would triumph once more. Only his wife knew
the extent of his apprehension.

What he wanted above all was to win this last fight and get
out of the front lines. He hoped to pay more attention to his communications consulting business in Toronto and to enjoy the easy
prestige of sitting on one of the Senate's investigative committees
with their ample budgets for fact-finding trips abroad. He wanted
to be able to relax a little, secure in the knowledge that he would
be described in the memoirs, diaries, and historical analyses of
the Pearson-Trudeau era as the best political operator of his generation. For twenty years the Liberal Party had been the central
obsession of his life, but he looked at his involvement with it now
as a job, a soul-shaking, body-breaking, disillusioning job that he
still filled surpassingly well.

II

WHEN DAVEY HAD FIRST COME TO OTTAWA in the spring of 1961
to serve as national organizer of the Liberal Party under the leadership of Lester Pearson, his attitude to politics was very different.
He was already thirty-four, with a dozen years' experience as a
successful sales manager at a Toronto radio station behind him,
but there was something endearingly naïve about him then, a boy's
unclouded charm that people remembered long after the naïveté
had been destroyed and the charm had turned into professional
bonhomie.

In those days he was a believer. He thought the Liberal Party
was an instrument of reform that would fulfil the heady expectations of his generation of go-ahead Canadians. He considered
Canada the best country in the world to live in, a place where
anything was possible — ever-increasing prosperity, full employment, universal post-secondary education, an open-door immigration policy, and countless other as yet unformulated benefactions
— given hard work, stout friends, good political organization,
and liberal reform ideas. In brief, his ideas epitomized the outlook of a group of politicians who were later called Pearsonian
Liberals, although a good many of them joined the party, as Davey
did, in the days of Pearson's predecessor, Louis St. Laurent.

Davey had been born in Toronto in 1926, on the same day as
the princess who was to become queen, as his mother was given
to saying portentously. His father, Scotty Davey, had grown up in
the small Southern Ontario town of Bradford, the son and grandson of cattle-drovers and butchers, people typical of the British
immigrants who settled in the area in the nineteenth century and
brought with them the Victorian attitudes that made the province
prosperous, insular, and stable to the core. Scotty had been bap-
tized Charles Minto Davey in honour of the Governor General,
the Earl of Minto, but a Bradford druggist he did errands for gave
him his nickname when he was twelve and it stuck with him until
he died.

Like thousands of other small-town boys of his generation,

Scotty gravitated to the provincial capital, Toronto, just after the First World War. Still in his teens and anxious to get on in the world, he quickly landed a job as apprentice pressman at the Toronto *Star*, then just consolidating its reputation as a social force under the direction of Joseph ("Holy Joe") Atkinson, who was a confidant and supporter of the Liberal leader, William Lyon Mackenzie King. One Sunday, not long after he arrived, Scotty spotted a pretty schoolgirl named Grace Curtis singing hymns in the choir of a Methodist church in the city's west end. He wangled an introduction and began an ardent courtship that was to last for seven years. Scotty was making seventeen dollars a week at the *Star* and the mores he and Grace adhered to dictated that they couldn't get married until they had saved up enough money for a house. She got a job in an office, he continued working hard at the *Star*, and every Friday they went to Shea's Theatre to see a show, and every Sunday they went to church and, afterwards, if the weather was good, they strolled along the boardwalk at Sunnyside Beach, eating double-dip ice-cream cones and talking about their future. When they were able at last to buy a house on St. Clements Avenue in North Toronto, they got married and settled down to live in the comfortable security of that district for the rest of their lives, withstanding the vicissitudes of the Depression and the war with equanimity and a firm belief in the efficacy of cleanliness, godliness, hard work, and caution.

When their only son, Keith, turned four they enrolled him in St. James–Bond United Church (by then the Methodists had joined with the Presbyterians to form the United Church), saw to it that he took the pledge of total abstinence from alcohol when he was nine, and were pleased when he helped found the Progress Bible Class when he was in his teens. The cattle-droving Daveys of Bradford had been Tories; the *Star* was fanatically Liberal; and Scotty Davey, who was working his way up the paper's production hierarchy, was determined to stay out of politics. (He eventually became production manager of the *Star* and worked there for fifty-five years.) The subjects discussed in the Davey household when Keith was a boy were sports of all kinds, newspapers, principally the *Star* and its arch rival, the Tory Toronto *Telegram*, and the social activities of the United Church.

Despite the heavy dose of Methodist piety in their backgrounds, the Daveys loved fun, and the reputation as a practical joker and all-round "good head" that their son made for himself in school never left him. He was the kind of adolescent who was slow about dating girls himself but who climbed over the wall of Casa Loma with a couple of buddies to make faces through the ballroom windows at the one boy from their gang intrepid enough to invite a girl to a big formal dance.

"When I look back at those days, I can hardly believe how insular we were," James Service, one of Davey's school friends and Liberal Party colleagues, said later. "At North Toronto Collegiate, there was one Jew in our class. He was the exotic." The only other foreigners the boys ever saw were the "Chinamen" in laundries and greasy-spoon restaurants. French Canadians were as remote as Fiji Islanders, except when their fathers started grumbling in the conscription crisis of the 1940s that they wouldn't fight for their country. England had declared war on Germany the same September Davey and Service entered high school. None of the fathers of the boys in their close-knit school gang had been to university, but they all wanted their sons to go. "We were to have security and success, and university education was the ticket to those destinations which everybody assumed was readily attainable if you really tried," Service said.

After high school, both Service and Davey enrolled in the old general arts course leading to a B.A. at Victoria College in the University of Toronto. It may have been the best period in the university's history to be an undergraduate. As an institution, Toronto was at its apogee in the years right after the war. Veterans swarmed the campus — men who had been matriculated from high school before the armed forces claimed them and who were now the beneficiaries of education grants called DVA Allowances, thought up by the Department of Veterans Affairs of the Liberal government of the day as part of its postwar reconstruction plans to still the discharged soldiers' discontents, counter unemployment, and divert the nation from the evils of socialism. The DVA students invested the lecture halls and junior common rooms with an atmosphere of intellectual scepticism and intensified ambition, against which the students of normal undergraduate age had to measure their intelligence. There were scores of gifted under-graduates (John Meisel, James Reaney, James Eayrs among them) studying under the many brilliant scholars on the staff (Northrop Frye, E. J. Pratt, Donald Creighton, Harold Innis, C. B. Macpherson — to name only a few). Still, it wasn't the intellectual ferment that delighted Keith Davey, but the general after-the-battles-are-over optimism in the air. He worked just hard enough at his courses to get by and devoted his enthusiastic energies to cheering at football games ("Tor-on-to, Tor-on-to, Tor-on-to Var-si-tee. We'll shout and fight for the Blue and White and the honour of the U of T!"), sitting on the student council, and conducting a well-publicized mock feud with the engineers on behalf of the men of arts.

Several of his friends were Liberals and he was persuaded in his final year, which coincided with the retirement of Mackenzie King as prime minister and the first election campaign of his successor, Louis St. Laurent, to go to some campus meetings held by the university Liberal club. "I never thought of Davey as having formulated any political ideas as an undergraduate," said Douglas Fisher, who was a DVA student at Victoria College at the time and later became a CCF/NDP MP and then a political colum-nist. "He was a good-time kid, plain and simple, and the Liberal club seemed to loom in his mind as another kind of Varsity team to whose aid all right-minded, high-spirited kids should come."

When he graduated in 1949, Davey's marks were so low he had to give back the Senior Stick, an honour awarded in the spring of the year to the graduating student who had contributed most to the life of the college; it was the first time in Vic's history that the stick had to be returned. (It was characteristic of Davey that he liked to tell this story about himself years later when he was a senator, leaning back in his leather chair, shaking his head, and laughing.)

After graduation, Davey didn't quite know what to do next. In high school he had been a sports writer for *Canadian High News*, and in college he had written letters to *The Varsity*, and hankered after a newspaper career. He decided against journalism on the grounds that he wasn't a good enough writer, went on to law school, dropped out after a few months, rejected his mother's idea that he might become a United Church minister, and quickly found his métier as a salesman for the popular-music radio station CKFH, founded by the sportscaster Foster Hewitt. He married Isobel Hart, a girl from Woodstock, Ontario, who had graduated from Vic in household economics, and they settled down to married life in North Toronto not far from his parents' house. In the next few years Davey intensified his interest in the Liberal Party, working as a campaign organizer in Eglinton, his home riding, and becoming president of the Toronto and Yorks Young Liberal Association. He loved the camaraderie of party politics; in the evening after work, he was on the phone talking constantly to his fellow Liberals, the first to volunteer for a job, the last to leave a meeting. Still, the real melding of his life with the Liberal Party's fortunes didn't begin until 1957, when he was already sales manager of CKFH and well on his way up the ladder of success in the communications business.

III

IN KEITH DAVEY'S MIND — and in the minds of most Canadians who were over twenty that year — June 10, 1957, was a benchmark date, identifying the kind of cataclysmic public event, like the declaration of a war or the assassination of a politician, that people remember afterwards in highly personal terms. What happened that day, of course, was that the Progressive Conservative leader, John Diefenbaker, narrowly defeated Louis St. Laurent's Liberals, overthrowing the government party after twenty-two years in office and ending the great Liberal era that had begun with the elevation of Mackenzie King to the party's leadership in 1919 and to prime-ministerial power in 1921. It was a popular triumph, enhanced nine months later when another election turned Diefenbaker's 1957 minority into the huge 1958 Conservative majority.

Diefenbaker's Conservative régime was to prove what the Ottawa bureaucracy of the day came to call ''an episode'', an interregnum that disrupted the Liberal hegemony for only six years. But at the time it was such an amazing rout that even Liberals might have been expected to recall it as a blow dealt by an avenging fate to a party too long in power. Grits being Grits, though, their tendency was to look back less in chagrin at their loss — or even in sorrow at the public's failure to see what a collective error in judgment it was perpetrating — than in zestful satisfaction at how quickly stout Liberals rallied to the party when confronted by defeat.

Nowhere in the country did they rally with such vigour as in Toronto, a city that was emerging as the economic centre of Canada and would later be described by the novelist Mordecai Richler as the middle-class capital of the world. Certainly the group of young politicians who were such an important part of what came to be called the Liberal revival of the late 1950s possessed what was clearly recognizable as the Toronto style.

In its initial stage, the group's chief organizer was a college friend of Keith Davey's, a sober young lawyer named Gordon Dryden. Dryden had been born on a farm near Guelph, Ontario, the great-great-grandson on his mother's side of an immigrant Scottish farmer who had settled there early in the nineteenth century and who came from the same stock as William Lyon Mackenzie, the leader of the anti-establishment Rebellion of 1837 and grandfather to William Lyon Mackenzie King. Dryden's maternal grandfather had been a staunch Grit, active in the affairs of his constituency, and vocally proud of his friendship with Mackenzie King, who valued such party stalwarts for their enduring loyalty and who was valued by them in turn for his enduring success.

Young Dryden had absorbed Liberal politics with his porridge. His grandfather owned an old battery radio with an aerial strung up to a spruce tree and the political news that it brought into the farmhouse during the Depression and the war provided the family with its chief entertainment. By the time Dryden was called to the bar in the late 1940s his Liberal persona was set: he was the unselfish, unquestioning loyalist. A Liberal to the marrow. Ready to serve in good times and bad. He made the party his hobby, his family, and, some said, his life. (Dryden was a bachelor until he was over forty, though for many years he nurtured a romantic attachment to Judy LaMarsh, who was at law school with him and later became a cabinet minister.)

When the election results came in on June 10, 1957, Dryden was shaken to the soul. He had spent the day working as a scrutineer in a poll in East York, a Toronto suburb, and the anti-Liberal mood of the constituents who trooped in to vote made him suspect the party was in deep trouble, a hunch that was confirmed as the votes were counted across the country. Just as soon as he could get away, Dryden telephoned Boyd Upper, a close friend and fellow Liberal. They decided to drive up to see the finance minister, Walter Harris, at his house in the small town of Markdale, north of Toronto, feeling, as they discussed the import of the results, like desperate riders on a mission to save the party's future.

Their immediate concern was that the Prime Minister, the seventy-five-year-old Louis St. Laurent, who was known to be "past his prime", as good Grits euphemistically described his advancing befuddlement, would be too upset to respond well to reporters' questions about the Liberal disaster. They thought that

Harris as a privy councillor might be able to get through to him on the telephone and head off embarrassment to the party. When Harris — who that night lost both his seat in Parliament and his long-cherished hopes of succeeding to the leadership — placed his call to St. Laurent in Quebec City, it quickly became apparent that Dryden and Upper need not have worried. Jack Pickersgill, the Minister of Citizenship and Immigration — Jack-the-Nimble as he was known after a quarter-century in the back and front rooms of power — was already with the Prime Minister. He had driven from Ottawa to Quebec City with his wife that day, showing himself ready, as he had been so many times before and would be so many times again, to go any distance in the sacred cause of Liberalism. Pickersgill hadn't expected the defeat, but Pickersgill would know what to say. This news triggered in Dryden and Upper momentary relief and immediate resolution. The party must be rebuilt!

Within days Dryden had set himself to writing a long "Memorandum Concerning the Liberal Party in Canada after June 10, 1957" suggesting ways in which a recovery might be effected. He went up to Ottawa at his own expense to present his memo to Lester Pearson, whom he caught in a poignant moment, sitting alone in an ordinary MP's office in the Centre Block surrounded by boxes of unsorted files that had been carted over from his expansive room in the East Block, where he had laboured so sunnily and for so long in the service of Canada, first as a public servant and then as secretary of state for external affairs in the St. Laurent cabinet, a diplomat famous throughout the world. He listened to Dryden sympathetically, accepted his analytical memo gratefully, and generally confirmed Dryden's belief that Pearson, the most progressive of the Liberals still in the House — and the least tainted personally by the political errors that had caused the defeat — was the man around whom recovery would have to be built. (The other St. Laurent senior ministers who had survived the election, Lionel Chevrier, Paul Martin, and Jack Pickersgill, were nothing but old pols in Dryden's view. Pearson was a prince.)

Back in Toronto, Dryden soon organized weekly meetings, first at the King Edward Hotel and later at the Board of Trade, calling on Keith Davey and several other Liberal friends from college days to come to the aid of the party, and to recruit others if they could. When St. Laurent stepped down in the autumn, they all pledged their support to Pearson for the leadership. By this time the group was known as Cell 13, though it sometimes numbered more and sometimes less than thirteen, and even Dryden later professed not to remember exactly why the name was chosen, except that he didn't want it to be called Dryden's Club, as it had been for a few weeks. "My grandfather told me," he said, "that if you want to last long and finish strong in politics, you don't get your name linked up with a faction."

It included several lawyers — David Anderson, Royce Frith, Dan Lang, Philip Givens, Richard Stanbury, Joseph Potts, James Trotter, and Judy LaMarsh, who had joined her father's law firm in Niagara Falls and was the only one not practising in Toronto; Paul Hellyer, a land developer who had been a cabinet minister briefly under St. Laurent and as a sitting MP was the only member of the group who held elected office; James Service, Keith Davey's boyhood friend, who was in the real estate business by now in North York; James Scott, the executive director of the Ontario party; Boyd Upper, a medical doctor and Dryden's close friend; Gordon Edick, who owned a small construction firm in the west end of Toronto and had happened into the group by chance and resolutely played the plain man and token Roman Catholic, or "bead teller" as he called it; and, of course, Keith Davey, who started out as just one of the boys but was to become the most successful Liberal of the lot. (David Greenspan and Jerry Grafstein of Toronto and James Coutts of Calgary, three lawyers who were still students at the time of Cell 13's formation, were considered afterwards in Liberal circles to be part of the group, but they were nearly a decade younger than the others and weren't closely associated with Cell 13's members until the early 1960s, when they no longer went by that name but called themselves new-guard Liberals instead.)

Several of the Cell 13 crowd had known each other at the University of Toronto in the 1940s and they were still talking about those heady days with deep nostalgia. (Remember the time Keith Davey talked Joe Potts into burning his coonskin coat on the front campus at noon? Remember when Gordon Dryden rigged

that Hart House debate on DVA Allowances by tricking the opposition into going to a torchlit protest rally beforehand so the Liberals could pack the house and win? Remember when the arts
men were feuding with the engineers and stole the chamber-pot
from the Lady Godiva Memorial Band? God, we had fun!)

But more important than these shared memories of the past
was a shared vision of the future that they had in common with
other members of Cell 13 who hadn't been at college with them.
They all belonged to an expanding class in English Canada, an
aggressive, optimistic, upwardly mobile bourgeoisie, beneficiaries
of the first push towards mass higher education that had taken
place just after the war. They were the natural constituency of the
Liberal Party that Mackenzie King had built and that Louis St.
Laurent had briefly enhanced with the gloss of his reputation as a
corporation lawyer. Most of them were just under or just over
thirty and they all wanted important careers. They were one or
two generations away from the farming hinterland but still wired
together by the Protestant ethic that had driven their rural ancestors to settle the country. Several of them besides Dryden had
Liberal family backgrounds. Frith's mother regularly cast the only
Liberal vote in her poll in eastern Ontario. David Anderson's
father was an upright farmer in P.E.I., known far and wide on the
island for his energetic children and his Liberal politics. Judy
LaMarsh's father was the leading Liberal in Niagara Falls. But
for most of them, inherited loyalties weren't all that important.
The old habit engrained in rural and small-town Canadian families of clinging to one party, generation after generation, didn't
interest them. This was a new era. They were urban Canadians.
Liberalism attracted them because of its aura of progressivism. It
was the know-how party. Their credo was a reaffirmation of Sir
Wilfrid Laurier's statement that the twentieth century would belong to Canada. They were convinced that in the second half of
the century, Canada would be a progressive egalitarian state led
by a meritocracy made up of people uncannily like themselves:
the century *would* belong to Canada and Canada would belong
to them.

If they had been asked at one of those Wednesday meetings
at the Board of Trade to analyse their ideology, they probably

would have come up with something very close to the positive
liberalism of Mackenzie King, though they looked on King, who
had been in his grave for less than a decade, as an embarrassment
out of the distant past, a strange old fogey who never would have
been their hero. They didn't meet to talk history or ideology, in
any case. They were pragmatists, not intellectuals, and they met
to talk practical politics. They were driven on not just by personal
ambition — though they were smart enough to know that the Liberal
Party had been good to lawyers, developers, and ad men in the
past and would doubtless be good to them in future — but by a
certain delicious shared belief not uncommon in reformers that it
was their duty to sweep out what they saw as an incompetent old
guard and replace it with a highly competent and incorruptible
new wave, consisting of themselves.

They quickly took over the Liberal Party organization in
Toronto by getting Keith Davey elected president of the Toronto
and Yorks Liberal Association and then placing their candidates
in all the key jobs on the provincial executive of the Liberal Party
in Ontario. What they wanted was to make the party truly democratic, to free it from the influence that big business had on
St. Laurent and that old-fashioned small-time party bosses had on
party organization, and to make it respond to an uncorrupted grass
roots. They felt the way to achieve this ideal was by building
towards it constituency by constituency, with Toronto as the
proving-ground.

As they set about this formidable task, they discovered riding
associations that were run haphazardly by hack politicians and
greased by petty payoffs. In the early 1950s the Liberals had been
in possession of a larger war chest of election funds than ever
before, thanks to the popularity in the country's corporate community of St. Laurent's powerful colleague, C. D. Howe. Gordon
Edick, who reorganized the Toronto riding of Parkdale in 1958,
found out to his disgust that in Howe's time, riding presidents in
Ontario would go down to Toronto's Royal York Hotel at the start
of a campaign to pick up their allotted share of the election funds
in thousand-dollar bills, dispensed by C.D.'s emissaries. These
men didn't actually carry the money in a Gladstone bag or hand it
over while smoking two-dollar cigars, but that was the sort of

aura they had about them. Tammany Hall in the twenties.

Within the ridings, payoffs worked in several ways. Workers would get money for everything from knocking on doors to scrutineering. Local service businesses — a print shop, say — would submit inflated bills and then kick back ten to twenty per cent to the riding association. Candidates would promise and deliver small-time patronage jobs to loyalists and their sisters and their cousins and their aunts. Edick's revelations of the practices that some of the old-time pols indulged in delighted the Liberal revivalists. They had seen American movies (*Mr. Smith Goes to Washington, All the King's Men*) and hankered after the American Democratic reformers (FDR on the radio! Harry Truman in the heat of the kitchen!), and the whole scenario appealed to their imaginations.

In a way, they went about political reform like college boys on a caper. The group turned into a classic male combine. Each member was loyal to the group and each was tagged with a persona like the kids in an Our Gang comedy. Frith was handsome, loquacious, interested in the arts, and often asked to appear on television; he was the showboat. Lang was a little older than the rest, had been to a private school, worked for an establishment law firm, and had an admirable ladylike wife; he was nicknamed senator years before he was actually appointed to the Red Chamber.

"We had two criteria for anything we decided to do," Frith remembered. "It had to be important and it had to be fun." Their common wisdom had it that the long climb back to federal political power would involve first regaining power for the Liberals in half a dozen of the provinces. This was the strategy articulated by Gordon Dryden in his memo to Pearson in June of 1957, in which he pointed out that the Liberals held only three of the ten provincial governments before the 1957 federal defeat. Their first goal was to win Ontario, and they tried out their new organizational techniques in the provincial election of 1959, only to see the Liberals defeated badly once again by the redoubtable Conservative premier, Leslie Frost. Never mind, they told each other on the telephone during the next day's post-mortems, we'll do better next time. But even at their most optimistic, and they were an optimistic crew, they calculated that recovery would probably take a decade.

In this they reckoned without a man who was shortly to link his interests with theirs, a man who came from a very different milieu, who knew a great deal more about the attainment of power and the organization of people than the Cell 13 collective had yet dreamed of, and who was to join them in recovering for the Liberal Party what its members thought of as its rightful place on the government benches in five years rather than ten. His name was Walter Lockhart Gordon.

AT THE TIME OF THE LIBERAL DISASTER in 1957, Walter Gordon was a Toronto accountant and management consultant and that was the way his background was described in newspapers and magazines during the decade that followed. To his familiars it was so inadequate a description of his essence that it always sounded like a joke.

Gordon's real calling was power-broking and in his prime he practised it brilliantly. By class, education, experience, and instinct, he was equipped to understand power — how it was acquired and how it worked — as well as any Canadian of his generation. He became a pivotal link between the old Liberalism of the King–St. Laurent hegemony and the new Liberalism of the Pearson-Trudeau era. Almost everything that had happened in his life before he was publicly identified with the party seemed to qualify him for the role.

Gordon was born in 1906, the first of the five children of Harry Duncan Lockhart Gordon, a young accountant who was later to become a lieutenant-colonel in the All Canadian Mounted Rifles, a much decorated hero in the First World War, and a very rich man in the decades that followed it. The Colonel's father had come to Toronto from Scotland in the 1860s, after first getting a degree from Cambridge and reading law in London at the Inns of Court. He had fitted into the colonial gentry of pre-Confederation Toronto with ease, and his son Harry married Kathleen Cassels, who belonged to one of the most illustrious English-Canadian families of the nineteenth century. The world Walter Gordon grew up in was the privileged and orderly society of the Toronto-centred English-speaking ascendancy in Canada, a world of winding Rosedale streets, panelled libraries, heavy silver on mahogany sideboards, dark ancestral portraits, parlourmaids, and clearly defined behavioural ideals. Canada was emphatically British still, and however much the Canadian rich chafed under that knowledge, they modelled themselves on the English governing class. Equanimity and excellence were admired. Continuity was desirable. Privilege brought responsibility.

Young Walter followed closely in his father's footsteps, apparently without complaint, though if he had any resentments, he never would have voiced them, having been trained to keep his expression composed, his mouth shut, and his back straight. (The straight back was crucial in the society Gordon was shaped by; his wife, Elizabeth, once remarked to a friend that her own girlhood had resounded with the much-repeated postural admonition "Brooches out, young ladies! And buckles in.") Walter was sent to his father's schools to be educated, first to Upper Canada College and then the Royal Military College at Kingston, and in January 1927, when he was not quite twenty-one, he joined his father's firm, Clarkson, Gordon & Dilworth, as an apprentice accountant.

Harry Gordon had been a partner in Clarkson's for only fourteen years but the firm itself had been prospering in Toronto since it was founded by an Englishman named Thomas Clarkson in the middle of the previous century, which made it very old and established indeed according to the way antiquity was reckoned in English Canada at the time. It had become — and would remain for decades — as the writer Barbara Moon described it "an unofficial but effective finishing school for young men of the upper class . . . what sociologists call an acculturating institution," where a chartered accountant was not just a professional roughly on a par with a high school principal as he might be anywhere else but "a Clarkson man", a gentleman who had been taught from birth if he were lucky, or during his apprenticeship with the firm if he were less so, how things worked in the Canadian elite.

Clarkson men masked their aggressive, innovative energies behind an acceptably circumspect façade of unrelenting hard work, iron-willed self-control, and unerring good manners. The firm led its field in Canada and was well known and much admired by businessmen on the eastern seaboard of the United States and in England, where it maintained close ties. The acumen of the senior partners, Harry Gordon and G. T. Clarkson, the founder's grandson, was relied on heavily by Canadian bankers, brokers, and entrepreneurs and by federal and provincial governments; they were hard-headed business advisers of impeccable reputation and Walter Gordon was to learn all they knew and eventually to surpass them in influence.

From the beginning of his apprenticeship, they saw to it that he was involved in government inquiries as well as in business investigations. (They also made sure that he worked even harder than the other apprentices, to stave off charges of nepotism.) In the thirty years between his first sixty-dollar-a-month, seventy-hour-a-week job as an articling student and his active involvement in Liberal politics after the election of 1957, not only did Gordon acquire a personal fortune, he also learned from the inside how the Canadian power structure worked.

His experience of government started when he was employed as a step'n'fetchit for the Liberals' Royal Commission on Customs and Excise in 1927 and deepened when he worked on the Conservatives' Royal Commission on Price Spreads and Mass Buying in the early years of the Depression. He spent an instructive ten months with that commission, looking into the Eaton's department-store empire and conducting a number of other industrial investigations. He also struck up what was to be one of the most enduring and important friendships of his life with Lester Bowles Pearson, a young External Affairs officer who had been seconded from his department to act as the commission's secretary. "Mike", as everybody called him, was nine years older than Gordon but still boyish in manner (as he was to remain for the next thirty years) and given to the kind of self-deprecatory wit that suited Gordon's own publicly circumspect, privately irreverent style.

Gordon was beginning to move away from the conservative confines of upper-class Toronto, the world of his father and "the Firm", and to develop a different kind of social consciousness. Canada had been hard hit by the Depression and Gordon had friends among the group of mostly upper-middle-class intellectuals who banded together in the League for Social Reconstruction (usually called the LSR) to make reform proposals for the country's economic, social, and political problems and who then went on to found the democratic socialist party the Co-operative Commonwealth Federation. One of those friends, Graham Spry, ran for the CCF in a by-election in Toronto East in 1934 and borrowed the Gordons' car for his campaign. Mike Pearson also had important connections to the LSR. Frank Underhill, one of his former colleagues in the history department at the University of Toronto where he had taught before joining External Affairs, was a key figure in the League, and several of its members had been at Oxford around the same time in the 1920s. Pearson and Gordon spent hours together in godawful hotel rooms in prairie towns while they were travelling with the price-spread commission talking about the LSR crowd's ideas on social justice, government intervention in the economy, and the need for Canada to get out from under the smothering weight of the Empire — ideas that were unremarkable in intellectual circles but very different from those of most of Gordon's contemporaries in the business world, men like Bud McDougald and E. P. Taylor in Toronto or Hartland Molson and Ward Pitfield in Montreal. Not long after the commission's work was over, Pearson was posted to the Canadian High Commission in London and Gordon once again was assigned by Clarkson, Gordon to a government inquiry; this one involved the automobile industry and it gave him a clear picture of Canada's problems vis-à-vis its other powerful trading partner, the United States.

Despite these early assignments, Gordon's real immersion in the workings of official Ottawa didn't begin until just after the declaration of war in September 1939 when he went to the capital on a few hours' notice and stayed more than two years. He worked first on the organization of the Foreign Exchange Control Board, then as special assistant to the Deputy Minister of Finance, the great Clifford Clark, under whose aegis he worked out a dominion-provincial tax-sharing agreement that was a model of financial logic and tough federal diplomacy. Later he acted as a part-time consultant travelling up to Ottawa from Toronto regularly for the duration. (Although Gordon was in his early thirties and had been an officer in the militia, he could not go on active service because he suffered from the miseries of gout, an ailment that plagued him for years.)

Even then, as a relatively young man, he had the kind of insouciant self-regard that came out of inbred class confidence reinforced by the knowledge that he'd been able to survive the rigorous professional training the Clarkson, Gordon partners had devised. He took charge of whatever problems came his way in Ottawa, deflating pomposities, cutting red tape, and generally behaving in a manner that endeared him to his colleagues who were caught in the exhausting, if occasionally exhilarating, pressures of trying to run a war. Gordon had a score of witty anecdotes about his wartime experiences that he liked to tell at table for decades afterwards in his elegant Toronto dining room while maids tottered around bearing heavy platters of roast lamb and crystal decanters of claret. In his even, ironic voice he would divulge his acute perceptions of the way that power worked in Canada in those days, recounting stories marvellously evocative of an era and a way of life, ostensibly self-deprecating but in their subtle way self-aggrandizing, describing as they did Gordon's triumphs over stuffy Bank of England officials, apoplectic admirals, overbearing waiters, and recalcitrant bureaucrats in London, Ottawa, Washington, and New York.

During the decade after the war, Gordon kept up his Ottawa contacts. He'd had a whiff of the pleasures of the power game and had made for himself a considerable reputation within the closely knit political-bureaucratic establishment of the era. Several times in that ten years he was offered appointments either to the public service or in the St. Laurent cabinet. He turned these offers down, partly because, although he admired St. Laurent, he disagreed seriously with the attitudes of his most important colleague, C. D. Howe, who was Minister of Trade and Commerce but widely known as "the minister of everything". Gordon knew that he couldn't thrive in any government Howe dominated, and besides he was busy getting rich in Toronto. He had made a great personal success at Clarkson, Gordon working as a consultant to important corporations across the country and at the same time investing cleverly in a stock market that was reaching peaks it hadn't scaled since the 1920s. Not yet fifty, in consistent good humour and good health, despite his gout, Gordon was approaching the prime of his time, and was now as much of an establishmentarian as any Canadian could be, apparently thoroughly enjoying the personal prosperity of his own middle age and the general prosperity Canada was experiencing in the boom.

In 1932 he had married Elizabeth Counsell, an elegant woman from a prominent Hamilton family who as the years wore on had developed a greatly admired personal style in dress and decoration. The Gordons weren't just another rich Toronto couple. In an elite that was generally provincial and self-satisfied, made up of millionaires whose money was derived from hogs, threshing machines, or insurance, and where an interest in the arts or ideas was thought to be effete, the Gordons were unusual. Gordon had turned into a highly civilized man, witty, intelligent, and sensitive. He had friends in the universities as well as in the business community and the Ottawa bureaucracy. He and his wife had three lively children, friends all over the world, membership in the best clubs, a penchant for travelling to exotic places, an impressive art collection, a Georgian house in Rosedale, and a farm called Seldom Seen in the horses-and-hounds countryside northwest of Toronto.

But behind his armour of social and professional success, impeccable moustache, and unassailable self-regard, Gordon harboured an eccentricity. He was a passionate nationalist. Gordon never liked to talk about the intellectual or emotional roots of his nationalist ideas. He preferred to describe them drily in sheerly practical terms. "At heart, Walter was really a romantic Scot," Alison Ignatieff, one of his close friends, once remarked. "But he had to hide it, to submerge that side of himself in favour of the canny Scot who was more acceptable in the world he grew up in." Once, when hard pressed by questions from a writer who was trying to get him to plumb the psychic origins of his economic nationalism, Gordon told a story about being enrolled for a brief period in an English preparatory school during the First World War when his father's regiment was posted overseas and he was nine. The English boys had been laughing at his accent and other colonial crudities for weeks, and one day when he could stand it no more he had taken several of them on in a fight behind the school gymnasium. Pinned at the bottom of the heap, he decided he didn't like these little snots who were piled on top of him. "There was nothing funny about being a Canadian. In fact, I would bloody well sooner be me than one of them, and that idea stuck with me for a long time." Having told this unembroidered tale, he looked distinctly uncomfortable, as though he had committed some kind of unacceptable gaffe. He lamely summed up by saying, "Besides, my family had been around in Canada for a while and I felt that I might have some idea of how the country should be run." He then went back with relief to describing the futile efforts he had made in the late 1930s to form a holding company that would buy out Canadian-owned firms in danger of being sold to Americans with capital raised in England, efforts that were abandoned at the outbreak of war and lost in the urgencies of the 1940s.

By 1955, these old concerns had turned into a suppressed anger at the federal government's complacent attitude towards the accelerating sell-out to foreign business interests of Canadian resources and industries. It seemed to Gordon that, despite the booming post-war economy, there was entirely too much foreign equity capital — mainly American — coming into Canada for the country's long-term good. He thought these developments presaged grave difficulties in the future — technological inferiority and industrial stagnation, unemployment, a mounting foreign debt, and a further relegation of the country to the ignominious role of resource production and little more. Nobody in the business community or the bureaucracy was publicly questioning the Liberals' postwar economic policies, which Gordon felt were far too reflective of C. D. Howe's continentalism. Howe was an engineer from Massachusetts who had absorbed Calvin Coolidge's great adage "The business of America is business," then added his own corollary, "and the sooner Canada lives by that rule, the better off we'll be." Gordon knew that if he mentioned his view that Canada's economy was being mishandled in the York Club where he had lunch in Toronto or in the Rideau Club in Ottawa, his confreres from the symbiotic elites of central Canadian big business and the federal government would think he had lost his grip. For them, Howe was a hero. "C.D." had been the most important Canadian civilian running the war; now, as St. Laurent grew more and more confused and depressed in office, he was the most important Canadian conducting the peace.

In the early 1950s, Canadians were indulging in an uncharacteristic euphoria induced by a belief in the ethic of progress that later seemed astonishingly naïve. The country's resources were widely viewed as unlimited and so was its future, with "a grateful population seen as advancing ever onwards towards a high-income nirvana", as the economist Abraham Rotstein described it. The cold-war situation, which had created a close bond between Canada and the United States through a common defence system, fed this mood. Canada was dependent on American might for defence reasons, so why not rely on American capital to speed our economic progress? Gordon questioned this reasoning. After years of examining the business prospects of his firm's important clients, he had begun to think that economic dependence on direct American ownership might turn out to be far more threatening to Canadian sovereignty than the country's earlier political dependence on Britain had been. He decided something should be done.

The way he went about doing something was indicative both of the era — when Canada's affairs were conducted almost entirely through discreet agreements made among friends — and of Gordon's particular technique of working the system, which was to seek unconventional ends by reassuring means. He was chairman of the executive committee of the Canadian Institute of International Affairs in 1955 and he prepared an article for its publication, the *International Journal*, expressing his concerns about the economy and calling for a royal commission, the traditional device used by parliamentary governments to handle a politically dangerous issue. Lest the article upset Liberal Ottawa, he sent a draft to Kenneth Taylor, the Deputy Minister of Finance. Taylor showed the article to his minister, Walter Harris, who had reasons of his own for questioning the primacy of C. D. Howe. Harris, in turn, showed it to the Prime Minister, Louis St. Laurent. It was decided between them that a commission might be just the ticket to provide the Liberals, a few of whom were vaguely aware that they might have grown a little torpid after twenty years in power, with some new ideas to throw to the voters in the next campaign. Gordon's only remaining problem was to get the commission past C. D., who was sure to regard any investigation of the Canadian economy as an investigation of himself. This feat was accomplished by finessing the necessary order-in-council through the cabinet when Howe was out of the country and then letting it be known that Gordon's appointment as chairman was Mr. St. Laurent's express desire.

The Royal Commission on Canada's Economic Prospects took over two years to complete, gave Gordon an overall knowledge of the country's postwar economy that few experts could match, and turned him into a national name. Superbly written in part by its research director, the poet-diplomat Douglas LePan, the Gordon Report stated clearly — as Gordon had intended it should — that increased foreign investment conferred on nonresidents an alarming measure of control over some of Canada's most important industries, so that there was a real danger eventually of "legitimate Canadian interests being overlooked or disregarded" — an idea that was heresy in the 1950s as the shrieks of businessmen immediately confirmed. Otherwise a solid expression of conventional economic research, the report reiterated the accepted belief that, barring an atomic war or a major depression, Canada was destined to wax ever richer, like some solid, stolid widow who had unlimited resources and the benefit of impeccable advisers managing her estate.

Despite the orthodoxy of most of the report's proposals and St. Laurent's vague assurances to Gordon that he needn't worry about the effect it would have on C. D., when the preliminary report was made public in December 1956 Howe persuaded St. Laurent to disavow much of it on the grounds that it might provide more ammunition for the Opposition than planks for the Liberal election platform. Rumours circulating in Ottawa that Gordon would be appointed to the cabinet after the report's release evaporated. Howe was so furious at Gordon for poaching on his preserve that he refused to speak to him at a wedding reception at the Country Club. ("Not speaking" was a practice rarely resorted to in those days in Ottawa; you could cut a rival's arguments to ribbons in a meeting but you did it with civility, so if you met at the Rideau Club's communal table at noon over the oysters on the half shell you need never feel embarrassed.)

The Conservatives were delighted at this sign of dissension within the government party and used it as a debating-point in the months leading up to the election of 1957. Ironically the Tories buried Gordon's final report, which was completed five months after they assumed office in June, because of its Liberal taint. They abandoned their traditional economic nationalist stance which had been co-opted by Gordon, whom Diefenbaker described as "the flossy Toronto taxidermist who stuffs the Grits with zany ideas". In the wake of the Liberals' defeat in June, Gordon decided he was fed up with federal politics in any case. The other senior partners in his firm, including his father, who was still active in business in his eighties, had been opposed to his close involvement with any one political party in the belief that partisanship would alienate other potential clients in the private and public sectors. Gordon had an important contract to fulfil with the Conservative government of Leslie Frost in Ontario and he retreated to Toronto. The only thing that still attracted him to politics in 1957 was his still-stubborn desire to put his economic ideas into effect and his friendship with Lester Pearson, a friendship that would involve him with the Liberal Party for the next decade and very nearly break his heart and ruin his reputation.

IN HIS TIME, LESTER PEARSON was a man admired by almost everyone who knew him. The qualifying "almost" is necessary because occasionally an acquaintance — usually a contemporary who had known him in the Department of External Affairs and watched his wondrous rise from a small-town Ontario Methodist minister's son with a flair for playing hockey to university lecturer to diplomat to cabinet minister to Nobel laureate to prime minister to apotheosis in the Liberal pantheon — would say wryly that behind Pearson's sunny smile and endearing malleability was a man of steely ambition with an enviable talent for getting others to do his bidding without rousing their resentment.

When he became leader of the Liberal Party in January 1958, Pearson was the *beau idéal* of the old Ottawa establishment made up of the intertwined elites of the bureaucracy and the King–St. Laurent cabinet. In a way, Pearson's life and the establishment's had a parallel pattern. When the establishment came to dominate the government between 1935 and 1949, Pearson was busy climbing the public service pyramid; when it was at its peak in the 1950s, he was the most famous Canadian in the world; and until he died in 1972, its ethos lingered on in the capital, although by then most of its original members had long since been superseded by younger men with somewhat different ideas and very different ideals.

It was an establishment of unusually talented men, the cream of the young Dominion's intelligentsia. The secret of Pearson's success within it, which surpassed that of even his most talented colleagues, is usually attributed to his unpretentious good nature, his willingness to compromise, and above all his good luck in being in the right place at the right time. But Harry Ferns, who worked on Mackenzie King's office staff before leaving Canada in 1950 for a distinguished career as a professor of political science at the University of Birmingham, thought otherwise. "Pearson did have a secret," he observed. "But it wasn't anything as nebulous as good luck. There were other Canadians tap dancing on the world stage in the 1940s and 1950s, some of them more gifted intellectually than he was. But he had an unusual manner that came straight out of his childhood training in a Methodist parsonage. He was able to project great respect for power while appearing to stand apart from it, as though he knew its worth but didn't want it for himself. This quality was understandably attractive to powerful men and a wide range of political leaders from Mackenzie King to R. B. Bennett and Louis St. Laurent clasped Pearson to their bosoms and eased his way in the world.''

For all Pearson's nearly universal popularity with his peers, his relationship with Walter Gordon was special. During the decades after their first meeting in the 1930s, while Pearson was growing famous and Gordon was growing rich, their paths crossed many times. When Pearson was posted to Washington, first as minister counsellor and then as ambassador, Gordon used to meet him often to talk about their wartime adventures and their burgeoning careers. Later when Pearson, as under-secretary and then secretary of state for external affairs, was engrossed in the formation of the North Atlantic Treaty Organization and in diplomatic brokerage at the United Nations, he would seek Gordon out to discuss international issues; and Gordon, in turn, would tell him what was going on in financial circles in London and New York as well as Toronto and Ottawa, offering him interpretations and information on economic developments. Their wives were friends, the couples had spent many happy days together at home and abroad, and at some point in this period, Gordon apparently came to feel responsible for Pearson's material welfare. He regarded Pearson as a wholly admirable man who might know his way around international negotiating tables but who was too much the innocent intellectual to be able to look after his own political or economic welfare. (Later on, when things went sour between them, Gordon's allies were left to wonder who was really the innocent.)

When Louis St. Laurent asked Pearson to leave the public service to become his minister for external affairs in 1948, Gordon tried to allay Pearson's fears about the financial risk of leaving behind his bureaucratic pension for the uncertainties of politics by raising money from business friends to provide funds for a modest annuity of $4,800 a year. Similarly, when Pearson was running for the leadership in 1958, Gordon became concerned about the lackadaisical state of his campaign. He organized a pre-convention dinner in honour of Pearson's newly acquired Nobel prize to get him a favourable press. Then, as a self-appointed, unofficial campaign manager he went about the Chateau Laurier at the convention, discreetly buttonholing delegates so that Pearson's first-ballot victory over Paul Martin would be sufficiently crushing to show the party united behind Mike.

Not that Pearson's triumph was ever really in much doubt. It was a curiosity of the postwar Liberal Party elite, whose members so valued political shrewdness in themselves, that they liked to think their leader was beyond politics, too pure for the little arts that engrossed their waking thoughts and haunted their slumbrous hours. Pearson-the-Pure-in-Heart had been designated for the succession by St. Laurent-the-Saintly and had accepted the imprimatur after a graceful show of reluctance. Martin, who had a better record of service to the party as an MP for twenty-three years and as an effective minister of national health and welfare, besides an outstanding academic background in law and international studies, was seen as a ward-heeling pol. He *wanted* power, curious creature, and he let people see this base desire.

It was Martin's unhappy lot throughout the St. Laurent and Pearson decades to bear the disdain that had been reserved previously for Mackenzie King, that "fat little conjuror with the appliqué smile", as he was described by Charles Ritchie, the diplomat. That King was a brilliantly intuitive leader responsible for the Liberals' long political reign didn't really seem to occur to most of the denizens of the party's upper reaches, and after his death they determined that his like would never be seen again in the leadership. Liberals loved to tell the story of Pearson attending King's funeral with Gordon and expressing astonishment at the crowds who lined the streets to watch the cortège. "They just want to be sure he's dead," Gordon said tersely and Pearson had to duck his head to contain his unseemly laughter.

Certainly none of the Liberal elite blamed Pearson when, in his much admired political innocence, he made his disastrous first speech as Opposition leader in the House of Commons right after the leadership convention in January 1958. On the advice of Jack

Pickersgill, he had put forward a motion that the Diefenbaker minority government should step down and hand power back to the Liberals without the benefit of an election. Delighted with this fresh evidence of Liberal arrogance, Diefenbaker called an election that dealt Pearson a trouncing of a kind no Liberal leader had suffered before. All his friends felt sorry for Mike and one of the most sorrowful was Walter Gordon, to whom he turned for advice on how to rebuild his decimated party.

Gordon manfully set about this task knowing nothing whatever about political organization. He treated the party like an ailing firm whose ills he had been called in to diagnose as a management consultant. What he found in the course of a study that took several months to complete was an institution deeply in debt, with its head office staffed by old-fashioned and in some cases incompetent individuals, producing outmoded policies that were unattractive in the face of the fresh services offered by the rival firm, the Tories. He wrote a succinct report describing these problems in November 1959 which read as though Pearson were the chief executive officer of a nearly bankrupt business that could be saved only through harsh and decisive action.

Somehow the harsh and decisive action fell to Gordon, since Pearson was engrossed in learning to be Leader of the Opposition in the House of Commons where he still felt like a neophyte. (Despite the fact that he had been a cabinet minister throughout the St. Laurent era, Pearson had spent so much time practising diplomacy he knew very little about domestic politics, including parliamentary procedure.) Later, when he and Pearson were estranged, Gordon expressed amazement at having been charmed into doing Pearson's political dirty work for him. Before he agreed to try to revive the Liberal Party, he did attempt to clarify in letters that read like government memoranda what his role and Pearson's policies would be, should the party be restored to office. Gordon knew his economic ideas were anathema to traditional Liberals. But their long friendship had led him to believe that Pearson's early humiliating experiences as a diplomat attending international meetings where Canadians were treated like colonial lackeys of the British, and his later difficulties with American policy-makers like John Foster Dulles and Dean Acheson, had turned him into a nationalist, too. There were many soothing understandings reached in conversations between the two men in the early months of 1960 on matters of trade, defence, and economic policy, and a firm promise was given that Gordon would be minister of finance in a Pearson government.

Gordon then set about rebuilding the party organization. His first action was to raise $200,000 to settle the Liberal debt, which required him to travel across Canada and make pleading noises in the boardrooms of the nation, a task he loathed and quickly completed. He then asked an old friend, Major-General Bruce Matthews, who was president of Excelsior Life and had a network of impeccable connections in the business community, to take on two jobs as both president and treasurer of the party. Matthews agreed to replace another old friend of Gordon's, Duncan MacTavish, an Ottawa lawyer who had worked for both King and St. Laurent as a fund-raiser and had grown tired in the cause of Liberalism. Gordon further shook up the staff of Liberal headquarters on Cooper Street in downtown Ottawa by firing all the people he had described as dead wood in his report to Pearson and began to look for fresh recruits as their replacements.

In the course of making his original study of the party, Gordon had been directed to the meetings of Cell 13. The group was dynamic and hopeful in a way older Liberals were not and Gordon decided its members had a lot to teach him about practical politics, even though he thought they were somewhat jejune in their attitudes. They thought he was amazing, a man of a rarefied sort they had never seen before who could top their wisecracks with witticisms and who knew intimately the intricacies of the upper reaches of Canadian society which they had yet to penetrate.

Keith Davey particularly took careful notice of Gordon's mannerisms, from the names he dropped and the management techniques he advocated to the phrases he used and the clothes he wore. He still dressed in the uniform that the Clarkson firm had insisted on when he was young — sober suit with waistcoat, rep tie, striped shirt, polished Oxfords, dark hose secured by garters — though he no longer felt compelled to wear a hat. (Before the war, Colonel Gordon, on encountering a hatless employee at the firm's front door, marched him to the petty-cash box, took out ten dollars, and sent him out forthwith to buy a fedora, lest Bay Street get the idea that Clarkson men were sloppy.) Davey soon abandoned the sports jackets and Lester B. Pearson polka-dot bow ties he had been wearing and took to ordering tailor-made, three-piece suits that weren't exactly in the Gordon style but near enough to signal to his friends that he was entering a new and more serious phase.

The two men had met briefly at the leadership convention in 1958 when Davey's frenetic efforts to swing every possible Toronto delegate into Pearson's camp drew Gordon's attention. After a few Cell 13 meetings, Gordon decided that Davey was the most useful member of the group for his purposes. He wasn't as rigid or as career-committed as the lawyers and his easy laughter and quick imagination appealed to Gordon, who had always advocated hiring graduates of the arts courses at the University of Toronto as apprentice management consultants. "Get them young, quick-witted, and flexible," he would say, "and you won't have any trouble teaching them techniques."

Gordon Edick, the contractor who was the outsider in the Cell 13 group, remembered vividly Gordon's effect on its meetings. "Most of those guys were big talkers having a good time playing politics. The group wasn't really going anywhere until Walter came along. He had experience sizing up men and delegating jobs. He realized that if you told Davey what to do, he'd do it. Keith was plenty smart despite his shenanigans and Walter put the bugger to work."

The next year, Gordon asked Davey to come to Ottawa as the party's national organizer. Davey's Toronto friends gave him a huge going-away party that was prominently reported, to his parents' pleasure, in pages of the *Toronto Daily Star*, and shortly afterwards he set out for the capital, eager to put into practice what was later called "the new politics" and to try to engineer for Gordon and Pearson the great victory he felt they deserved.

VI

BY THE TIME KEITH DAVEY arrived in Ottawa in the spring of 1961, the intellectual background for the new Liberalism had been set by two gatherings. The first was the Kingston Conference in September 1960, organized at Pearson's suggestion by Mitchell Sharp, a former civil servant who was then working as a business executive in Toronto. Two hundred members of the country's small-l liberal intelligentsia were invited to Kingston to discuss policy issues whether they believed in big-L Liberalism or not. The second event was the National Rally, a Liberal Party policy convention convened in Ottawa the following January under the chairmanship of Paul Hellyer, where resolutions directing the party slightly leftward were hammered out under the watchful eye of Walter Gordon's policy committee. The ideas discussed at both of these meetings were wide-ranging, as befitted such loosely constituted ideological groupings, but the overwhelming impression that emerged for public consumption was one of newness, vitality, and progressivism.

Pearson had brought to the party his optimistic internationalism, his belief that Canada had an exemplary role to play in the world through its peace-keeping efforts, its proposed recognition of Red China, the rejection of nuclear arms for its armed forces, and other initiatives of a conciliatory nature. Now he was apparently putting his imprimatur on a domestic policy thrust which had emerged from position papers prepared by a group of activist intellectuals who were working on the small staff of his opposition office: Tom Kent, an English journalist who had been employed by the *Manchester Guardian* before joining the Winnipeg *Free Press* as editor; Maurice Lamontagne, an economist educated at Laval and now teaching at the University of Ottawa; and Allan MacEachen, another economist who had been elected as MP from Cape Breton in 1953 and 1957, only to lose his seat in the debacle of 1958. The papers written by Lamontagne and Kent for the Kingston Conference had been attacked by businessmen and editorialists as socialistic, but their general direction — towards the completion of the welfare security system that had been begun under Mackenzie King — was consistent with the positive liberalism of Pearson, Gordon, and the Cell 13 crowd. Gordon's principal preoccupation, the redirection of economic policy away from the drift to resource-based continentalism and towards a more self-sustaining structure based on Canadian-controlled manufacturing, was endorsed by a long resolution passed at the rally under the heading "For a strong and independent Canada".

Contrasted with the stagnant politics of the late St. Laurent era and the ineptitudes of the Diefenbaker government, which were now becoming obvious, these ideas gave the Liberals a new glow as a party. They seemed to be promising a kind of Camelot of the North at a time when the Western world was excited by John F. Kennedy's promise of a reinvigorated and ennobled United States and when John Kenneth Galbraith was telling the hundreds of thousands who were reading *The Affluent Society* that modern capitalism could advance into the future with a human face.

In response to the favourable publicity given to the new Liberalism, the party's old guard, which had been all but routed in the defeats of 1957 and 1958, was largely silent. But that didn't mean it was dead. After Keith Davey had spent a few weeks at his new job, he formulated a view of the party that was very different from the one he had held in Toronto. One day he went to see his leader and said, "Mr. Pearson, I want to try out some impressions on you. As far as I can tell, the party has an old guard and a new guard, and it also has a left and right wing, so you've got the old-guard left and the new-guard right and so on through all kinds of permutations, with the same people sometimes changing groups on certain issues." Pearson looked at him for a few seconds and then flashed his famous grin. "That's right, Keith," he answered. "And it's up to you and me to get along with all of them."

Though his sympathies lay with the left-wing new guard, Davey then and later tended to back off from policy discussions, reasoning that his job was to get the party machinery ready for an election. It was a formidable task. Gordon had discovered that the party as it was constituted in the 1950s could hardly be described as an entity since it was a loose federation made up of ten provincial parties, organized on different principles and with widely varying degrees of effectiveness from the newly reformed, vibrant Quebec organization — which was successful provincially but largely indifferent to the federal party — to the nearly dormant Alberta party, which had elected only one federal MP in 1958. In the King–St. Laurent era regional barons had dominated federal party affairs — men like Stuart Garson from Manitoba, Jimmy Gardiner from Saskatchewan, and Joey Smallwood from Newfoundland, who were expected to use their provincial machines to deliver a federal vote and who expected in return to control federal patronage.

Gordon had decided the new party could be run more efficiently — like so many of the multi-faceted corporations whose reorganization he had advised as a management consultant — by establishing central control over the whole operation. He set up a Leader's Advisory Committee, with Pearson as chairman, which gave Gordon the power to direct the party's reorganization without having been elected to its official national executive. He and Davey concluded they would have to by-pass the provincial parties and organize their own campaign committees in each province under the direction of a local chairman appointed directly by Pearson and responsible only to him and his national campaign committee.

The practical political techniques that the newly centralized organization devised were an amalgam of what Gordon knew as a management consultant and what Keith Davey had picked up in his years as a poll captain, riding president, and campaign chairman in the Toronto riding of Eglinton, and as a member of the Cell 13 squad which had cleared the Toronto ridings of hangers-on under its "Work Or Resign" slogan. (Another of the group's slogans, conceived in 1960 for a membership drive, was "6-for-1 in '61", which made Walter Gordon shudder at its cuteness. Gordon had to admit that this kind of hokum worked, though; Toronto membership in the party was increased from three thousand to ten thousand in a single year.)

Gordon taught Davey that it was necessary to be superbly well organized, to hire bright people and delegate responsibility to them, to keep meticulous lists, to assess what he wanted out of a meeting before it began, and to manage the people attending it so they would come to agree with the ideas he was trying to put across. Davey lapped up everything he was told and his eagerness endeared him to his elders, no matter where they stood on the party spectrum. John Connolly, an Ottawa lawyer who belonged to the old Liberal establishment and had replaced Bruce Matthews as party president in 1961, remembered Davey afterwards as unique in his experience. Once they were standing together at an airport after seeing Gordon and Pearson off on some kind of Liberal mission. Davey was alive with the excitement of his new job and his new connections. After watching the departing plane taxi down the runway, he turned to Connolly to ask, "Say, do you think Mr. Gordon is a millionaire?" Connolly thought this was the damnedest question he had ever heard (*This fellow doesn't even know that only Americans boast about money*) but he answered gently, "Well, I think he's probably pretty comfortable." Davey pondered this response, missed its implications, and then pressed on, "Well, are *you* a millionaire?" Connolly was delighted with the question and with the enthusiasm Davey brought to party headquarters on Cooper Street.

Hundreds of other Liberals, older and younger than Connolly, were delighted with Davey too. He had a talent for mobilizing and motivating people, for making problems seem readily soluble, for optimism in the face of disaster. When Gordon sent him out to recruit, he would go after likely candidates as though he were a scout for the National Hockey League. He even used hockey lingo as part of his persuasive pitch. ("We want this guy on side," he would say to a local riding association about some smart young lawyer who had made a reputation on a municipal council, or "We think you would be a great stickhandler" to some go-ahead car dealer who was respected in his home town.) When Davey had a likely candidate lined up, Gordon would authorize the party treasurer to pay his way to Ottawa for an interview with the chief coach, Lester Pearson. In this recruiting drive, Davey was aided in Ontario by Dan Lang and Gordon Edick and in British Columbia by John Nichol, a businessman from Vancouver who was later president of the party and a senator.

Davey spent so much time out in the country, encouraging riding association executives, seeking out candidates, and going to meetings in school auditoriums and church halls, that he came to know by name hundreds of Liberals in every province. He introduced them to a Cell 13 device that had been tested in the 1959 Ontario provincial election under the catch-all title "The School for Practical Politics", which taught basic electoral skills to new candidates and their campaign officials. Nationally, these travelling show-and-tell demonstrations of canvassing, speaking, and advertising methods were called Campaign Colleges and were stage-managed cleverly by Royce Frith and David Greenspan, who had pioneered the techniques in Ontario.

By the time a general election was called in the spring of 1962, Gordon and Davey were able to point to a roster of candidates of such energy, intelligence, and experience that it was evident even to the old guard that the party had indeed been revitalized in the amazingly short space of four years. Among those who, as Gordon ponderously put it, "gave the lead to Canadians" by agreeing to stand for office as Liberals were people like Jack Nicholson and Jack Davis in British Columbia; James Coutts in Alberta; Hazen Argue, who had abandoned the CCF to run as a Liberal in Saskatchewan; Margaret Konantz in Manitoba; Maurice Lamontagne, Maurice Sauvé, Bud Drury, and John Turner in Quebec; and, in Ontario, Edgar Benson, Lloyd Francis, Lucien Lamoureux, Pauline Jewett, Larry Pennell, John Munro, Herb Gray, Eugene Whelan, Mitchell Sharp, Donald Macdonald, James Walker, Ian Wahn, and Walter Gordon himself.

Among hundreds of campaign workers attracted to the party in the same period were several young Liberals who were later to achieve public prominence: Ron Basford, David Smith, Michael McCabe, Duncan Edmonds, Stuart Smith, Ed Roberts, Richard Cashin, and Alec Campbell. Afterwards, when Gordon had suffered his great fall from grace, Gordon Edick still stubbornly insisted that most of the candidates and workers who rallied to the party in the early 1960s came as much for Walter Gordon and Keith Davey as for Lester Pearson. Whether they came because of Davey, Gordon, Pearson, or all three, they were a company of generally enthusiastic and largely liberal Liberals who revered their leader, believed in their party, and appreciated each other's ideas and company.

They were practising what Richard Gwyn, the political columnist, later called "the politics of joy". Partly it was a matter of the atmosphere Davey's personality created, partly it was the tenor of the times. In those years, it was possible for Liberals to convince themselves that turning John Diefenbaker out of office would be not just a political feat but a national service. Diefenbaker had proved himself a maverick prime minister. By his very nature as a small-town prairie lawyer and populist politician, he had quickly alienated the bureaucracy. By 1962 he had alienated the business community as well through such actions as the cancellation of the Avro Arrow aircraft project which scuppered the most promising technological development thrust of the decade, his unbecoming trench warfare with James Coyne, the Governor of the Bank of Canada, and the general uncertainties engendered by his economic policies. In response, accomplished Canadians began to rally in opposition, and Gordon, Davey & Co. were there to show them the way to win office.

Davey had read voraciously in the American popular political literature about new techniques in the engineering of consent that were being developed in the United States, principally mass polling and television advertising. A born fan, Davey loved John Kennedy and the New Frontier almost as much as he loved Lester Pearson and the Liberal Party. As he travelled across Canada on party business, he carried in his moulded attaché case a well-thumbed copy of Theodore White's book *The Making of the President, 1960*, which described minutely the technical details of Kennedy's electoral victory.

At Davey's urging, Gordon interviewed and then hired Kennedy's pollster, Lou Harris, to take soundings on the state of the Canadian electorate's psyche. Harris may have been an American with little knowledge of Canadian political or social intricacies but he was modern, and for a new-guard Liberal, to be modern was to transcend all other considerations. If you were modern, you were urban, educated, reform-minded, adept at dropping words like "participation" and "communication" into every other sentence, and, above all, hard-nosed. You believed in scientifically assessing ridings through statistical analysis. Older politicians knew — or thought they knew — by experience which were the hopeful and which the hopeless ridings. Under Davey, in an approach that was initiated by his friend Dan Lang and later became

second nature to Canadian politicians, previous voting data were
tabulated, the margin of loss or victory was determined riding by
riding, and the decision was made to "target" those "winnable"
ridings where the margin of defeat had been under two per cent or
where the riding had historically maintained a strong Liberal base.

"Don't waste resources where you can't win" was the kind
of adage that Davey formulated from these techniques and
translated into a strategic decision that was to have far-reaching
consequences for the Liberal Party in the next twenty years. Gordon
and Davey decided to concentrate their limited financial and
organizational resources on holding Quebec and making gains in
urban Ontario and British Columbia. Liberals on the prairies and
in the Atlantic provinces would have to rely on their own devices.
If some of the old Liberal strongholds held, great; if they didn't,
too bad.

"Elections aren't won on policy, they're won on issues"
was another crucial maxim Davey borrowed from the Kennedys.
The Liberal Party manifesto devised in the leader's office after
the Kingston Conference and the National Rally of 1961 covered
the whole gamut of policy issues of the day and suggested how a
future Liberal government would deal with them. But Davey knew
that to be effective in the short duration of an election campaign,
the Liberals would have to concentrate on dealing with just a few
points, the kind he liked to call "gut issues". These were the
concerns on the public's mind which the party's pollster could
quickly identify and its advertising team could turn into slogans
to be hammered home in paid advertising as well as in candidates'
speeches. The Toronto advertising firm of MacLaren's decided to
take the risk of working for the financially stretched Opposition
party and assigned a young employee, Richard O'Hagan, who
had formerly been a newspaperman, to work with Davey in Ottawa
on the party's advertising campaign and its publicity arrangements.

Teddy White's book had also illustrated how central to Jack
Kennedy's success the establishment of a good working relationship with the press had been, another technique that coincided
happily with Davey's natural talents. All those years of gossipy
discussions with his father about the Toronto newspaper world
and the inside knowledge about broadcasting he had gained from

working in radio meant he knew intuitively how to talk to journalists, how to flatter them and feed them inside information advantageous to the party.

When John Diefenbaker was able to hang on to power precariously after the election of 1962 despite the Liberals' impressive candidates and modern campaign techniques, Keith Davey's enthusiasm was undampened. He took comfort from the knowledge that the Liberals had cut the Conservatives down from the largest majority any party had ever held in the Commons to the ignominy of a bare minority. His glee held through the 1963 campaign when he exerted his wildest efforts to ensure Pearson a majority. (And some of those efforts were wild indeed. Davey was roundly criticized for dreaming up election gimmicks in the American mode such as a Truth Squad which saw three hapless Liberals trailing Diefenbaker to his campaign meetings in order to uncover his "lies", an Election Colouring Book with heavy line cartoon drawings of the Conservatives over scurrilous captions, and a flock of pigeons whose purpose was to carry the Liberal good news to rallies. The pigeons never arrived.)

After the 1963 election, when the Liberals attained a minority of their own, there was a brief period of euphoria. Pearson did a good job of satisfying both the old and the new guard in the party by his judicious cabinet-making. Gordon was made minister of finance, the job he had wanted for nearly a decade in order to put his economic ideas into effect. Mitchell Sharp was made minister of trade and commerce, Paul Martin got external affairs, Lionel Chevrier went to the justice department and Paul Hellyer to defence — the same roles they had held in the Opposition shadow cabinet. Pearson allowed two other stalwarts, Maurice Lamontagne and Jack Pickersgill, a choice of the remaining portfolios. Lamontagne asked for the presidency of the Privy Council and Pickersgill for secretary of state. Neither portfolio carried heavy administrative duties, which gave them both the freedom they wanted — Pickersgill so that he could devote his energies to matching wits with John Diefenbaker in his other job as the Liberals' House Leader in the Commons, and Lamontagne so that he could tackle the problem of English-French relations, which he and Pearson regarded as the new administration's most urgent problem. In the other appointments, there were surprises involving two of the most contentious figures of the new guard. Judy LaMarsh was given the difficult portfolio of health and welfare, but Maurice Sauvé, an economist from Quebec who had been involved with organizing the provincial Liberals before winning himself a seat in Iles-de-la-Madeleine in 1962 in defiance of the Quebec old guard, was given nothing. When the cabinet-making was over, the deputy ministers were called together and made to understand that the bad days of Diefenbakerism were over and a new and better era was beginning with the Liberals once more in command. Pearson went to London to confer with Prime Minister Harold Macmillan and to Hyannisport, Mass., to confer with President Kennedy. Six years in the wilderness of opposition had made even a minority victory seem sweet indeed. For Keith Davey the whole takeover process was "a real gasser" as he said to his friends, "just the way I'd always dreamed it would be."

Within two months, the politics of joy began to deflate like a helium balloon left to blow in a park after the rally's over. Walter Gordon brought down a disastrously incompetent first budget in May of 1963 — too quickly conceived in response to the urgencies of an election promise Pearson had made about a Liberal government that would change the country's course in Sixty Days of Decision — and watched it turn into a political boomerang. From that moment, when he had been in political office only a few weeks, Gordon's reputation began to fade in the face of the resolute opposition of the bureaucracy and the business community and their allies in the cabinet, Charles M. "Bud" Drury, the Minister of Industry and Gordon's brother-in-law, and Mitchell Sharp, who pounced on his nationalist ideas and set out to destroy them as impractical and just as ill-conceived as the budget itself. Gordon's old friend Pearson was soon beset by dissension between the factions in his cabinet, by John Diefenbaker's inspired attacks in the Commons, by opposition throughout English Canada to his proposal for a Canadian flag, by the urgent demands of an awakening Quebec which his "co-operative federalism" schemes couldn't assuage, and by a series of scandals involving his French-Canadian ministers. He was growing old and confused under pressure, this man who had been like a golden boy until he was sixty. He began to vacillate, sometimes supporting Gordon, sometimes responding to the ideas of the cabinet old guard and his former bureaucratic colleagues and current corporate friends, who were now seeing Gordon not as a brother in arms but as some kind of crazed visionary who was threatening their basic ideas about the economy.

"Pearson was never an economic nationalist," Jack Pickersgill said, looking back. "He was a status nationalist. He wanted the flag, the Order of Canada, ceremonial changes so Canadians could stop feeling like quasi-colonials. But he wasn't interested in economic affairs. He wasn't really that left-wing either. All the time he was in St. Laurent's cabinet he never showed the slightest interest in what we were doing about old-age pensions or equalization payments. He was interested in international affairs and in the ideas of his 'civilized' friends, who ranged all over the ideological map."

As time went on, criticisms of Gordon conveyed to Pearson by friends in Ottawa, Toronto, and Montreal were bolstered by opposition from politicians in Western Canada. Leading Liberals — Ray Perrault in B.C., Adrian Berry in Alberta, Gil Molgat in Manitoba, and Ross Thatcher, who became premier of Saskatchewan in 1964 — expressed their belief that Gordon's ideas were those of a socialist. (Confusingly, Westerners also said that Gordon was a central-Canadian protectionist guarding the interests of the Bay Street capitalists.) This internal warfare was more than Pearson could bear.

Domestic politics seemed to him grubbier than he had thought and he longed for the world of international diplomacy. He had never been interested in politicking — though he had done the necessary chores dutifully — and the hatred felt by Maryon Pearson, his wife, for the process was a party legend. She was given to wearing sunglasses on platforms, to glaring at voters when she could be persuaded to remove her "shades", as the new-guard Grits called them behind her back, and to insulting MPs, their wives, and their workers with a lethal wit — though she could be charming to people she liked. Once, when Pearson was still in opposition, Gordon Edick was riding into Toronto from the airport, sitting with the driver in the front seat of the Pearsons' hired limousine. As the car sped along the highway, he started yelling over his shoulder in the leader's general direction the kind of numerical rundown of party prospects all good sportsmen-politicians love. Mrs. Pearson turned to her husband and said in a queenly manner, "Who *is* this man?" "This man" was one of the party's most faithful workers and he had gone out to the airport in the first place out of kindness as a one-man welcoming committee.

Still, Liberals for the most part sided with Pearson rather than Gordon when the rift between them began to widen. No matter what blunders his government fell into, no matter how indecisive he might appear, Pearson remained lovable in most English-Canadian Liberals' eyes, a distinguished but approachable father figure. His door was open to party stalwarts. He usually appeared to be heeding their advice. When John Aird, a crucially important fund-raiser, and Gordon Dryden, the founder of Cell 13, for instance, felt there was an acute need to reform the system of party financing, Pearson obliged them by setting up a royal commission on the subject. He was always anxious to conciliate between Liberal factions, to charm dissidents with his decency, to make peace at all costs. In any case, Liberals were acutely aware that he had the power of his office behind him, the ability to make or destroy political careers.

Because of the minority government situation, Keith Davey was maintaining the party apparatus in a state of electoral readiness with the aid of Richard O'Hagan, who was now serving as Pearson's press secretary, and Jim Coutts, who had become his appointments secretary. The three men were kept busy stroking the egos of the Liberals out there in the hinterland, mindful of how much their aid would be needed when the party had to go to the country again. They passed on inside stories about the cabinet's vagaries and exploits, telling funny tales about the old-guard party regulars, Jack Pickersgill, Lionel Chevrier, and Paul Martin. Coutts was a superb mimic and he developed an imitation of Martin that always caused his audiences to howl with laughter, depicting the minister touring his riding and doing his famous trick of inquiring after the relatives of his constituents as though they were all dear friends. "And how is that fine woman, your mother?'' Martin was supposed to have asked a young farmer at an evening meeting, only to have him drawl in reply, ''Same as she was when you asked me that in town this morning, Mr. Martin. Dead.''

The trio was just as caustic telling stories about their own foibles — Coutts's penchant for Christian Dior pyjamas and tall women, O'Hagan's fondness for hand-made shirts and three-hundred-dollar suits, and Davey's continuing teetotalism. No matter how many political conventions, expensive restaurant dinners, or state receptions they attended, Davey and his wife, Isobel, resolutely resisted drinking alcohol anywhere or serving it in their house. John Nichol, the most active new-guard Liberal in B.C., got fed up with what he regarded as an untenable situation and one night, while sitting in the Daveys' living room in suburban Ottawa, said yes when asked if he would like a drink. Then, rather than waiting to find out whether he'd be offered coffee, Coke, or lemonade, he snapped open his brief-case on his knees and with a flourish brought out a bottle of expensive Scotch and two glasses, one for himself and one for his wife, Elizabeth.

Pearson enjoyed hearing about that kind of caper and his followers never hesitated to tell him of their goings-on. They forgave him his weaknesses as party leader not just because of the glorious reputation of his past but because of the warmth of his response to their needs as people, and his continuing espousal of the progressive Liberal policies being developed by his government — ideas for tackling regional economic disparities, setting up a universal medical-insurance scheme, making the federal public service bilingual — policies which seemed to them more achievable than Walter Gordon's ideas for repatriating the economy. Many of the Liberals Gordon had attracted to the party had never entirely accepted his economic theories anyway. It was his personal wealth and his managerial expertise that had impressed them. When his troubles with his first budget were compounded by a currency exchange crisis in the summer of 1963 and a brouhaha with David Rockefeller, the American titan, over his takeover of the Mercantile Bank's Canadian operation, Liberals began to fear that he was an inept dreamer and his bad luck might be contagious.

No matter what his friends said, Keith Davey remained stubbornly loyal to both Pearson and Gordon. Pearson he revered as his leader, Gordon he venerated as his mentor, "a super guy who taught me everything I know". Davey had become "a gut nationalist" as he called it because of his respect for Gordon's views and the fact that the *Toronto Star* espoused them editorially. He clung to the belief that Pearson would be able to govern well and to fulfil the promises he had made Gordon if only the party machine could wrest a majority government for him from the reluctant electorate. In September 1965, on the dubious strength of polls they had commissioned from Oliver Quayle (another American who had succeeded Lou Harris as their pollster), Davey and Gordon persuaded Pearson to go to the country once more. The campaign was a disaster. Pearson was a reluctant warrior, terrified of John Diefenbaker, who went around the country flailing at him wildly, hitting hard at his government's inefficiencies and the scandals involving his French-Canadian ministers. The Tories were able to consolidate the anti-Liberal feeling which had been growing on the prairies for several years and had proven unresponsive to Davey's modern techniques. In this campaign those techniques didn't work very well elsewhere either. There were embarrassing failures at rallies in terms of the size of crowds assembled and the workings of sound systems and the unsaleability of "poor old pooper Pearson" as the men in the Press Gallery took to calling the Prime Minister. Pearson, for all his charm, intelligence, and decency, wasn't, and never would be, appealing to a mass audience.

On election night, November 8, Keith Davey ran up and down stairs from his office on the ground floor to a meeting room on the second where Pearson was sitting with his wife and a few close friends, trying to make the bad news sound better. But within sixty minutes of the polls' close, the results were obvious, and after that awful hour Davey never really recovered the ebullience he had brought with him to Ottawa. He was like a cheerleader whose paper pompoms had got wet in the rain and run all over his white buck shoes. Pearson eventually went downtown to meet the press and acknowledge that the Liberals had only gained two seats more and were still faced with a minority situation in the Commons.

Watching the results in Toronto, Walter Gordon acknowledged that as campaign manager in English Canada for three elections which had failed to produce a Liberal majority, he felt directly responsible for the party's position. Furthermore, as an experienced player of power games, he knew that his influence in the government would now be severely limited. (Even before the disappointment of the results, Pearson had told several businessmen privately that he expected that in his next cabinet Robert Winters, a resolutely old-guard former cabinet minister now a Toronto corporate executive, would replace Gordon as his finance minister. True to his inconstant form, in public he insisted that he intended to keep Gordon on after the election, while telling bureaucratic friends that he was going to replace him not with Winters but with Mitchell Sharp.)

After the election, Gordon resigned from the cabinet and Keith Davey gave up his job as national organizer. They told themselves they were leaving behind them a modernized party machine that would stand the Liberals in good stead for decades. In the previous six years they had broadened the party's base in the urban areas of the country, centralized its operations in Ottawa, cut out some of the worst of the old petty-patronage practices, set in train important changes in fund-raising, taught new campaign techniques to dozens of candidates and hundreds of workers, and tried to make sure that there was an active constituency organization in every riding in English Canada.

That they had never even come close to Cell 13's goal of making the party open to the grass roots and were simply replacing one elite with another, or that their decision to centralize the party's operations would cause Liberalism grave difficulties in Western Canada in the future, they couldn't appreciate and wouldn't have admitted in any case.

Despite the brave front they put up, what they took away from their days of glory was a certain disillusionment that they disguised even from each other. They were both resilient men and they went on playing the roles they had assigned themselves — Keith Davey as Candide and Walter Gordon as Don Quixote. But it would be many years before their ideas would again have purchase within the Liberal Party.

Those times, both good and bad, seemed long ago and dismayingly far away to Senator Davey on the night of March 26, 1979, as he waited in the Senate for the news to be conveyed to the Speaker from the Governor General's residence that an election had been called. As he looked back, the Liberal Party's prospects in the 1960s now appeared enviable and the vacillations of Lester Pearson endearing. In this campaign, Senator Davey was directing a party machine in a very different state of readiness and a leader with a very different cast of mind.

PART TWO

PIERRE TRUDEAU AND THE POLITICS
OF PASSION
The Liberal Party, 1965–1972

THE MAN SLIPPING INTO RIDEAU HALL the night of March 26, 1979, on his way to a ceremonial conference with the Governor General was so sure of foot and so sleek of profile it was hard to believe that in six months he would be sixty years old. This was the fourth time in the eleven years he had been prime minister that Pierre Elliott Trudeau had come to this place for this purpose, the third governor general he had advised that, as leader of the Liberal Party of Canada, he intended to seek a mandate from the electorate.

This time his situation was more uncertain than it had ever been before. Despite his great advantages — the power his office bestowed on him, the historic strength of the party he led, the weaknesses of his opponents, the intensity of his lifelong will to win — in this election his disadvantages would seem to outweigh them.

He knew he could count on Quebec's overwhelming support, derived not just from ancient loyalties and a ruthlessly effective political machine but from a special regard for Trudeau as a French Canadian operating among "les autres", an attachment that was almost familial in its intensity even among Québécois who disagreed vehemently with his stance on federalism. But Trudeau also knew that the electorate in the nine other provinces was deeply uneasy about the country's situation and a large element within it had translated this unease into an anger focused on his person. Out there in English Canada where the election had to be won, in every tavern, day-care centre, church basement, post office, and golf club, there were people to be found who hated his guts, who really believed that Canada's prospects would improve instantaneously if he were swept from office.

Even within his own party, among the English-Canadian Liberal loyalists there was a feeling of ambivalence towards him that had been there since he first took office in 1968 and that now approached a kind of schizophrenia. In the disastrous by-election campaign of the previous October, when the party had lost all but

53

two of the fifteen seats contested, Liberals by the dozens had refused to turn out to work, saying openly to the organizers who phoned them, "Not while *he's* the leader. No way."

Trudeau was going into this campaign alienated from almost everyone but the small cadre around him. His failure to reach an agreement on constitutional reform at a last-ditch federal-provincial conference held in February meant he might never realize one of the most central of his original ambitions as a politician: the patriation of the constitution with an entrenched bill of rights that would guarantee the linguistic equality of French Canadians within the Canadian federation. His closest friends and ideological allies from Quebec were scattered. His cabinet had been stripped of its strongest English-Canadian ministers by a series of resignations and retirements. His young wife had staged a flamboyant public separation from him two years before and had been crudely betraying him in the capitals of the world ever since, her behaviour calling up from his adherents both sympathy and rage at his apparent inability to control her.

Throughout the winter, as the opinion polls continued to show the Liberals in disfavour with the electorate in every province but Quebec, there had been attempts made by the press to uncover rebellion in the Liberal ranks. There were constant whisperings in the party about the possibility that Trudeau might be deposed and be replaced by his former minister of finance, John Turner, who had resigned from his cabinet in anger in 1975 and who was thought to be fomenting dissension deliberately from his law offices in Toronto.

The rumours and the whisperings had come to nothing. For months Jim Coutts and Keith Davey, who were Trudeau's liaison with the English-Canadian wing of the party, had been telling dissatisfied Liberals that despite everything, Trudeau was the best weapon the party had, that the campaign would have to be centred on his leadership qualities, that he was brilliant on the hustings, that up against Joe Clark, the altogether ordinary young man the Conservatives had offered up as their leader, he would look like a titan, a prince, a colossus. Trudeau alone could save them all from the ignominies of defeat.

This argument usually silenced his detractors, at least while

Coutts or Davey was within earshot. Even Turner had to admit that Trudeau's intellect was unmatchable in Canadian politics, an instrument as sharp and pitiless as a sword, and everybody knew how effective that intellect had proven when set on the attainment of a goal. Pierre Trudeau had been a winner all his life and maybe he could win again, the Grits said grudgingly to each other as they shouldered once more the burden of loyalty to the leader that was part of the Liberal faith.

Most Liberals had never felt that Trudeau was "one of us" despite the dazzling speeches in praise of the party and its historic virtues that his staff had prepared for him to deliver in the previous three years. These feelings didn't stem entirely from the fact that he had come into the party in 1965 as an all too obviously pragmatic convert to the cause, an intellectual activist who had previously been bitterly and wittily critical of Liberalism.

Instead, it was Trudeau's attitudes that disturbed them, or what they would be more likely to call his style. After eleven years of his leadership, after the hundreds of appearances he had made at party functions, the thousands of opportunities Grits had seized to have a word with the PM, the dozens of analyses of his character that had appeared in print, and the scores of interviews with him on television that had supposedly revealed his inner being, most Liberals were still quick to say that they didn't really understand him.

After emerging from a Liberal meeting in Vancouver earlier that winter, called to discuss what could be done to improve the party's dismal prospects in B.C., Paul Manning, the candidate in Vancouver-Quadra, remarked to a journalist, "We decided that he's a weird bugger but a smart one and maybe he can pull it off," thereby summing up the considered opinion of countless numbers of his peers. On Trudeau's strengths the Liberals' hopes were centred in this election, and on his eccentricities, their fears.

II

MANY MONTHS BEFORE, during the seemingly interminable period when the Liberals were gearing up for this campaign, Richard O'Hagan, Trudeau's communications adviser, had convened a meeting in a suite in the Royal York Hotel in downtown Toronto, inviting for lunch in the Prime Minister's name half a dozen important English-Canadian publishers. Trudeau had a long history of bad relations not just with reporters and editors but with their employers as well, many of whom had been offended by his expressed indifference to their publications' expressed opinions.

O'Hagan had been labouring for nearly two years to try to repair the damage to Trudeau's image of this mutually sustained hostility, and the Royal York lunch was an important part of his plan. He had picked the guests carefully: John Bassett, the former publisher of the Toronto *Telegram*, now chairman of Baton Broadcasting, the owner of the Toronto television station CFTO-TV, and chairman of Inland Publishing Company Limited, which controlled half a dozen Ontario weekly newspapers; Brigadier Richard Malone, the publisher of the Toronto *Globe and Mail* and president of the FP chain of newspapers; Walter Dimma, the president of Toronto Star Newspapers Limited; Paul Deacon, publisher of *The Financial Post*; Michael de Pencier, publisher of *Toronto Life*; Gordon Fisher, the president of the Southam Press, owners of fourteen daily newspapers in cities across the country and the weekly *Financial Times*; and to give the gathering some extra zest, Gordon Sinclair, the venerable newsman still broadcasting daily his outrageous opinions on CFRB, the radio station with the largest audience in the Toronto area. (It was not the least of Sinclair's idiosyncrasies that he still stubbornly admired Trudeau after most of his fellow journalists had grown to dislike him.)

The lunch party started a little awkwardly shortly after noon. The guests avoided certain subjects — the antics of Margaret Trudeau, who was in the international press constantly describing her lovers, her ambitions, her clothes, her anatomy, in a way that no Canadian woman, let alone a prime minister's wife, had ever done before; their rage as corporate capitalists at the government's inability to come to grips with the problems of the stagnating Canadian economy; the Liberals' steady slippage in the opinion polls; the purpose of this lunch, which was presumably to court their editorial favour — all the topics that were really foremost in their minds. Small talk was traded, with Sinclair, Malone, and, above all, Bassett carrying the conversational burden while Trudeau sat up very straight on an ottoman in the sitting room of the hotel suite, sipping orange juice while most of the others drank Scotch, trying to look engrossed in the conversation, showing in his replies that he remembered people's names and backgrounds, as O'Hagan had told him he must. Finally, after some scattered talk about the price of newsprint and the shortage of oil, the company settled in at table. The *filet de boeuf* was served, the Bordeaux poured, and the men began to relax a little, to make easy jokes, to trade stories about their response to the Grey Cup football game which had taken place the previous Sunday in Montreal. Trudeau had attended the game and so had several others in the room; the rest, like nearly every other good ol' boy in the country, had seen it on television, enjoying the rites of autumn, watching the most important sports event of the year.

Somebody mentioned the presence of René Lévesque, the Quebec premier, in the stands of the stadium wearing a toque and there was a round of mildly derisive murmuring. (No matter how his other policies were perceived, Trudeau was still thought of in English Canada as the champion of federalism, and Lévesque, the avowed separatist, with his proposals for sovereignty-association and a unilingual Quebec, was regarded with fear and loathing as an unregenerate villain.) One of the guests, apparently expecting approval from his host, said in some bemusement, "Do you know the guy had never seen a football game before?" There was general hearty laughter at such an absurdity. But instead of responding as was expected with laughter of his own, Trudeau bristled visibly and looked at his guests with his eyes narrowed for a chilly silent second. Then he said in the nasal tone his voice characteristically took on when he was controlling his anger, "Why should he have? I had never been to a football game myself until I was Minister of Justice. It may be difficult for you people to understand but football is *not* a French-Canadian sport.''

For a few seconds, no one responded. O'Hagan, who had been watching the proceedings with anxious professional concern from the far end of the table, looked down at its starched white cloth and began to push the food around on his plate as if he were making a fork painting. (*O my God! Is it going to turn into a snarling match?*) Wine glasses were raised thoughtfully as Trudeau's response was absorbed. (*Is he defending Lévesque, his arch enemy? Is he saying he doesn't like football?*) Finally, the commanding voice of John Bassett was heard in the room. He began to talk smoothly about lacrosse, which was a French-Canadian sport, and about his youth in Quebec, where his father was president of the Montreal *Gazette*, and a majority shareholder in the *Sherbrooke Record*. Trudeau picked up the conversation. O'Hagan began to breathe more easily. Other voices joined in, and the moment passed.

There was more scattered talk about the possibility of recruiting a new group of Liberals in English Canada, about the unhappy mood of the West, the intractability of inflation, possible measures that might be taken to counter the separatists in Quebec. By the time the lunch was over an hour later and Trudeau had swept on to his next engagement, with his train of advisers following in his wake, the gentlemen owners of the press were ready to go back to their offices, if not entranced by Trudeau at least momentarily mollified. O'Hagan's purpose, which was admittedly modest — ''I just wanted to get them talking together to show them he doesn't have horns'' — appeared to have been accomplished. But all the same, there was something about the scene that lingered in the mind. Its elements seemed so symbolic of Trudeau's ''otherness'', of those mannerisms, attitudes, and experiences that separated him so drastically from the English-Canadian wing of his party and from so much of the country that he had conquered at the polls. What had always set Trudeau apart were his two most obvious attributes: his Frenchness and his intellectualism.

The country had been governed twice by prime ministers from Quebec before Trudeau took office in 1968. But both Sir Wilfrid Laurier and Louis St. Laurent had turned themselves into the kind of readily understandable stereotypes that soothed the

Anglos' racial unease. Laurier was the silver-tongued orator, the lawyer from the country town who loved the Empire and, until the racial conflicts that erupted in Canada during the 1914–18 war, praised all things British as beautiful whenever he had the chance. St. Laurent was Uncle Louis, the half-Irish Quebec City lawyer with the coolly precise private manner that made him the ideal token French Canadian in the corporate boardrooms, coupled with the comfortingly folksy public façade that made him acceptable in legion halls and church basements in the rest of the country.

Until Trudeau, the country had never before had a professed intellectual as prime minister, much less a French-Canadian Catholic intellectual. In English Canada, before Trudeau's rise, the intellectuals and the two old parties had tended towards mutual distrust. Among most academics, involvement with party politics — other than with the CCF and its successor, the NDP — had long been seen as suspect, and among politicians, intellectuals had been traditionally considered impractical on the whole, people best kept within the confines of the universities and the civil service, useful as policy-makers, grey eminences for cabinet ministers who could interpret their ideas, or as contributors of research papers to royal commissions, but temperamentally unsuited to the rigours of practical politics. The country had been too raw, too admiring of its doers and survivors, to recognize the importance of its thinkers. The intellectual as man of action was a concept that was mostly unheeded, if not entirely unknown.

Trudeau never seemed to come to grips with the implications of this incompatibility. Within his own milieu he didn't have to hide his intellectualism. In Quebec's hierarchical society, the intellectual had a definite place. (Too important a place, Trudeau himself once said: "As a people we have spun a thousand theories and remained almost completely impotent.") In the years he had been active in party politics, intellectuals of his generation and the one immediately after it had dominated politics in French Canada.

At the time Trudeau came to prominence in English Canada as a cabinet minister in 1967, the country was in an uncharacteristically open and optimistic mood. Both his Frenchness and his intellectualism were acceptable mostly because they came wrapped in a number of other attributes — physical prowess, a powerful sexuality which he enhanced with his calculated flirtatiousness, a talent for romanticizing his past, and a genius for sounding as though he knew how to solve Canada's bi-racial problems — his famous stance on federalism that had the nation's patriots wringing their hands in hope and the nation's bigots seeing him as the Frenchman who would keep the French in their place. All these things masked his real nature and defused the Anglo-Canadian public's natural mistrust of both the egghead and the French Canadian. It was only when the loving stopped entirely in the economic and national-unity crisis of the mid-1970s that English Canada began to see how alien Trudeau's attitudes were, how very different was the system of values of which he was a product, how much he remained in the country outside Quebec, after nearly a decade in the public eye, "un inconnu très connu".

For years Trudeau was believed to be not just bilingual but bicultural, a rare creature who could feel entirely at home in either of the nation's cultures. It took a long time and the dual dramas of John Turner's resignation as finance minister in 1975 and René Lévesque's election as Quebec premier in 1976 for the country at large to realize that, despite his effortless English, the subliminal signals Trudeau sent out, and the culture from which they were transmitted, were French. As a consequence, they were unfamiliar to the Richard Malones and the Gordon Fishers, or for that matter to the Joe Clarks and the John Turners, and so were the signals they sent him in exchange. If Richard O'Hagan had put together a working lunch for an English-Canadian politician, John Turner, say, in a Royal York Hotel suite in the late 1970s, the atmosphere would have been very different. First of all, publishers as powerful as the men gathered in that dining room would have talked to Turner often before on a continuing basis. He would have bounded into the room, pumped his guests' hands, greeted each one by his Christian name, asked after their wives and their balance sheets, told them half a dozen stories about his encounters with the great international figures of their time, sought their opinions on the economic situation, expressed his view, in strictest confidence, of the state of the country, and left them with the feeling that they were witnesses to history, stout allies in his once and future political battles, big men all of them attacking big issues and bent on wrestling them to the ground.

But for Trudeau, the publishers' lunch was not a political opportunity to be seized, it was an annoyance and a bore. He had never been willing to be droll, or deferential, to handle such men with calculated charm. He was attending this lunch because his political staff had told him he must. These men weren't intellectually stimulating, they weren't even articulate, he complained to O'Hagan later. They didn't have anything much but commonplaces to impart. Thank God for Bassett, he at least had enough élan to keep the conversation moving so it could be endured. What O'Hagan was too circumspect to tell him in reply was that the publishers hadn't said very much because they were ill at ease. Their conversation came out of the urgencies of the boardroom and the club lounge, not the common room and the Privy Council Office. They were corporate men, interested in power and money, not intellectual men interested in disputation and speculation. The forces that had formed Trudeau were so different from those that had formed the men at the Royal York that they were, in effect, foreigners to each other. What they needed was a diplomatic briefing before they met.

III

WHEN TRUDEAU FIRST BECAME A CELEBRITY in Canada during his drive to the Liberal leadership, a myth was made about his past life — a brilliant, seductive, very nearly archetypal myth — which persisted afterwards no matter how many further details were revealed that contradicted its simplicities. He had been born into a rich family — "as rich as the great English Montreal families like the Molsons, only not so famous" — was the way the Toronto *Telegram* put it, in the kind of statement that was thought insightful at the time. He was described as a superlative student, a fearless adventurer who had roamed the world in search of sensation, an athlete of formidable prowess, a writer of impeccable style, a playboy sought after by women, and a reformer who had done battle with Maurice Duplessis, the dark dragon of the Québécois past. Above all he was perfectly bilingual, with his French father and his English mother, his Jesuit education at home and his post-graduate education abroad, the pan-Canadian the country had been looking for, who fused the English and French into one, a kind of racial hermaphrodite, the unmatchable bicultural man. The myth was so appealing and so pervasive that it was difficult later to examine Trudeau realistically in relation to the family and the society out of which he had come.

Trudeau was always reluctant to talk frankly or revealingly about his past — in a way he was the creator and the keeper of his own myth — but he did make it clear to the newspaperman George Radwanski, in one of a series of unusually open interviews he agreed to give in 1977 as part of his staff's concerted effort to improve his publicity, that he thought of himself not as an Anglo-French hybrid but as decidedly French Canadian. This statement echoed an even stronger one he had made in the introduction to *Federalism and the French Canadians*, a collection of his essays published in 1968, to the effect that if he had not been born a French Canadian, he would have chosen to become one.

Certainly, to anyone who observed him closely as a politician over a long period, it was evident that despite his English-speaking mother and the years spent at Harvard and the London School of Economics, despite the extensive travelling and his superb command of the English language — he could be elegant, he could be slangy, he could turn a pun or enhance a phrase with a precision that put most anglophones to shame — his visceral response came out of his deep roots in Quebec society.

Plainly he drew strength from that solid phalanx of ten generations of Trudeaus stretching back more than three hundred years through Quebec's history to 1659. But plainly he also bore, as did every educated French Canadian of his generation, the psychological weight of the Conquest a century later. His father, Charles-Emile Trudeau, may have become a millionaire businessman, but his grandfather, Joseph Trudeau, was a unilingual, illiterate farmer from St. Michel de Napierville, who brought his produce for sale into the Bonsecours market in Montreal.

This grandfather and his wife Malvina, whom Trudeau remembered from his childhood as a strong peasant woman, a widow dressed always in black, were determined that their children should be educated. Their second son, Charles-Emile, became a lawyer in Montreal before the First World War, and after it a wealthy man through shrewd investment in a chain of gasoline stations which he eventually sold to Imperial Oil. But for all his prosperity, the world Charlie Trudeau inhabited in the 1920s and 1930s was very different from the world of the English-Canadian business class in the province.

In those years, Quebec was like two separate garrisons in its upper and upper-middle reaches. The old dominant English business class, with its great merchant families whose fortunes were made in the nineteenth and early twentieth centuries, may have been past its entrepreneurial prime but its social snobbery was at its peak while Pierre Trudeau was growing up. Its members were not about to open their houses, their institutions, or their hearts to upstart French Canadians. (They weren't receptive to upstart English Canadians either. Max Aitken and Isaak Walton Killam, two Maritimers who came to Montreal to make a start on the huge fortunes they eventually amassed, were both seen as Johnny-come-latelies and kept out of the best clubs. As for the upstart Irish and the Jews, well, my dear, they really *wanted* to keep to themselves, is what the Anglostocracy always said.)

Not only were the English and French bourgeoisies separated by the religious affiliations of the school systems, they lived in different areas (Westmount and Outremont); they went to different universities (McGill and the Université de Montréal); they belonged to different clubs (the Mount Royal and St. James's clubs, where the Anglo-Montrealers talked business, and the Club St. Denis); they supported different cultural organizations (at one point there were two symphony orchestras, one for each race); they attended different social galas (the St. Andrew's Ball and Le Bal des Petits Souliers); and they had very different ways of making money. The Anglos were in the big corporations, the trust and insurance companies, the shipping companies, and the breweries, on the bank boards and the stock exchange, with connections to London, Boston, and New York. There was a French elite on the bench, in the government, and in the Roman Catholic church, but not among the managers of the economy. The French-Canadian businessmen were for the most part *petits bourgeois*. They might own shops, gas stations, amusement parks, and small manufacturing firms, but they had few connections to the business world beyond the province, having been abandoned by French financial interests after the Conquest and ignored ever since. Their lesser place in the capitalist hierarchy was reinforced by the teachings of their own dominant institution, the Roman Catholic Church. French Canadians were an unspoiled people who belonged to the land and to God. Involvement in industry and commerce would sully their purity as a race.

In his memoirs, *What's Past Is Prologue*, Vincent Massey alluded to the separate but supposedly equal status of the two founding races in describing the customs of the Garrison Club in Quebec City. "One of [the club's] traditions," he wrote, "is the reservation of one room for English-speaking members and another for French-speaking members, with a communicating door between the two which is always opened on New Year's Eve . . ." and then added, approvingly, "The arrangement . . . illustrates the important principle that there are natural differences between French- and English-speaking Canadians. . . ." What Massey was saying ponderously was that the two groups comprised "parallel elites", as the sociologists call them; what he wasn't saying was that in the minds of the English, at least, there was no doubt which was superior.

After Pierre Trudeau became prime minister, Grace Pitfield — the mother of his régime's most prominent public servant, Michael Pitfield, who had been born into one of the old English-Canadian Montreal families and had relatives married into half the others — reminisced about French-English relations in her youth and early married life. "We didn't talk to the French Canadians very much in those days [the 1920s and 1930s]," she said. "Except for a few people like Georges Vanier [later the governor general] and his wife Pauline, they just didn't go to the places we went to or do the things we did. I mean, you never even *saw* them at the Ritz. Some of my friends had been at school with Grace Elliott [Trudeau's mother, who had been educated at Dunham Ladies' College in the Eastern Townships and was the daughter of an English-speaking businessman said to be descended from United Empire Loyalists]. They heard later that she had married a Frenchman. But nobody knew who he was and of course they never saw her afterwards." In brief, the Trudeaus were not "just like the Molsons", they weren't just like the old-rich French-Canadian families like the Simards or the Taschereaus either. They were the Outremont new rich, members of a small, recently prosperous urban middle class. Grace Elliott may have been gently reared, but her father had made his money in tavern-keeping and her husband in selling gas.

By most accounts, including his own, Pierre Trudeau's parents were very different temperamentally. In press descriptions they were often made to represent the stereotypical characteristics of the two founding races as well as the prototypical Victorian masculine and feminine virtues. What emerges from the hyperbole is a clear picture of Charlie Trudeau as a man of energy and flair, an entrepreneurial hustler who was physically and psychically tough. He didn't content himself with practising law despite the fact that, as a farm boy, his achievement of professional status was a considerable accomplishment. He wanted his share of the 1920s boom and he set out to get it in an imaginative way through a company he founded in 1927 called the Automobile Owners' Association. Despite the institutional aura of its name, it was a commercial venture that, for a ten-dollar fee, gave its members a road map, free towing, and reductions on oil and greasing in its service stations as shrewd inducements to the purchase of gas. It cashed in on the car craze of the period and boasted fifteen thousand members dealing with its thirty filling stations on Montreal Island when Charlie Trudeau sold it to Imperial Oil in 1933. According to Roddy Choquette, an accountant who acted as general manager of the AOA, Charlie Trudeau was paid a million dollars for his seventy-five per cent share, a sum Choquette believed he was able to double through other investments before he died. He put money into mining and steel stocks and into Belmont Park, a Montreal version of New York's Coney Island, as well as buying a share of the Montreal Royals, the baseball team whose games he loved to watch. He also loved boxing matches and playing high-stake poker as often as two or three nights a week at the Club St. Denis. In politics, he was *bleu* as his parents were before him, backing Camillien Houde for the leadership of the Quebec Conservative Party in 1929. Houde would drive up to the Trudeau business headquarters and say, "J'ai besoin d'oxygène," meaning he needed money, and Charlie Trudeau would dispatch Choquette to the safe in the back office to get a hundred dollars while he gossiped with Houde out front.

What Grace Elliott thought of her husband's business success and sporting life has never been publicly described. Until her son became leader of the Liberal Party, she was able, as ladies of her time were taught was appropriate, to keep her name out of the papers except on the occasions of births, marriages, deaths, and appointments to the boards of cultural institutions. She has been repeatedly depicted as restrained, delicate, and puritanical — the kind of genteel woman admired as a type in both English and French Canada for a couple of generations after Victoria, the queen who had created the ideal, had died. Certainly Grace Trudeau's interest in music and art, and the kind of household she ran, seemed to have little connection in style with the rough worlds of professional sport and small business through which her husband cut such a swath. She always talked in a low voice and liked other people to follow suit. She encouraged her children to have musicales on Sunday evenings, she invited other ladies in for afternoon tea, she cherished a Dresden china set, she kept her wedding trousseau lingerie wrapped in tissue for more than half a century, and she lived throughout her married life and protracted widowhood in Outremont — first in a modest dwelling on Durocher Street, then in a larger brick house on McCulloch Avenue that was built around the turn of the century and was still furnished in the dark wood and petit-point chairs of that period when she died in 1973. Above all she was intensely religious, a faithful attendant at Mass, fierce in her devotion to Catholicism, an other-worldly woman married to a worldly man.

Despite the temperamental differences between his parents, Pierre Trudeau always turned aside questions or suggestions that might characterize his childhood as conflictual. He remembered being delicate, a boy who had to do rigorous exercises to build up his health, who felt puny in comparison to his country cousins, tough boys growing up on farms, much as his father had done a generation before at St. Michel de Napierville. As an adult Trudeau vividly remembered holiday scenes from his childhood in his relatives' big farmhouse kitchens, where his uncles, with beads of sweat standing on their foreheads from the heat of the stove, carved huge roasts or turkeys and their noisy families crowded around the table, waiting hungrily to be served. At home in Outremont, even among the petit-point chairs, his father was still the dominating presence, a strong disciplinarian who would return late in the day to ask penetrating questions about what Pierre and Suzette and Charles, his sister and brother, had accomplished at school, before going out again to play poker or do deals. He taught the boys to box, and took them hunting and fishing, and in the summers when they were staying in the country, he would come on weekends bringing an entourage of rowdy, laughing, swearing men, sometimes athletes he had an interest in, baseball players from the Montreal Royals or a young boxer he owned a share of named Leo-the-Kid Roy.

From all accounts Charlie Trudeau would have been a formidable father for any boy — demanding, successful, seemingly all powerful in his own milieu, "afraid of nothing" as his ac-

countant, Roddy Choquette, claimed — but doubly formidable
for a boy who was sensitive, intelligent, inclined to be sickly, and
forced to comply at least part of the time with the very different
standards of behaviour set by his mother. Charlie Trudeau must
also have been enormously attractive to his children in his vivacity,
his certainty, and his warmth. He was a great hugger, Pierre
Trudeau once said, and he is repeatedly described as full of life,
as though all around him there was laughter, noise, and light.
Then suddenly he died, with dramatic swiftness, of pneumonia
contracted at the Montreal Royals' training camp in Florida in the
spring of 1935 when he was forty-seven and Pierre was fifteen.

After Trudeau became famous as a federalist, it was fashionable in Quebec to say that this death of his father in his mid-
adolescence altered his life radically, swinging his allegiance to
the English side of his dual inheritance. Separatist sympathizers
like Michel Chartrand, the radical union official who had been a
schoolmate of Trudeau's, liked to say that he wasn't really a French
Canadian at heart but English like his mother. His middle name
Elliott was spat out as part of the "proof" of his Englishness and
his alienation from Quebec.

Yet however often it may be repeated, the theory of Trudeau
as a closet WASP doesn't bear scrutiny. Trudeau at fifteen was a
French Canadian born, bred, and educated. His mother may have
been primarily English-speaking — which made English as ready
on his tongue as French — but her own mother was a French
Canadian; she had been sent to a convent before the ladies' college claimed her in her teens and she lived as a devout Roman
Catholic among French Canadians all her life. After her husband
died, she continued to send her sons to Jean de Brébeuf, the classical college run by the Jesuits where Pierre Trudeau studied from
the age of twelve until he received his baccalaureate at twenty.
Trudeau went on from Brébeuf to the Université de Montréal and,
according to his close friends Gérard Pelletier and Jacques Hébert,
his family was never regarded as assimilated by their peers.
Pelletier particularly was at pains to point out that such people
went to English schools, and to McGill, and moved away to
Westmount. All of Trudeau's friends from his childhood and his
early manhood were French Canadians: Pierre Vadeboncoeur, Guy

Viau, Roger Rolland, Jean de Grandpré, Guy Marcotte, the much younger Philippe de Gaspé Beaubien. His most influential teachers were the priests Father Robert Bernier and Father François Hertel from Brébeuf. Most of the writers he quoted throughout his public life were French, from Buffon (whose famous phrase "the style is the man himself" Trudeau used to such effect in his leadership race), to Edmond Rostand (whose romantic lines from *Cyrano de Bergerac* Trudeau could still quote at length and with startling accuracy forty years after he'd memorized them).

It seems more likely that the difficulties created in Trudeau's life by his father's early death were less a conflict between the French and English elements warring within the bosom of a single boy than a prolonged crisis of identity — the classical crisis with its "who am I and what will I be?" questions that most adolescents must deal with but that in Trudeau's case seemed to take another fifteen years to resolve. If it's the adolescent's job to forge himself an identity out of the multiple, sometimes shifting, often contradictory needs of his own character and the demands of his parental adjudicators, if he must, as Freud and Erikson have it, prove his own strength in relation to his parent to show himself the equal in manhood of the all-powerful father of his childhood, then Pierre Trudeau was indeed marked both by Charlie Trudeau's flamboyantly masculine life — so Latin in its relentless machismo — and by his dramatic early death.

From his friends' scattered revelations of how Trudeau behaved from 1935 to 1949, there emerges a picture of a late adolescence and young manhood riddled with contradictions, a boy forced to construct an elaborate public façade behind which he could play out his internal doubts, hopes, and fears. In the past he had often been combative — physically aggressive and lippy — with the other boys and his teachers at school. Now he began to create the swaggering persona that he donned occasionally ever afterwards as a device to distance himself from others. Even though his father was no longer around to goad him on, his need to excel scholastically and athletically seems to have grown more rather than less intense. Classmates remembered him picking senseless fights at school and on streetcars, calling himself Pierre *Esprit* Trudeau for a while in honour of Pierre Esprit Radisson, the explorer, roaring around on a motorcycle and sleeping on the roadside. He did well at his studies, competing relentlessly and sometimes winning top honours, though the notion that he was always the best student in his class was disputed later by other Brébeuf students who came forward to claim they had beaten him in their time. He learned to dive, to box, to read music, to look at art and architecture with an educated eye. He read Racine and Corneille and set out to lose his Québécois accent in order to achieve the perfection in classical French that these writers' style represented in his mind. He tried to perfect his English as well and took elocution lessons to ensure that his voice in both languages was mellifluous and firm.

Because of the isolation of Quebec society and his family's comfortable financial position, he was affected only peripherally — in a way that few young men of his generation in English Canada could be — by the great international events that shook the 1930s and 1940s. The Depression didn't touch the Trudeaus financially; in fact it marked the period when their money was made. There was never any evidence that they lived luxuriously, except for the fact that after Charlie Trudeau sold out his business to Imperial Oil, the family went on an extended trip to Europe, and the year he died, they intended to join him in Florida for the Easter vacation. Grace Trudeau was frugal by temperament and she had married a far-from-rich young lawyer whose fortune wasn't made until he was well into his forties. After her husband died, the income from his investments made it possible for the Trudeaus' family life to continue as before in material terms, with the dark house on McCulloch Avenue still offering its middle-class comforts. The expensive education Charlie Trudeau had shrewdly considered important for his sons continued to be encouraged and so was the sports program to strengthen them physically. Pierre was sent for a summer to the rigorous Taylor Statten wilderness camp in Algonquin Park, one of the few occasions before he went into politics when he came into contact with the English-Canadian elite. The offspring of the Toronto well-to-do who spent their summers at Taylor Statten were astonished by his penchant for quoting Beaudelaire and by his prowess as a canoeist.

Similarly, the Second World War was less a cataclysm in

Trudeau's life than a nuisance. He had considered studying psychology but there was no such course offered at the Université de Montréal and he couldn't go abroad because of the war. His father had always said he should get a legal degree as a base for anything else he might want to do, so he enrolled in law at the university in 1940. Like many French Canadians of the educated class he resisted enlistment in the armed forces by serving with the Canadian Officers Training Corps instead, all qualms stilled by the belief — so prevalent in the province as to be the conventional wisdom — that Quebec had been betrayed once more by the English-Canadian politicians into sending her young to be butchered in a foreign war. When the federal Liberals put up a French-Canadian army major-general named Léo Laflèche, whom they wanted in the cabinet, in a by-election held in Outremont in 1942, Trudeau openly and eloquently supported his opponent, Jean Drapeau, the candidate for the Bloc Populaire, the anti-war party, and later the notorious mayor of Montreal. Drapeau lost the election and Trudeau went on with his studies, graduating in 1943, and then practising law for a year in Montreal before going to Harvard as the war came to an end to study in the master's program in political science.

For the first time he emerged from the sheltering cocoon of Quebec and realized that the life he had led had been parochial after all, despite its emphasis on classical excellence. To his chagrin, he found that the political science students at Harvard knew more about law as a discipline than he did, that he had been educated for a small-time life as a Quebec *avocat*, a trade he had already discovered he hated. For all the rigour he had exercised in training himself to be a superior student, a stronger athlete, a more clearly cultivated speaker in English and in French, he could be outdone by contemporaries who belonged to a more open society.

For the next twenty years he worked fiercely, almost compulsively, at throwing off the parochialism that he became aware of at Harvard. Not the least important aspect of the myth attached to Trudeau after he became a star was the notion that, because he rarely held conventional jobs in the decades between the time he left his Montreal law firm and the year he joined the Liberal Party, he was some kind of rich idler, chasing women and driving ex-

pensive cars, diverting himself with the travelling and the capering
that never stopped. Trudeau actually spent those years in the
rigorous pursuit of the kind of knowledge and experience that
might have served as a model curriculum for the ideal leader of a
democratic state, as conceived by an educator who knew more
about Plato than about *Realpolitik*. His pursuits were rarely idle.
He was strongly motivated in everything he did, apparently driven
on by an intense need to prove himself superior and to find a role
that would satisfy the messianic streak in his nature.

As his twenties wore on, his flair for self-dramatization grew,
along with his highly developed self-discipline. It was as though
he was knowingly setting out to make himself into a hero in the
classical mould, an Orestes, a Moses, a Ulysses — cast out in the
world from his tribe, wandering in the wilderness, setting himself
tests of endurance both physical and intellectual, and then returning
to the tribe transformed, the possessor of special insight, the owner
of an aura.

At Harvard for two years and later at the London School of
Economics, he engrossed himself in the study of government, the
relationship between the governed and the governor, the meaning
of liberty, the rights of the individual as against the imperatives of
the state. Contemporaries who met him in seminars and common
rooms remembered that he seemed to have read everything from
Aristotle to Acton, from Marx to Mosca, from Mill to Keynes. It
was as if, emerging from the constrictions of French Canada, he
fell in love with some of the basic tenets of English political
thought, becoming a passionate convert to English nineteenth-
century liberalism with its stress on the importance of individual
freedoms, its opposition to highly concentrated power, and its
belief in checks and balances.

Between Harvard and the London School of Economics, he
had stayed for a time in Paris at La Maison Canadienne, attending
classes at the Ecole Libre des Sciences Politiques, talking, frol-
icking, and drinking coffee in the cafés, soaking up the fervid
intellectual atmosphere of postwar Paris, where the personalists
and the existentialists were engaged in a kind of savants' sacred
combat for the soul of postwar France through an endless stream
of books, plays, and erudite essays in little magazines. Trudeau

found the Sorbonne inferior in what it offered in its post-graduate programs, as so many foreign students did. One of the most important aspects of his Paris stay was a friendship formed with a contemporary from Quebec, Gérard Pelletier, who was working for a student relief organization. They had met before when they were both student editors at classical colleges but now they became close friends, sparking each other's ideas in a dialogue about religion, politics, and Canadian society that was to continue for the rest of their lives.

Again Trudeau was remembered by his contemporaries from these post-graduate days in Cambridge, London, and Paris in contradictory terms. Some saw him as an ascetic on a spiritual search, others as a dilettante given to wild pranks, sometimes got up in ragged trousers, sometimes in custom-made silk shirts, shy but intensely aware of the effect he was having. Roger Lemelin, the Quebec novelist who later became publisher of *La Presse*, met Trudeau in Paris and talked with him about the success of Lemelin's book *Au pied de la pente douce*. Much later the novelist remembered: "He attended a reception that Georges Vanier [the Canadian ambassador to Paris] gave for me . . . and the first remark he made to me was, 'How is it that you, a boy from a poor background, have created this marvellous novel and I with all my advantages have created nothing?' "

Trudeau showed then and later an acute ambivalence about his money, the not uncommon response of the intellectual with inherited wealth. When he was at Harvard, he wrote to his close friend from Brébeuf, Pierre Vadeboncoeur, who later became a union official and an impassioned critic of Trudeau, to say that he was thinking of getting rid of his share of the Trudeau inheritance. Vadeboncoeur wrote back to dissuade him, suggesting he would need money for his political work. To be free of the imperative to choose a career and earn a living immediately seemed both a pleasure and a burden; it gave him the leisure to do the extensive studying and travelling he craved but it also set him apart from his peers. As a student, he seemed to want to prove that money was not important to him, that he could travel the world for nearly a year on a couple of thousand dollars, or live for a month on a few hundred francs, just as his contemporaries did.

This attitude was resented by those who knew about his inheritance, especially when he grew older apparently without ever understanding the financial strictures other people faced either as impecunious students or later as the parents of young families. They complained that he never seemed to realize that not caring about money was a luxury most people couldn't afford. He gained a reputation as a tightwad who rarely repaid his acquaintances' hospitality, who always insisted on splitting the bill for meals in restaurants. When he was middle-aged he would still stay for days at a time in the apartment of a friend living on the salary of an assistant professor, and absent-mindedly leave without so much as buying a bottle of wine. "Pierre was always angered by people who thought his money was limitless, some mogul's great fortune, which it wasn't, or that it had brought him intellectual or career advantages which he felt it never had," a close woman friend said. "Both his mother's training and his spartan temperament inclined him to frugality, with the occasional extravagance, as when he bought expensive cars; in the same way his training and temperament made him continually restrained emotionally, with the occasional extravagance in behaviour — dressing up in costume, or standing on his head at a party — some showy act that didn't have much to do with his inner life. They were diversions, sly jokes."

When he became a public man, Trudeau disliked discussing money as much as he disliked discussing any other intimate detail of his life. The facts that he did reveal were the stuff of romantic fiction, kept a little mysterious, a little *outré*. The famous trip he made around the world in 1948–49 after ending his post-graduate studies wasn't just the grand tour that was (and is) a commonplace for young men with a certain kind of background and education. He travelled more widely than his peers, beyond Europe to the Middle East and the Orient, and underwent a series of incredible adventures, physical, spiritual, and intellectual. He fought with border guards, took up with rebels, swam the Hellespont, sojourned with holy men and political leaders — and made certain that wonderful photographs were taken of him and preserved for posterity.

It all smacked of the young André Malraux and it all made

wonderful copy later. What rarely merited more than a line in those ubiquitous newspaper stories about the fantastic adventures of P. E. Trudeau was the fact that when his year of travel was over in 1949, Trudeau came back to Canada to seek a job in the Privy Council Office in Ottawa. It was just after the Liberals' triumphant victory in the election of 1949. He was thirty that year, a crucial age for any man. He was choosing to come to work as what was called a policy adviser — a kind of apprenticeship post — in the cabinet office of Louis St. Laurent, the first French-Canadian prime minister in nearly forty years. His purpose, he later said, was "to see how the cogs of democratic government worked". It must have seemed an auspicious place for an ambitious man to begin an important career. And it must have proven a catalytic experience, a period that tested his patience and his pride, and fixed indelibly in his mind certain facts about his country's power structure.

The Ottawa of Louis St. Laurent was an English town, dull, provincial, and not so much prejudiced against Quebeckers as wary of and patronizing towards them. The role that they played in that Ottawa was secondary, the Prime Minister's presence notwithstanding. St. Laurent at sixty-seven was already an old man. He had always disliked politics and only Mackenzie King's insistence after the death of his Quebec lieutenant, Ernest Lapointe, that in all conscience he had to come forward to be Quebec's representative in Ottawa for the sake of Canadian unity in wartime had got him into it in the first place. He was sure his first term as prime minister would be his last, and he soon fell prey to one of a series of depressions that were to plague him during his eight years in office. In brief, he was hardly a leader of bursting energy prepared to make sweeping changes in the power structure on behalf of the French-Canadian race.

In his cabinet, the important ministers in 1949 were all largely King appointees or protégés and all anglophones: C. D. Howe in trade and commerce as the government's mastermind of the domestic economy, Lester Pearson as its star abroad as minister for external affairs; Doug Abbott, an Anglo-Quebecker who liked to boast of his Yankee ancestors from Vermont, as the finance minister (to be followed by Walter Harris); Brooke Claxton in health and welfare and then in national defence; and Jimmy Gardiner as the minister of agriculture. (Jimmy Sinclair, who was later Trudeau's father-in-law, was still a promising MP from Vancouver who wasn't made minister of fisheries until 1952.) The Quebec ministers were given minor roles — ministries rich in patronage (the post office and public works) or pomp (the solicitor general and minister of veterans' affairs was Hugues Lapointe, the son of King's Quebec lieutenant, Ernest Lapointe). The most important portfolio held by a French Canadian in St. Laurent's first cabinet was bestowed on Lionel Chevrier, the minister of transport, who wasn't a Quebecker in any case but a Franco-Ontarian. (After the election of 1953, Jean Lesage, a lawyer and backbench MP who was a favourite of St. Laurent's, was brought in as a promising junior minister in resources and development, and Chevrier left the government to be president of the St. Lawrence Seaway Authority for the next four years.)

The milieu in which Trudeau himself was working — the world of the public servants who in the St. Laurent years were at least the politicians' equal in influence — was even more an English-Canadian enclave. Norman Robertson, Lester Pearson's contemporary from the Department of External Affairs, had been recalled by St. Laurent from London, where he was serving as deputy high commissioner, to become his clerk of the Privy Council. Clifford Clark was the deputy minister in finance, Graham Towers the chairman of the Bank of Canada, Arnold Heeney the under-secretary in external affairs, and Maxwell Mackenzie was C. D. Howe's deputy in trade and commerce.

In brief, the whole power web was English-Canadian right down to the man in the middle, Jack Pickersgill, who was in charge of the Prime Minister's Office, serving as St. Laurent's chief adviser and go-between for the politicians and the public servants. Pickersgill saw to it that there were more French Canadians in the PMO under St. Laurent than there had been under King, but their roles were minor. Jules Léger was seconded from External Affairs to serve as Pickersgill's second-in-command, Pierre Asselin was made private secretary (he did the translating and the political liaison work with St. Laurent's riding), and Annette Perron was the personal private secretary (she did the typing). The few token

French Canadians who were successful in the bureaucracy — men like Georges Vanier, who by now was the ambassador in Paris after a distinguished military career, and Marcel Cadieux and Jules Léger, who were promising officers in External Affairs — were anglicized not quite to the point of assimilation but almost.

Trudeau himself was assigned to assist Gordon Robertson, a young civil servant formerly with the Department of External Affairs, in the preparation of background material for a series of projected constitutional conferences with the provinces that would work out a method of amending the constitution in Canada itself so it didn't have to be done by the British at Westminster. The federal government intended to propose at the same time a constitutional amendment to entrench minority educational rights and the provisions regarding the use of the French and English languages contained in the British North America Act of 1867, an entrenchment which in Jack Pickersgill's phrase was "tantamount to a limited bill of minority rights". (As part of this job, Trudeau made a summary of existing federal-provincial relationships that covered more than fifty pages and served him in good stead as basic research for the expertise he developed afterwards in constitutional matters. Neither he nor Robertson could have imagined that thirty years later they would still be engrossed in the same problems, though from a different vantage point, with Trudeau as prime minister and Robertson as the secretary to his cabinet for federal-provincial relations.) The work on the constitution took over a year and ended when two full Dominion-provincial conferences failed. The prime cause of the failures was the intransigent opposition to the federal proposals for constitutional reform of the premier of Quebec, Maurice Duplessis, who was to prove a more important influence on Pierre Trudeau's political development than Louis St. Laurent.

Before Trudeau came to work in Ottawa, when he was just back from his adventuring year abroad and still sporting the handsome beard he had grown during his travels, he had driven to the Quebec town of Asbestos in the Eastern Townships to take a look at a bitter miners' strike that made the area a focus of interest in the province for months. His friend Gérard Pelletier was working as a journalist for *Le Devoir* and had been assigned to cover the

strike. Pelletier introduced him to Jean Marchand, a union leader
who had been organizing the asbestos workers for five years.
Pelletier and Marchand both came from working-class backgrounds,
Marchand from Quebec City and Pelletier from Victoriaville, a
textile town not far from Asbestos. Through brains, guts, and
grinding hard work, they had both scratched their way to university
degrees, and were now deeply involved in trying to change the lot
of labour in the face of the accelerating industrialization of postwar
Quebec. Marchand was tough, shrewd, combative, and experienced.
Pelletier was intelligent and idealistic, a left-wing Catholic devoted to the cause of social justice. They both had young families
and small salaries. Trudeau, though he was less than a year their
junior, still seemed like a privileged boy to them with his sandals
and his self-absorption — but an eloquent boy with a dramatic
flair who got up one night in a local mining hall and inflamed the
crowd with his rhetoric. In the Trudeau myth, this encounter between the three men took on the aura of the first meeting of a
messiah with his chief apostles. At the time, Trudeau was the
least dominant figure of the three. He spent three weeks in the
area. Marchand and Pelletier were there for almost six months.
None of them knew what a watershed the strike would prove for
their generation of activists in their struggle to free Quebec from
the shibboleths of its past.

During the strike's aftermath Trudeau kept returning to
Montreal from Ottawa on weekends, keeping up his contact with
Pelletier and several other reform-minded friends. By November
of 1951, he had decided to abandon the capital and a promising
career there to come home to Quebec. All he said directly about
this move was that you couldn't be involved in Quebec politics to
the extent that he had become and continue to work as a public
servant. But it was plain from his other testimony and from his
close friends' conversations that there was more to the decision
than that. For a man of Trudeau's *fierté*, the route to success for a
French Canadian in Ottawa — which required a compliance, a
bending of the self to the anglophone institutional will — must
have been so repugnant as to be untenable. St. Laurent was already seen by many Quebeckers of Trudeau's age and general
persuasion as one of the straw men English Canadians used for

their purposes in business and politics. During the height of the
trouble at Asbestos, he had allowed his minister of labour to turn
aside the strikers' difficulties with the bland statement that it was
a provincial matter. It was becoming increasingly obvious that he
was going to reach the same kind of accommodation with Duplessis
that King had come to in the mid-1940s. Pierre Laporte, who had
been a classmate of Trudeau's at Brébeuf and was one of the
regulars in the weekend discussions of reformers at Charles
Lussier's house on Rockland Street in Montreal, was writing in
Le Devoir that St. Laurent might be involving Canada in another
major war by sending troops to Korea, that he might turn out to
be a liar about conscription as King had been before him. Trudeau
himself witnessed an "unbelievable . . . great fight to have a sign
put up in the East Block reading *Bureau du Premier Ministre* as
well as Prime Minister's Office," a fight that loomed in his mind
as symbolic of St. Laurent's sad impotence in the face of the
English-Canadian establishment. Ottawa was grey, complacent,
and alien — a kind of living death. Quebec was alive with ideas
and on the verge of a struggle operatic in its scope, a struggle
against evil, ignorance, and oppression that was uniquely suited
to the needs of the man Trudeau had become.

Once when he was asked what was the most important and
exhilarating event in his life — which of his great political or
personal triumphs — Trudeau replied that the most moving thing
that had ever happened to him was not a single event but a
realization he came to over a period in his late twenties and early
thirties (which coincided in part with the time he spent in the
PCO) that he was "a whole person . . . my own judge and my
own master". He called this a recognition and acceptance of "the
concept of incarnation . . . as the personalists put it." In brief, he
had experienced an epiphany. He didn't have to be a fawning
vendu in Ottawa, or a lawyer in Montreal grovelling before the
Anglo business monolith, or a professor in one of the provincial
universities, kow-towing to the clerical hierarchy. He could do
what he liked, become who he wanted to be.

The reference to the personalists — which the interviewer
who asked him the question ignored — was crucial. While Trudeau
and Pelletier were living in Europe in the late 1940s, they were

excited, as were so many young Catholic intellectuals of the time, by the personalist review, *Esprit*, which was politically vague but morally certain. Its founder, Emmanuel Mounier, exhorted Catholics to activism in the world, to a confrontation with the bourgeois values of the traditional Catholic Church, to anti-materialism, a transcendence of selfish interests, a reliance on individual conscience rather than conformity to rules, and a militant Christian response to the spread of world communism. In personalism, Trudeau found important answers to the conflictual elements in his thinking — his ambition to prove his courage and strength as an activist (which was hampered by his refusal to bend himself to the indignities and superficialities of the professions available to French Canadians) and his intense religiosity (which warred with a disdain for the repressive behaviour of the Quebec clergy). Earlier the priests at Brébeuf had told him he was a protestant Catholic, always questioning authority. In espousing personalism — or at least in adding it as a motivating idea to the mixture of theories and philosophies he had already assimilated — he was deciding to become a radical Catholic, bent on social reform. He would practise law specializing in civil liberties and labour cases, and he would write.

As early as 1947, Pelletier and Trudeau had discussed founding a Canadian version of *Esprit*. In 1950, with an *équipe de la revue* of eight other like-minded Catholics to act as an editorial board, they published the first issue of their magazine, which they called *Cité libre*. They were confirming that they were a generation who had thought hard about Quebec's problems and decided to say, in Pelletier's words, "Damn it, we'll stay home and change the place."

The immediate target was the régime of Maurice Duplessis, the Union Nationale premier first elected in 1936 and re-elected in 1944 after a Liberal interlude, who had become a metaphor for the oppression of freedom in Quebec, a symbol of the French Canadians' collusion in maintaining their own inferior economic and social position within the Canadian confederation. The magazine was published irregularly over the next decade (it became more frequent after 1960) with a small editorial team and a faithful group of regular contributors which included, besides Trudeau and Pelletier, who were the mainsprings: Pierre Juneau, Charles Lussier, Roger Rolland, Jacques Hébert, Pierre Vadeboncoeur, Jean Pellerin, Marcel Rioux, and later Pierre Vallières. The first issue ran five hundred copies. (Each of the ten founders was given fifty copies to sell for fifty cents each.) At its peak in the late 1950s and early 1960s its circulation never surpassed three thousand. Its direct effect was on an intellectual elite; it was no more widely read among politicians than the *Canadian Forum* was in English Canada. But like the *Forum* it was a seedbed for political ideas that were to have an important effect for decades after their first dissemination.

The *Cité libristes* were only one element in the postwar opposition to the established order in Quebec. There were many other reformers who drew their strength from other institutions: men on university faculties and in trade unions who were former students of Father Georges-Henri Lévesque, the celebrated Dominican priest who was founder and dean of the faculty of social sciences at Laval; writers and editorialists who responded to the leadership of André Laurendeau, the editor of *Le Devoir*, members of L'Action Catholique or of L'Institut Canadien des Affaires Publiques or of La Ligue d'Action Civique. In the 1950s these reformers interlocked in complex ways, regrouping over and over again, taking in younger members, losing adherents to individual ambitions or ideological quarrels, centring their involvement on various causes, convening discussion groups and writing for various publishers and publications (Jacques Hébert's *Vrai* as well as *Le Devoir* and *Cité libre*, plus *Les Editions du Jour* and *Parti pris*.) They were involved with each other and in the politics of their province with an intensity that the English-Canadian Liberals who met them later and who came out of a very different tradition rarely understood. These Quebeckers belonged to a small, cohesive society, with an introverted history and a highly developed cultural life that the English Canadians knew very little about and could not share. French Canadians had been arguing for generations about the meaning of the Conquest, the importance of their survival, the role of the church vis-à-vis the state in their domination, the dreams and delusions engendered by the racial pride that had such a hold on their collective imagination.

Trudeau was never seen as a leader of these reformers, though he threw himself into this long-simmering discussion after it began to boil in the aftermath of the strike at Asbestos and he kept on feeding the fire under it throughout the 1950s with a series of brilliant articles and editorials, mostly in *Cité libre*. Ostensibly he was engaged in the practice of law, taking on only work that appealed to him, such as the defence of his friend Jacques Hébert, who was involved in a lawsuit after the publication of his book *J'accuse les assassins de Coffin*, or legal negotiations for Jean Marchand's Confédération des Syndicats Nationaux. Actually, his chief preoccupation was an intensive analysis of French-Canadian society and the formulation of solutions to its problems. Excerpts from his writings in the 1950s and early 1960s were often taken out of context after he became prime minister and used by his enemies to hoist him on his own petard. People who took the trouble to read them as a body of work recognized them as a remarkable testimony to the lucidity of his writing style, the cohesiveness of his political philosophy, and the doggedness of his intellectual application. Far from being petty *pensées*, tossed off between athletic exploits and sexual adventures, his writings were clearly the product of hundreds of hours given to intensive research and painstaking thought. They displayed a deepening, highly developed, disciplined mind; not the mind of a research scholar but that of a political thinker who was developing the notion of "a functional politics" — which was the title of his first essay in *Cité libre*.

Trudeau's introduction to *La Grève de l'amiante*, a collection of papers on the Asbestos strike, published as a book in 1956, involved a carefully documented thesis concerning the distortions of French Canada's development over the previous half-century — its economy, its education, its religious and social institutions, and its politics — an analysis so clear that it must have taken months of concentrated effort to formulate. (Trudeau spent another six months living in hotels in Paris and London writing it. The hotels were cheap digs of the kind students habituate. Outside, Trudeau parked his Jaguar.)

He wrote of Quebec as a society run by a reactionary elite who had kept it backward in their own interest, who had failed to recognize the importance of the rapid industrialization of the previous half-century, who had used phony nationalist arguments and corrupt electoral practices to scare the people into submission, who had turned themselves into cannibal kings — *rois nègres* in the inspired analogy of André Laurendeau — making deals with the federal government and failing to realize that their blithe acceptance of foreign development capital would cost them future control of the province's resources.

Trudeau believed that democracy had never put down deep roots in the province and that federalism — that is, taking part in the governing of Canada as a whole — was Quebec's best chance for economic progress and for freedom from authoritarian structures. He agreed with the English political theorist Lord Acton that the best form of democratic government lay in the federation of various ethnic groups into one state. It was his addendum to Acton's theory that Canadian federalism had proven particularly worthy of regard through its devotion to protecting distinctive cultures without impoverishing them. He wanted French Canadians to take advantage of their partnership with English Canadians, to make their own equality within the federal system. He saw the fascination with nationalism of so many French-Canadian politicians and thinkers as crippling; they must involve themselves in the greater world.

That he himself wasn't more prominently involved in the world in the 1950s was fuel for the charge of dilettantism hurled at him so often later by his enemies. But his behaviour in that decade had a simple explanation. Trudeau could hardly have become an active politician in a period when "Duplessis seemed eternal in Quebec," as his friend Alex Pelletier, the Quebec writer and film-maker, once remarked. The Liberal Party, the official opposition to the Union Nationale, was still provincially weak, helpless in the face of the "non-aggression pacts" federal Liberal MPs had made with the Union Nationale. In the fifties, voting "*bleu à Québec, rouge à Ottawa*" was a commonplace. Trudeau did toy with the idea of creating a party of the democratic left, taking a prominent part in 1956 in the formation of Le Rassemblement, a league of various Quebec groups who were dedicated to democratic education and action. It withered away two years later without ever becoming a political force, much less a political party. (This association was seen as a leftist front in Quebec, though it attracted people across the political spectrum. Along with his studies at LSE under Harold Laski and his travels to Russia and China, his role in Le Rassemblement later gave rise to the nonsensical charge that Trudeau was a communist.) Not only was Trudeau denied a more active role in politics, he couldn't get a job as a professor. He applied to the Université de Montréal for a job on four occasions and each time he was refused, apparently because of the opposition of the university's rector, Cardinal (then Archbishop) Léger. He might as well have been on the blacklist in McCarthyist America or a dissident in the Soviet Union: there was no work for the unorthodox. (Trudeau was offered a teaching job at Laval in 1949 by Maurice Lamontagne, who was chairman of the Department of Economics, but he turned it down to work in Ottawa. Later, Lamontagne and his mentor, Father Lévesque, were forced out of Laval by Duplessis and there were no teaching jobs available to Trudeau except in English institutions.)

Despite the currency Trudeau's ideas were given in Quebec reform circles in the 1950s, he was regarded, even by some of his allies, as an intellectual idler. He was apparently so anxious to have his accomplishments appear effortless that few people knew how hard he worked. He was seen as an inveterate traveller, frivolously in search of sensation, though his trip to Russia in 1952 produced a long article; his trip to China in 1960 with a group of French Canadians invited by the Peking government resulted in a witty, lively book co-authored with Jacques Hébert; his further journeys elsewhere in Africa and Europe turned up in learned papers as footnoted asides on other societies and their governments. He continued to drive his mind hard, reading omnivorously in political, legal, and social theory. It was as if he were in search of greatness and he wasn't quite sure where and when it would come. While he waited, he affected when possible an insouciant manner.

He was living at home in Outremont with his mother when he wasn't travelling or staying in various chalets in the Laurentians, first in a colony of his friends from *Cité libre*, later on a piece of land he bought for himself. He had taken on Charlie Trudeau's

job as head of the family, squiring his mother to concerts and
plays and overseeing the management of the family finances, a
job neither his sister, Suzette Rouleau, who was now married to a
dentist, nor his brother, Charles, who was an architect, were
equipped to do. He was also busy developing in his thirties and
early forties a reputation as an amorous adventurer.

Earlier, in his twenties, when most of his contemporaries
were getting married, he was largely solitary and extremely shy.
His women friends were other students with intellectual interests,
girls who were acceptable to his mother and a far cry from the
showy women who compelled his interest in middle age. He was
expected to marry Thérèse Gouin, a serious, well-bred girl who
later became a professor of psychology at the Université de
Montréal. He was friendly in Paris with Andrée Desautels, who
was later a professor of music; they went on chaste holidays
together on his motor bike. In Montreal, he occasionally squired
among others Sylvia Knelman (later Ostry), a young woman from
Winnipeg who was studying economics at McGill, though they
usually went out as part of a trio with a mutual friend. When
he worked in Ottawa he dated a diplomat's daughter for a while
and talked shyly to the young women from the civil service who
ate their lunches on the lawns of Parliament Hill on hot summer
days and retreated to the parliamentary cafeteria in winter.

More than twenty-five years later a woman remembered her
first glimpse of the young Trudeau at a jazz dance class they both
attended. From across the practice room she was struck by the
compelling attractiveness of his face and the strength and grace of
his body. He asked her out several times for coffee, or to go to
Belmont Park, where he had a free pass on the rides because of
his family's investment in the project. She found him brilliant but
emotionally withdrawn, his sensuous pleasure in his body as
displayed in the dance class nowhere in evidence between them.
"He seemed to be so repressed then that if he had ended up as a
monk, I wouldn't have been surprised," she said. Another woman,
the wife of a distinguished French-Canadian federal public servant
already climbing the bureaucratic ladder in Ottawa when Trudeau
was working in the PCO, commented on Trudeau's reputation as a
roué a quarter of a century later. "In those days no one would

have believed this transformation could come about. He was self-effacing and shy, like a young *curé*. His skin was bad, pockmarked from acne, and though he was in some ways attractive, it was not in the fashionable mode of the time. You have to remember that Jean-Paul Belmondo came along much later and made the *beau laid* the rage. In those days Charles Boyer and Jean-Pierre Aumont were the ideals. Jean Lesage, the MP, or Jean Fournier, who was an external affairs officer, were the kind of handsome, charming men who appealed to the women. Whatever else he was, Trudeau was not a social success.''

Ten years later, his reputation as a radical tilter at Duplessis's powerful windmill established, Trudeau had outgrown or at least found a way to mask his former shyness. He was seen around Montreal at balls, in bistros, and at parties given by his now middle-aged friends, accompanied by a variety of women, most of them beautiful, accomplished, and much younger than himself. By the time he began to teach public law at the Université de Montréal in 1961 — the professorial job that had eluded him till Duplessis's death — he was already a cult figure with the undergraduate women, sexy in a way that only a professor can be to sophomores spinning their unresolved longings and unformulated ideas into unrealizeable dreams. Most of his liaisons were brief, a few encounters and little more. Some turned into lasting friendships. One, with a beautiful and vivacious woman named Madeleine Gobeil, whom he met through the Pelletiers when she was a student of nineteen and he was thirty-eight, continued until he was married thirteen years later. When they met, Trudeau had already gained a reputation for not liking women past thirty; they were too serious about the future, they made demands on his privacy and his time. (When his wife left him in 1977, the year she was turning twenty-nine, a former love said with a bitter laugh, ''Poor thing, she was getting too old.'')

Undaunted by admonitions from his friends that he should settle down now that he was almost forty, he drove fast cars, wore remarkable clothes, indulged in what then seemed like exotic pursuits such as yoga, karate, and meditation, which added to his hard-won reputation for physical toughness and emotional independence. Nina Bruneau, a Montreal woman who met him at a ball when she was eighteen and he was thirty, and saw him often in French-Canadian intellectual circles later on, remembered that after becoming politically engaged herself, "I began to see Pierre at all kinds of political events. . . . The image he gave was that of an autonomous man, but one not yet totally involved. In 1958 when Jean Lesage was nominated [as leader of the Liberal Party in Quebec], there was Lesage in the centre of the crowd with René Lévesque running around for the CBC. Pierre . . . was just sitting in a trench coat off in a corner, watching. He looked like the conscience of a nation but he was still a man in the shade." As late as 1964, a distinguished French-Canadian professor told the English-Canadian historian Ramsay Cook that "Trudeau is easily the most talented intellectual in Quebec, but he [has] frittered away his gifts in aimless intellectual nonconformity and bohemian pleasures."

The remark was in direct opposition to the opinions of two of Trudeau's most intimate friends, Pierre Vadeboncoeur and Madeleine Gobeil, both of whom believed he had wanted political power for most of his adult life in order to put his ideas into effect. A year later, the appearance of aimlessness was discarded. To the astonishment of his acquaintances, if not his close friends, Trudeau joined the Liberal Party and set out to learn how to turn its power to his purposes.

WHEN TRUDEAU BECAME A LIBERAL in the late summer of 1965 in the company of Jean Marchand and Gérard Pelletier, their conversion lit a brush fire of interest across the country. In English Canada, the editorialists hailed them as "the three wise men". In Quebec, they were called *"les trois colombes"*, literally "the three doves", though "sitting ducks" might be a better interpretation of the feelings of their compatriots. Their collective decision to join a party they had so disdained in the past had been made by a tortuous process over a period of several years.

Their original disgust for the Liberals had been due to the blatantly undemocratic nature of the party's Quebec wing in the heyday of Mackenzie King when he had delegated responsibility to the man who was called his Quebec leader but was really a kind of viceroy in charge of a backward reach of the Liberal kingdom. King's first Quebec lieutenant, whom he cared for like a brother, was Ernest Lapointe, his second, Louis St. Laurent. They delegated control at the constituency level to a group of bosses. There were no constituency associations open to public membership. Instead, each riding had *un organisateur* and *un trésorier*, who were sometimes one and the same person, filling the roles of campaign organizer, patronage dispenser, and bagman. Two *organisateurs en chef* — one in charge of the eastern constituencies around Quebec City, the other overseeing the western ridings from Montreal — served as middlemen between the riding bosses and the Quebec leader, reporting to Ottawa regularly and keeping in touch locally with public opinion and political needs. (There were six English ridings in Montreal district that were outside this system; instead, an anglophone Quebec minister was put in charge.)

Patronage was the essential fuel of this hierarchical party machine. As Trudeau had discovered in Ottawa, Quebec ministers were always given at least two of the cabinet portfolios — public works, post office, transport, justice — that were richest with patronage possibilities. The local bosses dispensed *whisky blanc* and jobs on the docks and the big bosses dispensed judgeships and Scotch at the Reform Club. At election time, cash was doled out to pay workers and to bribe voters with tons of coal and bags of groceries. The candidates were usually named by the bosses and awarded with renomination for their docility and loyalty. They were supposed to be above electoral bribery and devoid of political ideas. As Trudeau wrote, "The shameful incompetence of the average Liberal MP from Quebec was a welcome asset to [an English-Canadian-dominated] government that needed little more than a herd of donkeys to file in when the division bells rang. The party strategists had but to find an acceptable stable master — Laurier, Lapointe, St. Laurent — and the trained donkeys sitting in the back benches could be trusted to behave."

In their ridings the bosses wielded the power and did the dirty work, and under their aegis, Liberal meeting-rooms in Quebec towns were like lodges similar to the legion halls of English Canada, noisy with the camaraderie of political gossip larded with political largesse. (These shenanigans are vividly described in the memoirs edited by Norman Ward of C. G. "Chubby" Power, the MP for Quebec South for nearly forty years, who was Lapointe's *organisateur en chef* for the Quebec City region. A man of merry demeanour, prodigious thirst, and unusual organizational ability, Power saw himself as a reform Liberal — indeed, he ran against Louis St. Laurent for the party's leadership in 1948 as an anti-establishment candidate — but his attitude to the petty corruptions of the Quebec machine was accepting, rather like that of the *colon* amused by the peccadilloes of the natives.)

Distinctions between the federal and provincial wings of the party were blurred, with the same people usually working for both at the local level. In the teens and twenties of the century, the provincial Liberals' needs had been dominant, especially during the long period when they held power in Quebec City under Sir Lomer Gouin and L. A. Taschereau, and the federal Liberals were out of power or only shakily in office in Ottawa. But after Taschereau's defeat in 1930 and King's resounding victory in 1935, the balance changed. The federal wing was ascendant, so much so that it almost destroyed the provincial party, manipulating the selection of its leader, Adélard Godbout, in 1936 and interfering massively in the 1939 election, which the provincial Liberals won. Having turned the provincial Liberals into dependent puppets, the federal Liberals proceeded to do them more harm than good, sabotaging their later electoral prospects by implicitly, and occasionally explicitly, supporting the policies of their political enemy in the province, Maurice Duplessis. Non-aggression pacts were reached between federal Liberal MPs and Union Nationale members in overlapping ridings. After Godbout lost the provincial elections of 1944 and 1948, he was retired to the Senate in Ottawa and a young federal MP, Georges-Emile Lapalme, became the provincial leader as the choice of the federal organization, though he was treated little better by it than Godbout had been.

Louis St. Laurent had never been interested in political organization, and during his period as Quebec leader and then prime minister the system Lapointe had built up steadily deteriorated. In the election of 1957, it was obvious that the federal Liberal Party was in ruins in Quebec as well as everywhere else. The next year, Diefenbaker won an astonishing fifty seats in the province with Duplessis's help — when Le Chef smelled a Tory victory, the old entente between the Union Nationale and the federal Liberals was discarded entirely. Liberal ranks in Quebec were ravaged, dropping from sixty-two seats in 1957 to twenty-five in 1958, the lowest number of Liberal MPs from Quebec in any Parliament in this century.

Many of the fifty Conservative MPs from Quebec were Union Nationale castoffs, members of a slate Duplessis had cynically provided for Diefenbaker. The situation was particularly repugnant to one of the small band of federal Liberals who were busy trying to help Pearson recover from the humiliation of his defeat. His name was Maurice Lamontagne and he was to have a profound effect on Pearson's Quebec policy. Lamontagne was the economist who had been a student and close colleague of Father Lévesque's at Laval. An ardent anti-Duplessis reformer from the time he finished his post-graduate work at Harvard in the 1940s, he had enraged Duplessis with a book he wrote in 1954 on Canadian federalism. By then Lamontagne had moved to Ottawa as an adviser to Jean Lesage and stayed on to work for Louis St. Laurent in the Privy Council Office. He kept up his interest in provincial politics and was part of a group who had been pushing for reforms in the provincial Liberal Party under Lapalme. When Lapalme resigned the leadership in 1958, exhausted and embittered by federal Liberal betrayals, Lamontagne decided his successor should be Jean Lesage. Lesage had been a golden go-getter from the time he graduated from the Laval law school in the late 1930s and had been assiduously groomed in Ottawa, first as a parliamentary secretary to the ministers of finance and external affairs, and then as a junior minister. St. Laurent had been noticeably remiss in bringing along able French Canadians and Lesage was the only really promising survivor of the 1958 debacle in Quebec. Pearson was reluctant to let Lesage go but Lamontagne convinced him the Lesage leadership in Quebec could be the road back to power federally as well as provincially.

Lesage was quickly able to capitalize on Lapalme's efforts to democratize the provincial party's structures, and after Duplessis died suddenly in September of 1959, he gained tremendous momentum with his reform efforts, attracting candidates, funds, and editorial support, including a favourable article in *Cité libre* by Trudeau. His famous victory in June of 1960 brought to power an aggressive team of reformers that included many men who were to dominate Quebec politics for the next couple of decades: Paul Gérin-Lajoie, Claude Castonguay, Pierre Laporte, René Lévesque, Jacques Parizeau, and Claude Morin. They were called *une équipe de tonnerre* and their thunderous success heartened the Liberals in Ottawa as nothing else had done since Diefenbaker humiliated them in 1957.

In Quebec there was a kind of euphoria. The labour unions' long battles of the 1950s were bringing impressive results in wage settlements and working conditions. The dominance of the church in secular life was being challenged, not just by intellectuals but throughout the society. Sweeping reforms were being proposed for the educational system. The civil service was undergoing a reorganization from top to bottom, with many bureaucrats from Ottawa being invited to come home to Quebec to bring about a new era. Patronage practices, notably in the construction industry, were under scrutiny. Duplessis's old habit of paying off newspapermen was discontinued. Marchand was invited to give advice out of his experience as director of the Confédération des Syndicats Nationaux to the government's economic council. (He was later asked to stand as a provincial Liberal candidate, though the offer was subsequently withdrawn by Lesage.) Pelletier was hired as editor of *La Presse*, the largest daily. Trudeau was made a professor of law at the university and a member of the Institut de Recherches en Droit Public. It looked like a new dawn.

Within two years the federalists among the old anti-Duplessis reformers became alarmed as separatist sentiment grew with the formation of L'Action Socialiste, L'Alliance Laurentienne, and Le Rassemblement pour l'Indépendance Nationale. The Lesage Liberals began to pander to this sentiment, running a snap election in October 1962 on the nationalistic slogan *"maître chez nous"*. At the same time, a few of Pearson's federal Liberals were making still tentative but all the same conscientious efforts to take a fresh look at Quebec's needs. (The efforts were sufficiently tentative that as late as 1960, at the Kingston Conference that year, the question of Quebec's discontent wasn't raised as a separate issue, though the gathering was billed as a "study conference on national problems".) Nevertheless, Pearson's key adviser, Maurice Lamontagne, was seriously concerned by what was happening in Quebec.

In December 1962, during the Diefenbaker minority government, Lamontagne wrote for Pearson a strong speech on the Quebec situation, calling for a royal commission of inquiry, and talked him into delivering it in the House of Commons. It had an electric effect in Quebec, and suddenly there was talk in Montreal about a large reform group who were anti-separatist running for the Liberal Party in the next federal election, expected within months. "There were going to be fourteen or fifteen of us," Trudeau remembered, "Guy Favreau, Jean-Louis Gagnon, Jean-Paul Lefèvre, as well as Marchand, Pelletier, and Trudeau. Several others came to meetings. We thought there was safety in numbers, we didn't want to be swallowed up."

Because of his popularity as a labour leader, Marchand was the chief object of the Liberals' blandishments. For years, he — as well as many of his reformer friends — had been drawn intellectually to the CCF and then to the NDP, but they were prevented from joining the socialist party by their recognition that it couldn't make political gains in Quebec. Trudeau had been a friend of F. R. Scott, a founder of the League for Social Reconstruction, grey eminence of the CCF, and director of Recherches Sociales, the group that gave Trudeau and his collaborators the grant to publish their book on the Asbestos strike in 1956. He had also contributed to *A Social Purpose for Canada*, a collection of socialist essays edited by Michael Oliver, a CCF academic who later became president of the NDP. But he had become disenchanted with the NDP over its Quebec policy, which endorsed a special status for the province. Now it was Trudeau who provided the rationale for the reformers' new attraction to federal Liberalism in a murderous attack on separatism published in *Cité libre* in 1962 called "New Treason of the Intellectuals". In this piece he urged Quebeckers once more not to hide in their home province but to prove themselves in the larger context of Canada, repeating his conviction that the reason they had continued to be inferiors within confederation was the folly of nationalism. Separatism for him was retrogressive, the old nationalism done up in a different guise. He believed that all the concessions French Canadians had squeezed out of Ottawa over decades of wrangling could have been achieved in one cabinet meeting by a French-Canadian minister as adroit and as powerful as C. D. Howe.

"If Canada as a state," he wrote, "has had so little room for French Canadians, it is above all because we have failed to make ourselves indispensable to its future. . . . With the sole exception of Laurier, I fail to see a single French Canadian in more than three-quarters of a century whose presence in the federal cabinet might be considered indispensable. . . . Similarly, in the ranks of senior civil servants, there is probably not one who could be said to have decisively and beneficially influenced the development of our administration as has . . . an O. D. Skelton, a Graham Towers, or a Norman Robertson. . . . The Anglo-Canadians have been strong by virtue only of our weakness."

Despite this powerful exhortation by Trudeau and its acceptance by Marchand, negotiations between the Ottawa Liberals and the federalist Quebeckers broke down in early 1963 over what they saw as a betrayal of principle by Lester Pearson. Pearson

was on record as being opposed to nuclear warheads but under
pressure from his defence critic, Paul Hellyer, and others whom
he never named (but whom Trudeau suspected were agents of the
American State Department), Pearson made a speech in January
declaring that the guided missiles already on Canadian soil should
be armed with nuclear warheads in order to honour the NORAD
and NATO agreements under which they had been accepted by
Diefenbaker in the first place. In response, Trudeau wrote an
outraged and outrageous attack on Pearson and the Liberals that
was still being used by dissenting Grits as proof that he wasn't a
party man long after he became prime minister. (It still stands as
one of the most devastating descriptions of Liberals in our time as
"men . . . who tremble with anticipation because they have seen
the rouged face of power". In vituperation, Trudeau has few
peers.) Because of Trudeau's outrage, Marchand decided against
running for the Liberals. Of the fourteen or fifteen reform-minded
Quebeckers the Liberals hoped to attract, only Guy Favreau and
René Tremblay took the plunge. Trudeau himself further alienated the Quebec Liberal machine, who had never wanted him in
the first place, by ostentatiously supporting the candidacy of
Charles Taylor, a McGill professor and personal friend who was
running for the NDP in the Montreal riding of Mount Royal. After
the election, Trudeau, Marchand, and Pelletier went back to the
dubious comforts of intense late-night discussions on the future
of Quebec in Pelletier's house in Outremont. They were joined by
André Laurendeau, the editor of *Le Devoir*, and René Lévesque,
the former CBC television star, now a star minister in Lesage's
cabinet, who sometimes used the group as a kind of brains trust.

That same year, Trudeau started to take part in yet another
series of discussions, this time with a group of younger intellectuals in meetings sparked by a man whose fortunes were to be
inextricably linked with his, a Montreal lawyer named Marc
Lalonde. After meeting for several months, the group wrote a
federalist manifesto called "An Appeal for Reason in Canadian
Politics" which was published in *Cité libre* in the spring of 1964.
It appeared simultaneously in the *Canadian Forum* in an English
translation rendered by another young lawyer named Michael
Pitfield, an English-speaking Montrealer then carving out a gov-

ernment career in Ottawa, and a close friend of Lalonde's.

By now, Trudeau, Marchand, and Pelletier were sick of their endless discussions. The Quiet Revolution was quiet no longer. There were separatist bombings, a separatist robbery of an armoury, and a disastrously unpopular visit by the Queen in October 1964 that made Quebec look like a seething colony. These incidents and others were destroying the dream of a modern democratic state that they had sought to realize for so long and that they thought Lesage's victory had presaged. In Ottawa, the reform Liberals in the Quebec caucus were being savaged by the Opposition and by the old guard, and were clearly in need of reinforcement. When the federal Liberals came wooing Marchand again in 1965, it seemed to him and his friends that the time had come to put their ideas into action. The Liberal Party, in Trudeau's view, was the only place they could jump. It was to be used, he said, "not as an end but a means, not a goal but an instrument".

During the week after Labour Day, just after the November 1965 election had been called, Pelletier, Trudeau, and Marchand took part in a dramatic late-night negotiation with the federal Liberals, represented by Guy Favreau, Maurice Lamontagne, and Maurice Sauvé, at the Windsor Hotel in Montreal, and then announced their agreement to run for the party at a press conference next day. Their old friend René Lévesque had urged them to go as a group lest they be swallowed up by the still-powerful old guard in the Quebec caucus or turned into *rois nègres* by the anglophones. ("I have no doubt that the three of them were sincere in believing they could reform the Liberal Party at the time. I thought that too when I became a Liberal in the late 1950s," Lévesque said later when he was the péquiste premier of Quebec. "But the Liberal Party is the greatest whorehouse in the western world and you know what happens when you try playing piano in the parlor of a place like that. Pretty soon, you're in the thick of the fray upstairs.") *Cité libre* published a sorrowful editorial about the defection of their colleagues, and Trudeau and Pelletier wrote a concise piece of tortured prose in response, explaining their remarkable decision. Editorialists brought up the fact that Pelletier had once called the Liberal organization *"la poubelle de Montréal"* — the garbage can of Montreal. Other friends reminded them of

Trudeau's own earlier statement that historically the Liberal government looked on Quebec MPs as "little more than a herd of trained donkeys" to be kept in line by a stable-master.

Marchand, Pelletier, and Trudeau brushed off the witticisms and the warnings. They had no intention of becoming cannibal kings, trained donkeys, or even stable-masters. They meant to be as powerful as C. D. Howe. To achieve this goal they were counting heavily, as Marchand said many years later, on Trudeau's knowledge of Ottawa, his impeccable command of the English language, and his presumed understanding of the English-Canadian style.

THE APPREHENSION with which the three wise men approached
official Ottawa after their election to Parliament in November 1965
had its roots in bitter experience. Most Quebeckers of their generation who had spent time in the federal capital could recount
stories of insults suffered there at the hands of members of the
English-speaking ascendancy. (Later, younger French Canadians
who had come to maturity after the Quiet Revolution called these
tales ''atrocity stories'' and laughed at them in disbelief.) Marchand had never forgotten the ignominy that befell him once in the
1940s when he arrived in Ottawa as the sole Quebec representative
in a delegation of trade unionists from across the country. The
group had been cordially received by Humphrey Mitchell, the
minister of labour in the King government. But once the formal
greetings in the minister's office were over, Mitchell singled out
Marchand, whose English was heavily accented and, in those days,
rudimentary. Oozing concern like lemon curd from a cake, the
minister suggested in front of the whole group that Marchand
might be ''more comfortable'' meeting instead with a certain
''mon-sew-er'', a minor official who was also French and who at
that very moment was awaiting him eagerly down the hall.
Marchand allowed himself to be led away, feeling like a servant
sent to gossip below stairs while the serious business was conducted by his betters in the drawing room over cigars.

The Ottawa he came to with Pelletier and Trudeau nearly
twenty years after that episode was a city in a state of transition —
and Marchand was a man in a state of certainty, forty-six years
old and at the pinnacle of his career. In many ways the old establishment that Trudeau had encountered fifteen years before in the
PCO appeared to be in charge once more after the uncomfortable
hiatus of the Diefenbaker years. Its *beau idéal* had become prime
minister. Its chief fixer, Jack Pickersgill, was the minister of
transport and a dominant voice in cabinet. Its financial branch
was firmly in command of economic policy now that Mitchell
Sharp was ensconced as finance minister, with Maurice Lamontagne

relegated to the Senate and Walter Gordon on the back benches. The French-Canadian ministers were still in the patronage portfolios (Guy Favreau in justice, Lucien Cardin in the post office) and the French-Canadian officials still in the minor deputy-ministerships. But appearances were misleading. The establishment's power was threatened by changes of many kinds, not the least of them the aspirations of the new Quebec. It was no longer acceptable to hire a few malleable French Canadians and make them token members of boards or token senior bureaucrats and feel that the needs of the other culture had been filled. Official Ottawa was wriggling with embarrassment at its past failure to give Quebeckers their rightful place in the governing process.

The preliminary report of the Royal Commission on Bilingualism and Biculturalism, on which Marchand had served as a commissioner, had been published the previous year warning of the grave threat to Canada's future that French-Canadian dissatisfactions posed. Lester Pearson had said openly that he believed he was the last Canadian who could be elected prime minister without being able to speak fluent French. (Astonishing as it might seem that Pearson, the famous diplomat, was functionally unilingual, it was not an unusual deficiency in members of the Department of External Affairs in his heyday. Pearson's colleague and great friend, Norman Robertson, who served the department with distinction in its most important jobs for more than thirty years, and was clerk of the Privy Council during Trudeau's employment in that office from 1949 to 1951, could not speak French either. Once, when Robertson was under-secretary of state and the virtues of an official due for promotion were being discussed, it was mentioned that the man spoke French fluently, as well as a couple of other languages. Unimpressed, Robertson drawled, in his carefully cultivated mid-Atlantic voice, "All of them, no doubt, with the facility of a headwaiter." Robertson and Pearson were born and raised in the era when the English ruled the world and even their colonials could feel superior — especially if they had studied at Oxford and had met its exigencies with distinction.)

Ever since 1962, when he had been pushed into making his path-breaking policy speech on the Quebec situation by Maurice Lamontagne, Pearson had been seeking to remedy his feelings of inadequacy towards Quebec by finding an acceptable and capable French-Canadian lieutenant to play the advisory and organizational role that Lapointe had played for Mackenzie King. He had been thwarted in this desire during his first term in office both by the fierce factionalism that raged within the Quebec wing of his party (where the old-guard/new-guard fights were constant) and by a series of scandals involving several of his French-speaking ministers and their assistants that made them look accident-prone, if not actually corrupt, and made Pearson himself look foolish. His attempts at conciliating the aspirations of Jean Lesage and his quiet revolutionaries through the piecemeal policies of "cooperative federalism" had been largely unsuccessful. Having tried and failed to make first Lionel Chevrier, then Maurice Lamontagne, and finally Guy Favreau into his own Ernest Lapointe, Pearson in late 1965 was at the end of his tether. The future of Canada was at stake, he kept saying in public, and so was the future of the Liberal Party, his political advisers kept saying in private. Without a better showing in Quebec the party's chances of forming a majority government after the next election were no better than they had been in the previous three. Jean Marchand looked like the Liberals' last, best hope.

Marchand was appointed immediately to Pearson's cabinet as minister of manpower and immigration. Within a year he had the Quebec caucus under his control, its old guard having been subdued and its new reform group whipped into a semblance of harmony. Favreau had been retired to the bench and Marchand was named Quebec leader. These accomplishments were a tribute, of course, not just to Pearson's determination to come to grips with his Quebec problem but to Marchand's own political savvy gained in the rough struggle of his life as a union organizer with the Confédération des Travailleurs Catholiques du Canada (later the Confédération des Syndicats Nationaux).

The son of a poor Quebec City widow, Marchand had worked his way through university by taking jobs as a stenographer for the Quebec Provincial Police and a clerk at Canada Steamship Lines. His mentor was Father Georges-Henri Lévesque, who had taught him at Laval and consistently encouraged him after he plunged into the union movement as a combative iconoclast of twenty-four. By the time he became a Liberal politician, Marchand had nearly twenty-five years' experience in motivating men and it showed. He wasn't a gentle professor like Lamontagne, whose parliamentary career was tragically destroyed by the foolish judgment he had shown in buying furniture on time from some petty thugs who went bankrupt with his unpaid account on their books. And he wasn't a *naif* like Guy Favreau, whose distinguished past as a legal counsel hadn't taught him how to deal with the backstabbers in his own caucus, or the lethal attacks of Diefenbaker's Tories in the House, or the unreasonable demands of his distraught leader, Pearson, who loaded him with too much work, giving him a cabinet portfolio, the House leadership, and the Quebec lieutenancy all at one time. Instead, Marchand was street-smart and tough as a longshoreman. He knew who had to be controlled and who had to be flattered and who had to be elbowed aside. He was earthy, vivacious, fearless, funny, and charming. When he was asked what he liked best about Ottawa, he answered in a flash, "The fast train to Montreal," and the Anglos, far from being affronted, were delighted at the insult. In the years from 1965 to 1968, Marchand lived in a state of grace in Ottawa. He was a man whose time had come.

"He may have felt he was relying on my knowledge of government," Trudeau said in the autumn of 1978 looking back on the mid-1960s, "but without him I would not have survived six months in Ottawa. Pelletier and I accepted our disabilities — we felt it was important for Marchand to have a cabinet seat. He had a political reputation of his own, a power base. Pelletier and I felt we needed to learn a lot. I wanted a year and a half at least [without any sort of official role to play]."

Trudeau realized that he knew far more about political theory and the governing process than Marchand did but far less about real politics than any poll captain in any riding in downtown Montreal. Marchand had made sure that a seat was found for him in 1965. The party's Montreal organizers thought that he wouldn't be acceptable in any of the available French-Canadian ridings because of his anti-clerical reputation, so a complex arrangement was worked out with the Montreal Jewish community's Liberal elder statesman, Lazarus Phillips, a distinguished lawyer who had met every prime minister since Laurier and raised money for every Liberal leader since King. Cartier had traditionally been the Jewish riding in Montreal but the incumbent MP, Milton Klein, realized that the riding's Jewish population was dwindling and he badly wanted to switch to Mount Royal, an English riding held by the Speaker of the House of Commons, the Honourable Alan Mac-Naughton, who was due to retire. The Quebec organization had all but agreed that Mount Royal should be the new Jewish seat and two other promising would-be Jewish candidates, Dr. Victor Goldbloom and Dr. Stuart Smith, also wanted Mount Royal. Despite the pressures, Phillips held out for Trudeau as his preferred candidate. Eventually only Smith contested the Mount Royal nomination against Trudeau and lost. (He later became Liberal leader in Ontario.) Goldbloom went into provincial politics. Klein went back to run for the party once more in Cartier in 1965 and later supported Robert Winters for leader at the 1968 convention as a protest against both Lazarus Phillips and Pierre Trudeau.

Once Marchand had shepherded Trudeau safely into Parliament, he made sure that he wasn't stuck on the back benches. In late December of 1965, Trudeau was staying in a hotel in London, where he had gone to celebrate New Year's after a skiing holiday in Switzerland, when he got a long-distance call from Ottawa. Lester Pearson came on the line and asked Trudeau graciously whether he would serve as his parliamentary secretary. Trudeau casually told the astonished Prime Minister he would let him know, but he didn't think it was the kind of job he wanted. Marchand was furious, dismissing Trudeau's doubts with the bluntly expressed opinion that Pearson's political difficulties meant he was willing to help the Quebeckers, everybody knew the real power was in the Prime Minister's Office, and access to real power was what the three of them needed. He had pushed Pearson to get the job for Trudeau. Trudeau damn well better take it. Marchand not only made sure that Trudeau went into the PMO, he also insisted that the MPs in the Quebec caucus, most of whom — old guard and new guard alike — looked on Trudeau as an intellectual turncoat out of place in the party, paid him all due respect. It was like the tough kid in the gang looking after the smart kid, the one with the glasses and the book.

At the suggestion of Trudeau and Pelletier, Marchand instituted a series of lectures to the Quebec caucus to provide background information on issues of the day so that its members could function as more than the "trained donkeys" of Trudeau's sarcastic description. At these sessions, Trudeau was a star performer, displaying his gift for lucid analysis. In contrast, at the meetings of the entire Liberal caucus, where the English Canadians held sway, he was generally quiet, watchful rather than assertive, biding his time.

AFTER HIS REMARKABLE RISE to the apex of power in 1968, when Trudeau had become a national symbol of arrogant virility and dazzling nonconformity, it was hard to believe how shy and uncertain he had appeared when he first arrived in Ottawa in 1965 and was seen in the company of professional politicians and experienced power manipulators for the first time. Before a thousand newspaper stories had declared him a glamorous bachelor, and a hundred television cameras had worked their peculiar magic on the sharp planes of his unusual face, he was noteworthy mainly to those who recognized the quality of his mind. If the political pros in the Liberal Party in either the old or the new guard had been told at any time during his first eighteen months in Parliament that he was leadership material they would have roared with derision.

In the spring of 1966, Keith Davey, as a newly appointed senator, still harbouring an affinity for any Liberal who was described as reform-minded, invited Trudeau for lunch and regaled him with advice on how to make it in the big time. Trudeau sat quietly through the meal, suffering the advice politely, rejecting the proffered intimacy firmly. "After about fifteen minutes, I figured he was nothing but an egghead," Davey said later. "You know, the kind of guy who can tell you why it's raining but doesn't know when to come inside. The snappiest thing about him seemed to be that he wore an ascot. There was no way it looked like he was going to be my kind of guy."

Davey had been told about Trudeau by Richard O'Hagan, who was still functioning as Pearson's press adviser when Trudeau arrived in the PMO as the parliamentary secretary in early 1966. O'Hagan came home one night a few weeks later and said to Wanda, his wife, "Listen, let's give a dinner for this guy — he's got something." The dinner was duly given and completely dominated by Patrick Watson, then one of the CBC's biggest television stars, who took over the conversation and the attention of Trudeau's close friend and partner for the evening, Madeleine Gobeil, who was by now a lecturer in French literature at Ottawa's Carleton University. Whatever the "something" was that Trudeau had, it escaped the notice of most of the twenty-odd people in the room who knew very little about Trudeau except that he was Jean Marchand's sidekick and was filling a largely ceremonial job in Pearson's office.

Pearson himself hadn't met Trudeau before he joined the Liberal Party. But he was a friend of Pearson's old friend, Frank Scott, and was well thought of by Gordon Robertson, the Clerk of the Privy Council. Trudeau had impeccable manners, he had been to the right universities, and praise God, he was given to reticence rather than to the hysterical displays of emotion which Pearson had suffered from his Quebec colleagues in the previous three years. All this made him entirely acceptable in the role of parliamentary secretary, despite his insulting attack on Pearson in 1963 after his about-face on nuclear policy.

The job, as Marchand had predicted, was central to Trudeau's rapid advance. It gave him status in the Quebec caucus and meant he had access to the combined operation of the Prime Minister's Office and the Privy Council Office, the ideal place from which to refresh and expand his understanding of how the federal government worked. Two of his closest intellectual allies were also working in the PCO. Marc Lalonde, the Montreal lawyer, was in Ottawa two or three days a week, first as a member of the PCO task force, then as a part-time adviser to Pearson on federal-provincial affairs. (The next year he was to become a full-time policy adviser to Pearson.) Michael Pitfield had just become an assistant secretary to the cabinet, after serving as secretary to two royal commissions as well as aide-de-camp to the Governor General. Between them Lalonde and Pitfield had a formidable knowledge of Ottawa and the changes it had undergone in the fifteen years Trudeau had been away, and they shared his belief both in federalism and in the idea that the government's operations had to be radically modernized. Their experience had persuaded them that the old bureaucratic-political axis with its generalist approach to government problems may have been effective in the 1940s and 1950s, but was inadequate to cope with the complexities of the 1960s. They were enamoured of cybernetics and of other technocratic ideas that they saw as a means to make government both more efficient and more democratic and that fitted in perfectly with Trudeau's views on "functionalism". Like him, they approached everything on a rigorously intellectual basis and despite the fact that they were theoretically deeply concerned with democratization of the governmental process, the gritty business of party politics was unfamiliar to them.

Trudeau had a number of other friends in Ottawa during his pre-leadership years, some of whom he had known before his election: Eugene Forsey, then the director of research for the Canadian Labour Congress, a constitutional expert, and a long-time member of the CCF, who had split with the NDP over its special-status policy on Quebec; Allan Gotlieb, the head of the legal division of the Department of External Affairs; Roy Faibish, now a broadcast executive but formerly an executive assistant to Alvin Hamilton, the Minister of Agriculture in the Diefenbaker ministry, the Tories' most innovative idea man; Bernard Ostry, who had met Trudeau in London in the 1950s and who was now working at the CBC in public affairs, and Sylvia Ostry, his wife, by now an economist with the Economic Council; Morris Miller, another economist from McGill, who'd been in Russia at a conference Trudeau attended in 1951 and now worked in the Department of Finance; Blair Fraser, the Ottawa Editor of *Maclean's*, who was also a friend of Frank Scott's and who shared Trudeau's interest in wilderness canoeing. They were all people of an intellectual bent; none of them was a politician in the sense that Keith Davey's crowd of reformers understood politics. Certainly none of them was a Liberal. Madeleine Gobeil used to say to Trudeau regularly when he would meet her for dinner after a day on Parliament Hill, "Well, how were the sharks today?" and Trudeau would make some joking reply to the effect that he had eluded their teeth for the moment. This was the way he appeared to his friends then, a good man in a grimy trade, watching the muddy field of party politics bemusedly from the sidelines. To the Liberal Party's old hands, he was briefly the subject of attention of the kind accorded promising freshmen MPs but soon dismissed as not really a "comer".

Even when he went into the cabinet as minister of justice in the spring of 1967, a major portfolio that Pearson was persuaded by Marchand to bestow on him, Trudeau kept out of the limelight for several months, working hard at learning the department's business. He set out to supervise the last stages of the major revisions to the Criminal Code that were under way in Justice at the time and hired Ivan Head from the University of Alberta and Carl Goldenberg, a Montreal lawyer and veteran of government inquiries, as special advisers for an extensive review of the constitution. During the centennial summer celebration when his ministerial colleagues were cavorting at dinners, balls, and sundry other ceremonies held in honour of kings, queens, and visiting world statesmen, he was holed up with briefing papers in his departmental office learning his job. An Ottawa woman who knew him slightly was amused one summer Saturday to see him wandering the grounds alone at Expo 67 in Montreal clad in sandals and khaki pants, licking an ice-cream cone, completely unnoticed in the crowd.

In September he made an important speech to the Canadian Bar Association on a proposed constitutional Bill of Rights that was widely reported in the press partly because he got into a slanging match with a Quebec City reporter at a press conference afterwards. He was beginning that fall to attract media attention because of his unusual clothes, his athletic prowess, and his apparent disdain for convention and acclaim. But it wasn't until his announcements in the House of Commons in December of a new divorce bill and an omnibus bill to overhaul the Criminal Code that he became the subject of the famous burst of publicity, beginning with the widespread use of his remark ''There is no place for the state in the bedrooms of the nation,'' that launched his public drive to the Liberal leadership. In less than two months he was a declared candidate; in a little more than four, he was prime minister.

Pierre Trudeau then and later was usually portrayed as a man who did not want power but had it thrust upon him. His admirers liked to characterize the series of events that cast him into the limelight and from there into the leadership as sheer happenstance — the two important bills that the justice department had been working on for months but that just happened to be released in

December 1967, the precise month of Pearson's long-awaited announcement of his retirement; the expertise he had painstakingly gained over nearly twenty years on the most important issue of the day, constitutional reform, expertise that just happened to be revealed at the federal-provincial conference in February 1968 when he pitted himself against Daniel Johnson, the Quebec premier, and dazzled the onlookers and the press; the surprise enthusiasm expressed for him by Joey Smallwood, the premier of Newfoundland, who controlled the most docile political machine in Canada and who had been wowed by Trudeau during a trip he made to St. John's before the constitutional conference at a time when Smallwood's original choice, Robert Winters, had not yet entered the race; the spontaneous displays of support for his candidacy from the intellectual and arts communities in English Canada, among people who were normally indifferent or opposed to the Liberal Party; the last-minute withdrawal from the leadership race by Mitchell Sharp, the Minister of Finance, who threw his support to Trudeau and defused the fears of some of the cautious delegates at the convention who might otherwise have voted for Robert Winters, Trudeau's strongest opponent, and tipped the balance in his favour. These events were presented by Trudeau's advocates as luck and nothing more. But his detractors — and they were legion in the Liberal Party even in 1968 — saw them as deliberately planned manoeuvres by a masterly strategist, an amateur far shrewder than the pros.

Liberals who backed Robert Winters or Paul Hellyer or John Turner pointed out bitterly that Marc Lalonde had been meeting with various advocates of Trudeau's for months, long before Pearson's announcement, plotting a campaign strategy. They believed that Pearson had been pressured by Lalonde into deliberately making Trudeau look good by the timing of the Criminal Code revisions and the federal-provincial conference on the constitution. (In a way, Pearson confirmed this part of the theory in an interview with Martin Sullivan, a *Time* correspondent, in 1968, admitting that he had given Trudeau a series of boosts and had been surprised to find him "not just an intellectual but a tough, Tammany Hall politician". Confusingly, he told his friend Bruce Hutchison, the newspaperman, that he had not boosted Trudeau at all. By the time his posthumous memoirs covering the period were published in the 1970s, all that was committed to print was that Pearson was anxious that there should be a French-Canadian candidate, he had told Trudeau if he won the leadership he would have his blessing, and he had let ''a few of my friends know I was well disposed towards him.'') Long after his victory, Trudeau's opponents, notably the supporters of John Turner and Paul Hellyer, continued to feel the presentation of him as a reluctant leader was sheer image-making, claiming that his leadership campaign was brilliantly plotted to attract press attention without appearing to do so, contrived to look uncontrived, right down to the last wet-eyed, short-skirted Trudeau hostess in the crowds at the convention hall. As an example they were quick to point out that Marc Lalonde had persuaded Pearson before the February 1968 federal-provincial conference to dispatch Trudeau, as yet not a declared candidate, to each of the provincial capitals to call on the premiers in his role as justice minister. These meetings generated easily the kind of widespread television news coverage declared candidates were desperately trying to manufacture. They thought Lalonde had played on Pearson's guilt about Quebec — particularly his dismay at the destruction of the careers of Guy Favreau and Maurice Lamontagne — into giving Trudeau unfair advantages.

Certainly Lalonde was central to Trudeau's leadership organization, along with Pelletier, who had thought he should be leader since 1966, and Marchand, who went all out for Trudeau once he decided not to run himself. But many talented people rushed forward to support Pierre, to persuade Pierre, to aid Pierre despite a previous lack of interest in — even a disdain for — the Liberal Party. In Toronto, Mashel Teitelbaum, an artist, and his wife, Ethel Teitelbaum (who later became more deeply involved with the party as an organizer and ministerial assistant), persuaded their friend Ramsay Cook, the historian who had known Trudeau for several years, to begin a Trudeau-for-leader movement that eventually attracted other academics and artists as well as broadcasters and journalists. In Ottawa, Trudeau's friends, both old and new, were intrigued with the idea that such a man could lead a government. Roy Faibish offered his advice, as did Michael Pitfield and Allan Gotlieb, who was a civil servant, and Bernard

Ostry and Patrick Watson, who were experts in broadcasting. Eugene Forsey wrote an endorsement of Trudeau's leadership. Roger Lemelin, the Quebec novelist, turned up with a tin of special tooth whitener mixed by his dentist so Trudeau's smile would be more dazzling. In Edmonton, Mel Hurtig, the publisher, supported him vigorously. In New York Joyce Wieland, the artist, persuaded a number of Canadians-in-exile to rally to him. As a group, these people represented a formidable agglomeration of talent, and a surprising number of them felt it was their doing that Trudeau decided to go for the leadership, that it was their advice he heeded, their words that had overcome his seeming indifference. They joined together enthusiastically with already active Liberals who saw themselves as the new progressives, notably Donald Macdonald, Edgar Benson, Bryce Mackasey, Russell Honey, Martin O'Connell, and Robert Kaplan, the MPs; Allen Linden and William Kilbourn, academics with Liberal connections; Gordon Gibson, Tim Porteous, Eddie Rubin, and Pierre de Bané, who were ministerial assistants in Ottawa at the time.

When he was asked a decade after the event about his decision to run for the leadership — did he really want it or was he persuaded by his friends? — Trudeau was ambiguous, portraying himself as never having been power hungry but as knowing he was capable of exercising power all the same. "It's true," he said leaning back, arms spread-eagled along the back of a leather sofa in his office in the Langevin Block in September 1978, "that I had some reluctance to go for the leadership. I felt it was too early. I thought I would be an epiphenomenon with no roots and no power base in the Liberal Party. I wasn't known in English Canada, except for a few people in the universities. This was the real source of my hesitation. It was certainly not that I had an inferiority complex."

Whether or not he had ever considered himself as a possible prime minister before the race to succeed Pearson began, one thing was clear when Trudeau became Liberal leader on April 6, 1968: he felt beholden to no one in the Liberal Party. He had not made any deals with the other leadership candidates or curried the favour of any of the acknowledged power brokers. Certainly he didn't ask for the support of any of the English-Canadian reform politicians from the early 1960s who at the time of the convention no longer formed a cohesive group. Their sometime leader, Walter Gordon, had been discredited long since as a powerful force in the party. His retirement from the Pearson cabinet after the 1965 election to the Liberal back benches was followed by the ignominy of having his proposals on both the economy and medicare defeated at the October 1966 Liberal Party policy convention by continentalist Liberals led by Mitchell Sharp. After Pearson, under pressure from the Ontario caucus of the party, invited Gordon back into the cabinet as a minister without portfolio in January 1967, Gordon found that the influence he had formerly commanded as Pearson's close friend and adviser couldn't be recovered.

In May of that year, Gordon disgraced himself in Liberal eyes by making a speech in Toronto voicing his opposition to the United States' actions in Vietnam. This speech caused Pearson to fall into an unaccustomed rage and to rebuke him publicly. What Gordon said was that Vietnam was "a bloody civil war" in which American involvement could "not be justified either on moral or strategic grounds." It was hardly a radical notion to put forward as late in the war as 1967, but the attitudes Pearson had acquired in the Department of External Affairs during the rise of the American Empire in the 1940s, and 1950s had left such a mark on his thinking that he regarded Gordon's forthright expression of his opinions as insufferable "meddling in the affairs of a foreign country". That the United States itself was "meddling in the affairs of a foreign country", and in a rather more significant way, was something he was willing to discuss in private; he had made a chiding speech on the same topic himself at Temple University in 1965 urging an end to the American bombing of North Vietnam and been sharply rapped on the knuckles by Lyndon Johnson for his efforts. But the strength of Gordon's opposition — his outright questioning of the American behemoth — was unacceptable because it broke both diplomatic rules and cabinet discipline.

Gordon's speech and Pearson's reaction to it strengthened the position within the party of the Liberal ministers — notably Robert Winters, John Connolly, Mitchell Sharp, Bud Drury, and Paul Martin — who were opposed to Gordon's views on the economy and worried that his influence over Pearson might continue. They made sure that Pearson didn't honour the promise he had made at the time Gordon was reinstated to cabinet that he would be put in charge of the Privy Council Office staff and, with it, the cabinet agenda. The only specific duty Gordon was given involved organizing a task force of eight economists, led by Mel Watkins, a professor at the University of Toronto, who were charged with investigating the impact of foreign investment on Canadian industry. Gordon and Pearson continued to be polite to each other but their friendship of thirty years was finished, and with it, Gordon's power in the party. (The friendship was never repaired, though when Pearson was dying in the autumn of 1972, Gordon went up to Ottawa to say good-bye to him at the urging of their mutual friend George Ignatieff, the diplomat.)

By the time the jockeying for the Liberal succession had begun to accelerate in the fall of 1967, Gordon was seen as having very little to deliver to potential leadership candidates. As the man who had centralized the organization of the party, he was unpopular in Western Canada, where delegates could be picked up. As an economic nationalist, he was disdained in the business community in Toronto, where the big-money donations were to be had. As a politician who had suffered a string of losses, he was out of favour with the media, except for the *Toronto Star*, whose publisher, Beland Honderich, continued to expect his staff to publish Gordon's every public utterance as though it was "an announcement of the second coming", as a *Star* editor of the time put it.

After the 1965 election, Gordon had thought briefly about running for the leadership himself. He had discussed the idea with Pearson several times before their rift over the Vietnam speech, and he had once gone so far as to gather together a group of his closest political allies to assess what kind of support they thought he might command. Gordon Edick, the Cell 13 member, remembered it as an uncomfortable meeting with Gordon canvassing the men in attendance and getting evasive responses: "Nobody else had the nerve to tell him the truth, but when he got to me, I just said, 'Walter, you're too damned old.' I could feel the tears in my eyes when I finished. But he accepted it as the God's honest truth."

Undaunted, Gordon attempted to exert influence over the choice of leader in the hope that he could keep the party left of centre and his ideas on repatriating the economy alive. His own preference was Jean Marchand, with whom he had developed a strong rapport. He saw Marchand as the most important member of the left-leaning group in the cabinet which included in his view Judy LaMarsh, Allan MacEachen, Larry Pennell, Edgar Benson, and, after April 1967, Pierre Trudeau. Gordon often went out to lunch or dinner with Marchand, sometimes in the company of other members of the Quebec caucus, and Gordon would prevail on the whole company to speak English since his grasp of French was tenuous and he hated doing anything badly. Such was the power of his charm — and the charm of his still powerful self-confidence — that Marchand never resented this but teased Gordon relentlessly, if respectfully, about his linguistic ineptitudes. Gordon liked Marchand for his tough mind and his reform ideas but he also firmly believed, as 1967 wore on and the Quebec situation worsened, that in choosing their next leader the Liberals had to honour their party tradition of alternating between French and English Canadians.

After Marchand decided in early January 1968 that he would not stand for the leadership because of his faulty English, his uncertain health, and his wife's distaste for life in Ottawa, he pressured Gordon to support Trudeau. Gordon was reluctant. He felt Trudeau was too inexperienced politically and too unpopular in Quebec, and when he told Marchand about his doubts, the Quebec leader replied, "Well, okay. On the inexperience, that could be an advantage considering the public's view of experienced politicians. In any case, he has the brains to learn fast. On the popularity, I can fix that. Give me three weeks. If I say he should be popular in Quebec, you wait. He will be." When Gordon realized Marchand was adamant, he began to pester Trudeau to try to get him to define his attitude towards economic nationalism. At one encounter, he asked him his opinion of the recently published Watkins Report (named after the chairman of Gordon's task force on the structure of Canadian industry). Trudeau had long condemned all forms of nationalism. On this occasion, he waffled a little, saying ambiguously that he had read the report and its general principles made sense, but he had not had a chance to study it thoroughly, a response that did little to overcome Gordon's lack of enthusiasm for Trudeau's candidacy.

More than ten years later during a discussion about the Liberal Party in the fall of 1978, Trudeau still remembered Gordon's reluctance to support him, saying, "He made it abundantly clear to me that he would go all out for Marchand but not for me." What Trudeau did not mention was that during the leadership campaign, Gordon put to him an awkward question that was being voiced by Trudeau's enemies in Liberal circles constantly at the time, but that none of his friends had the nerve to raise with Trudeau himself. One day early in the leadership race, when the two men met in the government members' lounge behind the curtains of the House of Commons chamber, Gordon said to Trudeau, "Pierre, do you know what they are saying about you? They are saying you're a homosexual." Coldly furious, Trudeau gave what he later developed into his standard response to this charge, a sarcastic statement to the effect that whoever said that about him should leave him alone in a room with his wife for a couple of hours and what transpired there would provide his rebuttal.

Scurrilous rumours about Trudeau's sexual proclivities spread in English Canada despite the vigorous denials of Trudeau's French-Canadian colleagues, who thought the charge was an Anglo-Canadian canard. Alex Pelletier, a woman who had known Trudeau for twenty-five years, told an interviewer that spring, "Every girl in Montreal is sitting at home tonight in case Pierre will call. . . . he has had many girls, beautiful ones, and at least two times he nearly got married." Jeanne Sauvé, a journalist and broadcaster, who was later to be a member of Trudeau's cabinet, found the whole idea absurd. "Listen," she would say in discussing it in her street-smart, tough-kid manner, "I worked at the CBC for years in Montreal and I know homosexuals. I can smell them. And nobody who knew him ever thought that of Pierre."

The dismay that these charges engendered among many Quebeckers was expressed with clarity by Carole Corbeil, a bilingual Montrealer who was a schoolgirl in 1968. "In those Trudeaumania days [Trudeau was] so stylishly outré, so elegant, that he gave a magic aura to the hybrid state of speaking two languages. . . . At that time English Montrealers were still in their Pepsi-epithet stage, and this man on television was no Pepsi. Crazy as it may now seem, not looking like a Pepsi once carried a lot of weight in our bourgeois drawing rooms. You could look French-French, you could be intellectually nationalistic, but the English could always get to you by bringing up the Pepsi [label]. The English in this case were my three stepbrothers and stepfather. And so while the French contingent of the family — my mother, sister and I — were beaming at the shimmering idol on the screen, the English contingent was having a hard time coming up with a dismissive phrase. Finally, my English stepfather, his large frame reclining so gracefully in his armchair, turned to my French mother with rehearsed disdain. 'That guy,' he said, precisely dismissive and flicking an ash from his cigarette, 'belongs in a hairdressing salon.' My exquisite mother looked a bit taken aback. 'Oh, George,' she said in her soft absent voice, 'what makes you say that?' 'Well,' he replied with the weight of Westmount authority, 'he's not married and he's *French*.' "

Trudeau's attraction to women in 1968 had nothing much to do with which of the two official languages they spoke. English-Canadian women went wild over him and often met with the same kind of male dismissal of Trudeau's charms that Corbeil experienced in Montreal. "Boy, is he sexy," a Toronto journalist said watching him on a television monitor during the leadership convention. A professor watching with her considered the idea dispassionately, and then replied, "Well, I suppose you might say that. But you have to admit it's in a curiously *androgynous* way."

Whether the rumours about Trudeau's alleged homosexuality were prompted by cross-cultural misunderstandings, male jealousies, or political rivalries, they continued and were picked up in Quebec by Conservatives and Social Crediters in rural ridings who made sly allusions to Trudeau's overhaul of the Criminal Code, which had included changes to the laws governing homosexual conduct. A Conservative candidate in the Beauce, Gilles Beaudoin, to give an example reported at the time, said at a public meeting in his riding, "Let's call a spade a spade. This is a bill for queers and fairies," and then added, casually, that Pierre Trudeau was unmarried.

There were other allegations made about Trudeau, notably by the ultra-right-wing Canadian Intelligence Service, in Flesherton, Ontario, which published an article in March 1968 written by an "undercover agent of the RCMP" accusing him of being associated with Communist causes and calling him "a rabid admirer of Mao", charges so stupidly phrased and so redolent of McCarthyism they were generally dismissed and may even have won liberal support for Trudeau within and without the Liberal Party.

In the end, Walter Gordon did support Trudeau for the leadership, finding his ideas preferable to the more conservative views of the other front runners, Paul Martin, Robert Winters, and Paul Hellyer. But he didn't bring with him the votes of Keith Davey or any of the other Liberals he had been close to in the early sixties. Davey, Dan Lang, David Greenspan, Gordon Edick, Robert Andras, and Judy LaMarsh campaigned all out for their old friend from Cell 13, Paul Hellyer. Allan MacEachen was a candidate himself. The two French Canadians who had been close to the Gordon reformers, Maurice Lamontagne and Maurice Sauvé, weren't in the Trudeau camp; Lamontagne stayed out of the proceedings and Maurice Sauvé supported Paul Martin. Jerry Grafstein worked on John Turner's campaign. John Nichol as president of the party was chairman of the convention and officially neutral. Richard O'Hagan was in Washington serving as the minister-counsellor in the Canadian Embassy and didn't come to the convention. Neither did Tom Kent, who had twice failed to get himself elected as an MP, and was now a public servant. Jim Coutts, who was studying at the Harvard Business School that year, came to the convention only as an observer, watching the balloting on television in a room in the coliseum in the company of Maryon and Lester Pearson.

Most of the 1960s reformers did see Trudeau as an "epiphenomenon" as he feared they would, only they used blunter language to express their opinions. Judy LaMarsh summed it up when during the balloting period she urged Paul Hellyer within sound range of the CBC to take his support to Robert Winters, saying "Don't let that bastard [Trudeau] win it, Paul. . . . He isn't even a Liberal." Experienced politicians in the Liberal Party — whichever faction they belonged to — were openly puzzled by Trudeau's success.

("What's this guy got anyway?" John Turner was heard to ask over and over.) None of the modern techniques that they had so ardently believed in and so wholeheartedly deployed during the long campaign and at the convention had had the desired effect. The laboriously contrived and elaborately presented policy positions put together by their advisers. The books they had ghosted and published. The years spent cultivating contacts among the party's small-time bosses and big-time power-brokers in the hope they would deliver delegate votes. The gimmicks like the giant pizza baked for Paul Hellyer with "44" on it traced in slices of pepperoni to remind Liberals that Hellyer was still a young man — four years younger than Trudeau, although he had been around Ottawa since the St. Laurent years and people thought he was much older. The catchy songs adapted from Broadway musicals. The teenagers in cheerleader costumes who looked just like the girls at the American party conventions of 1960 and 1964. The hospitality suites where the booze and the gossip flowed. Even the speeches with the Kennedyesque cadences ("Now is not the time for mellow men," John Turner said). They were all to no avail. Trudeau won the leadership by acting the humble intellectual, "creeping into the convention like Jesus Christ," as Frank Walker, the editor of the *Montreal Star*, described it, relying on spontaneous demonstrations, which were actually carefully planned, on dazzling displays of superior reasoning power in both languages at workshop sessions, on distributing to delegates a tabloid newspaper featuring testimonials from other intellectuals and a drawing by the painter Harold Town, on a calculated indifference to the press that unaccountably gained its favour — in short, by breaking all the rules they had learned out of the American books and, by God, winning, winning big.

That Trudeau won because he was both shrewd and lucky in his timing — that an intellectual could also have moxie — was amazing to traditional politicians. Trudeau and his close friends knew that English Canada had suffered a series of electric shocks from Quebec in the 1960s. They counted on transmitting to the delegates the belief that Trudeau was the ideal man to soothe the country's fears by heartening them with his certainties about federalism. And, of course, their artful strategy worked.

ONCE TRUDEAU HAD WON THE LEADERSHIP, he quickly called an election and Liberals, whether they had voted for him or not, rallied to the cause. John Nichol became campaign co-chairman with Jean Marchand, and Bill Lee, who had been Paul Hellyer's executive assistant in the Pearson years, acted as tour manager. Most of Trudeau's opponents at the leadership convention went back to their ridings, rounded up their supporters, and set to work for a Liberal victory. Years later, Davey was to say that the campaign was "not an election at all, it was a coronation. It didn't teach Pierre Trudeau anything about politics or about the Liberal Party. All he had to do was to show his face and make his speech about the Just Society and participatory democracy and all that jazz. He didn't need the Liberal Party to win and he didn't know what the Liberal Party was all about."

Certainly it was a curiously deceptive campaign. Because he talked so persuasively about democratizing the party, making it more open to the ideas of "the people", Trudeau's inherent elitism was disguised. New candidates vied wildly for nominations, certain that they had the qualifications to meet his prescription for the politician of the future who would be adventurous and flexible, governing pragmatically from a set of principles. Because his "just society" concept included the amelioration of regional disparities, Westerners in numbers unprecedented for many years were attracted to Liberalism, and his ignorance of Canada west of Ottawa was covered up. Because he was a consummate actor and moved with ease and apparent pleasure among the crowds who flocked to him as if he were a pope, his basic introversion and misconceptions about human needs were never apparent. Trudeau's campaign was theatrical and, in the end, superficial, but his opponents Robert Stanfield, the Conservative leader, and T. C. Douglas of the NDP were written off by most commentators as the plodding politicians of Canada's yesterdays. Trudeau was the man for tomorrow.

Despite their pleasure at the Liberals' huge electoral victory in June — their first majority since 1953 — some party insiders were apprehensive about the leader. They had been mildly disturbed by Trudeau's insensitivity to party form shortly after his leadership victory when he had deprived Lester Pearson of his "day in the House" — the occasion when the expected tributes on his retirement could be paid by members of all parties. Trudeau called the election as soon as the Commons met after he was sworn in as prime minister, cutting off any opportunity for members to rise on points of privilege and make speeches in Pearson's honour. Pearson bitterly resented Trudeau's action, though he referred to that day in a characteristically light-hearted manner afterwards as an occasion when he was left clutching an undelivered speech of thanks to tributes that were never delivered. David Lewis, the veteran NDP member, thought it was an insult not just to Pearson but to the gentlemanly traditions of the House of Commons itself.

Trudeau was equally indifferent to the less gentlemanly if more urgent traditions of hustings politics. John Nichol, who as party president had been close to Trudeau for the eight weeks of the campaign, told his political friends stories about the way the leader behaved in private that showed him to be a very different man from the accessible and diffident hero presented in the press. Late in the campaign, Trudeau had wanted to cancel a swing through the Western provinces because he was tired and didn't think it was necessary since he was ahead in the polls. Nichol had been furious; hundreds of Liberals — candidates and their workers — had been working for weeks preparing for him to come. Only a shouting match and a threatened resignation forced Trudeau to complete his campaign schedule. On another occasion, Nichol had accompanied Trudeau to a reception of Liberals who were gathered in Ottawa for a campaign strategy meeting and Trudeau had stood irresolutely at the door of the hotel suite where the party was being held, saying he didn't want to go in and break into conversations, everybody was having a good time, couldn't he just go home? Nichol explained that everybody was having a good time partly because they were expecting his imminent arrival; they wanted to go back to their provincial campaign committees and say they'd had drinks with the leader and given him crucial advice.

How could this *be* that the man who was so reticent in private was so charismatic in public? Out on the campaign trail, travelling in Trudeau's entourage was like being with a Caesar. At one big rally in the Toronto-Dominion Centre in June — the kind of outdoor gathering of cheering thousands the new politics' practitioners had tried so often to amass for Pearson in the three earlier elections of the sixties — Nichol had stood on the roof of one of the buildings with a couple of journalists and watched the scene below. The square was crammed with ten thousand office workers on their lunch hours, and in the windows of the towering buildings surrounding the square, hundreds of others were pressed up to the glass. Trudeau bounded up onto the platform like an actor coming on stage, bands played, the speakers introduced him in hyperbolic banalities, and Trudeau launched into a stupefyingly dull fifteen-minute lecture on the future of cities, the kind of speech that if delivered by Lester Pearson would have prompted groans even in his own entourage. But with Trudeau, it was like a Roman triumph. When he was finished, the crowds shouted his name over and over and it blew eerily down the windy canyons of Bay Street — Troo-doe, Troo-doe — in a way that Nichol and his companions found discomfiting. What was going on? A kind of mass auto-eroticism. It was the same everywhere that Trudeau went in English Canada: in a curling rink at Kamloops, a park in Saskatoon, at a shopping centre in Winnipeg when he stood on a truck dolly with James Richardson, the scion of the city's most famous family, and the Liberal candidate in Winnipeg South. At the end of every paragraph he uttered, the stolid Manitobans roared their approval.

When these rallies were over, Trudeau always wanted privacy, time to meditate, exercise, read, memorize the next speech. He didn't seem to realize that the leader had to talk to local Liberals, that their feelings would be hurt if he didn't speak to their wives warmly and ask after their views respectfully. Nichol gave in to Trudeau's need to be alone, reasoning that he was tired from the astonishing events of the previous six months, he was new at his job, he'd soon get the hang of what was expected of him. What Nichol didn't know was that Trudeau would continue to misunderstand party traditions and party politicians for the next four years.

WITHIN A FEW MONTHS of Trudeau's twin triumphs in 1968, many of the Grits who had belonged to the old Gordon-Davey network began to call themselves Pearsonian Liberals, not just because they had come into political prominence first in the early days of Pearson's leadership but because the designation allowed them to distance their ambitions from what was going on in Ottawa. The truth was that Trudeau and his gang of amateurs had taken the party away from them, and they found themselves politically passé before most of them had even had time to settle into middle age.

Their disorientation was due partly to the unexpectedness of Trudeau's rise. For the first time in party history, the succession to the leadership had not been preordained. Before Pearson each of the Liberal leaders had been able more or less to direct the choice of his successor. Edward Blake had designated Wilfrid Laurier and Laurier had designated Mackenzie King — or so King claimed — and King had designated Louis St. Laurent and St. Laurent had designated Lester Pearson. But at the end of the Pearson years — after the Liberals' ten-year-long scramble to regain their elusive objective of majority power — the party had been so factionalized and the cabinet so ridden with ambitious men that even if Pearson had been inclined to king-making he would have had difficulty in pointing to a natural successor and making his choice stick.

As a result, when Trudeau won the leadership and the country by cunning and charisma there was an understandable unease among formerly powerful Liberals who weren't sure where they stood with this new guy. (Opinion polls of rank-and-file Liberals taken after the convention had shown them to be well satisfied with the choice of the new leader. After all, here was a big winner, promising a just society and a participatory democracy. But the perceptions and needs of the rank and file in 1968 were very different, as always, from those of the power brokers.)

Trudeau was quick to say later that he had understood the situation. "I knew I was inheriting a failing and a factionalized party," he said in 1978. "And I was well aware of how shallow were my own roots in it. I did everything I could to knit it up, offering my opponents places in the cabinet and contriving new lines of communication to the rank and file. . . ." It was true that when Trudeau took office and engaged in what the sociologists call a circulation of elites — the new leader's classic action of replacing a deposed power group with men of his own choosing — he did so after much deliberation and with a supremely rational plan. He was convinced of the need to democratize the governmental process by breaking the grip of the bureaucratic establishment on decision-making and policy formulation and he meant to use the Liberal Party as an important instrument in this democratization.

In his cabinet-making he appointed many of Pearson's former ministers — notably MacEachen, Turner, Hellyer, Greene, Martin, and Sharp, all of whom had been rivals for the leadership, and Drury, who was not — as well as judiciously rewarding his own supporters. Marchand and Pelletier were given important posts, as were the English-Canadian MPs Donald Macdonald, Edgar Benson, and Bryce Mackasey, who had come forward to support him early in the race. He gave Eric Kierans, who had provided the only new thinking and real policy alternatives to the leadership campaign, the portfolio of communications. He also paid heed to regional considerations, putting in his first cabinet Art Laing and Ron Basford of British Columbia, Bud Olsen of Alberta, and Robert Andras from Northern Ontario, all men who had opposed him but had been elected from areas that demanded representation.

Once he had his ministers in place, he proceeded with the drastic reforms of the cabinet system that were meant to endow the politicians with greater power vis-à-vis their senior bureaucracies. At the same time he set in train a number of other elaborate schemes for keeping in touch with the party and the country, schemes his staff called communicating channels. There was political cabinet, which involved regular meetings of ministers with party officials, including the party's new president, Richard Stanbury, and national director, Torrance Wylie. He established the troika system, which involved an advisory group from each province consisting of three members — a cabinet minister, a caucus member, and a representative of the provincial party's membership — who were meant to be in charge of the party's affairs in their areas. He set up the regional desks in his own office which were supposed to relay directly to him non-party intelligence ("Whatever that means," Keith Davey said at the time). Above all, he encouraged the exercise in "participatory democracy", which the party president Richard Stanbury had enthusiastically touted as the cornerstone on which to build a new mass Liberal Party. This ambitious scheme comprised three phases — first, a thinkers' conference held in a remote and idyllic B.C. spa, Harrison Hot Springs, in November 1969, when several hundred party activists and several dozen experts of varying ideological hues tried to re-enact the 1960 Kingston Conference on a grander scale; then a period of grass-roots consultation when the rank and file of the riding associations were meant to respond to the thoughts of the Harrison thinkers and generate draft resolutions; and finally, a climactic policy convention in 1970 when hundreds of resolutions in twelve policy fields were passed amid great excitement on the very questionable assumption that the delegates were deciding the fate of the country for the next two decades.

Rationally it all made sense. It was a model plan for a model party in some idealized democracy, taking a little from the British Labour Party, a little from the Social Democrats in Germany, a little from various other parties in various Scandinavian states, and quite a lot from the small group of reformers in Quebec and Ontario — notably Claude Frenette, Jerry Grafstein, Mark MacGuigan, Maurice Sauvé, and Allen Linden — who had been pressing for a democratization of the party's internal structure throughout the Pearson years.

The trouble was it didn't work. It didn't take sufficiently into account the fact that the Liberal Party was a federation of eleven provincial and territorial organizations with very different needs, traditions, and memberships. (It was difficult, for instance, for a centralized political bureaucracy working on regional desks to process information from political cultures as diverse as the fiefdom Joey Smallwood ran in Newfoundland and the rough, tough, raw capitalist-versus-socialist world of British Columbia where the Liberals had been in bed with the Socreds for years, desperately trying to keep warm and alive.) It ignored the reality that Canada was a country where brokerage politics was the rule and what was needed was not a rigid system but an intuitive leader with a feel for the country and personal contacts among its elites. Trudeau had neither, as he himself knew very well.

"My staff [as of 1978] has tried to get me phoning around the country to three hundred people or so regularly in order to keep in touch," he said ruefully. "They say 'Paul Martin, John Turner, Mackenzie King used these techniques. How are things in Matane? How are things in Melville?' I would have done this [from the beginning] if I had had three hundred Liberal friends. I didn't have thirty. I needed to rely on a system to fill me in."

Within three years Trudeau's system had shown itself to be dismally unreliable. The participatory exercise had foundered by the fall of 1971 when it had become obvious that the resolutions passed with so much fanfare at the party convention of 1970 were being disregarded in the policy-making of the government and had been rejected by cabinet as the basis for the party's next election campaign. Political cabinet had degenerated into a series of interminable, largely futile meetings where party officials and cabinet ministers — already exhausted from too many cabinet committee meetings — snarled at each other. The troika advisory groups had turned into patronage-dispensing agencies and little more, and the regional desks had become yet another source of rage for the Liberal caucus, whose members thought their functions as elected officials had been usurped by the Prime Minister's Office.

Party politicians have an unerring instinct for the exact locus of power, and long before the press began to complain about the pervasive influence of the PMO in the first Trudeau régime, there were whisperings among Liberals that what really mattered was not participation exercises or communication channels but an open line into the tight little group of officials who surrounded the PM. Trudeau had staffed his office with participants from the various intellectual discussion groups of his past. Marc Lalonde had become his principal secretary. Ivan Head, who had been hired for his constitutional review in the justice department, was his legislative assistant and foreign policy expert, and Jim Davey, a physicist from Montreal who had been involved in a series of discussions in Trudeau's office in 1966 and 1967, was his program secretary. These were his principal aides along with Gordon Robertson, the clerk of the Privy Council and secretary to the cabinet, and Michael Pitfield, the most important of the deputy secretaries. Below their level were a dozen others from the private sector and the civil service who had had rarefied educations (there were six Oxonians in Trudeau's circle, and half a dozen others who had been at either Harvard, the London School of Economics, or the Université de Paris), people who by training or background had been during most of their adult lives as remote from the Canadian reality outside the intellectual elites of Montreal and Ottawa as Trudeau was himself.

As a group, they were self-contained, secretive, and snobbish. They wrote speeches for Trudeau that read like articles in learned journals. (His old colleagues from *Cité libre*, Roger Rolland, who had worked for Radio Canada, and Jean Lemoyne, who was a prize-winning author, were hired to write for him in French; Tim Porteous, a younger intellectual who had met Trudeau at a conference in Africa in the 1950s, tackled the writing of the English speeches along with Ivan Head.) They shared his obsessions with the problems of separatism in Quebec and government process in Ottawa. They believed, as he did, that Canada's problems had to be assessed *rationally* through task forces and study groups. Foreign policy, fiscal policy, social policy, and, above all, the constitution were all reviewed painstakingly. But the Trudeauites became so entangled in their reviews and assessments that action was delayed frequently to the point of absurdity. They set up in the East Block a sort of counter-bureaucracy, a prime-ministerial staff of four hundred and fifteen people, three times as many as Pearson had employed. They approved of the cabinet-committee system he had established at the urging of Michael Pitfield, a system that was meant to make the decision-taking procedures in government more democratic but that kept ministers so busy arguing their departments' legislative proposals with each other that they had little time for politics — and little stomach for raising their crassly political concerns in front of a leader who would demolish any argument based on ''hunch''. The PMO group thought that backbench MPs should be satisfied with the rigid rules imposed on their weekly caucus meetings, which effectively cut off political arguments and caused the former mayor of Toronto, Philip Givens, to declare that as a backbench Liberal MP he felt "as useless as tits on a bull". In brief, Trudeau's staff knew very little about and basically despised party politics. Politics was boring, trivial, and a waste of time for an intellectual elite involved with "the larger questions".

Trudeau himself hated political talk and party gatherings partly because of the unease in social situations which never left him despite his elevation to high office. If he couldn't perform — as an orator, an athlete, a dancer, a Lothario, the leader of a teach-in, or in some other dramatic role that distanced him from intimate contact with strangers — he didn't know what to do. It wasn't possible for him to rely at Liberal functions on the briefing papers his staff prepared for him for encounters with cabinet ministers and bureaucrats. He had no facility for telling anecdotes or discussing sports or responding to passionate statements. When a riding association president from Calgary would tell him earnestly about Western rage, repeating ideas he had heard a hundred times, he would give a bored and boring answer about all the meetings he had attended with Western premiers in which "attempts to delineate these problems had been held to see what the limits of the solution may be in so far as the federal government is concerned." What the Westerner really wanted was for the Prime Minister to make some personal remark showing concern that the outlying area of the country be attracted to and understood in the centre, that steps be taken to recognize Western distress about oil prices/freight rates/grain marketing; he wanted to know that Trudeau had been discussing this thorny problem with Hu Harries, MP for Edmonton-Strathcona, or somebody else they knew — some human response to their nagging concerns, a response the Westerner could repeat to his cronies.

Trudeau had been pleased that most English-Canadian Liberals, like most English Canadians, had rallied to him in the most dramatic incident of his first régime, the October Crisis of 1970, involving the kidnappings of James Cross, a British diplomat, and Pierre Laporte, a Quebec cabinet minister, by the Front de

Libération du Québec, a separatist terrorist group in Montreal.*
(When one small group of intellectual party activists remonstrated
with him at a meeting in November 1970 about the handling of
civil liberties in Quebec during the crisis, he was furious at their
"stupidity", their bleeding-heart liberalism.) But for the most
part he seemed to pay little heed to what the party thought. He
ignored occasional objections to his policies voiced by party
members as the maunderings of the uninformed, in the same way
that he disdained most people outside his small technocratic circle. In a famous show of temper in the House of Commons, he
told Opposition MPs that they were nobodies "fifty yards from
Parliament Hill", dismissing the complaints of people such as
John Diefenbaker, the former prime minister, as well as rumblings
among his backbenchers that he was ignoring Parliament. He was
unimpressed when journalists and political scientists began to write
that he had created a presidential office in the East Block. After
all, he was a liberal democrat, with a philosophical position. He
knew how much democracy a democracy could stand.

His belief in the efficacy of systems left him with no idea
of the importance Liberals attached to informal contacts between
the leader and party members. He didn't know anything about
what John Nichol called "psychic patronage", the art of keeping
his supporters happy and involved by personal contact. He thought
it was enough to attend formal party meetings and to make dull
speeches at fund-raising dinners, to shake hands with the party
faithful as he moved through the crowds in a kind of royal progress.
He had no inclination to be more personal with his followers than
that, to tell them of his ideas, to ask about theirs, to remember the
contributions they had made to his campaigns, or to compliment
them on their business or legal or political triumphs. He was an
intellectual interested in concepts of governing, at ease mainly
with bureaucrats of superior intelligence or with fellow Quebeckers
who were also federalists. For other people he had very little
time, no matter how important they were or had once been to the
Liberal Party.

Except for formal exchanges on ceremonial occasions,
Trudeau didn't keep in touch with either Lester Pearson or Jack

*For a further discussion of the October Crisis, see Part 5.

Pickersgill, who knew more about the Liberal Party's history than anyone extant. (Pickersgill liked to say that he "divided political leaders into two groups: the intuitive and the rational. King and Pearson were intuitive. St. Laurent was rational. This Prime Minister [Trudeau] seems to think you can govern by geometry.") Their former colleague, Walter Gordon, saw Trudeau only two or three times during his first two years in office, and then only by asking for an interview, leaning on his prestige as a privy councillor. The two men discussed the possibility that Gordon might take on the chairmanship of the proposed Canada Development Corporation. Shortly afterwards, Gordon was publicly critical of the government's handling of the economy and he never heard from Trudeau again. ("When I told them I thought it was a hell of a mistake to slow down the economy in an attempt to deal with inflation, they [Trudeau's advisors] treated me like I was an elderly crock who didn't know what it was all about.") Gordon busied himself with his company, Canadian Corporate Management, in Toronto and with keeping his ideas alive through the establishment in 1970 of the Committee for an Independent Canada and the writing of his memoirs.

His protégé, Keith Davey, was focussing his energies on an investigation of the mass media in Canada, which he conducted as chairman of a special Senate committee. This project took more than two years and resulted in the publication in December 1970 of *An Uncertain Mirror*, a half-million-word report that was contentious, well written, and lively, and earned Davey dozens of columns of print in the newspapers of whose owners his committee was so critical. The Trudeauites ignored it. When Davey asked Lalonde what he thought of the report, Lalonde said off-handedly that it seemed to him irrelevant.

None of these people had ever been friends of Trudeau's and they were all realistic enough to respond philosophically to their deposition from the corridors of power. What they didn't realize for a long time was that even with his supporters, Trudeau drew on the talents of only those whose abilities fitted his needs.

Eddie Rubin, a lawyer from Montreal who had been his special assistant in the justice department, a lively young man with a glittery eye who had put up a thousand dollars of his own money to rent an office for Trudeau's leadership campaign, was frozen out of important discussions in the PMO because he was known to talk to the press; six months after Trudeau was named leader, he left Ottawa to return to the practice of law. John Nichol and Bill Lee, who played important parts in the election campaign of 1968, didn't hear from Trudeau for more than three years after it, which left them at first puzzled and then furious. (Both of them later quit the party; Nichol even quit the Senate.) Trudeau never expressed to people either his gratitude or his regrets. He regarded both their involvement in political life and their departure from it as being their own business. He felt it was just chance that within three years of his election as leader all his opponents, other than John Turner, were either devoted to his cause or out of politics completely. By 1971 Robert Winters and Joe Greene were dead. Paul Martin was acquiescent in the Senate. Both Paul Hellyer and Eric Kierans had quit the cabinet and then the party over disputes with Trudeau. Allan MacEachen and Mitchell Sharp were dutifully thumping their desks when the leader spoke in the Commons and expediting his decisions in the Privy Council chamber. Only Turner had kept up a personal power base in the party and an independent public reputation.

AT THE BEGINNING OF 1972, when he realized it was soon going to be constitutionally necessary to hold an election, Trudeau assumed the party machine could be kicked into gear by the simple act of informing the regulars there was going to be a campaign. What he did not understand was that the party machine had rusted from neglect. For four years he had nourished a misunderstanding of how party politics worked. He had not recognized that the two old-line parties were loose aggregations of people held together by little more than their hopes for personal advancement through the electoral and patronage systems, their feelings of friendship for each other, and the vicarious excitement to be derived from being close to power — of being able to say "I know a guy [e.g. a cabinet minister, an MP, a member of the PM's staff] who talks to the PM all the time and he told me that . . ."

In the 1960s, when first Keith Davey and then John Nichol were in charge of keeping the party happy, they took soundings across the country continually, listening to complaints from the constituencies and promising to repeat them to the PM forthwith, keeping an eye out at the same time for party workers who deserved or needed an appointment, for MPs who were in trouble organizationally, for organizers whose parents had a golden wedding anniversary coming up, for riding association presidents who needed a cabinet minister to come to a fund-raising function, and so on. This wasn't just a matter of gregarious personalities emoting. Davey and Nichol were struggling with the reality of minority parliaments and they were compelled to keep the machine oiled in order to fight the four federal elections held in the six years from 1962 to 1968. Their task was made easier because they both knew instinctively how to make politics fun. They loved the game and they loved their leader, even though Pearson was no fonder of politicking than Trudeau was. But as a small-town minister's son, Pearson was canny enough to realize that people have to be cultivated if you're going to maintain their goodwill, and charming enough to persuade first Davey and then Nichol to do his spadework for him.

Trudeau did not even recognize the need for a Davey or a Nichol, who would regularly and systematically stroke the party on his behalf, calling a network across the country on the telephone to drop Ottawa rumours and make them feel like insiders. Instead, he thought all the liaison work was being handled through his co-ordinating channels. It was his belief, in any case, that people should involve themselves politically only if they found it intellectually important and/or morally satisfying.

After John Nichol adamantly refused to be anglophone co-chairman of the campaign in 1972 when Trudeau telephoned him after years of silence, the Prime Minister gave the job to Robert Andras, a cabinet minister from Thunder Bay who was a loyal Liberal but a long way from an organizational wizard. (Andras was a car dealer, recruited during the early 1960s revitalization, and he was accustomed to running only his own riding campaign.) In any case, Andras's advice was consistently overruled by Trudeau's own staff, mainly Ivan Head and Jim Davey, who had no experience with electoral politics other than the coronation election of 1968.

The 1972 campaign was a near disaster. It had a slogan ("The Land Is Strong") of memorable absurdity, concocted by a hapless advertising team at MacLaren's agency in Toronto, trying to meet Trudeau's staff's insistence that he was running not an ordinary election campaign but a "dialogue with the people". (The slogan inspired dozens of jokes; one of the best of them originated with a farmer in southwestern Ontario who heckled a Liberal candidate with the statement, "If you had any sense you'd know it's horse shit, not Liberal shit, that makes the land strong.") Trudeau's speeches were written by his personal staff, speeches that failed to address the puzzling and persistent economic problems that were already troubling the electorate. The campaign was badly planned at the national level — Ottawa didn't even produce a strategy paper for the provincial campaign chairmen to use — and understaffed by volunteers in the ridings because so many Liberals had been alienated by Trudeau's attitudes and policies. In brief, it was a campaign that ignored most of the basic precepts of electoral politics.

Trudeau and his closest staff members felt that he didn't need to worry about the party. "The people" would understand. They didn't seem to realize that "the people", like the party, were puzzled by his seeming indifference to the feelings of large blocs of Canadians. He had infuriated liberal church people and university groups who were making efforts on behalf of the Ibos' struggle for self-determination in Nigeria when he had started off a long response to a question by saying "Where's Biafra?" He had shocked the staid by mouthing "fuck off" at the Opposition in Parliament. He had alienated farmers by responding to a question on grain marketing with the rhetorical challenge "Why should I sell your wheat?" And he had maddened Ukrainians by equating the struggle in their homeland with Quebec separatism. All of these statements had a "rational" basis, which any one of his staff would wearily explain to inquirers as though they were retarded, and which, they felt assured, "the people" would understand.

Months before the 1972 election, when a journalist who had long been an acquaintance of Trudeau's suggested to him during an interview in his East Block office that there was some disappointment with his administration, his eyes blazed with irritation and he jumped up from behind his desk and pointed out the window at the crowd of tourists hovering around the official limousine waiting to take him to lunch. "See that," he said, beckoning her over to the window, "*they* are not disappointed — it's only cynics like you who are."

You didn't have to be a cynic to realize that the attainment of power had altered Trudeau's character, or at least the face he put on it for the world. He had always been intellectually confident but his social diffidence had tempered his manner. Now the sweet reticence had vanished and was replaced by a display of overweening pride that astonished his old friends. To people who had known him prior to 1968 he was the hero as victim of hubris; to people who had accepted the absurdly hyperbolic image the various media were projecting, he became a little gilt god.

Power-mongers who had previously ignored him now turned

pink with pleasure as soon as he came into the room. Women swarmed to him, mouths moist, eyes translucent. Parties were lit up by his presence. In the days when he was a shy MP, it had been possible for him to slip in and out of official gatherings and escape the notice of everyone but his close friends. Once in early 1967 just before he became minister of justice, he was asked to the house of a well-known journalist for a reception in honour of the publisher of a powerful Toronto newspaper who was in the capital to take a preliminary look at the probable candidates for the Liberal Party leadership. Trudeau came late, alone, and seemingly reluctant, and stood in the hall, holding a glass of sherry that a harried bartender had filled too full, coolly regarding the antics of the as yet undeclared contenders — Martin, Hellyer, Winters, Turner, and the rest — who were crowded into the living room, talking, laughing, and gesticulating in their attempts to capture the publisher's attention and his editorial favour. After exchanging a few pleasantries with the hostess, and sipping his sherry carefully, Trudeau remarked that the guest of honour seemed to be fully occupied, and as for himself, he thought he would leave now, thank you very much. He vanished into the night without anybody but the journalist's wife and the bartender even knowing he had been there.

The next time he came to that same house a few months after his elevation to the leadership, he arrived in a limousine, with RCMP outriders to clear the way, a rose from the Governor General's greenhouse in the lapel of his evening clothes, and a beautiful girl in a long white dress, Jennifer Rae, the daughter of Saul Rae, the Canadian ambassador to Mexico, on his arm. When he entered the house the phalanx of guests — who were, give or take a few faces, the same people who had been there the year before — parted like the Red Sea, and his commonplace remarks to the hostess in the hall were passed from group to group and room to room as though they were rubies, or at least rubrics no mandarin could afford to ignore.

For the next three years, a period which coincided with his first intense involvement with and then marriage to Margaret Sinclair, the post-adolescent daughter of the former cabinet minister Jimmy Sinclair, he seemed to exist in a kind of bubble of unreality. It was not that he did not work hard; as prime minister he was tireless in his attention to the details of his job, a bureaucrat's bureaucrat. His staff, made up almost entirely of like-minded people, rarely contradicted him, and his arduous official responsibilities and his personal life — the secret courtship and surprise marriage to a very young woman — alienated him from the realities of even his own world of the intellectual elite. He saw his old friends only rarely. Most of the English-Canadian intellectuals who supported him had quickly fallen away, appalled by his intransigence over Biafra in 1968 and his ruthlessness in the October Crisis of 1970. Quebec intellectuals — other than the small band of federalists who came to Ottawa with him — were turning increasingly to separatism as the solution to Quebec's problems in any case. They reiterated their charges that he was becoming more and more anglicized and cut off from his home province.

Once, at a rare dinner for some Montreal friends, when a lively discussion of old times and new ideas was being conducted in rapid French, one of the guests — a veteran of the anti-Duplessis wars, a feminist, a strong woman — noticed Margaret Sinclair sitting at the end of the table looking uncomprehending among these people from another culture and another generation. When she remonstrated with Trudeau, asking whether they shouldn't speak English out of courtesy to his little friend, Trudeau replied patronizingly that there was no need to worry about her, she wouldn't know what they were talking about even if they were speaking English.

This same kind of dismissive paternalism prevailed in his attitude to the electorate. He couldn't see that the various innovations his government had brought about were puzzling to Canadians who didn't understand them: the Official Languages Act, which signalled the all-out attempt to make French Canadians equal in the civil service; the emphasis on constitutional change, which ended in the failure of the Victoria Conference in 1971; the imaginative Opportunities for Youth Program, which offered young people chances to do at home the kind of socially committed work normally reserved for overseas aid ventures; the Local Improvements grants, which stimulated countless innovative activi-

ties in communities across the country; the alterations in the role
of the Unemployment Insurance Commission intended to broaden
the safety net extended by the country's income-support system.
They were good programs, they did not need to be explained. As
a leader he was trusted, his bond with the people would hold, and
if it did not, well, *tant pis,* they could get someone else to lead
them. This was the politics of reason, Trudeau maintained, without
comprehending that his stubborn inflexibility was unreasonable,
that what he was really practising was a politics of passion —
passionate concern with only those issues that interested him,
only those people who met his standards, only those ideas that
matched or extended his own.

When his bond with the people did not hold and his government was reduced to a minority position on October 30, 1972,
Trudeau went into a state of shock that lasted for many weeks.
Ironically, he was rescued from his plight by the intervention of a
group of Liberals from Toronto — several of the 1960s reformers
plus some newer recruits — who were exactly the kind of professional party politicians Trudeau had previously so disdained.

Keith Davey was one of that group who set out to teach Trudeau
the rudiments of Liberalism nearly five years after he became
their leader. The man who provided the refinements, the post-
graduate course in politics as it were, was James Coutts, who was
appointed Pierre Trudeau's principal secretary and principal adviser in 1975 and spent the next four years teaching him some
tricks that even Davey didn't know. What no one could be certain
of — on the night the long-delayed election of 1979 was finally
called — was whether Coutts's tricks would prove Trudeau's
salvation or his downfall.

PART THREE

JIM COUTTS
AND THE POLITICS OF
MANIPULATION
The Liberal Party, 1972–1977

I

THE TWENTY-SIXTH OF MARCH, 1979, that miserable Monday when Pierre Trudeau finally called the federal election he had been postponing for more than a year, was not the kind of day James Coutts, his principal secretary, enjoyed. Coutts had been working for weeks activating the battle plan for the campaign to come, and the last-minute details he had to attend to on Monday were dispatched with his usual efficiency but not his usual zest. Coutts loved to conduct every aspect of his life with what he thought of as style. He didn't like sandwiches at his desk, whiners on the telephone, pessimistic forecasts, or criticisms of Liberalism; and he had been forced to put up with all of these annoyances on the twenty-sixth of March.

What he really liked was having his secretary summon important Liberals to eat lunch with him on Sundays in the mock splendour of the Park Plaza dining room not far from his clever little house in downtown Toronto where he usually spent his weekends. Or ordering up mineral water with a twist of lime from room service at the Inn of the Provinces where he stayed in Ottawa during the week, before settling down in his suite to gossip the late-night hours away with a Liberal crony from out of town. Or sauntering over to enjoy a long lunch at the Chateau Laurier across the road from his office in the Langevin Block after a morning spent in agreeable tasks, such as advising the PM on an important appointment or consulting with the Clerk of the Privy Council on the cabinet agenda.

Ever since he had become Trudeau's right-hand man in August 1975, Coutts had made the Chateau Grill his personal lunching club. Such was his importance in the city in the late 1970s that his presence there had turned the restaurant into a more fashionable place to eat at noon than the Rideau Club or Le Cercle Universitaire. He was seen in the Grill as often as three or four times a week, always in the fourth alcove on the east side of the room, his fair head clearly visible in the gloom beneath the green flocked hangings that gave the place the aura of a bordello in a

story by de Maupassant. He would sit on the velvet banquette like
an Irish landowner on rent day, bestowing his benign interest on
the waiters ("How's your wife, Pasquale?"), ordering the same
food and drink (martini straight up, minced steak medium rare,
sliced tomatoes, black coffee, and then, oh sin, oh sweet sublimity,
a fat chocolate cream from the silver bonbon dish that was brought
only to the tables of the favoured), dropping his pearly perceptions for the benefit of his guests, waving in acknowledgement as
privy councillors and deputy ministers respectfully passed by, his
clear eyes surveying, small presence commanding, the room that
lay before him. It had taken Coutts a quarter of a century to propel
himself to that table and he was shrewd enough to savour its
significance.

He knew that within a few months of his second coming to
the capital — he had been Lester Pearson's appointments secretary
from 1963 to 1966 — people had begun to say he was a political
wizard, capable of concocting strategies that would have taxed
the ingenuity of Jack Pickersgill in his prime. In a way, Coutts's
devotion to Liberalism was very much like Pickersgill's. He was
a party man, first, last, and always. He served Liberal prime ministers because he believed in Liberalism. It was almost as if he
had encompassed the party's past, sponged up its primordial lessons, and turned them into personal truths.

Outside the concentric circles of the Canadian elites, he was
very little known before he came to Trudeau's office, though during the second year he was in town, journalists filing background
reports from Ottawa who were accustomed previously to attributing
rumours of intra-party deals to "the Prime Minister's chief honcho,
Senator Keith Davey" took to writing sentences that began, "The
Prime Minister's closest political advisers, Keith Davey *and* Jim
Coutts, are known to have urged him . . .". Inside the party itself
Coutts's name began to be mentioned more often than Davey's as
the arch "fixer", the man operating in the vortex of power and
operating surpassingly well. A dozen scenes were telegraphed
along the Liberal information exchange: Coutts conducting the
search for Margaret Trudeau the weekend she ran away from home
with the Rolling Stones and gave her Mountie escort the slip;
Coutts meeting secretly with Jack Horner, the Alberta MP, when

he was skittish as a brood mare about leaving the Conservative Party for a seat on the Liberal front bench, promising a Senate seat if all went wrong at the next election and a cabinet portfolio in the meantime; Coutts having lunch with Dr. John Evans, the president of the University of Toronto, helping him screw up his courage to run for the Liberals in Rosedale; Coutts gravely discussing with the Prime Minister what to do about the "j'accuse" letter that betrayed the indiscretions of Francis Fox, the Solicitor General and MP for Argenteuil–Deux Montagnes, who had signed another man's name on an Ottawa hospital form in order to obtain an abortion for a woman who was not his wife; Coutts ringing up Al Johnson, president of the CBC, during a federal-provincial conference on the constitution to complain that the proceedings were not being broadcast on the English network, a failure he described as a blow to national unity, which in his eyes meant a blow to Liberalism as well; Coutts dropping in on deputy ministers' meetings, Anti-Inflation Board meetings, cabinet committee meetings, with messages from the Prime Minister, messages from the hinterland, messages from the party regulars, to be stuffed in the ears of his elders and his equals. All for the party's good.

Coutts, Coutts, Coutts. How did he get to that banquette in the Chateau? What did his success mean?

COUTTS WAS IN HIS LATE THIRTIES when he came to work for Trudeau, but his looks remained remarkably boyish, so that it was possible to imagine him easily as an undersized, rosy-cheeked fourteen-year-old, riding his bicycle down a side street in his home town of Nanton, Alberta (population 1100), on that idle summer Sunday in 1952, when the direction of his life was set. He had stopped to gaze over a hedge at the guests enjoying a backyard breakfast in honour of the Alberta provincial Liberal leader, Harper Prowse. The hostess told him to "Get off that bike and come on in, you hear, Jimmy! Harper's going to speak." Harper did speak, eloquently, about the miracles of eternal progress, the importance of "little people", and similar sacred touchstones of Liberalism, and young Coutts was hooked for life by the romance of the moment and the force of the Liberal myth.

Coutts's father, Ewart, sold insurance and real estate in Nanton, a CPR town fifty miles south of Calgary, and his mother, Alberta, worked in dry-goods and variety stores and at playing the piano in a movie house. Jim was a lively boy, imbued with Western hustle and fascinated by the goings-on of the townspeople, both proclivities that he could indulge while he made money after school running the projector at the Broxy Theatre or sweeping floors and setting type at the *Nanton News*. ("I've always had hunches about people," he said when he was an adult. "Somehow I just know what they are going to do in certain situations, and that comes out of being a kid in a town where you knew everybody and could watch their behaviour for years.")

Politics for him was a ticket to the world outside Nanton, where the goings-on were even more fascinating, where he could stretch his mind and perfect his talents, where a face like a kid in a toothpaste commercial and a mind like Niccolò Machiavelli's were both formidable assets — especially when you knew instinctively the advantages to be wrung from one and the importance of concealing the other.

When he was in his teens and twenties, Coutts loved poli-

140

ticians and politicians loved him. He was adorable in those days, with his red-blond hair and his china-blue peepers, getting up at riding association meetings to cut short the ramblings of his elders with his surefire jim-dandy ideas; volunteering to work for Joe McIntyre, a mine manager and local riding boss, when he ran for the Liberals in the 1953 federal campaign and reaping publicity out of the fact that there he was, a campaign manager, at the tender age of fifteen; fetching up at the University of Alberta a few years later as Liberal prime minister in the model parliament along with another boy from southern Alberta, named Joe Clark, who was a member of the Tory opposition. A few years after that, when Coutts was just out of law school and articling in a Calgary firm, he was elected national president of the National Young Liberal Federation and began to form the cross-country network of friends who were to prove so important later in his life.

By the time the federal campaign rolled around in 1962, when the Liberals were all set to save the country from John Diefenbaker, Keith Davey talked Coutts into running as the candidate in his home riding of Macleod. He lost resoundingly but cheerfully. (In fair times and foul, good Liberals are supposed to be cheerful, and Coutts learned early on how to be a good Liberal above all else.) The next year Davey, who liked Coutts's sunny style and reputed left-Liberal leanings, named him campaign chairman for Alberta, a job no one else wanted, mainly because the province had been hostile to Liberalism since 1921 when the United Farmers of Alberta had swept the Liberal Party out of power provincially apparently forever. Again Coutts performed optimistically and well, helping elect Harry Hays, the former mayor of Calgary who had been cajoled into running by Keith Davey, almost against his will and certainly against his better judgment.

That was the campaign when Keith Davey's natural ebullience ran away with him and he thought up a series of gimmicky ideas, including the anti-Diefenbaker Election Colouring Book, which might have wowed them on the U. of T. campus in 1948 but left the editorialists dripping sarcasm and the politicians plainly hostile in 1963. When Coutts was sent copies of the colouring book — which featured a series of wiseacre cartoons of John Diefenbaker with captions like "This is the Prime Minister and his Cabinet. They have just disagreed with him. He doesn't like people to disagree with him. Colour the P.M. purple." — he promptly telephoned party headquarters in Ottawa from Calgary, deep in the heart of Diefenbaker's West, and said without preamble, "Listen, Davey, colour me *pissed off.*" It was entirely in character for Keith Davey to love the line and to go around Ottawa repeating it to everybody he met, with proud glee at Coutts's acuity.

Later that spring when Coutts was invited by Lester Pearson to work in Ottawa, on the recommendation of Davey and Gordon, he already had a reputation in Liberal circles as a wit, "a natural", "a great little guy". Few people realized how circumspect he had been at checking out what he was getting into and how determined he was to learn from every experience that came his way. He was twenty-five years old and he already knew the basic lessons about how to climb the ladder of success — the "greasy pole" as he was given to describing it — who you needed to know, how you ought to dress, the ways in which to ally yourself with other men on the move. He had asked his friend Tony Abbott, an easterner who had been working in Calgary when Coutts was articling in a law firm there, to introduce him to his father, Mr. Justice Douglas Abbott, finance minister in Louis St. Laurent's cabinet, long since gone to his reward on the Supreme Court bench.

Before beginning his job in Pearson's office, Coutts had trotted along to consult the senior Abbott in his august red-carpeted chambers about what to expect from political Ottawa. Abbott told him that a political assistant's job could be an invaluable training but to keep his mouth shut, and his eyes open, and on no account to stay at that level in Ottawa too long. Two years preferably and certainly no more than three. After that, Abbott warned him, you're liable to turn into an Old Faithful, to get hooked on the trappings of power and to be of diminishing use to the party and of no use at all to yourself. Best to get out and make a stake in the business world and run for office when you have an established reputation of your own.

Coutts stayed three years in Pearson's office and afterwards he remembered them as the most valuable learning experience of his life. From the beginning he was entranced with Pearson and his wonderful anecdotes about international affairs and cataclysmic events, his self-disparaging wit, his seemingly casual attitude to the power of his office, his liberalism. Pearson made Coutts feel like an instant insider and Coutts was able to watch the government system from the centre and to figure out how it worked. Weekdays he sat in Pearson's outer office on the second floor of the East Block, keeping the Leader's appointments calendar, making friends with the powerful, and the has-beens, and the would-bes, who waited there before passing through the ancient green baize doors on their way to talk to "good old Mike". Evenings he went to big cocktail parties and to little dinners and to have drinks in hotel bars, soaking up news of what was happening from middle-echelon civil servants, minor diplomats, Press Gallery reporters, Liberals from the outlands. He was friendly to everybody, from the political assistants in ministers' offices to the wives of his associates in the PMO, who found Coutts cosy, funny, and altogether — well, adorable was the word. He watched monetary crises and cabinet scandals and the rise and fall of the reputations of many men. He came to understand who did well at politics and who did badly and why. And he accomplished all this without making his elders uneasy or his contemporaries jealous. He was so popular, in fact, that when a television documentary called *Mr. Pearson* was made by Richard Ballentine at the urging of Pearson's press secretary, Richard O'Hagan, in 1964, nobody minded that Coutts seemed to figure prominently in frame after frame, though Pearson joked that it "looks as if my grandson is running the country."

By the spring of 1966, when the Gordon-Davey group had fallen apart after the disappointment of the previous fall's election, Coutts had served his apprenticeship. He announced to his friends that he was not going to go back to Calgary to practise law since he had met the tough admission standards of the Harvard Business School and meant to amble down to Cambridge, Mass., to get his M.B.A.

During the next two years at Harvard, Coutts made friends with other young and ambitious managerial men from all over the United States and Canada, went to seminars on corporate management and political power given by famous American academics — Henry Kissinger and Richard Neustadt among them — and finished his degree with creditable standing.

He then went to work briefly in New York City with the management consultancy firm of McKinsey and Company and, among other duties, took part in a study of the organization of John Lindsay's mayoralty office. In 1969 McKinsey sent him to Toronto. But functioning as a factotum in a U.S. branch-plant office was not to Coutts's taste and he soon struck out on his own with half a dozen other young men, some of whom had also been to Harvard. They formed the Canada Consulting Group, which was described in its handsome brochure as a firm of ''management consultants to the Private and Public Sectors''.

The Canada Consulting Group had a ''business philosophy'' which was formed on Harvard principles. It set out to meet the needs of ''top managers'', to provide them with ''strategies . . . to keep [their] organizations effective in a changing environment''. In brief, they were hiring themselves out as troubleshooters to the men in the executive suites, advising a vice-president here and a deputy minister there, instigating analytical studies, proposing ''concepts'' that would help Canadian businessmen ''turn the profit corner'' and Canadian bureaucrats ''actualize'' their political masters' plans, using Harvard Business School jargon and Harvard Business School techniques to dazzle their clients a couple of decades after these notions had begun to wow them in New York and Washington.

It was the perfect setting for Coutts at that point in his career, and, coincidentally, the perfect finishing-school experience for a man who was to find himself chief fixer for the prime minister of Canada five years later. Canada Consulting allowed him to draw on his professional education and his practical understanding of Ottawa and to connect once more with the cross-country network he had made in his student Liberal and appointments-secretary days. It also taught him how the Canadian business world worked. John Aird, the Liberal senator and fund-raiser; Tom Kent, the former policy adviser to Pearson who had become first a deputy minister and then the president of the Cape Breton Development Corporation; Paul Desmarais, the chairman of Power Corporation in Montreal; Tony Abbott, who was working for Jake Moore, the president of Brascan; Maurice Strong, executive director of the Environment Program of the United Nations Secretariat; Sylvia and Bernard Ostry, who were fast becoming the best-known civil servants in Ottawa, she as the chief statistician and he as assistant under-secretary of state; and Michael Pitfield, deputy secretary to the cabinet, who had all the right connections in English Montreal. All these people were old friends who were able to provide entrée for him. Coutts went to Africa to do studies at the behest of Strong. Coutts went to Cape Breton at the behest of Kent. Coutts stayed with Desmarais at his hunting lodge on Anticosti Island. Coutts met Aird's business friends and discussed with Aird, the prototypical old Toronto establishment man, all the little details of his career. Coutts went up to Ottawa to consult with government officials and conducted important studies of Central Mortgage and Housing and of the power of deputy ministers; and all his old friends in the bureaucracy, from Michael Pitfield on, were pleased that Jimmy was doing so well.

Coutts had a talent for other kinds of friendships, too. He loved the arts world and the media world and the glitter that went with both. His old friend Martin Goodman, who had been in the Ottawa Press Gallery in the 1960s, became the editor-in-chief of the *Toronto Star* in the 1970s, and Goodman's wife, Janice, an interior designer, helped Coutts decorate his Toronto house. His old friend John Roberts, who had been an executive assistant to Maurice Sauvé during the Pearson years, had become MP for York-Simcoe and married Beverley Rockett, a Toronto fashion photographer, and Coutts did his Paul Martin and Mitchell Sharp imitations at their parties. Coutts went to the ballet and to the commercial art galleries downtown and filled his house with Canadian paintings. Coutts was seen with beautiful women at beautiful parties and in beautiful bars. Coutts began to wear bright-red braces to hold up the trousers of his well-cut suits and to snap them at odd moments as a kind of deliberate put-on, lest anyone think he was taking himself too seriously or that he had forgotten his small-town roots. Coutts went on sailing holidays in the Grenadines, and to weddings of Harvard classmates in Virginia, and to hear Mabel Mercer singing at the St. Regis in New York.

And Coutts kept away from politics "like an addict keeping away from his drug", as he himself described it. Keith Davey was still his closest friend and he saw other Liberals, particularly John Aird, George Elliott, the party's advertising man, and John Nichol, John Roberts, and Tony Abbott, almost as often as he had of old. But, essentially, in the first Trudeau régime, Coutts's most important party connections — the self-described Pearsonian Liberals — "were out of the play", to use their euphemism. For four years the Prime Minister ignored them and they were lying low. They still talked politics constantly. They still kept track of whose career was on the up and whose was on the down, who had the leader's ear, who brought on his fury or his frowns. But no matter how knowledgeable they were about the party's affairs, none of them could have forecast in 1972 how radically the situation of Liberals would be altered after the election in October of that year when Trudeau was returned shakily to office as leader of a minority government with a margin of only two seats over the Tories.

III

WITHIN HOURS OF ABSORBING the first shock of the Liberals' poor showing in the 1972 election, the Toronto lawyers Jerry Grafstein and Gordon Dryden were on the phone to each other urgently discussing what could be done "to save the Party". Though neither of them had ever run for office, both men were still almost as devoted to the Cause as they had been in the heady days of the new politics. Grafstein was now thirty-seven, a successful communications lawyer, the kinetically energetic, chronically enthusiastic son of an immigrant Polish Jew who had owned a catering business in London, Ontario; Dryden was now forty-eight, a dutiful tax expert working for the Unity Bank, still known for his loquacity, his loyalty, and his horse sense. What they shared was a kind of mystical approach to Liberalism. They were not just true Grits but true believers. For them the party was a vehicle for progress, a marvellously adaptable institution that was able to renew itself generation after generation for the greater good of Canadians. They were given to reminding their confrères, in bad electoral times like these, of Mackenzie King's rule of thumb that if you straddle the centre and lean to the left in Canada you will triumph. They believed implicitly that whenever the Liberal Party turned right — as they thought it had in the first Trudeau régime — it lost its way and its natural constituency. Grafstein and Dryden decided during that post-election conversation that something had to be done to save the party from the forces of reaction, and they set about convening a meeting of Liberal friends in Grafstein's office on Richmond Street West to decide just what that "something" should be.

Many such meetings were held over the next few weeks with a dozen people in attendance at most of them — Keith Davey, Jim Coutts, Dorothy Petrie, Kathy Robinson, Chris Yankou, Martin O'Connell, John Roberts, Boyd Upper, Tony Abbott, Bob Kaplan, Gordon Floyd and, of course, Dryden and Grafstein. None of them was quite as mystical in his attitude to the party as Grafstein and Dryden were — though Coutts once told Grafstein that it was his belief that there were two hundred good men in Canada, something like the Twelve Just Men of Judaism expanded into a great big Liberal team, who would come together instinctively when Liberalism was in trouble in order to put it right. But they all thought of themselves as progressive and ultra-loyal Liberals and they were all intensely pragmatic in their approach to politics.

They quickly came to a conclusion — worthy of Canada Consulting — that as a group they had three priorities: first, to re-establish their political presence in the party by devising a winning plan for the next campaign; second, to convince the Prime Minister that he needed the group; and, third, to get Keith Davey named co-chairman of the National Campaign Committee. They were tough goals because of Trudeau's known disdain for professional politicians and because of Davey's deflated reputation as an organizer.

The Senator was dragging with him, nearly a decade after the fact, the blame for Lester Pearson's failure to win a clear majority in the three elections of the early 1960s. It was an article of the modern Liberal faith that the leader was never blamed for disasters; the leader had to be beyond reproach. St. Laurent was not blamed for 1957; it was C. D. Howe's fault for being so arrogant. Pearson was never faulted for the failures of 1962, 1963, and 1965; it was Keith Davey's fault or Walter Gordon's fault for not getting him a majority; they gave him the wrong advice, they let him down. This same attitude was put to work for Trudeau after the near defeat of 1972. It was his advisers, Ivan Head, Jim Davey, and the rest of the technocrats in the PMO, who were blamed for having "isolated the PM from the political process", as if he were some passive object without free will.

Despite the drawbacks his reputation as a three-time near-loser represented, Davey was still the best-known and best-liked member of the Toronto group, both inside and outside the party. He possessed what the American senator Eugene McCarthy once described as "the perfect political mentality — that of a football coach, combining the will to win with the belief that the game is important." Even after seven years on the sidelines, Davey had maintained his network across the country among Liberals in the party's English-Canadian progressive wing.

That network was lobbied vigorously by the Toronto group on Davey's behalf in the early months of 1973; pressure was put on every MP, senator, and party organizer the group knew to "speak to the PM about Keith". Eventually Davey was granted an interview with Trudeau and went to his office, "briefed to the eyeballs" with a list of "seven reasons, Mr. Prime Minister, why you should *not* appoint me your campaign chairman." It was a gimmick that was "a real stopper — it caught his interest, definitely," Davey reported to Coutts on the phone.

As part of the same campaign to get Davey appointed, John Roberts, who had a temporary job in the PMO as a policy adviser, arranged a dinner for the Toronto group at 24 Sussex Drive. The Torontonians made their pitch, summing up what had gone wrong with the campaign just past ("no juice, no guts, no fight") and pledging that they would work their fingers to the bone and their brains to the nub in the campaign to come ("lotsa juice, lotsa guts, lotsa fight") if the leader saw fit to use their talents and heed their advice.

After a few minutes of this rhetoric, Pierre Trudeau cast upon the assembled company his cold, cold eye and said in quizzical tones, "Look, when my friends and I came into politics in 1965, we had a fire in our bellies — we wanted certain things for Quebec. But I don't understand what motivates you guys. What's in it for you anyway?"

The Torontonians were furious: they felt they were being insulted, treated as though they were nothing but ward pols on the make. Abbott wanted to say, "Well, we had a fire in our bellies in World War II when you were riding around like a goddam fool on a motorcycle wearing a Nazi helmet," and Grafstein felt like hollering, "Listen, I was a Liberal — a *real* Liberal — when you were attacking Mr. Pearson in *Cité libre.*" But they contained their anger, having promised themselves that they weren't there to score debating points, they were there to "save the party". Instead, they patiently explained to Trudeau what the party meant in their lives — the whole "vehicle for progress, circle of friends" number they did so well.

Trudeau was sceptical, but he was also desperate. Having first succumbed to a deep shock that lasted for several weeks after the election, he had roused himself to go over the 1972 results riding by riding. He and his French-Canadian colleagues, particularly Marc Lalonde, were convinced they were the victims of an English backlash against French power. At the same time, Trudeau knew he needed to take deliberate political action to win back the allegiance of English Canada.

He set about trying to mollify the various English-Canadian power groups in a way that caused Jean Marchand later to say sadly, "At first he was wonderful, like a philosopher's ideal leader. But after 1972, he had to become too political." In his cabinet-making, Trudeau had appointed John Turner finance minister in the hope that the business community, which had been distraught over the actions of the previous minister, Edgar Benson, would be mollified. He had made approaches to the New Democratic Party with promises of Liberal legislation compatible with their goals in return for their agreement to maintain him in office despite the minority situation. And in response to the complaints of his English-Canadian MPs, he changed the makeup of his office, substituting for the technocrat intellectuals of his first régime a more politically experienced staff that included two defeated MPs, Martin O'Connell and John Roberts, as well as Eddie Rubin, his sometime assistant from the justice department. (Rubin had been practising law in Hong Kong for three years until his firm, Phillips & Vineberg, which had its head offices in Montreal, agreed to bring him back to Canada for the minority government's duration.) After many consultations and much thought, he finally decided in the spring of 1973 that the Toronto group was the best vehicle available to provide him with organizational and political advice, and he telephoned Keith Davey to ask him to be co-chairman with Jean Marchand of the campaign committee for the next election.

Davey was in the Senate lounge watching a Stanley Cup playoff game on television when he was summoned to answer Trudeau's call. After asking him to take on the job, Trudeau said politely he hoped he wasn't interrupting Davey's dinner. Davey told him he was watching hockey and added that the Buffalo Sabres were winning the game. There was an awkward pause at the other end of the line and then Trudeau said, "Oh, I see. What inning are they in?"

The Liberal Alliance of the Sixties

When Mike Pearson shuffled his cabinet in April 1967, he appointed three young ministers, Trudeau, Turner, and Chrétien, who embodied the chief elements of a bicultural alliance that was to dominate the Liberal Party for a decade to come.

The Pearsonians: Politicians of Joy

Walter Gordon and Mike Pearson were friends and political allies, and so were Keith Davey and Jim Coutts, who came to Ottawa to work for them. They wanted to make the Liberal Party into an instrument for political reform.

The Trudeauites: Politicians of Passion

Pierre Trudeau and Marc Lalonde (*left*, in the winter of 1968) and his friends and allies Jean Marchand and Gérard Pelletier (*below*, the same spring) also sought to make the party into an instrument of reform. But the reforms were very different, and so was the way they viewed the party.

The Rival

Turner, at the leadership convention in 1968, was the Liberal loser who hung in and held on to his delegates, securing a power base in the party that was unshakeably loyal and setting up a rivalry that was equally enduring.

The Winner

Trudeau at the leadership convention in 1968 was the Liberal winner who took all: the delegates' votes, the establishment's support, the media's attention, on a day when it seemed the kissing and the cheering would never ever stop.

The Party Unites

Behind the newly elected leader in April 1968 the powerful Grits
of the day form a solid phalanx of support, all discord suppressed,
all disappointment swallowed. The future belongs to the winner,
it's the Liberal way.

CP Photo

Trudeau dances at a gala at Government House with his friend of
dozen years, the beautiful Madeleine Gobei

An Era End

CP Photo

Trudeau dances at a gala at the National Gallery with his friend of a dozen weeks, the beautiful Margaret Sinclair.

Davey loved that story. In fact, he loved any kind of story that showed up intellectuals as impractical, not to mention ignorant, about ordinary affairs. It reinforced his equanimity about losing the Senior Stick and dropping out of law school. "I'm no egghead," he would say emphatically; "that's what makes me valuable as a political adviser — I'm just an ordinary guy." That this was a fiction, that he was, in fact, shrewd, competent, and unusually empathetic, Davey would never admit. He figured his "ordinary guy" stance allowed him to josh Trudeau constantly, to tell him things that more pretentious advisers would have been too wary to suggest, to play the bad-news messenger no leader could afford to shoot.

In the year following Davey's appointment, Trudeau and the Toronto group were fused into an electoral team under the Senator's prodding, with Coutts figuratively hovering at his elbow providing expert managerial advice. In the end, Trudeau learned their tricks and they learned his.

Davey convened a series of dinner meetings with Liberal workers so that Trudeau could hear their complaints, their ideas, their inchoate yearnings. Trudeau learned to keep quiet when the yearnings got sufficiently inchoate to arouse his ire. What Davey was doing was trying to rehearse the Prime Minister for the stance he wanted him to take during the campaign to come: he had to show an understanding of Davey's belief that "the public likes a politician to be a politician." Davey wanted Trudeau to project a double image of contrition (forgive me, for I have sinned in my arrogance) and pugnacity (but I'm the best man for the job).

For his part, Trudeau convinced Davey that secrecy was a virtue; under the pressure of constant reminders from Coutts, the Senator managed to restrain his normal impulse to talk openly to everyone he met, including members of the press. In the 1960s, Davey had been known in the Parliamentary Press Gallery as the "best leak in town", a much-repeated description that once prompted a sour reporter to reply, "Hell, that's no leak, that's a gusher." Now, in the 1970s, Davey went about his work in Ottawa and elsewhere with a lapel button stuck inside his wallet that read "Stifle Yourself", so that every time he reached for a credit card, his new behaviour pattern was reinforced.

During this whole period Trudeau was anxious that no "elec-

tion psychosis'' be created. He was busy handling a volatile minority situation in the House of Commons with the nimble aid of
the House Leader, Allan MacEachen, and he didn't want an election triggered before both he and the party were ready. Behind the
scenes, preparations went on and some of Liberalism's oldest
precepts were brought into play. Patronage of one kind or another
was used to dazzling effect, to repay the worn-out and to make
way for the ambitious, just as it had been used for decades by
Grits on the ''Them that has gives and gits'' principle. Dozens of
Pearson Liberals were drawn back into active party work so that
their skills and connections could be called on once the election
writs were issued. Campaign jobs were roughly outlined and
assigned in secret to the ablest people available. Finally, in early
May the minority Liberal government engineered its own defeat
and was released, at last, from the grip of the NDP, which as a
condition for its continuing support in the Commons had forced
the Trudeau cabinet into more progressive legislation in eighteen
months than had been passed in the previous four years. The
Liberals had indexed personal income taxes, announced a new
energy policy, set up the Foreign Investment Review Agency, established the Food Prices Review Board, passed the Election Expenses Act, raised old age pensions and family allowances, and
initiated a precedent-setting inquiry into a proposed gas pipeline in
the Mackenzie Valley, under the direction of Mr. Justice Thomas
Berger, a former NDP MP from British Columbia.

   Once the election was called, the Toronto group let it be known
to the press that the Prime Minister had not wanted it at this time
(which was partly true, since Trudeau disliked campaigns and
never wanted an election) and pretended the party apparatus was
in disarray. In fact, the party was so geared up for the election
that in the next eight weeks the Toronto Liberals were able to
conduct the campaign of their dreams, the campaign that rivalled
in their fevered minds the Kennedy campaign of 1960 for sheer
professional style. Davey operated from his Senate office in
Ottawa, directing and co-ordinating the national and provincial
campaigns by telephone, with particular attention paid to Ontario,
the crucial province, where Dorothy Petrie was in charge of the
campaign committee, replacing Clem Neiman, who had the job

in 1972. (Davey and Petrie functioned so well as a team that six months after the campaign was over, the Senator left Isobel Davey, his wife of more than twenty years, and Mrs. Petrie left her husband, an accountant named Bill Petrie, and both sought divorces. They were married in December of 1978.)

To fill what he regarded as the campaign's other key appointment, the party's liaison man travelling with the Prime Minister, Davey had told Trudeau that the best person would be Coutts. Coutts pleaded reluctance on the grounds that the job would take too much time away from his business, until Davey arranged to have Trudeau himself telephone to convince Coutts his presence was crucially important.

"When I heard about that phone call I practically choked," another member of the Toronto group said later. "It was so much a Davey-Coutts caper. Deals within deals. Everything Coutts had observed over the months we had been negotiating with Trudeau convinced him that to have purchase with this guy you had to be bringing him something, not just asking him for something, you had to have your own base. Coutts didn't want to look eager and he figured his return to a public role in politics could come later when he had built up his financial stake, unless the conditions were absolutely right. At the same time, Davey knew that Trudeau was worried about having Coutts in such a key advisory position in case his own staff was disturbed. Finally, everybody was finagled out of their fears. Davey got what he wanted. Coutts got what he wanted. Trudeau got the adviser he needed. And it was seen as an all-around triumph."

Coutts had known Trudeau when he was Lester Pearson's parliamentary secretary and Coutts was still in the PMO as appointments secretary. But they were a long way from cronies, and, like most of his Liberal friends, Coutts was wary of Trudeau. But, unlike most of them, Coutts knew how to make a personal connection with the Prime Minister. He spoke the language of technocrats, he had read the requisite American journals and the touchstone books, he had been to Harvard, he had travelled widely in Europe and Africa, he knew some French. He was tough, he was witty, he was smooth. He was able to bring twenty years of political experience in English Canada to the job. And if Trudeau wanted to be cold-eyed, well, what the hell, Coutts could be cold-eyed too.

What Trudeau wanted was to win, and Coutts knew how to help him do it. He accompanied Trudeau by train, plane, limousine, and cable-car for eight weeks and he talked all day long. He talked to Trudeau's staff, smoothing their feelings. He asked Ivan Head to write major policy statements and Jim Davey to give him advice on transportation policy, fitting their ideas into speeches written by an expert team that included Head himself as well as Alan Grossman, a former writer for *Life* and for Democratic politicians in the United States.

Weekends Coutts talked non-stop to Davey in the suite where they holed up in the Carleton Towers hotel in Ottawa. Weekdays Coutts talked to Davey back in Ottawa by telephone, as often as four times a day, describing what was going on, fitting in the "tactics" with the "strategy", i.e., what do we do today that will fit in with our overall game plan? Coutts talked to Liberals out in the country, that vast network of strivers and achievers who were giving their all lest the party lose and they lose with it. Most of all, Coutts talked to Trudeau, cajoling, persuading, informing, entertaining, reminding him at every stop who was important locally, what kind of one-line joke the crowd might respond to, which policy might attract notice from the press.

They made an odd pair, sitting at the front of the Liberals' chartered DC-9 campaign plane: Coutts with his fair hair over his coat collar, his face still rosy, his eyes as lively as a twenty-year-old's, Trudeau with his angular cheekbones, his expression opaque as a Chinese mandarin's, his mouth an austere line. Under Coutts's influence, Trudeau not only bounded onto platforms and made crassly political speeches every day, it got so that he actually enjoyed them. It seemed as if Coutts had made another friend, or at least an admirer of his considerable talents.

Looking back, Coutts decided that a crucial moment in their relationship came in the railroad station in Rimouski, Quebec. Very early in the campaign after the Trudeau entourage had just finished an old-fashioned campaign-train swing through the Maritimes, Jean Marchand and Gérard Pelletier, Trudeau's old friends, climbed aboard the train to report to the Prime Minister, like barons reporting to their prince on how things were going in this part of his fiefdom. Coutts immediately rose to move into the next train car but Trudeau called out that he should stay, and turning to his confrères remarked that Jim spoke French and they needed his advice. Coutts knew that the Liberal French never talked to the Liberal English about strategy: to be in on the inside talk about Rimouski as well as Red Deer was a sign of acceptance beyond his expectations. He also knew better than to give the slightest sign that he thought this was unusual. So he snapped his red galluses for good luck and casually sauntered back to sit down.

None of the other members of Davey's campaign team had roles quite as visible or as delicate as Coutts's but they all ran full out, their collective enthusiasm fuelled in equal parts by their lust for victory, their fear of failure, and the fun they were having together. Grafstein conducted a lively ad campaign from Toronto through a newly formed organization called Red Leaf Communications. Dryden, as party treasurer, managed the flow of money. Policies were made by an ad hoc committee that included Jack Austin, a lawyer from Vancouver who was now Trudeau's principal secretary, and Eddie Rubin, as well as Martin O'Connell, Davey, and Coutts. The policies concocted were highly political in content, co-ordinated closely with what Keith Davey was hearing from his professional pollster, Martin Goldfarb of Toronto, who had been talking to the electorate for months trying to gauge their concerns. During the course of the campaign, Trudeau promised easier home ownership for the aspiring middle class, more equality for women, fairer freight rates for the West, an industrial-development strategy, and a broadened social security system for the aged — all "progressive" legislation that was designed to attract the left-wing vote from the NDP. When he was attacked in Calgary over oil prices, in Metro Toronto over the planned Pickering Airport, and almost everywhere on inflation, Trudeau responded brilliantly, turning aside his hecklers with strength, charm, and some elegantly elliptical evasions of his past record. The party's most popular English-Canadian cabinet ministers, John Turner, Eugene Whelan, and Bryce Mackasey, were persuaded to stump the country tirelessly on the Liberals' behalf and the French-Canadian cabinet ministers were persuaded to stay home. (When a party worker mistakenly booked Jean Chrétien to give a speech at a riding meeting in Ontario, she was reprimanded; French power was being downplayed, though it was the raison d'être of the leader's political life.)

In brief, the Toronto group scripted a role for Trudeau and he, the consummate actor, was able to play it to perfection. They turned him into something they themselves could admire: a fighting leader, a gentle father, an adoring husband, and an all-around "beautiful guy" as his bride of three years, Margaret Sinclair Trudeau, described him in a speech in Vancouver. This was no arrogant intellectual, the Liberal strategists told the Liberal troops and the bug-eyed press. This was a misunderstood man, running as an underdog, a supporter of the little man, fighting against the heinous wage-and-price-control policies of Robert Stanfield, the Conservative leader, that awkward, not-so-beautiful guy, who was forecasting economic doom and who wanted to freeze wages to forestall it. Tory times are bad times, remember! Liberal times are boom times! Trudeau cares!

The whole campaign drove home this theme. The standard Trudeau speech, contrived to make him seem if not folksy at least accessible, ridiculed Stanfield mercilessly for his honestly considered solutions to the country's economic problems. The television free-time films, made under the aegis of Jerry Goodis, the Toronto advertising-agency president and a member of the Red Leaf conglomerate, idealized the new "loving" Trudeau. Goodis called them "straight propaganda, featuring ordinary Canadians in fedoras and glasses, ethnics, country people, kids — films full of uglies and one beautiful guy." By contrast, Stanfield was made to look old and David Lewis to look irrelevant. Neither was able to regain the kind of momentum they had achieved in the 1972 campaign, when Stanfield had been so effective attacking the Liberals from the right on their Unemployment Insurance Commission policies and Lewis had attacked them from the left, using his "corporate welfare bums" phrase as a basis for his critique of Liberal economic policy. Fresh photo and story "opportunities" were provided for the press and the television cameras: the three days of old-fashioned whistle-stop campaigning on the train in the Maritimes, ethnic group picnics outdoors in the wonderful June weather, shopping-plaza rallies packed with party supporters cheering themselves hoarse, hand-shaking and cheek-kissing with voters in outdoor markets, all with generous visual access to Margaret Trudeau, who was actually stumping the country with her husband for the first time.

Since Trudeau's marriage in 1971, he had been obsessively concerned that his wife, Margaret, not be exposed to press scrutiny. On a state visit to Russia in May 1971, shortly after their wedding, his press secretary, Peter Roberts, had instructed the accompanying journalists on their first morning in Moscow that they were on no account to speak to the bride, and this directive had held, with a couple of exceptions, ever since. But now, Mrs. Trudeau, dressed as an artless young mother in simple blouses, skirts, and earth shoes, was seen on the television news almost nightly, speaking out on her husband's behalf, shaking voters' hands, or publicly hugging her nursing baby, her second son, Sacha, who was only six months old. Her presence inspired some of the most favourable prose ever printed about a Canadian public figure — prose that when read later, particularly in juxtaposition with Margaret Trudeau's own book about the period, *Beyond Reason*, sounded as much like Liberal propaganda as the party's own effusions. June Callwood, one of the country's best-known journalists, wrote in *Maclean's* that Margaret was "a perfectly preserved flower child" who listened at rallies "with an ethereal smile and rapt eyes full on her husband as he delivered his speeches", a woman "whose truthfulness and trust are like the artistry of a high-wire act, all guts and beauty". (This was written just six week before Mrs. Trudeau went to a celebrity tennis match in the United States and fell in love with the prominent politician she referred to as "my American", her attempted suicide with a kitchen knife at the prime minister's weekend retreat at Harrington Lake, and her subsequent admittance for severe depression to a hospital in Montreal.) "She was so flaky, even then, we were scared as hell every time she spoke during that campaign," one of the Liberals from Toronto said later, "but we were counting on her being mostly seen and not heard."

In Quebec, Mrs. Trudeau was seen very little and heard not at all, since her French was thought by the Quebec campaign committee to be inadequate and her manner a little outré. In fact, the Quebec campaign was left to Quebeckers, as English-speaking Liberals had left it since the time of Laurier. It was under the direction of Jean Marchand, as it had been in 1968 and 1972. All he took from the national campaign was the redesigned Liberal logo, a big ''L'' with a little maple leaf tucked in the corner, part of the Grafstein group's clever graphics for advertisements and campaign posters, a logo that said implicitly the flag is Liberal, the country is Liberal, we're the Government Party. All Marchand promised in return was that he would deliver the party between fifty and sixty of the seventy-four Quebec seats, a promise as sure as God makes the maple sap run in the Eastern Townships in March.

In sum, the Liberals drew on nearly every political axiom in their considerable repertoire and their concerted effort worked. On July 8 the party won a majority, a victory far more telling than even the most optimistic among the original Toronto group had ever dared hope. For the first time in twenty years and eight campaigns, the Liberals ended a campaign with a higher percentage of the electorate's support than the polls had given them at the start.

A few days later, a triumphant dinner was staged at 24 Sussex Drive in honour of the ''key players'' in the campaign, the kind of celebration Trudeau had never held in his life but that Coutts and Davey believed in as crucial for maintaining morale. A group photograph was taken on the lawn behind the house, to be mounted later on the office walls of several of the English-Canadian Liberals, their hour of glory frozen in an eight-by-ten glossy and framed in aluminum, with Pierre and Margaret standing in the middle of the group, hands clasped in front of them, smiling demurely into the camera like a Presbyterian minister and his sweet young wife at a church elders' picnic.

After dinner, toasts were proposed and speeches made, contrived of inside jokes and fulsome flattery for all concerned, and finally Trudeau got to his feet amid loud applause. He paid tribute with becoming if unaccustomed modesty to the party that had just rescued him from the ignominy of a defeat that had seemed almost certain since 1972 and then told a story that proved to the assembled company that he had indeed been "humanized" by the campaign.

Trudeau said that his first experience with politics had been through his father, Charlie Trudeau, an ardent Conservative. What he remembered best from the election nights of his childhood was his parents' friends damning the all-too-often-successful "Liberal machine" with righteous fury. These outbursts had so impressed him that until he was well into his teens he had visualized the machine as some huge Rube Goldbergian device that whirred, clicked, and threw off sparks which had a diabolical influence on the electorate.

Above the loud laughter this story inspired, Jean Marchand called out, "But Pierre, haven't they showed it to you yet?" The Anglos in the room greeted that sally with even louder laughter. For them a "machine" was what had existed during the bad old days of C. D. Howe and Jimmy Gardiner, and that existed still in Quebec, though they would never have been so indiscreet as to say this in front of French Canadians. But *they* weren't a machine. *They* were a company of stout-hearted friends with admirably liberal ideas, and they left Sussex Drive that night on a wave of euphoria.

They felt a new Liberal alliance between French and English had been forged. They thought they had taught Trudeau what Liberalism was all about and delivered him from the technocrats who held him captive in the PMO. They were certain he would henceforth run a government that would be consistently more "political" and therefore more "progressive", more reflective of his real nature and of their lifelong belief in liberalism.

What they did not realize was that Trudeau had never been the captive of anyone, that he had run his government from 1968 to 1972 in the way that he himself thought best, that his approach to people would remain elitist, and that, in fact, he did think of them as a machine. They did not know either that the next five years would turn into a bad dream for the Liberal Party, that before those years were over they *would* behave like machine pols, and would argue desperately among themselves about whether their leader should be told that for God's sake and the party's he really must step down. But all that was far in the future. On that victorious July night in 1974, they all went happily home bathed in self-satisfaction, bilingual bonhomie, and the afterglow of the *vin mousseux*.

IN THEIR OWN TRIUMPHANT post-election discussions, Coutts and Davey agreed that Trudeau now knew the importance of keeping in touch with the party and congratulated themselves on having set up a series of "structural interfaces" to make sure he would continue to consult Liberals on a regular basis. But they also realized that Trudeau was never going to be what they called a "gut politician" in the way John Turner was, the kind of guy who just rings you up to shoot the breeze, nice and easy and how ya doin' boy? Still vivid in their minds was the attitude Trudeau had displayed in the early meetings they had convened for him with party members in 1973, behaviour that had caused their old Cell 13 friend Gordon Edick — the man who sometimes functioned as their ambulatory "grass-roots opinion" — to say Trudeau was "the most perverse s.o.b. I've ever seen in my life. As soon as you give one sign you don't agree with all his actions and ideas, he chews you up and spits you out."

To counteract Trudeau's tendency to treat party affairs and party members at best mechanically, at worst contemptuously, Davey and Coutts decided Trudeau should be persuaded to rely on the Senator to be his "nose" in English Canada between elections as well as during them. Once the campaign committee was disbanded, Davey had no official title other than Senator. Trudeau had offered him the post of government leader in the Senate but he had declined and the job went to Ray Perrault instead. (The only reward Davey sought for successfully managing the 1974 campaign was legislation to abolish the so-called Canadian editions of *Time* and *Reader's Digest* as a move to improve the advertising base for real Canadian magazines. Even with Trudeau's blessing, it took two years and many legislative hassles to get a watered-down version of this mildly nationalistic measure passed as Bill C-58, an amendment to the Income Tax Act. Still, it was something of a triumph for Davey and his former mentor, Walter Gordon, that Ottawa was forced into even this mildly nationalistic legislation in the face of U.S. State Department opposition and intensive lobbying by the *Digest,* which managed to save its position by reorganizing itself as a foundation.)

In the months following the 1974 election, Davey kept on making regular appointments to see Trudeau, to have lunch or coffee with him so he could tell the PM news about the party's affairs and its members' views, draw to his attention articles in the English-Canadian press and trends in the English-Canadian business community that were politically important, comment on what was being said in the parliamentary corridors and the government lobbies — in brief, to fill him in on all the little details that usually bind party politicians together and keep them in touch with the public mood.

Despite his best efforts, Davey soon began to feel the arrangement wasn't working, that Trudeau was unaffected by his stories about ordinary guys and their ordinary concerns, unmoved by his suggestions about who he should be appointing to important jobs, who ought to be invited to dinner at 24 Sussex, which books and articles must be read.

Trudeau made a number of decisions that left Davey uneasy: the appointment to the important position of clerk of the Privy Council of Michael Pitfield, whose friendship with Trudeau had already caused unfavourable comment in the press and grave mutterings in the bureaucracy; plans for a $200,000 swimming pool at 24 Sussex; an order for a new $76,000 Cadillac; permission for Margaret Trudeau to accept an invitation to visit Japan on a trip the press estimated would cost $20,000 to be paid for by Japanese businessmen trading with Canada; gloomy statements in his traditional New Year's interview with the CTV television network to the effect that 1975 was going to be a bad year economically and Canadians would have to lower their expectations, remarks that didn't fit in with the extravagances of his own life. Trudeau had no feel for the English-Canadian outlook, Davey realized, and it couldn't be instilled in him during one or two conversations a week.

When the job of principal secretary in the Prime Minister's Office fell open in the summer of 1975, Davey was relieved. He advised Trudeau to hire Jim Coutts so that he could benefit from hard-headed political advice on a daily basis. Davey felt Coutts would be able to influence the Prime Minister in a way he himself could not; after all, Davey said to their mutual friends, Coutts was bilingual, Coutts was an intellectual, Coutts knew what all those charts they had in the PMO were supposed to mean, and Coutts as a bachelor could be on the job sixteen hours a day.

Coutts himself was both apprehensive and intrigued. He had planned to withdraw from active politics after the 1974 campaign while he built up a personal fortune which would be useful later on when he decided to launch a political career. He was earning close to $200,000 a year from his Canada Consulting partnership and his investment income, and his political activity was proving a financial disadvantage. Not only did it cut into his working time, he was beginning to believe it hampered his firm. As much work as he and his partners could handle was available from the private sector, and he was sick of the carping he heard that government contracts came to Canada Consulting because of Coutts's political connections. After all, the firm had contracts with the Conservative government in Ontario and with the NDP in Saskatchewan, and recognition of his partners' competence went far beyond the Liberal Party.

On the other hand, nothing gave Coutts the heady feeling he had experienced during the 1974 campaign; after that, even the biggest business deal seemed oddly flat. He weighed the decision carefully, as he had been taught to at Harvard. "Do I want to commit the next time block of my life to this job?" he asked himself and the answer came out yes.

The job of chief aide to Liberal prime ministers of Canada was a role that had been played by many men under many titles in the previous fifty years, some of them politicians, some of them civil servants, but all of them supposedly more concerned for the leader than for themselves. Mackenzie King once wistfully described in his diary his version of the perfect prime minister's man as "someone in whom I could have the fullest confidence and could trust . . . as implicitly as myself . . . someone who was discreet and would not let it be known he was even there."

The closest King ever got to this ideal was O. D. Skelton, the Queen's University professor and biographer of Laurier who became his under-secretary of state for external affairs in the 1920s.

He was King's closest adviser on both domestic and foreign issues as well as the founder of the modern civil service. When Skelton died in 1941, King wrote in his diary that he would sorely miss his "sterling rectitude" and the "fine sense of security" his presence always brought.

After Skelton's death, King relied for advice on a troika: Norman Robertson, who was O.D.'s successor as under-secretary; Arnold Heeney, who was the Clerk of the Privy Council; and Jack Pickersgill, who was second-in-command of King's office staff and then its chief after the war, though he was called special assistant to the prime minister rather than principal secretary, a title he disliked. Pickersgill held the same job under Louis St. Laurent for a time and discharged it brilliantly before he publicly declared himself a Liberal by running for Parliament in the Newfoundland riding of Bonavista-Twillingate in 1953.

Lester Pearson never got around to appointing a chief of staff of any kind. The uncertainties of his minority governments — coupled with his ambivalent attitude to politics — meant his office was run on a curiously helter-skelter basis and he took his internal political advice from Tom Kent, who was called his policy adviser, as well as from Walter Gordon and Keith Davey. It wasn't until Trudeau was elected in 1968, determined to establish an orderly operation to fulfil his majority mandate, that the title "principal secretary" was dusted off and bestowed on Marc Lalonde. Trudeau wanted to end the ambiguous position of the people employed in the PM's office. He determined that none of them would be public servants, all would be his personal staff and hence clearly partisan; civil servants would be relegated to the Privy Council Office and kept at arm's length.

After the debacle of the 1972 campaign, Liberals began to say the principal secretary's job should be filled by a political tactician rather than by a political theorist like Lalonde. In the 1972-74 minority period, Martin O'Connell, the defeated Toronto MP, held the job, and from 1974 to 1975 Jack Austin, a Vancouver lawyer, former executive assistant and then deputy minister of energy, mines, and resources, headed up the office until he resigned after being attacked in the press for his part in a B.C. mining deal and was then appointed to the Senate. In short, the list of men who had served as chief aide to Liberal prime ministers before Coutts took it on in August 1975 was long and distinguished. Probably no one else ever came to the job with so clearly defined an idea of how it should be done. What Coutts wanted above all was to run "a professional shop". He was not an intellectual as his best friend, Senator Davey, fondly imagined. He was a Harvard M.B.A. What he was versed in was technique. Any task, however formidable, was "do-able" (a favourite word) in Coutts's view if only you could find the right technique. What he loved was not policy or principle, not causes or issues, but management. At this stage of his life, Coutts was less inclined to ask those around him — as Davey was known occasionally to do — "Is this decision right?" He was asking, "Is it smart politics?"

Smart politics in 1975 was to bring to Pierre Trudeau's attention in as technically proficient a manner as possible the viewpoint of English Canada so that electoral victory for the Liberal Party would be "do-able" once more. In taking on the principal secretary's job, Coutts didn't expect to be the Prime Minister's creature but he didn't expect to be his friend either. The years in Pearson's office had taught him that if you're "worrying about where you fit into the PM's scheme of things, you're no good to yourself or anybody else." In the Pearson years there was what he called "a gashouse gang" quality to the PMO, everybody scrambling in undefined jobs with seemingly informal attitudes, waiting for Pearson to tell them how dependent he was on them to make his life bearable. "Help me, I need you" was a sentiment Pearson expressed countless times in countless ways, confident of the effect of his charm.

Coutts observed from conversations he had with Pearson's contemporaries that the Prime Minister had displayed this same attitude to the External Affairs crowd when he was under-secretary and then secretary in that department, and that now these same old buddies were of minor importance to him. Before he went to Trudeau's office, he cannily decided that "You can't feed on your relationship with your boss; it puts you in bad shape as a person. People all over Ottawa, secretaries, executive assistants, policy advisers, feed on the great men, basking in their fame, making endless sacrifices for them, and getting their jollies from their little words of praise. As a consequence, they become defensive of the great man, protective of him, and they don't tell him the bad news. I'm never going to be like that.''

He made it a condition of his acceptance of the job that, under his aegis, the Prime Minister's Office would be highly political, in fact as well as in theory. Despite his extensive professional knowledge of how government worked, Coutts still maintained a touching faith as a politician who had come up through party ranks that a leader intimately in contact with the Liberal grass roots would be in touch at the same time with the needs of the nation. To this end it was his express purpose to "cheer up the PMO . . . make it a vital link between the PM and the party, the party and the bureaucracy, the party and the cabinet and caucus, a switchboard for processing information vital to keeping those at the centre in touch with the country.''

Before he came to Ottawa, he and Davey decided that one of the reasons the Prime Minister was behaving much as he had before his defeat in 1972 was that remnants of Marc Lalonde's old technocratic approach to party politics had hung on in the PMO. The regional desks, manned by people from various parts of the country who were supposed to produce "input" for the Prime Minister on what their regions wanted, still did their work in a desultory way. Coutts knew that MPs resented this fiercely, saying the regional desk men sometimes behaved as if they were more important than the parliamentarians in their influence on Trudeau. He decided to change the operation drastically, cutting back its numbers and making regional liaison more flexible. As for the PMO policy unit, established under Michael Kirby to co-ordinate long-range planning, he disagreed completely with its purpose, which was to have alternative policy ideas generated for the Prime Minister by his own staff. Coutts believed that there were several sources of policy ideas already built into the parliamentary system: cabinet ministers and their departments, MPs, and Liberal Party members meeting in convention. He disbanded the policy unit entirely in order to "prevent the PMO from second-guessing the cabinet and caucus''. Michael Kirby left Ottawa to join the Institute for Research on Public Policy in Halifax; Joel

Bell, an economist who had done work for the Gray Report on the costs and benefits of foreign investment and had been hired by Jack Austin to act as Trudeau's economic adviser, left to work for Petro-Canada, the government-owned petroleum company; other lesser regional-desk and policy-unit employees were farmed out to ministers' offices or encouraged to seek private-sector jobs.

Coutts then carefully set about putting together his own team in the PMO, a group who could be expected to keep their cool, as he put it, to do their jobs well under pressure, and to develop the right techniques. He whittled the staff to eighty, a dozen or so less than it had been under Lalonde, and the bulk of them were either secretarial or clerical help, employed in the correspondence unit to answer Trudeau's mail. Only about a tenth of the eighty were central to Coutts's operation. They were the group he thought of as his hand-picked pros. In the next few years this group was to set the tone of the government party in the same way Jack Pickersgill and the mandarins of old had set its tone in the King–St. Laurent era.

Most important were the three assistant principal secretaries who did liaison with the regions — that is, they were news gatherers and travel arrangers who gave the Prime Minister a little policy advice on the side. One of them, Tom Axworthy, a Manitoban who had joined the party when he was an undergraduate in the 1960s attracted by Walter Gordon's economic nationalism, took on responsibility for the Western provinces in the PMO. Colin Kenny, who had served in the office as a regional-desk officer, was appointed to look after party affairs in Ontario. The third man, Brian Flemming, a Halifax lawyer who had a dazzling curriculum vitae, including a nearly successful candidacy against Robert Stanfield in the election of 1974, was hired to deal with the needs of the Atlantic provinces.

(This new regional arrangement left only one part of the country without an overseer appointed by Coutts. As Tom Axworthy said ingenuously, "Coutts doesn't control Quebec." It still came under the aegis of the Quebec leader, though arrangements for the Prime Minister to attend party functions there were made through Michel Rochon, a social scientist and former member of Kirby's policy unit, who was put in charge of the PMO correspondence division under Coutts. Rochon eventually left to teach at the Université de Montréal and was replaced in the correspondence division by his assistant, Helen Dacey Wilson.)

In addition, Coutts kept his eye on the Prime Minister's personal support staff: Ivan Head, his foreign policy adviser, who stayed until he was made president of the International Development Research Institute in 1978; Joyce Fairbairn, his legislative assistant; Bob Murdoch, his executive assistant, who made sure his appointments schedule was adhered to; Marie-Hélène Fox, who took over as the patronage secretary from her brother, Francis Fox, after he left to run for Parliament in 1974; Cécile Viau, the personal secretary; and Mary MacDonald, who had been Lester Pearson's executive assistant and was now called a special adviser.

Coutts also set out to change the press office, which was in a state of depression and disarray. From the beginning of his first régime, Trudeau had been disdainful of the press, the press had grown to loathe him, and his press office staff had been caught in a trap between the two, terrified by Trudeau and prone to agree weakly with whatever dark thoughts about his régime the journalists were murmuring. Coutts and Davey decided the man to turn this situation around was their old friend Richard O'Hagan, who had been Pearson's press secretary and had gone down to Washington in 1966, when the "gashouse gang" was dismantled, to an enviable job as minister counsellor for information in the Canadian Embassy. Coutts chivvied O'Hagan into coming back to Ottawa, first for three or four months on an emergency basis to handle information services for the Anti-Inflation Board when it was set up in the frantic period in October 1975 just after the imposition of wage-and-price controls. O'Hagan agreed reluctantly to stay on in the Prime Minister's Office in early 1976, after Coutts created for him the title Communications Adviser to the Prime Minister, a job far beyond the usual press officer category with a salary of $40,000 a year and prestige to go with the title.

The other formal change Coutts made as principal secretary was to set up a political planning committee to meet every Tuesday without fail from nine to ten o'clock in the morning with the inner cabinet (the same group of ministers who belonged to the all-important Priorities and Planning Committee of the cabinet which met Tuesdays at ten), plus officials from party headquarters and Keith Davey in attendance. The business of this political planning committee was to discuss from a tight agenda devised by Coutts the factors, large and small, that could affect the Liberals' chances of winning the next election.

The next election was primary in Coutts's mind from the minute he arrived in Ottawa in 1975, even though in all likelihood it was at least three years away. News of fresh disasters left him unmoved in his dedication to this goal of a big electoral victory, even though the next eighteen months brought one crisis after another to the Liberal government. Within weeks of Coutts's arrival John Turner, the heir apparent to the Liberal leadership and the most prominent English-Canadian minister the Liberals had, resigned his post as finance minister for what he publicly described as private reasons and privately described as public ones. (Turner let it be known to his many friends in the business community that he bitterly disagreed with Trudeau's management of the government, particularly his attitude to economic affairs.)

In the confusion following Turner's departure from the Department of Finance, Trudeau was forced to reverse the main promise of his 1974 campaign, and to announce to the country on Thanksgiving night that wage-and-price controls were to be imposed immediately to offset runaway inflation. Once this startling action had been partly absorbed by the public, Trudeau went on television in December for a year-end interview and made speculative remarks about the free market not working any more, sending the business community into a mild hysteria and causing a flight of investment capital. (Charges were immediately made once more in the dining rooms of the nation's clubs that Trudeau was secretly a socialist. At the same time, Trudeau's continuing consultations on the economy with representatives of labour and business were causing countervailing charges to be made in the common rooms of the nation's universities that Trudeau was a covert corporatist.)

In February of 1976 the Conservatives held a leadership convention and won a round of favourable publicity, a boost in the public opinion polls, and a new leader in the person of Joe Clark, Coutts's old antagonist from the University of Alberta, who was presented as a sterling young man with a sterling young wife, a law student named Maureen McTeer. To make matters worse for the Liberals, their own leader's wife, Margaret, was in the news again after a brief period of calm while she had borne her third son, Michel. This time the response was not nearly as favourable to her unorthodoxies as it had been before. During the parliamentary winter recess in January 1976, Margaret accompanied Trudeau on a trip to Latin America, impulsively sang a ditty she had composed at a state dinner in Venezuela to the amazement of the assembled dignitaries, flirted outrageously with Fidel Castro in Cuba, appeared at official functions brassiere-less in a cotton T-shirt and jeans, and when she returned to Ottawa telephoned a hot-line radio show to defend her actions between the show's commercials and crank callers.

Liberals began to argue about whether she was a political asset or a liability, whether her behaviour was just that of a free spirit or of a selfish, spoiled young woman now out of control. As the winter and spring months passed, Mrs. Trudeau openly defied her husband's obsession with privacy, appearing one night at the Press Club on Wellington Street in Ottawa to order a drink and begin a now familiar "let's-be-soul-mates-and-chat" act with the men at the bar. When the Prime Minister appeared to take her home hastily, she exhorted the bartender to "Give the man a soda pop — that's about his speed." Stories about her bizarre behaviour surfaced all over the country. Old friends from her university days at Simon Fraser in Vancouver talked openly about her taste in hallucinogens. Party regulars began to whisper to each other that she was a manic-depressive who would not take the drugs prescribed for her illness.

As if the worsening economic situation and the disastrous state of the leader's marriage were not enough trouble for the Liberals, other serious problems quickly arose. The summer of 1976 brought a bitter air strike by the country's anglophone air controllers when their French-Canadian colleagues' demands for bilingualism in the skies set off open English-Canadian hostility towards the government's whole bilingual program. Then Jean Marchand quit the cabinet and so did Bryce Mackasey, Bud Drury, Mitchell Sharp, and James Richardson, resignations which were made for varied reasons but which, taken together with Turner's departure of the year before, fed the public belief that Trudeau could not get along with people, particularly strong-minded English-speaking people. What was more, it appeared that he didn't care, either about the country's economic difficulties or about the views of his colleagues. Instead of showing the restraint he had called for from Canadians, he set off on a trip to Yugoslavia, Jordan, Israel, and Italy with Margaret which infuriated all those who had listened conscientiously to his admonitions to tighten their belts. It seemed to Liberals in those years that the Trudeaus were always travelling — to the sun, to the ski slopes, to the yachts of the international rich. Coutts kept saying that for a man of his wealth, sophistication, and onerous responsibilities, Trudeau travelled very little. But nobody bought the line. "Who does he think he is," English Canadians were asking each other, "some kind of maharajah?"

The press, smarting under complaints that they had been fooled by the Grits' image-making in the 1974 campaign and by Margaret Trudeau's original disingenuous demeanour, had long since turned nasty. Journalists were no longer inclined to "explain" the government's position; they were on the attack. Day after day the editorial writers, columnists, and news commentators were bitterly and tellingly critical, the news reports on radio and television were doom-laden, the headlines in the newspapers unfavourable.

Finally in September of 1976, the cumulative results of the Liberals' problems hit home. The party's popularity fell to a thirty-year low in the Gallup poll; only twenty-nine per cent of decided voters said they would vote Liberal if an election were held then as against forty-seven per cent who said they would vote Conservative. (At the same time forty per cent could not name the new Conservative leader, confirming what every shrewd Grit thought he knew anyway: that the hostility was not to the party but to Trudeau.) In the wake of that poll, the Prime Minister set out on a fence-mending tour of Atlantic Canada to explain his economic measures, and encountered crowds unprecedented in the ugliness of their hostility to him. At a service club lunch, the audience refused to stand when he finished speaking; in one crowd there was a placard with a swastika on it, in another a home-made sign reading "We need Trudeau like we need VD." Days later, the Liberals were trounced in two by-elections: in Newfoundland a former Liberal-turned-Conservative named John Crosbie won the riding of St. John's West, and in Ontario Jean Pigott, a woman who managed a large bakery business, won John Turner's old seat, Ottawa-Carleton. After these results were announced, Jerry Grafstein got on the phone to Keith Davey to say hotly, "We're going down the tubes, man. What's the matter with Coutts?"

Coutts felt there was nothing the matter with Coutts. He refused to lose his composure. The situation was tough but it could be managed. To every problem there was a solution. Is the cabinet bereft of English-speaking ministers of stature? Never mind, let's have a shuffle and bring in some new faces like Coutts's old friends John Roberts (who became secretary of state) and Tony Abbott (who became minister of consumer and corporate affairs). Is inflation frightening the populace? Let's have a million-dollar advertising blitz to promote economic restraint. Is the party angry at the PM? Let's set up a series of morale-boosting meetings and conferences at which the Prime Minister will deliver speeches on the glorious history of Liberalism. Are business and labour in a flap? Let's have their leaders in to meet the PM. Is the press hostile? Well, let's get the leader to talk informally to journalists and publishers at the kind of intimate meetings those guys love. If we just do our best, keep our cool, and wait it out, Coutts told Davey, Grafstein, and whoever else asked, our luck will change.

When the Liberals' luck did change, with the surprise election of the separatist Parti Québécois in Quebec in November 1976, Coutts didn't flicker an eyelid or murmur an "I told you so". He simply proceeded to advise Trudeau to press the Liberals' advantage as the party of national unity, to capitalize on the renewed fear of Quebec separatism that the election engendered. Within the next several months, Trudeau made a series of major speeches on Canadian federalism, including one before the U.S. Congress in Washington that caused an effusion of praise from President Jimmy Carter, Vice-President Walter Mondale, Senators Edward Kennedy and George McGovern, and several important American political columnists and newspaper editorialists. Canadians basked in this praise as if it were the Florida sun. The

Americans said he was a great man; it must be so. Even in the previously hostile press, Trudeau was described as the champion of confederation. There was talk in Liberal circles of recruiting a national non-partisan "unity team" that would include Ed Schreyer, the NDP premier of Manitoba, Jack Horner, the Conservative MP from Alberta, Claude Wagner, the Conservative MP from Quebec, and Alec Campbell, the Liberal premier of Prince Edward Island. When this scheme failed, a Task Force on Canadian Unity was set up to travel coast-to-coast to report on the state of the nation's discontents.

With this flurry of positive action, the opinion polls began to rise. Everything seemed to be going in the Liberals' favour in 1977, even the final "freedom trip" of Margaret Trudeau, who ran away from home in March to Toronto and New York to be with the Rolling Stones at concerts and other kinds of capers. After the Trudeaus were formally separated in May, Trudeau was the beneficiary of waves of sympathy from the electorate for his dignity in handling the situation; his emotional pain in the spring of 1977 altered his face and turned him into a romantic figure once more. He was no longer the arrogant s.o.b. He was the wronged husband, the faithful father, the hero felled by domestic sorrow of a kind that could be readily understood.

Coutts and Davey began to make plans for an early election. They paid Martin Goldfarb to do an extensive survey of the electorate in June and assess attitudes towards issues. They discussed their Western strategy (in which the recruitment in March of Jack Horner was only the first step); they worked hard at attracting new candidates in Ontario to replace the anglophone ministers who had departed. They even discussed what would be the best seat for Coutts to contest when he made his first bid for elected office since his hopeless try in 1962. Alberta beckoned him home; visions of Jimmy Gardiner, the Minister of Agriculture who had held the West for Mackenzie King, danced in his head. But in the end reason prevailed and Toronto-Parkdale, a solidly Liberal seat, was provisionally chosen.

Despite all these favourable indicators, Trudeau refused to go to the country in a September election as Davey and Coutts urged. At a press conference he said calling an election would

look like opportunism, and his caucus backed him up in this opinion. In the quiet of his office he told Davey and Coutts he had not
yet been able to come to terms with the failure of his marriage.
He wanted time to think and to be with his children; he couldn't
face the demands of a campaign.

Coutts and Davey were daunted, since Goldfarb had warned
them that the Liberals' high standing in the polls was probably
temporary. But their chagrin was soon swallowed. They went back
to politics as usual, figuring with their usual optimism that this
was one good moment for the party, another would come to them
in time. Davey set out to make greater efforts in readying his
campaign team and his campaign strategy. Coutts agreed that he
would stay on in the PMO and forget about winning a nomination
so that he could work at his contacts inside and outside the government with constant energy and subtle strokings. He knew that
he had become the *ne plus ultra* of principal secretaries, the PM's
man beyond compare.

He did not know that by the time the long-awaited election
was finally called in 1979, what he had persisted in thinking of as
"sound management of ongoing problems" would be seen by
reporters in the Press Gallery as plain trickery. That his politics
would be described as the politics of manipulation. That he would
be called cynical, Machiavellian, and worse. That he would be so
intensely disliked within Liberal Party ranks that some people
who had been his friends for fifteen years, who had admired his
managerial skills enormously when he first displayed them in the
PMO, would start to say in dismay that he had been altered
alarmingly by the power of his position. That Liberals by the
hundreds would believe he had become a captive of the remote
elitists who had surrounded the PM from the beginning — people
epitomized in the collective Liberal mind by Trudeau's Clerk of
the Privy Council, Peter Michael Pitfield, who on the night of
March 26 was waiting at Rideau Hall to play his own role in the
dissolution of the Thirtieth Parliament.

PART FOUR

MICHAEL PITFIELD AND THE POLITICS OF MISMANAGEMENT
The Liberal Party, 1977–1979

WHILE JIM COUTTS was orchestrating the dissolution of the Thirtieth Parliament from the Prime Minister's Centre Block office on the night of March 26, 1979, his colleague Peter Michael Pitfield, Clerk of the Privy Council and Secretary to the Cabinet, was at Government House overseeing the technicalities of the ceremony going on there between the Prime Minister and the Governor General. It was just the sort of occasion that Pitfield revelled in — a secret meeting in splendid surroundings involving a romantic, ritualistic exchange between important people who respected his intellect, and relied on his judgment.

Pitfield had been elevated to the role of Clerk in January of 1975, when he was only thirty-seven. It was a controversial appointment from the moment of its announcement the previous October and Pitfield had remained a controversial figure in Ottawa ever since. This was partly because of the importance of the Clerk's job, which had been seen as the most powerful post in the federal bureaucracy for nearly forty years; partly because of the personality of Pitfield; and partly because of the nature of the capital itself.

Ottawa is a city that talks incessantly about power: who has it, who wants it, who's misusing it, who's losing it. The talk starts first thing in the morning as soon as the buses begin to lumber around Confederation Square and the sun glances off the windows of the West Block. As the day wears on, the buzz becomes very nearly visible, blowing in the wind like the sulphur fumes that used to waft over the area from the paper company on the Ottawa River's farther shore.

Everybody talks about power. Secretaries talk in the corridors of the Commons at a quarter to ten on their way to the cafeteria for coffee; commissionaires gossip at the main door and the sound reverberates from the vaulted ceilings, rivalling the chatter of schoolchildren lining up for official tours. MPs harangue each other while sprawling on leather sofas in each other's offices or hovering over the cold buffet in the parliamentary restaurant at noon. Deputies arrange to lunch late at Le Cercle Universitaire so they can sound out each other's weaknesses while glancing over their shoulders to see who else is talking there and to whom. Lobbyists reserve tables in the alcoves of the Chateau Grill and over underdone beef and overpriced Bordeaux float deals in voices that sound like chain-saws. Ministers greet each other behind the gold curtains of the Commons chamber after Question Period, exchanging innuendos and anxieties. Diplomats display their volubility in Rockcliffe houses between six and eight, eating anchovies and uttering banalities with effortless sophistication in two languages and fifty-four accents. Hostesses call their best friends for advice while writing out place-cards for little dinners at eight, hopefully placing the assistant deputy minister's wife, who is famous for intelligently listening, between the privy councillor who is famous for continuously yapping and the ambassador who is famous for unstintingly imbibing. Late at night backroom boys and executive assistants of varying shapes and political hues meet in dark downtown bars to complain confidentially about the press, the Leader, the cabinet, and the drawbacks of their lives and wives. Everybody talks, talks, talks about power all day long, spreading rumours, flying kites, seeking leaks, formulating strategies, and telling lies.

In the late 1970s one of the prime topics of all this talk was Michael Pitfield and the power he supposedly wielded far from the sound of wagging tongues, right at the city's quiet core in the Langevin Block where the offices of the Prime Minister and the Privy Council intertwine. It was said, among other things, that Pitfield held the Clerk's job only because he was the Prime Minister's friend, that his ideas prevailed over those of the cabinet in the governing of the country, that he had undermined the neutrality of the public service, that he was aloof, erratic, and out of touch with the real world.

For all his notoriety, few people in official Ottawa knew Pitfield really well. He rarely went to the parties, official and unofficial, that were so important a part of the city's working life and he was uneasy when he did go out, preferring to engage in intense talk about large issues with people he had known for years. Certainly only his close colleagues knew how bewildered he was by the uproar his actions as Clerk had caused. He had been trained from infancy to hide his feelings and do his duty, never to apologize and never to explain, to act, in brief, like the child of privilege he unquestionably was.

Pitfield was born in 1937, the seventh and last child of a rich Montreal family, and the weight of that family's expectations had always weighed heavily on him. His father, Ward C. Pitfield, had grown up in Saint John, New Brunswick, the descendant of United Empire Loyalists, and had gone into the securities business in Montreal after the First World War as an associate of Izaak Walton Killam and Max Aitken, two of the great magnates of the era, before he formed his own firm in 1927.

Ward Pitfield had married a wilful, attractive young woman named Grace MacDougall, the daughter of Hartland MacDougall, a stockbroker. Descended through her mother from the nineteenth-century Montreal shipowners and ships' agents, the Refords, Grace Pitfield was related to just about every other important family who lived in the Square Mile, the several blocks in central Montreal where huge mansions were built for the very rich around the turn of the century. Her brother Hartland had married a Molson of the brewing family, her sister Lorna had married a Price of the pulp-and-paper fortune.

No other city in Canada has ever produced anything quite like the smug gentry of old English Montreal. They inhabited a world where people intermarried unto the third and fourth generation, and looked to England for their role models and to the American eastern seaboard for their business partners and friends. Later, their descendants, both actual and spiritual, were called "the White Rhodesians of Westmount" and in its heyday their society did have about it the aura of a colonial ruling class. Its members rode to hounds, played polo, went to balls, met their friends for lunch or tea at the Ritz-Carlton Hotel, spent the summers in Cartierville, Murray Bay, or St. Andrews-by-the-Sea, and took pleasure in blackballing upstarts who wanted to join their clubs. Rigorous modes of behaviour were followed (no gentleman talked politics in the presence of a lady) and rigorous snobberies observed (families who had grown rich in certain trades or through sharp practice were cruelly snubbed).

Although Ward Pitfield was an outsider to this world both by

birth and by temperament, he made a marked impact on it through
the sheer force of his handsome presence and his daring in making financial deals, qualities that were remembered long after he
died in 1939 at the age of forty-seven of a rare disease called
actinomycosis, contracted from chewing a piece of straw while
on a tour of the stables on his large estate, Saraguay, at the city's
western edge.

After her husband's death, Grace Pitfield carried on, a magnificent widow of indomitable will, determined to see to it that
her children would be brought up with a knowledge of the mores
of their class and a proper sense of their duty to their country. In
her mind duty seemed to imply a transcendence of self, a devotion to a higher imperative. She spoke often and admiringly of the
regiment of Montreal men who had marched off to war in 1914 to
do their duty for the Empire on the battlefields of France and
were never seen at the Ritz again. Her sense of social obligation
did not extend to politics or the public service; those were occu-
pations for the middle classes. Gentlemen made money and set
examples.

Michael, who was only two when his father died, was her
most precocious and most sensitive son. He was devoted to his
mother, he absorbed her values, he was determined to do her
proud; and she was determined that his obvious brilliance should
be cultivated by the right teachers with the right ideas.

She sent him first to Lower Canada College, where he was
desperately unhappy, a bookish boy among the sports. (The family chauffeur had to take him by the hand and lead him there in
tears.) She then found for him the perfect setting, the Sedbergh
School in Montebello, Quebec, where under the care of sympathetic
teachers he whizzed through the curriculum in record time,
finishing his university entrance requirements at the unusually
young age of fourteen. To start him off on the path she had chosen for him, she arranged an interview with Cyril James, the
principal of McGill, a distinguished economist with a string of
honorary degrees and a *Chevalier de la Légion d'Honneur*. Young
Michael came out of James's office traumatized with shock; McGill
was not the place for him, he declared. He had found the learned
man *with his feet up on his desk*! His mother was secretly pleased;

Michael always was a stickler about things like that, she said. It turned out that no Canadian university would accept a student that young in any case, so Pitfield went to St. Lawrence University in Canton, N.Y., and spent a few difficult months as a cadet at West Point as one of several British Commonwealth students accepted there each year, on the recommendation of Averell Harriman, a family friend who was later Governor of New York. In 1955 he came home to Montreal to devote himself to the law. He articled with a downtown firm and simultaneously took classes at McGill, where his mother was on the board of governors, a body that was still trying to preserve the ethic of the old Square Mile as if it were a medieval manuscript. In the law school Pitfield came under the influence of two men who both later served as its dean: Frank Scott, the professor, poet, civil libertarian, and founding member of the CCF; and Maxwell Cohen, who was to become chairman of the International Joint Commission and already had extensive experience with government as a member of various federal commissions and advisory boards. Pitfield began to be fascinated by constitutional law and the peculiarities of the Canadian federal system, and to talk about the obligation of the privileged to the state.

His mother decided that these ideas were something he had to get out of his system before settling down to an illustrious career in the St. James Street world she knew so well. When he was twenty-two, and newly graduated with his law degree, a job was found for him in Ottawa as a senior clerk and then as an administrative assistant in the office of Davie Fulton, the Minister of Justice. Fulton was one of the few true Tories in Diefenbaker's motley cabinet, the scion of a distinguished Conservative family that numbered a premier, a chief justice, and an attorney general in its ranks. He was a gentleman, he had been at Oxford, he had a philosophical disposition, a distinguished reputation, and a future as a possible prime minister. He attracted to his office during the Diefenbaker era a cadre of promising young men — Ian Pyper, Christopher Dobson, Marc Lalonde, Lowell Murray, Brian Mulroney, and Peter White — all of whom in one way or another were to make their marks in Canadian life.

Even in this company, Pitfield was a striking figure. Very

tall and lanky, with a long, narrow head, he had a wardrobe of suits of the kind that middle-aged men of his background ordered from the same bespoke tailors in London who had outfitted their fathers and, if God spared the world from the socialists, would survive to outfit their sons. He was an unnerving conversationalist in those days, so advanced intellectually and so rarefied socially that most of the populist Tories of Diefenbaker's Ottawa regarded him as a curiosity. He set himself up in an apartment that duplicated the rooms his father had lived in at the Ritz before his marriage, and he could be found there in the evenings, clad in tweeds and English leather slippers, listening to Beethoven ("I love the Eroica but I suspect it's a young man's romanticism that I will soon outgrow"), pouring brandy into *ballons* for a few select friends, and allowing his conversation to wander from Max Weber to Marcus Aurelius ("You'll remember the passage where he's talking to himself," he'd say, and everyone would nod nervously as though they really did), from the difference between *crème caramel* and *crème Chantilly* to the constitutional subtleties propounded by Ivor Jennings and their relevance to the Canadian state.

He was sometimes seen at dinners around Rockcliffe and galas at Government House squiring slender, toothy girls who usually turned out to be wearing sapphire-and-diamond pins that had belonged to their grandmothers, and he had a maddening habit of dropping names. "Walter Lippmann was saying to me last weekend," he would remark, "'When a friend goes into politics, he can be a friend no more.'" Or, "I see you're reading the new book by Lady Diana Cooper. Mother was staying with her when she wrote her first." He would come to the parties of his contemporaries, held in the rented houses they could afford, where the surroundings were cold-war modern (swirled plaster on the ceilings, beige broadloom on the floor), and look painfully surprised when the hostess would appear with the pot of chili con carne and the glasses of Spanish red. Often he would fortify himself against such indignities by turning up very late, bearing a perfect Boursault and a vintage Côtes de Beaune Villages. Nearly everybody who met him was either dazzled or dismayed.

Still, the languid façade was misleading. Pitfield was ambitious, energetic, and disciplined. During the year he spent in Fulton's office he decided that the government service was a superior calling and he determined to learn to be a professional governor of the highest order, in the way a man of similar bent in another era might have determined to be a field marshal or a bishop.

As he saw it, every job or project he undertook in the next few years contributed to his knowledge of the governmental process. The stint in the Department of Justice taught him the nuances of the relationship between a cabinet minister and his deputy. At the same time he took night courses at the University of Ottawa — in company with another of the assistants in Davie Fulton's office, Marc Lalonde — towards a master's degree in public law. The next job he moved on to was the secretary's post on the Royal Commission on Publications, under its chairman, Grattan O'Leary, the newspaperman who was later a Conservative senator. In the year he spent directing the commission's research staff, Pitfield learned about the problems of communications in Canada and the hard realities of Canadian-American relations. After that, as secretary to the Carter Commission on Taxation, he had an intensive training in fiscal policy and the way the Ottawa bureaucracy's economic establishment operated.

While he held the royal-commission job, Pitfield lived at Government House, serving as an attaché to Governor General Georges Vanier and spending his leisure hours drawing up for His Excellency expert interpretations of such constitutional fine points as "When is a vote of non-confidence valid?" or "When does a minister's personal behaviour demand his resignation?" When McCartney Samples, an official in the British High Commission, asked him how he could bear to stand around there at endless stuffy parties acting like a trained flunkey, Pitfield replied in the incongruous slang he sometimes affected to take the curse off his orotund prose, "Well, I plan to be around Ottawa for a while and I want to case the joint."

Pitfield knew that everyone of importance in the capital eventually fetched up at Rideau Hall to be given at least drinks and canapés and at most royal assent; and, besides, his mother had been a girlhood friend of Her Excellency's and the food was rather fine. (Pauline Vanier was the daughter of a judge and a member of one of the small group of French-Canadian families who were "seen" by the Square Mile.)

During this period, Pitfield was growing out of his pedantry and his snobbery, expanding intellectually and socially through talking to people whose ideas the Square Mile would have found, if not horrifying, certainly distant from their own. He kept up his friendship with Marc Lalonde, who was now back in Montreal, practising law and concerning himself with the state of the Canadian federation. Through Lalonde, who came from a family of French-Canadian farmers and saw himself as an activist reformer, Pitfield's social conscience was aroused and he began to move away from the conservatism he had espoused in his teens and early twenties when he was given to spouting Edmund Burke. He had also become fast friends with Grattan O'Leary and spent hours in his company. O'Leary was a brilliant, witty talker; his recollections of politics went back to his arrival in Ottawa in 1911 as a poor Irish boy from Quebec who sat in the House of Commons spellbound while Laurier orated late into the night. His astute perceptions of politicians' motives and his engaging manner, made up of equal parts merriment and melancholy, were a revelation to Pitfield, who had never known anybody so ready to laugh at other people's foibles and his own.

(A decade later, when Pitfield married Nancy Snow, a young woman from Toronto he had met through an interest in scuba-diving, he asked Lalonde to be his best man. As it turned out, Lalonde couldn't get to the ceremony in time because his plane was unable to land in a winter storm. Senator O'Leary, who was at the church as a guest, was a last-minute substitute. They were a strange sight waiting at the altar for the bride to come up the aisle — Pitfield, six foot three and still slightly gawky at thirty-four, and O'Leary, five foot four and a wonderfully preserved eighty-three. At the reception afterwards when Pitfield responded to the toast to the bride by talking at great length about Talleyrand, O'Leary watched benevolently. Pitfield's choices of groomsmen were an indication of how far he had come from the world of his childhood, and the boys he had grown up with — those boys who had laughed at his intellectual proclivities and called him "the professor'', who had gone into the Bank of Montreal or the big brokerage houses, or the downtown law firms, married the sisters of their classmates at LCC or their fraternity brothers at McGill, and spent their leisure playing tennis and planning strawberry-and-champagne fêtes as Junior Associates of the Museum of Montreal.)

Through his friendship with Lalonde and with Fernand Cadieux, a Montreal intellectual of great originality who influenced many of his contemporaries before his early death, Pitfield became peripherally involved with the deliberations of the French-Canadian federalists who formed the Committee for Political Realism in Montreal in 1963. As a public servant, he couldn't sign the Manifesto they published in *Cité libre* the next year, but he translated it into English so it could appear simultaneously in the *Canadian Forum*. (Ramsay Cook, who was on the *Forum*'s editorial board at the time and was one of the few intellectuals in English Canada with a deep interest in Quebec, was told by Marc Lalonde that he could get the translation from a contact in Ottawa by telephoning a certain number. Cook was astonished to discover when he dialled the number that he had called Government House and that the translator was an attaché to the Governor General.) Pitfield had met Trudeau before the committee's deliberations at a conference of L'Institut Canadien des Affaires Publiques in the early sixties but they didn't really become friends until 1965.

By that time, Pitfield was convinced that the only way to prevent Canada from falling apart was to get leading Quebeckers to come to the federal capital and assume their rightful place in governing the nation. He took part in some of the many conversations Marchand, Pelletier, and Trudeau carried on when they were trying to make up their minds to join the Liberal Party. When they arrived in Ottawa as newly elected members of Parliament, Pitfield found that despite the time Trudeau had spent in the Privy Council Office fifteen years before, they were novices in their understanding of how the capital worked. They didn't know, for instance, the difference in importance between the roles played by Louis Rasminsky (then the Governor of the Bank of Canada) and Bob Bryce (then the Deputy Minister of Finance). He took it on himself to give advice to the trio about the way Ottawa really worked, and since Trudeau was in the Prime Minister's Office as Pearson's parliamentary secretary, it was Trudeau to whom he talked. (Pitfield was by this time working in the Privy Council Office as an assistant secretary to the cabinet, preparing briefing papers for Lester Pearson.)

Two years later, in 1967, when the French-Canadian federalists began to look for a candidate to put forward as their champion in the Liberal leadership race, Pitfield took part in some of the intense conversations Marc Lalonde held about the strategic and tactical problems involved in realizing their goal. As late as December of that year, though, Pitfield told two friends, Fernand Cadieux and Roy Faibish, that he was afraid the Liberal Party wouldn't accept any French Canadian as leader, that perhaps a new party should be started with Lalonde himself as its head. But as the Trudeau campaign caught fire in January and February of 1968, Pitfield decided that it would work, that it *must* work, if Canada were to survive.

FOR YEARS PITFIELD HAD SEEMED to many of his friends to be seeking, as Grattan O'Leary expressed it, "to find some one as superhuman as the lost father of his imaginings, some person or some cause that could live up to the ideal Ward Pitfield represented in his mind." First it was Davie Fulton, then O'Leary himself, then Georges Vanier that Pitfield idealized. In the Trudeau who emerged as Liberal leader in 1968, the man of passionate pride and stubborn conviction, Pitfield finally found his true hero and his great cause. Trudeau would save Canada and Pitfield would help him run the kind of government the country needed and deserved.

Later, he was always surprised when the Tories accused him of having become a Liberal. He felt that in encouraging Trudeau to seek power he was not a partisan but a patriot. Party considerations weren't important when Canada's future was at stake. Besides, he hadn't raised money for Trudeau or campaigned actively for him, which would have been inappropriate acts for a public servant. All he had done was talk to him and his advisers — particularly to Lalonde, who'd been his close friend for a decade — about the problems with the government process that were concerning so many people in Ottawa at the time.

What Trudeau thought about Pitfield was as hard to fathom as what he thought about anybody else. When he appointed him clerk of the Privy Council in 1975, and was taunted in the House of Commons by the Conservative MP George Hees, who asked if the appointment had been made on merit, Trudeau said drily, "Very great merit." French Canadians — not just separatists but federalists as well — believed that Trudeau's early life had turned him into a snobbish Anglophile and that it was Pitfield's background in the Square Mile that was the real merit in Trudeau's eyes. Certainly that background — coupled with his intellectual gifts — made Pitfield unique in government circles and unusually self-assured in his interpretation of Canadian society.

By the time the two men first became friends in the mid-1960s, Pitfield was living a block or so from Government House in a nineteenth-century house which he had renovated into what he liked to call a *garçonnière*, complete with wingback chairs in chintz, mahogany campaign chests, polished brass, antique prints, and an extensive, eclectic library. But he still spent most of his weekends in Montreal at his mother's house and met the friends of his uncles and his brothers at lunches, dinners, cattle shows, and fêtes. He could talk with great insight and intimacy about the moneyed class in both Montreal and Toronto, where the sons of old Montreal were already moving along with the first flight of capital from the province of Quebec. His father's firm, now Pitfield Mackay Ross, by then had its head offices in Toronto and his brother, Ward C. Pitfield, Jr., was its president. He knew the businessmen of the establishment, their antecedents, their deals, their connections in the United States and the United Kingdom, and the fears that fed their boardroom deliberations. He concocted elaborate theories about their power and its interlocks, based on his readings in elite studies as well as his personal observations.

How close Trudeau and Pitfield were as personal friends was the subject of endless speculation in Ottawa in the 1970s. The speculation first began in earnest when Pitfield accompanied the Prime Minister on holidays while they were both bachelors, serving as his staff adviser, along with an RCMP security guard and a secretary who handled arrangements and correspondence. After both men were married in 1971 (Trudeau in March and Pitfield in December) their wives became confidantes, and this caused further murmurings about friendship and favouritism. What the murmurings didn't take into account was that the two women were close in age and circumstance and they talked, according to Margaret Trudeau herself, about the difficulties of coping with young children and a life confined by the dictates of officialdom. Very little was made of the fact that Trudeau was also friendly with Ivan Head, his foreign policy adviser, who often acted as a competitive participant with him in the sports that Trudeau enjoyed — diving, swimming, skiing. Other Ottawa couples were friends of the Trudeaus: Tim Porteous, who had left the PMO to join the Canada Council, and his wife, Wendy, saw them frequently, and Gordon Gibson, his first executive assistant in the PMO, who was later Liberal leader in British Columbia, and his wife, Valerie, skied with them in the Gatineau; and no one found either relationship unusual.

The angry gossip about Pitfield seemed to spring from his rapid advancement in the Privy Council Office and the weight that Trudeau gave to his advice over that of older, more experienced bureaucrats. When complaints were made to Trudeau that this was unseemly, he would reply that he and Pitfield weren't friends in the way that he and Gérard Pelletier were friends; they came from different backgrounds and were eighteen years apart in age. In any case, friendship had very little to do with it. It was Pitfield's intelligence and competence that commended him.

The two men were able to come to agreement on government matters quickly because their thinking processes were so much alike. "Pitfield was valuable to Trudeau because he was his intellectual equal," a close colleague of both men said. "He was one of the few people who weren't terrified when the PM started one of his Jesuit-at-large grilling sessions. If Trudeau questioned an idea he put forward, he would argue back, without becoming agitated or aggressive. Trudeau respected that ability. Respected it, hell, he enjoyed it. Dialectic was meat and music to him."

Pitfield had always had great self-confidence when he was functioning in a familiar setting in front of a receptive listener; the mannerisms of his youth were softened by success and what remained was something close to personal grace. He still talked well on subjects of amazing variety. He shared Trudeau's intense concern with constitutional reform. He took an interest in eastern philosophy. He had read the Greeks, he was knowledgeable about protocol, he had opinions on hotels in London, country houses in France, the personality of the Queen Mother, baroque music, absurdist drama, Nelson's naval battles, the Napoleonic code, and just about anything else a statesman of Trudeau's interests might possibly want to discuss. But the subject that really engrossed Pitfield's restless intelligence was government. His ideas about the governmental process in Canada and how it should work had been evolving for nearly a decade when Trudeau became prime minister in 1968. They were integrated ideas, lucidly expressed, and they were to become the ideas that prevailed in Ottawa in the 1970s and that were to cause so much anger in that city and in the country beyond.

It was an irony that Pitfield, who was not a Liberal — "I know nothing whatever about the Liberal Party," he would always stubbornly insist, though there was precious little else he would admit to knowing nothing whatever about — was the source of so much of the advice that was to have an important effect on the way the party was perceived in English Canada as the 1970s lurched to a close.

PITFIELD'S INFLUENCE ON TRUDEAU was noteworthy in part because in their conversations before Trudeau became prime minister the two men had agreed that the best government would be one in which the politicians and the public servants would function at arm's length, playing distinctly different roles. But their close intellectual relationship as politician and public servant had parallels in every other Liberal régime and indeed in every other modern government. In practice, the politician functions as the centre-stage extrovert embodiment of policies; the bureaucrat is the behind-the-scenes introvert who both conceives policies and puts them into effect. In Canada, the relationship had traditionally been particularly intimate, since the modern public service was the creation of a Liberal prime minister and had provided the Liberal Party with seminal ideas for more than forty years.

The original Ottawa mandarins — as members of the group that was dominant in the federal public service during those forty years came to be called when their era of glory was drawing to a close — had always found Mackenzie King exasperating. But their importance in Canadian life was the direct result of his genius for finding and using clever men. (When Senator John Connolly, the Ottawa lawyer and government leader in the Senate from 1964 to 1968, who had been a close friend of many of the mandarins, was describing long after what held the group together, he said, not entirely jokingly, "Well, they could always get together at somebody's house and talk about the mysterious success of that crazy little s.o.b., Mackenzie King.")

King himself had started out as a bureaucrat in the Department of Labour — though a distinctly partisan one in the manner of the period — before becoming a minister in Laurier's cabinet in 1909. He saw the public service as a natural "stepping stone to the ministry" and that's what it became in his political lifetime. Lester Pearson was the most famous of the bureaucrats who were transformed into Liberal politicians, but seven other civil servants became Liberal ministers between 1940 and 1963.

191

From the time of Confederation until the end of the First World War, the civil service had been run according to the patronage principle, with its upper levels changing abruptly according to which party was in or out of power after an election, not just to give the victorious party's supporters rewards for their efforts but to ensure the new cabinet loyalty in the government's ranks. Reforms brought in by the Union Government in 1918 were meant to put a stop to this practice. They were based on a primitive theory of meritocracy — the supposition that a public servant could start out as a stock clerk and work his way up to the deputy minister's office. When King became prime minister in 1921, he quickly realized that if he were going to guide Canada out from under the shadow of the British Empire and turn it into a modern independent state, this system wasn't good enough. He needed the advice of Canadians with intelligence, imagination, and first-rate educations. His first step towards realizing this goal was to hire as a counsellor and then as under-secretary in the Department of External Affairs O. D. Skelton, a professor of political science from Queen's University in Kingston. (It wasn't just a happy chance that Skelton had explored the roots of Canadian Liberalism in his biography of Sir Wilfrid Laurier, or that he and King were in agreement in most important areas of policy. Skelton had taken as his mentor Adam Shortt, another Queen's professor, whom Laurier had appointed to the Civil Service Commission in 1908.) Skelton had the makings of a born public servant; he was clever, unobtrusive, eclectic in his interests, selfless, and hard-working. King was his own minister for external affairs and Skelton ran that department for him, as well as acting as his grey eminence for nearly two decades until his death in 1941. To strengthen the civil service at its top levels the profession's first entrance examinations were initiated in the late 1920s, and several successful applicants were hired to form the nucleus of the country's brand-new diplomatic corps.

While King was out of office for five years in the 1930s and R. B. Bennett was prime minister, Skelton stayed on and served the Tories well, thereby proving to King's pious satisfaction that the civil service he had created was non-partisan, in the British rather than the American tradition. In 1932, Skelton persuaded another Queen's professor, Clifford Clark, to come to Ottawa as deputy minister in the Department of Finance. Clark, in turn, took a deep interest in the annual "generalists' examination" which was open only to university graduates and was intended to produce a talent pool from which to draw top-level administrators. Skelton and Clark kept lists of those who showed themselves outstanding in these exams, and their names and talents were kept on file. (When Robert Bryce — who was later to become the most admired mandarin of them all — came home to Canada in 1937 after studying economics first at Cambridge and then at Harvard, Clark kept him in mind while Bryce was working at the Sun Life Assurance Company in Montreal, and then brought him to Ottawa to work in Finance in 1938.)

Between them, Skelton and Clark created a public service made up of men who were outstandingly intelligent and who were to have a remarkable effect on the development of modern Canada. Most of them came as young university graduates to the backwater capital of an undeveloped country whose foreign policy was made by the British, whose monetary policy was dictated by the money markets in New York, and whose economic policy was non-existent. In the next quarter of a century, they helped the politicians guide Canada through a depression and a war and saw it gain honour in the world in the 1950s — the peak period of their own lives — of a kind that it had never had before and has never had since. They came to be called the best public service in the world, and with all due immodesty they believed themselves worthy of the accolade.

Some of the outstanding men recruited in the 1920s and 1930s included: Lester Pearson, Arnold Heeney, Hugh Keenleyside, Norman Robertson, Escott Reid, Alexander Skelton, Donald Gordon, Hume Wrong, Dana Wilgress, Graham Towers, John Holmes, Hector MacKinnon, Jules Léger, Herbert Norman, Louis Rasminsky, Wynne Plumptre, Charles Ritchie, Robert Bryce, John Deutsch, Kenneth Eaton, J. R. (Bob) Beattie, Harvey Perry, James Coyne, Ross Tolmie, and Jack Pickersgill. They were joined during the war or immediately after it by a second generation of like-minded men, among them A. E. (Ed) Ritchie, Marcel Cadieux, Claude Isbister, George Davidson,

Gordon Robertson, John Baldwin, Simon Reisman, Douglas
LePan, Ernie Steele, George Ignatieff, Dave Mansur, Mitchell
Sharp, Marshall Crowe, Jake Warren, Max Mackenzie, and
David Golden. The last of the "great men" mandarins as
Michael Pitfield called them was A. W. (Al) Johnson, who didn't
come to Ottawa until 1964, when he joined the federal public
service as an assistant deputy minister in the Department of
Finance. He was later secretary of the Treasury Board, deputy
minister of Health and Welfare, and president of the CBC.
Johnson was the same age as the mandarins who joined the
service at the end of the war. He had much the same social
background (his father was a minister) and a similar education (a
Ph.D. from Harvard), but he had worked for the Saskatchewan
government of T. C. Douglas for eighteen years and the
mandarinate — though he had its considerable respect — was
always a little alien to him.

The group had two important divisions: Skelton's protégés,
the External Affairs men, were generalists for the most part, while
"Dr. Clark's boys", as they were called, were trained economists,
makers of monetary and fiscal policy in the Department of Finance and the Bank of Canada. It was small enough in its early
days for most of the people who belonged to it to become fast
friends. As the government expanded, they moved out to staff
new departments at the top levels, though External and Finance
continued to be thought of as the pinnacles of their profession.

What distinguished these men besides their intelligence and
the protracted length of time they spent in government was their
sense of mission. (Most of them entered the public service in
their twenties and stayed until retirement age, sometimes serving
on commissions or boards until they were well into their seventies.)
"They were just so damned smart and so damned devoted," said
John Connolly, looking back in admiration, "the cream of a generation, and they were able to believe in the importance of giving
their lives to the service of their country in a way hardly anybody
did who came into the service later when altruism was a forgotten
force. They provided Liberal governments with ideas that kept
them going for years."

Much was made of the Queen's University connections in

this group, in part because Queen's had had an illustrious history of involvement with government since the time of its famous principal George Grant. Besides Shortt, Skelton, and Clark, Queen's men included John Deutsch, who worked at the Bank of Canada and for the Rowell-Sirois Commission as well as in the Department of Finance and was later chairman of the Economic Council, and W. A. Mackintosh, who worked in Finance during the war and was the author of the 1945 White Paper on Reconstruction. But the rest did their undergraduate work at a variety of Canadian universities. What was probably more important in the formation of their attitudes was that so many of them had postgraduate educations abroad at Oxford or Cambridge or the London School of Economics.

By the time the mandarinate had been clearly identified in the 1960s, it was usually assumed, because of their rarefied educations, that most of its members had been born rich, a charge they bitterly resented. Aside from Bryce, Towers, Wilgress, Coyne, and Charles Ritchie, who were the products of upper-class or upper-middle-class homes, the rest came from middle-class, small-town Canada; they had been born in rural areas of Ontario, the Maritimes, and the Prairies, into parsimony if not deprivation as the children of ministers, teachers, veterinarians, doctors, and farmers. Rasminsky was a Jew, Deutsch a German Roman Catholic farmer's son, Léger and Cadieux were French Canadians, but the rest were mainly Methodists or Presbyterians who had been imbued with the Protestant work and duty ethic. They got their impressive educations because they had been outstanding students, winning scholarships from the Rhodes Trust or the Imperial Order Daughters of the Empire, scholarships that were meant to turn the colonial intelligentsia into the Empire's loyal public servants.

They went into the public service because the jobs were the best available and the pay was marginally better than in the universities. (In 1935, successful applicants were being offered $1600 a year, three or four hundred more than any university could pay them as instructors even if the available jobs matched their specialties.) For the rest of their lives, though, they remained intellectuals by inclination as well as by training and

there was always an aura of the gentleman-scholar about the
group. Their jokes were donnish jokes, their language redolent of
common rooms. (When George Davidson, who had been educated as a classicist, was plucked from the Treasury Board, where
he was deputy, and persuaded against his will to accept the
onerous burden of the presidency of the Canadian Broadcasting
Corporation in 1968, he sent Lester Pearson a one-line note that
read, *Caesar morituri te salutamus!* ["Caesar, we who are about
to die salute you!" — the salutation Roman gladiators addressed
to their emperors when they entered the arena to do battle unto
death.] He then dined out on this witticism for several weeks
thereafter without bothering to offer a translation, secure in the
knowledge that at the tables he frequented, everybody would get
the joke.)

In keeping with their high intellectual tone and their low
salaries, the first wave of mandarins tended to be disinterested in
the making of money. Few of them had any direct knowledge of
business, though Clifford Clark had left Queen's in the 1920s to
become vice-president of a U.S. investment firm specializing in
real estate. The firm went broke in the crash of 1929, an incident
that sent Clark back to Queen's laden with debts, his disdain for
money-grubbing confirmed.

In 1945 when Max Mackenzie, a partner in the Montreal
chartered accountancy firm of McDonald, Currie and Company,
who had worked in Ottawa during the war, was offered the job of
deputy minister in the Department of Trade and Commerce, he
asked for a salary of $12,000, which he felt was an adequate if
hardly extravagant remuneration for the job. He was appalled to
be told that Clark, who had been Deputy Minister of Finance for
thirteen years and was the government's chief economic adviser,
wasn't making that much. When Clark died a few years later,
there wasn't enough money in his estate to pay off the mortgage on his house, so C. D. Howe arranged with the mortgagee
that his widow would have to make only interest rather than
principal payments for the rest of her life. Clark's dedication and
unworldliness were much admired.

To the mandarinate any display of acquisitiveness or ostenta-
tion was dismaying. When Simon Reisman came back to Canada

after serving as a captain in the army during the war, with an M.A. in economics from McGill and further study at the London School of Economics, and was offered $2400 a year for a job in Finance, he objected, saying that wasn't enough money to support his family. Mitchell Sharp, who was doing the final interviewing on the department's behalf, stared at him for a few seconds and then said slowly, "Well, Mr. Reisman, that's all you're worth to me. It's a rare privilege to work in the Department of Finance and you should make that part of your calculation."

The mandarins thought of themselves throughout their working lives as nationalists, but their Canadianism was shaped by their reactions to the attitudes of the British who were their mentors and their scourge. Hume Wrong, who had been a colleague of Lester Pearson's in the Department of History at the University of Toronto and preceded him into External Affairs, once wrote, while attending an international conference where he felt overwhelmed by the public servants from Whitehall, "We should not be here at all as our instructions could be summarized as 'Say nothing and do nothing'. . . . Dining alone this evening, I developed a plan for the perfect representative of Canada. Our delegate would have a name, even a photograph, a distinguished record, even a secretary — but he would have no corporal existence and no one would ever notice he was not there." Despite the irony of its tone — and the tone was typical of the mandarin class as a whole — that sentence masked a deep anger and frustration. The mandarins had a shared passion: they disliked British condescension intensely and they wanted out from under the Empire. They were able, they were proud, and they were fed up with being treated as colonials.

This feeling had begun to take shape while they were at Cambridge or Oxford in the 1920s and 1930s, when their accents had been mocked and their undergraduate educations scorned. It was buttressed when they came into contact with O. D. Skelton, whose biographies of Sir Alexander Galt and Laurier had exposed the perfidy of the British, who were so loath to grant Canada any kind of autonomy and created in him a lifelong antipathy to them. It grew greater after they assumed responsible public service jobs and came into close contact with their British counterparts. George

Ferguson, a newspaperman who went to Oxford on a Rhodes scholarship after seeing action in France in the First World War and who was a friend of many of the mandarins, once described how difficult it was for his generation to forgive the British for their easy superiority to Canada and Canadians. When he was an old man in the mid-1970s, his eyes still reflected his rage at how he and his countrymen had been treated at Oxford: "We felt we had served with the best soldiers in the world," he said. "We had given ourselves wholeheartedly for the ideal of Empire and we were treated as though we belonged below stairs. I never forgot this and neither did most of the Ottawa men — whether they had seen service themselves or just heard about the war from their relatives. It burned our souls in a way we couldn't forget for years."

As late as 1944, Charles Ritchie wrote in his diary that he had dined in London at the Masseys' (when Vincent Massey was Canadian High Commissioner) with Rab Butler, the British politician, and then went on to say, "I like him better each time I see him. . . . All the same, he and his fellow Tories understand nothing about Canada. It is discouraging to find this ignorance in the intelligent ones like Rab. A small instance — Rab was trying to show that he appreciated Canada's position in the Commonwealth and said to Mr. Massey, 'To show you what I mean I have several times in speaking of Canada [to Canadians] referred to it as "your country". Quite separate from us.' This was said in good faith. Any Canadian's reaction would be, 'Why the hell wouldn't you — it *is* our country. Isn't it or is it?' "

To counter this kind of overbearing attitude in the British, the mandarins told themselves that they belonged to a North American Canada, to the New World, the world of the future, not to the world of the Empire, the world of the Dominions — that was the world of the past. They seemed largely blind to the possibility that by identifying themselves with the continent rather than the country they were in danger of falling into the arms of another empire. By the end of the Second World War, their continentalism had become so pronounced that even Mackenzie King was alarmed. He confided to his diary that Canada always had to keep the balance between the two great powers and he feared that the disregard for the British and the high regard for the Americans rampant among the Ottawa elite would harm the country. It was an idea the mandarinate would have laughed at if they had been able to read his thoughts at the time, as they had mocked so many of his intuitions.

Beyond their anti-imperialism, the other attitude the mandarins held to was a general rejection of old-fashioned laissez-faire dogmas in economic affairs. They had observed the horrors of the Depression. They had been exposed to left-wing ideas at Cambridge and Oxford. For the most part they were drawn not to Stalin's five-year plans and communism's obsession with working-class control of the state but to Roosevelt's New Deal and Keynesianism's belief in using the state to regulate the economy and so avoid the boom-and-bust gyrations that had plagued capitalism for decades. By implication it was they, the experts, who would decree how the state could be managed. Bob Bryce had absorbed Keynes's theories with tremendous enthusiasm when he studied with the economist at Cambridge three years before his landmark *General Theory of Employment, Interest and Money* was published in 1936.

Under the aegis of Clifford Clark these novel approaches were put into effect in a guise that was acceptable to the essentially cautious Canadian society these men sprang from. Clark set up the centralized banking system. He agreed with the Rowell-Sirois Commission's proposals to transfer powers from the provinces to Ottawa because greater central direction of the Canadian economy was vital to engineer a recovery from the Depression. With the dollar-a-year businessmen as temporary co-managers of Canada, they orchestrated a completely new economic system for the duration of the war effort — a kind of state capitalism that enthusiastically accepted such anathemas to free-market economics as wage and price regulation, exchange controls, and rationing. Clark wrote the legislation that introduced family allowances in 1944, one of a series of Liberal social welfare measures concocted both to head off the rising popularity of the CCF on the political front and to introduce on the economic front a measure of stability in the public's purchasing power — a sort of permanent stimulant to consumer spending.

In these policy thrusts it was not so much that the mandarinate had the support of the Liberal ministry as that they were able to talk the most powerful ministers into giving them support; they weren't underlings in policy-making, they were equals in a partnership. They were able to influence King first through Skelton, then through Norman Robertson, who was under-secretary after O. D.'s death, later through Arnold Heeney, who was Clerk of the Privy Council, and Jack Pickersgill, who was King's special assistant. They were highly influential with C. D. Howe when he was Minister of Transport before the war, Minister of Munitions and Supply during it, and Minister of Trade and Commerce afterwards. Their general view of Howe was that he was not a policy-maker at all, he was a Yankee doer, a competent man who despised red tape, and who was able to take their ideas and put them into effect and draw the business community along with him. That Howe was too anti-intellectual to share their general world view didn't matter very much. Because he agreed with many of their concrete objectives, he went along with some of their most cherished notions about achieving them — in the public sector if need be. This apostle of private enterprise became the man who expedited the founding of the CBC, and who set up Trans Canada Air Lines, Atomic Energy of Canada Limited, and the Polymer Corporation. He took the White Paper on Reconstruction written by Clark's close colleague from Queen's, Bill Mackintosh, in 1944 and put it into effect. Howe was a manager. The mandarins were the thinkers and the policy-makers.

"The point was," John Deutsch said thirty years later, "that Howe was a great operator, with important business connections. He knew how to make things run. You could tell him you needed some airplanes and he would build airplanes but why you needed them — how they fitted into some grand design — was a question of policy, the kind of airy-fairy question he didn't care for. King was extraordinary at recognizing talent and squeezing it for his purposes. He let Howe do what he was best at. He let the regional political barons in his cabinet do what they were best at. And he let the public servants do what they were best at. And he sat there like a fat spider in the middle knowing he had woven the web."

In the 1950s, with King dead, the economy booming, and

Louis St. Laurent and C. D. Howe presiding over the government like chairman of the board and chief executive officer, respectively, of some great business corporation, the mandarins began to change and so did their relationship with the politicians. King had kept the political factor supreme in running his governments; he had given the bureaucrats their head but, behind the scenes, he had controlled them as well as their ministers. By now, though, the mandarins as a generation were well into middle age and had grown complacent with success; their ideas were unchallenged in government and their network spread through all the elites in Canada. Their former colleagues Lester Pearson and Jack Pickersgill became ministers and there were other men in cabinet, notably Douglas Abbott in Finance and Brooke Claxton in National Defence, who suited them equally well. Moreover, St. Laurent, who had no real taste for gritty politics, was much more inclined to side with his bureaucrats in any dispute than with his ministers.

They now had important connections in the corporate world as well; the dollar-a-year men who had come to work in Ottawa in 1940 and 1941 were back in the business worlds of Montreal, Toronto, and Vancouver and had remained their friends. Because so many of the mandarins had been educated abroad, or had served in diplomatic missions and as delegates at international gatherings, their connections in the United States and the United Kingdom were excellent too. They were fond of telling stories about Sir Stafford Cripps and Lord Keynes, about Dean Acheson and George Kennan, about their triumphs at United Nations assemblies and International Monetary Fund meetings.

They were close to the great Liberal journalists, George Ferguson of the *Montreal Star*, Kenneth Wilson of the *Financial Post*, Bruce Hutchison of the *Vancouver Sun*, Grant Dexter of the Winnipeg *Free Press*, and Blair Fraser of *Maclean's* magazine. These men interpreted the world the way the mandarins saw it, and Fraser particularly wrote the kind of lucid, ironic prose they liked to read. Like them, Fraser was aghast at parish-pump politicking. He was clever, he was witty, he was an internationalist. "If it weren't for Blair, there wouldn't be anything to read in that rag at all," the establishment wives used to say about Canada's national magazine, which was then at its apogee. They preferred the *New Yorker*, the *Nation*, the *New Republic*, magazines published below the border in the world they had grown used to, the international world far from the dusty prairie towns, the northern resource outposts, and the raw cities of the Canadian boom, the places where they had grown up and that *Maclean's* was now trying to mythologize.

By this time they were living very well, not ostentatiously, of course, but in a civilized manner. In the 1930s they had formed a fishing club at Five Lakes in the Gatineau Hills where they went to relax. (Clifford Clark had scouted out the land and bought it very cheaply and a rough lodge was put up as a communal effort.) Now, belonging to Five Lakes became a symbol of success, the club an important place to meet, hammer out ideas, reach a consensus. They were able to afford houses in Rockcliffe Park and to furnish them with good pieces bought on their travels and Canadian paintings acquired inexpensively before the rich realized their value. (David Milne was a favourite; he was promoted by Vincent Massey, who served as a kind of go-between for the upper class and the mandarins, though both groups secretly laughed at his more-English-than-the-English pretensions. Still, they liked to tell the story of Lord Salisbury, who had confided that he found the Canadian High Commissioner's punctiliousness somewhat alarming. "Dear chap, Vincent, but he does make one feel a bit of a savage," he was supposed to have said of this austere descendant of robust Ontario entrepreneurs.) They themselves were sticklers for good manners and correct dress. They wore the international civil servant's uniform of three-piece dark suit, white shirt, and steel-rimmed spectacles, and their wives had knobs of hair, good educations, and a firm grasp of protocol.

In the 1930s and early 1940s, when they were younger and poorer, the mandarins had been accustomed to eat as a group in the Chateau Laurier cafeteria. Several of them, sitting around there one noon hour in 1940, had thought up the Wartime Prices and Trade Board. Afterwards Simon Reisman remembered what the atmosphere had been like at the end of the war. "External Affairs, the Department of Finance, and the Prime Minister's Office were all located in the East Block of the Parliament Buildings in those days and almost any noon hour you could walk down to the

Chateau cafeteria and this big guy with a white chef's hat would be standing there, cutting slices of beef off the arse end of a steer. You'd get that, a piece of blueberry pie, and a glass of milk and then sit down at a table with your peers and discuss the questions of the day. The other, older men would be sitting at a table nearby and they would sometimes call a young guy over and ask his opinion so they could assess him at the same time. It was such a homogeneous group you wouldn't believe it now.''

It was only later in the 1950s, when the mandarins had been infected by their own successes at home and abroad, and the public service began to grow larger, that their network became an exclusive clique, its members joining the Rideau Club and the Country Club, drinking martinis at La Touraine, eating oysters for lunch, and talking about the magnificent Brie at Vincent Massey's Sunday-evening supper dances at Government House.

What was really important about the mandarinate was not its famous mannerisms but the pervasiveness of its influence over the St. Laurent government. It got to the point where a powerful deputy minister who had conceived a policy he wanted made into law would address himself for support not primarily to his minister (or his "political master" as deputy ministers jokingly called the pols in mockery of Whitehall), but to his peers. Six or eight key deputy ministers ran Ottawa in the 1950s and early 1960s; they would hammer out a consensus acceptable to their shared overview of what was good for Canada, get the aid of two or three key ministers, and smoothly ram the policy through the weekly meeting around the cabinet table.

At this stage, the co-operation of the Clerk of the Privy Council was crucial. He was the man who put a policy on the cabinet agenda for debate. When he had the job, Jack Pickersgill was said to be so adept at handling policies that might just possibly be displeasing to some of the people's representatives that he could calculate not only the right day to put them before cabinet, but the right moment. Legend had it that he would wait for an antagonistic minister to duck out to the washroom and the policy would have been described, discussed, and approved almost before the minister had had a chance to button up his fly.

WHEN MICHAEL PITFIELD first encountered the bureaucratic power structure in Davie Fulton's office in 1959, it was still functioning very much as it had for the previous quarter-century, despite the Conservative victory of two years before. Diefenbaker came to office deeply suspicious of the mandarins because of their support of and influence over the Liberal Party and his feelings were shared by two of his most influential ministers, Alvin Hamilton, who served first in Northern Affairs and later in Agriculture, and Gordon Churchill in Trade and Commerce. But the Tory prime minister soon developed an unshakable trust in Robert Bryce, who was Clerk of the Privy Council at the time, and no mass firings or partisan hirings took place. (One important public servant, Mitchell Sharp, deputy minister in Trade and Commerce, did quit the government, chiefly over a disagreement with his minister, Gordon Churchill, about wheat policy. He was replaced as deputy first by John English, who died within a short time, and then by Brigadier James Roberts, who had been a fellow officer of Gordon Churchill's during the war, and was the only public servant brought in by the Tories at a senior level. Sharp went to Toronto to become vice-president of Brazilian Traction and eventually ran for the Liberals in the Toronto riding of Eglinton. Once the Liberals were elected in 1963, and Sharp became minister in the department where he had formerly been deputy, Roberts was deftly removed from the scene and transferred to a post at NATO, showing the essentially Grit colouring of Ottawa's "non-partisan" public service tradition.)

Far more prominent than accusations of partisanship was the charge made against the mandarins by the Tories that they were too powerful, that they had usurped the politicians' function. "You've got to watch these guys or they'll hornswoggle you," was the way Alvin Hamilton expressed this antagonism. In general, Diefenbaker's ministers felt outclassed by these men who were so experienced in governing, who in general had educations far superior to their own and connections in the post-war Canadian elites that they couldn't match.

At the same time, younger public servants started to complain that the mandarins as a group were old-fashioned, inefficient, and inbred, that the generalist educations which had served them so well in forming an "overview" of the dramatic problems of the Depression and the war were inadequate to deal with the intricacies of an expanding government in a technological age. Their homogeneity as a group, their ability to control the public service hierarchy, and their generally perceived snobbishness gave them the aura of a caste. External Affairs particularly was seen as the centre of an effete elite and its great guru, Norman Robertson, as the embodiment of the mandarin style. Marshall Crowe, who came into the Department after the war (when it was still called the Department, as the British Foreign Office was called the Office), remembered feeling stifled there by 1960 after he came back to Ottawa from a posting in the Canadian Embassy in Moscow to serve once more under Norman Robertson, then finishing his final stint as under-secretary. For a variety of reasons, after fifteen years in External, Crowe decided to take a job in Toronto as an economic adviser to Neil McKinnon, the president of the Canadian Bank of Commerce. When he went to tell Robertson his plans, the great man responded in horror, making it plain that quite *frankly*, it was *unthinkable* that a man from The Department would go into a *commercial* bank. Surely if Crowe had a hankering for the *tedium* of the banking world he would want to go into the Bank of Canada. Then he added wearily that if this were the case he, Robertson, would phone Graham (Towers, the Governor of the Bank) on Crowe's behalf. Crowe somewhat heatedly responded that he felt it was high time that he got out of External and that some fresh breezes ought to blow into the department's own dustier corners before its denizens choked to death, and then departed happily for a period in the world of private banking before coming back to Ottawa in 1967 to work in the PCO.

In response to the various criticisms being made against the system, Diefenbaker appointed J. Grant Glassco, a former partner in Clarkson, Gordon, now with Brazilian Traction, to head a royal commission to investigate the government's operations. Aided by J. E. Hodgetts, a University of Toronto political scientist, Glassco finished this task toward the bitter end of the Diefenbaker régime in 1962. The report of his Royal Commission on Government Organization urged the modernization of the public service and a marked decentralization of power within it. This was to be accomplished by the adoption of currently fashionable corporate business techniques such as PPBS — planning programming budgeting systems, an unmanageable phrase that was to echo in Ottawa for the next fifteen years — and by setting up a new watchdog agency, separate from Finance, to keep the departments' spending under control. The notion that the bureaucracy was old-fashioned, unbusinesslike, and inefficient had been formalized by means of one of the mandarins' own favourite tools, the royal-commission report.

Any illusion the mandarins cherished that the Liberals' return to office in 1963 would signal a return to the halcyon days of the public service was soon dissipated. The general feeling in the Pearson government was that inbreeding with the senior public servants had caused the St. Laurent régime to seal itself off from the electorate and had led directly to its defeat. Despite his own roots in the bureaucracy, Pearson swept into power with a highly developed program conceived as a result of the Kingston Conference, and with Tom Kent, one of that program's chief architects, ensconced in his office to be sure these policies were put into effect whether the bureaucrats liked them or not. The politicians would tell the bureaucrats what it was they were to do. Kent had strong ideas about social policy, a keen intellect, an Oxford education, and a great deal of scorn for the old St. Laurent Liberals' combine with the public service. Walter Gordon had equally firm ideas about the policies he wanted realized in the Department of Finance and equally firm doubts about the ability of the public service to carry them out, which led him to hire three outside experts to write his first budget — with disastrous results for all concerned.

When so many of their ideas proved difficult to turn into law, the Pearson Liberals, instead of admitting they were trying to do too much too fast, blamed the senior public servants, calling them intransigent, wilful, and anti-democratic. In turn, the bureaucrats said that because so many of the Liberal politicians had been bureaucrats themselves they were know-it-alls, trying to do two jobs at once. Many of them became deeply critical of Pearson in private, saying that he had never understood economic issues as his colleagues Norman Robertson and Hume Wrong had; that because he had been involved in international affairs for so long he refused to take advice in that area while at the same time trying to cover up his ignorance in domestic affairs; that his great facility for conciliation did not work in a fractious cabinet made up of ministers of such diverse ideological bents as Walter Gordon and Jack Pickersgill, Robert Winters and Maurice Sauvé, Judy LaMarsh and Arthur Laing; that he wasn't strong enough to be a prime minister.

Clearly the old symbiotic relationship was strained beyond repair. For the next few years discussion raged in Ottawa among the new generation of politicians and public servants, not just about the need for change — that was acknowledged everywhere — but about the principles on which it should be based and the form it should take. The emerging consensus was that the bureaucracy had to be brought under closer political control, that it should be more accountable and more efficient, that it was intellectually exhausted and needed to be infused with new people, more representative of modern Canada, preferably with experience in the world of business or with specialist educations suitable to the new techniques of governing.

These ideas were in the air in the capital throughout the 1960s; they were discussed constantly in public service and political circles, particularly by Alvin Hamilton and his executive assistant, Roy Faibish, both during and after the Conservative régime; by Michael McCabe, who was Mitchell Sharp's executive assistant in Trade and Commerce and then in Finance; by Paul Hellyer and his executive assistant, William Lee, in National Defence; by Maurice Strong, who had come from the business world to be head of the Canadian International Development Agency; by Walter Gordon, who prepared a memo for Pearson on the subject when he re-entered his cabinet in 1967; and by dozens of others who were either young or progressive or both. In short, Michael

Pitfield was not the only advocate of public service reform in the 1960s. But, by a series of circumstances, he was to play the most visible part in working out the system whereby reform was effected in the years from 1965 — when he was first appointed as assistant secretary in the Privy Council Office by Lester Pearson — to 1979, when he was functioning as the beleaguered clerk of the Privy Council in the government of Pierre Trudeau.

PITFIELD FORMALLY TOOK PART in the process of reforming the public service first in 1967 when he was sent by Lester Pearson to the United Kingdom and several European Economic Community countries to study their overall planning systems and to make a report on how he thought they could be adapted to Canadian needs. Some of the ideas formulated as a result of this study, and other Privy Council Office deliberations, were put into practice while Pearson was still prime minister, notably a partial overhaul of the cabinet committee system that had been functioning in a desultory way since the Second World War. But the major governmental reforms were not instituted until after 1968; they bore the clear imprint of Pierre Trudeau and his alter ego, Marc Lalonde, both of whom were in constant conversational contact with Pitfield as his ideas evolved.

Trudeau and Lalonde had been scornful of the way government was run under Pearson; to their minds it seemed that cabinet decisions were made on evidence that was all too often emotional and illogical. Part of the trouble, they believed, was that several of Pearson's important ministers were in thrall to their deputies, presenting policies to cabinet they themselves too often had little influence over, and responding to other ministers' policies out of general ignorance. Government policy-making should not be haphazard; it should be planned. But beyond that they were also conscious, as Trudeau had written before he came to Ottawa, that the capital's hierarchical structure had excluded French Canadians almost completely from the most powerful positions. They thought public service reform — along with the Official Languages Act (which came into effect in 1969 though the groundwork had been laid by Pearson), the constitutional reform they were so energetically seeking, and the appointment of Quebeckers to important economic ministries — would remedy some of the inequities in federalism by breaking up the old English-speaking bureaucratic clique.

These matters were discussed at some of the many gather-

209

ings Trudeau held in his office before he sought the leadership, meetings which were really the forum that hammered out so many of the ideas that he brought with him to office in 1968, as the Kingston Conference of 1960 had been the source of social policy ideas for Pearson. In accordance with his firm belief in the importance of planning, Trudeau had a list of twelve "priority problems" on his agenda in June 1968, problems that included such large issues as external affairs, energy, the environment, and consumer protection. After they were ranked in order of urgency by the cabinet, the second of them turned out to be "personnel policy in government", that is, the management of the public service. (The first priority was communications between the governors and the governed, a fact that anyone who spent time in the secrecy-ridden atmosphere of Trudeau's Ottawa found ironic to contemplate a decade later.)

The public service — and the decision-making process along with it — were to be reformed by three means: by strengthening the power of the Prime Minister's Office and redefining its relationship with the Privy Council Office; by remodelling cabinet procedures; and by exercising firm control over senior appointments in the bureaucracy, a power which of course belonged to the prime minister legally but had been largely wielded by the mandarinate when it was in its powerful prime.

Under previous prime ministers, the PMO and the PCO had become so intertwined that officials frequently could not remember in later years who had worked where. (Bob Bryce, for instance, in discussing in 1979 the economic advice that had been given to St. Laurent when Bryce was Clerk of the Privy Council, was not sure whether Maurice Lamontagne had been employed as a civil servant or as a political adviser to the PM.) The Trudeauites wanted this unseemly combine broken up. They wanted the political and the bureaucratic functions clearly distinguished. They saw the PMO as the prime minister's *political* support staff, set up to help him discharge his complex duties in the cabinet, the Commons, the Liberal Party, and the country at large. They believed his office should come under a clearly partisan chief of staff, the principal secretary, and that it needed a greatly expanded staff to take over certain functions being handled by the PCO (the answering of letters addressed to the prime minister, for instance, which in their minds were definitely political functions).

They saw the Privy Council Office as the cabinet's secretariat. It was to have three main divisions — operations, plans, and federal-provincial relations; its purpose was to help the cabinet in systematic decision-making and to ensure that its decisions fitted into a coherent overall policy. (The PMO would provide the prime minister with political advice using the same "fact base" as the PCO, but by removing from it the need to make decisions on what was good for the Liberal Party, the PCO would be "purified".) Cabinet decision-making was to be made more efficient, more rational, and at the same time more collegial through an elaborate committee structure. There were four line-level or policy committees — economic policy, social policy, government operations, and science, culture, and information; and five staff-level or co-ordinating committees — priorities and planning, federal-provincial relations, legislation and House planning, treasury board, and security and intelligence, which was established after the FLQ crisis of 1970. There were also numerous ad hoc committees to deal with problems as they arose.

The central idea of these reforms was admirable; its aim was to be sure the people's business was conducted by the people's elected representatives. Civil servants would not be able to combine any more to produce a consensus policy among themselves and then do a snow job on a vulnerable cabinet minister. The minister would tell his deputy he needed a policy. The deputy would go to his department, set its technical experts to work, and then produce several alternative policies for the minister to take to the cabinet committee concerned, where the options would be carefully explained and argued out among the ministers in that committee with the help of their officials. Only then, when the policy had been thrashed out and all its ramifications explored — and possibly sent back for revision to the department involved — was it to be brought to the full cabinet for further discussion if that was warranted or merely for review if it was not. Theoretically, in Trudeau's Ottawa, no official would ever be able to say to a politician, "Mr. Minister you should do this because I am your wise deputy and I know what's right." He would say, "Mr. Minister, here are your options — you and your colleagues must decide.''

The prime minister himself would have the benefit of expert but partisan advice from his own officers in the PMO so that he could provide a further check on the system, another countervailing force. He would be chairman of a collective executive rather than an all-powerful first minister. Ministers would be spared cut-throat competition on whose policies would have priority. The goal was consensual conclusions arrived at democratically, drawing on the most complete data available.

Similarly, on public service appointments, the prime minister was no longer to be given the final word on which up-and-coming civil servant was thought worthy of a deputy-ministership by the senior mandarin group. When a deputy-ministership or equivalent job fell open, the prime minister was to ''take soundings''. He would consult the Clerk of the Privy Council, who would consult the Public Service Commission, a body that the mandarinate had largely ignored. He was to talk to the minister whom the appointed deputy was meant to serve, and to the minister who was chairman of the cabinet committee before which the official would be required to appear. He was to discuss the problem with his principal secretary for ''private sector considerations'' and ''political input'' — i.e., is this a job for which we should bring in some outside expert from the business world, or will this appointment satisfy the party's long-term goals, such as the more equitable sharing of the top jobs among French and English Canadians? Only then would he decide. By keeping the PCO itself small and circulating its staff out into the departments, cliques would be discouraged. Empire-building would be prevented by requiring deputies to circulate from department to department at fairly frequent intervals and by reviewing their performances regularly. In brief, the deputies were to be managers, not mandarins. Michael Pitfield didn't conceive this system all by himself and it would never have been put in place without Pierre Trudeau's fascination with cybernetics and his belief in the efficacy of planning, an idea that was in intellectual vogue in the 1960s. But Pitfield became the system's most eloquent exponent and was seen in Ottawa as its chief architect.

If the system was admirable in concept, in practice it soon displayed serious flaws. "It was a model that belonged in a university, not in the real world," one of the deputies who climbed to the top of the public service ladder in the 1970s under this system said at the end of the decade. "Like so many of the ideas that the Trudeauites conceived, it was completely rational but deeply impractical. It was based on the belief that you could construct a system and then force not only people but events to fit themselves into it. It required a breed of supermen, and a universe unfolding as it should. Instead, it produced a world that was an administrative nightmare, and it drove able people out of public life. After ten years of it — and all the so-called refinements Pitfield introduced along the way — the public service was depleted, the calibre of its personnel's performance markedly inferior. No one would deny Pitfield meant well, that he was a man of the highest integrity. But he was just so unreal in his expectations. And Trudeau bought his unreality because it was couched in such rational terms."

This was a typical statement of the generally acrimonious attitude to Pitfield that had developed in Ottawa by the late 1970s. It was an attitude of which Pitfield was painfully aware, though the hostility puzzled him deeply when he considered the fact that the major changes in government organization had been made when Gordon Robertson was Clerk of the Privy Council and Secretary to the Cabinet from 1963 to 1974.

Robertson was a product of the old mandarinate clique. He had been brought into External under Norman Robertson in 1941 and had come up through the system. He had lines out to the remaining mandarins in the early years of the Trudeau régime. He was not the acknowledged dean of the public service, as Robert Bryce had been when he was Clerk, but he was accessible to the deputies, a smoother of differences rather than a creator of ideas. Furthermore, one of the two deputy secretaries in the PCO was Marshall Crowe, who was in charge of operations in the office; Crowe had also come up through the old system, and while he was convinced of the need for reform, he was a very practical man with the sense to be an advocate of the new system and at the same time respectful of the deputies' opinions.

As a result, any hostilities the senior public servants had towards the new system were not directed at Crowe or at Robertson — who repeatedly said they had urged caution on Trudeau in evolving the new governmental process. Instead, doubts were expressed as whispered criticisms of Trudeau's "smart boys" in the PMO and the PCO. Marc Lalonde, his principal secretary and iron-willed strong man, was both respected and feared; but Ivan Head, the foreign policy adviser, Jim Davey, the program secretary and wild-eyed futurologist who produced the flow charts, and most of all, Michael Pitfield, the deputy secretary in charge of plans who concocted the grand designs behind the priorities exercises, were mocked for their pretensions and pseudo-scientific sophistication. Pitfield was seen as being not a public servant at all in the old sense of the word but a hybrid creature, part politician, part bureaucrat; he never seemed at ease in his contacts with the senior bureaucrats. He was both shy and snobbish, and the deputies were enraged by the news from the East Block that Trudeau called him "Michel" during meetings, consulted him regularly outside office hours, and gave a dinner party for him after his marriage in 1971 — all expressions of esteem in the Prime Minister's eyes that had never been extended to any of them, despite their vast experience and clear seniority.

Throughout the régime's early years when Trudeau was riding high, the bureaucrats kept their hostilities both to the system and to Pitfield fairly quiet. They watched as the Department of External Affairs was systematically shorn of its great power by the foreign policy review the Trudeauites undertook; while they had sympathy for individual old friends in External, they weren't as a collective entirely sorry. External had been, as Norman Robertson had conceived it, the "seed bed" for the civil service. For thirty years it had sent the best and brightest of its officers out into the other departments; when Allan Gotlieb was appointed a deputy in 1968, he was the twelfth External man elevated to that category. But by 1970 Canada's role in the world was greatly diminished and so was External's reputation in Ottawa. Trudeau was supposed to have said sarcastically that the department was costing too much for the kind of information on international affairs it was providing, information that was no better in his view than what he could read in *Le Monde* or the *New York Times*.

It was also widely known in Ottawa that Lalonde felt diplomats lived too lavishly, with their servants, their fancy cars, and their large residences abroad, and that this offended his puritanism. Mandarins toiling away in Ottawa in other less glamorous departments, and with puritanical consciences of their own to assuage, tended to agree with him. Frightened by the rumours that Trudeau and Lalonde believed External had used French Canadians as mere tokens, they applied themselves diligently to French lessons and to furthering the careers of the francophones in their own departments. They laughed uneasily when diplomats returning from abroad for briefing meetings told them that the power of Trudeau's foreign policy adviser from the PMO, Ivan Head — who was called Mini-Kiss for the supposed similarity of his influence to that of Henry Kissinger in the United States — had turned them into mere factotums, bookers of hotel rooms and providers of duty-free booze for visiting ministers and officials from Ottawa.

Still, despite External's experience, despite the countervailing advice being given the Trudeau régime by advisers in the PMO, and despite the cabinet committee system where the senior public servants were required to perform at their ministers' sides, justifying their policies before their peers, the important deputy ministers felt their roles were undiminished on the whole. It was still possible to have strong relationships develop between ministers and officials: Bob Bryce and Edgar Benson in Finance, Allan Gotlieb and Eric Kierans in Communications, Simon Reisman and C. M. Drury at the Treasury Board, Jake Warren and Jean-Luc Pepin in Industry, Trade and Commerce, Bernard Ostry and Gérard Pelletier in Secretary of State, and in the post-1972 period between Al Johnson and Marc Lalonde in Health and Welfare and Simon Reisman and John Turner in Finance. The underlying hope of the senior civil servants was that the new system would settle down, "the smart boys" would get bored with their power games, and their own importance to the system would continue much as before.

In the minority government period after Trudeau's near defeat in 1972, it seemed as if this hope might be realized. Trudeau was preoccupied with politicking. He was dependent on the NDP to maintain his minority government in office and, under the exigencies of meeting its demands, long-range planning — so central

to his first term in office — was abandoned. His personal advisers
were dispersed. (Lalonde had run for office in 1972 and had been
replaced as principal secretary by Martin O'Connell, a former
minister; Pitfield was made deputy minister of Consumer and Corporate Affairs and the scuttlebutt in Ottawa was that he would
never survive outside the hothouse of the PCO; and Jim Davey was
banished with his flow charts to the Department of Transport.
Ivan Head remained as an adviser but was "defanged", in the
bureaucrats' word.) As a result, there was a reversion to policy-
making as crisis management and the public servants' advice was
directly sought and quickly heeded by ministers. By default, the
old machinery was at work again, as if it were some auxiliary
generator in a blackout.

But in October 1974 — after Trudeau had won back a majority in the July election and had convened the Thirtieth Parliament
— when he announced the appointment of Pitfield to the Clerk's
position, there was an explosion of rage in Ottawa among the
upper reaches of the bureaucracy reflecting frustrations that had
been building up for years. The general feeling among the last
remnant of those who had come into the public service under the
old order was that the new system just had not worked and was
not workable. The senior civil servants were bothered by the
growth of the bureaucracy, which instead of being brought under
control as the Trudeauites had promised was now like a swollen
elephant on the rampage, with a valiant little band of senior public
servants riding precariously on top. New departments had proli-
ferated, old departments had expanded, and new bureaucrats had
been hired by the hundreds. In ten years the public service had
increased by fifty per cent, but what appalled the old bureaucratic
caste just as much was the number of highly paid officials in that
group. In the period from 1969 to 1975, those earning $20,000 or
more increased by thirteen hundred per cent. The official response
was that these people needed to be offered blandishments, or
private industry and provincial governments would attract them
instead; the days of devotion to duty and acceptance of modest
remuneration were long gone. These people also apparently had
to be housed in expensive office towers with acres of broadloom
and forests of plants, quarters that were a long, long way from

the cubbyholes in the East Block in which the original mandarins had toiled. Furthermore, the system of advancement had changed. Young civil servants weren't marked by their betters as promising and promoted on that basis. Instead, they entered into a fierce competition among themselves for the posted available jobs; they had no loyalty to individual departments, or to their colleagues, only to their own careers. Technocrats were preferred over humanists. The Official Languages Act was demanding functional bilingualism. Francophones were thought to be favoured for advancement and anglophones were suffering a general paranoia. The complaints went on and on.

More important than any of these charges in the mandarinate's eyes was the contention that the "collegial" approach to decision-making had created a shambles, that far from providing good government during the first Trudeau régime, it had slowed down the governmental process disastrously. As an illustration that the system had failed, the older bureaucrats pointed out that the Liberals had been caught without a firm energy policy in place when the OPEC crisis blew up despite the elaborate planning system, that its Information Canada and regional desk exercises as a means of keeping in touch with Outer Canada had proved a farce and been largely abandoned, that ministers were too busy going to committee meetings and administering their departments to keep in touch with their constituencies, and that the "political" advice given the PM by the PMO on the PCO "fact base", far from being a worthy substitute for the ministers' own political instincts, was so bad that the Liberals had almost lost the election of 1972.

The old bureaucrats said Trudeau had never understood the politician-public-servant relationship anyway. The politician, in their view, should know in which general direction he wants to move the country and then seek policies to fit that overall framework. Instead of saying to the public service, "What sort of energy policy should we have in the 1970s?" Trudeau ought to have stated, "We want self-sufficiency in energy — provide me with the policies that will give it to us." The good public servant in their view should never try to usurp the minister's function; he finds out from him the policy direction he wants to move in and then sets out to tailor a policy or a number of alternative policies that would work. The minister, having conceived the general policy, then becomes its defender in the media and in the House of Commons. He has to answer for his views in a democratic forum; if the public doesn't like him they can throw him out of office. The public servant, in turn, is the policy-maker only in the nuts-and-bolts sense; if he's bad at his job, the minister can discharge him. In brief, the ministers should trust their deputies to present the viable options and their own political sense to choose among them; otherwise they are in danger of being bogged down in administrative detail. Trudeau's habit of taking advice in his own office from experts who weren't responsible to a minister and were inexperienced in practical terms wasn't "collegial", efficient, or accountable. It was exclusive and inefficient and it threatened a basic tenet of cabinet government — ministerial responsibility.

The senior deputies had expected that Trudeau would appoint as the Clerk to succeed Robertson someone who understood the old system but would be willing to adapt it — either Gerry Stoner or Basil Robinson or Marshall Crowe, who had left the PCO to become chairman of the Canada Development Corporation and then of the National Energy Board. Instead, the return of Pitfield to the PCO meant, as one of the most senior of the mandarins said bitterly, "the complete abandonment of the old system before the new one has been made to work. It signals bad times for Canada, bad times for the public service, and bad times for Pierre Trudeau."

THE DEPARTMENT that felt most threatened by Pitfield's ascendancy was the department that had the most to lose — Finance, where the team of John Turner as minister and Simon Reisman as deputy had been trying to stave off encroachments on their territory through the sheer force of their personalities and the ancient power of their fiefdom.

Simon Reisman was the eighth deputy minister of Finance since Confederation, the first Jew in a long line of stern-faced WASPs, whose portraits in dark frames hung in the anteroom of the department's new executive offices in the Bell Canada building, floating there eerily under the fluorescent light among the Mies van der Rohe chairs. Reisman had a reputation in Trudeau's Ottawa for being the most outspoken official in town, a man given to cussing, yelling, laughing, and smoking fat cigars. He was famous for dominating any gathering he took part in, fascinating the onlookers with the vitality of his conversation and the vehemence of his disagreements with all who opposed him — from the U.S. Secretary of the Treasury and former Governor of Texas, John Connally, who crossed him once at a meeting in Washington, to Tommy Shoyama, one of his own assistant deputies in Finance, who was as soft-spoken as Reisman was loud. (Once, at a federal-provincial meeting of officials, Reisman got into an escalating argument with a prickly official from the province of Alberta over the question of oil-pricing. Shoyama, ever the diplomat, leaned over to whisper in Reisman's ear that maybe he should take it easy; to the astonishment of everybody in the room, Reisman turned and hollered noisily into Shoyama's tranquil face, "Listen, Tommy, knock it off! When I need your fucking advice, I'll ask for it.")

Without being in the least like the original members of the old mandarinate, Reisman was very much aware of their tradition and very much devoted to it. He had worked under Clifford Clark just after the war when Clark still ran Finance with only a handful of officials whom he called his "helpers". There were some brilliant men among those helpers — John Deutsch, Mitchell Sharp,

Ken Eaton, Doug Fullerton, Claude Isbister, for five. But by common agreement the most brilliant of them all was Robert Bryce, and it was to Bryce's mantle that Reisman had aspired all his working life. Bryce, he once said admiringly, "was a one-man band. He could do everything better than anybody else could do anything." For thirty-five years Bryce had been a towering figure in the capital, a man whose advice was indispensable to prime ministers, cabinet ministers, and public servants alike. Bryce had served in Finance in various roles until he was appointed clerk of the Privy Council in 1953, a job he held until Walter Gordon asked to have him appointed his deputy in Finance in 1963. (Bryce had been unable to leave the PCO in time to help Gordon formulate his first budget and some said this was why it proved unworkable.) There were dozens of stories told about how Bryce had drafted budgets that were models of ingenuity almost single-handed, how Bryce had conducted difficult fiscal negotiations with only the notes that would fit in his back pocket, how Bryce had dug his heels in on this policy or that policy, always urging restraint, usually prevailing when the politicians were on a spending rampage, stepping in to save them from their follies and guide them past their fears. Ottawa remembered that Lord Keynes had admired Bryce for his perspicacity when he was up at Cambridge and that Clark had been respectful of his brains. Ottawa knew that Louis St. Laurent, the public servant's prime minister, had regarded Bryce as the prime minister's public servant.

Many stories were told about Bryce's influence with St. Laurent. Once when Ottawa was involved in negotiating tax rental agreements with the provinces in the late St. Laurent period, Bryce had become deadlocked in a serious disagreement with the then finance minister, Walter Harris. They had argued and argued and then decided to take their disagreement directly to the Prime Minister. It turned out that St. Laurent was in Quebec City, so Bryce and Harris went down to the railway station to await his return, pacing up and down the platform and continuing their discussion. Once St. Laurent got out of his railway car Harris put his case to him right there on the platform, and Bryce repeated his — which St. Laurent had already heard — and the whole matter was settled in minutes, in Bryce's favour of course. Ottawa also remembered what happened when Bryce's advice was *not* heeded. Bryce had begged St. Laurent to prevent Harris from raising the old age pension before the election of 1957 and had watched the subsequent electoral disaster helplessly when the minister was called "Six-Buck" Harris over the increase, which cost him his seat and wrecked his political career.

Bryce had kept Finance supplied with ideas when he was Clerk in the PCO from 1953 to 1963 and had kept track of the PCO when he was deputy in Finance from 1963 to 1970; Bryce had dazzled Diefenbaker and been heeded by Pierre Trudeau. Official Ottawa revered Bob Bryce; he was a hero in its eyes — unobtrusive, bloody-minded, completely confident, always calm, and as unfailingly generous with his respect for his peers' opinions as he was parsimonious with the public purse.

If the style of his successor, Simon Reisman, was very different from Bryce's his aspirations were the same: he wanted to be known as the unchallenged economic adviser to the government. When he was appointed in 1970, it looked as if Reisman might get his wish. Despite the Trudeauites and their belief in countervailing advice, the deputy in Finance was still the number one economic policy-maker in town. Reisman had the confidence of the ministry as a whole and when Turner took on the Finance portfolio in 1972 he figured he had the best minister of the lot as his champion. He had bolstered the department's policy-making proficiency by hiring a number of new officials, including Marshall (Mickey) Cohen, a Toronto tax lawyer, and three academic economists, William Hood, Ed Neufeld, and David Slater. The cabinet committee system infuriated Reisman, but he was generally able to buck its restrictions through his own adroitness and his department's strength. After he had been deputy for several months, official Ottawa started to say, "Well, Bob Bryce may have had his way nine out of ten times, but things have changed. Simon only has his way *eight* out of ten."

But by the spring of 1974 the joke had worn thin. Things really had changed and Reisman felt beset by a myriad of troubles. ("Listen," he would say in response to inquiries about his well-being, "compared to me, Job had it easy.")

First of all, the international economic situation had taken a baffling turn and the old solutions that Bryce had learned at the knees of Keynes and Reisman had learned at the knees of Bryce didn't work any more. Prices were running up everywhere in the world even though anti-inflationary programs were producing recessions and raising unemployment in most capitalist countries, especially in the United States, with whose economy Canada was so closely intertwined. The awkward word "stagflation" had been coined by embarrassed economists when they couldn't explain the Keynesian impossibility of simultaneous inflation and unemployment; now stagflation was being described as "entrenched".

In addition, the Canadian situation had its own peculiar twists. Shared-cost programs worked out with the provinces in the 1960s in the expansionary days of the Pearson government were presenting Ottawa with continuously increasing bills, especially in health and welfare costs, that were alarming in the new economic climate. Trudeau's early promises of social justice had triggered an additional explosion of social programs, which everyone had assumed would be easily borne on new waves of economic growth, waves that were no longer expected with quite so much assurance. New departments had been set up (Regional Economic Expansion, Consumer and Corporate Affairs), old departments expanded (Health and Welfare, Manpower and Immigration), and new ministries of state invented (Urban Affairs and Science and Technology) to realize these goals.

Not only were these proliferating bureaucracies "spending the big bucks", as Reisman said, to achieve the Liberals' expressed political aims, they had also become decision centres, directly challenging the old monolithic power of the Department of Finance. Finance's authority had already been eroded by the Treasury Board, which had been split off from the department and was now a central agency on its own, entrusted with monitoring government expenditures. It had brought in its own high-priced, high-powered economists, under the direction of Douglas Hartle, an adept University of Toronto professor, who had challenged the orthodoxies of Finance's macroeconomics with the new computer-based wizardry of econometrics. The provincial relations section of the PCO was increasingly involved in the economic act too, now that the provinces were becoming more and more obstreperous in their demands, and it had the advantage of a direct advice line to the Prime Minister through the Clerk of the Privy Council. All the ministries whose mandate affected the economy were steadily building their own expertise instead of relying on Finance: Energy, Mines and Resources, for instance, took on its own economists to provide the minister with special advice for a green paper on energy urgently being researched in response to the new oil situation. Not only did Reisman find himself unable to control the economic policy advice being tendered the government; sometimes he didn't even know what that advice was.

As if these accumulating complexities weren't enough to bear, early in 1974 Reisman was also troubled by political pressures. Under attack in the House from the Tories on the charge that the government was profiting from inflation, John Turner, his minister, had decided the previous year to introduce the indexing of personal income tax, which had ''reduced the government's elasticity on revenues'' — i.e., cut back its tax monies just as it needed more. Now Reisman's preference for fiscal conservatism had to be overcome to produce a pre-election expansionary budget — a budget that would eventually be blamed as an important cause of the severe inflation that followed in the closing years of the decade. (Canada alone of the Western countries refused to suffer the consequences of the American recession that year. Reisman said later that it was the cabinet ''big spenders'' led by Marc Lalonde and Al Johnson, his deputy in the Department of Welfare, who were responsible for that budget and that his own minister, Turner, had been unwilling to be painted as a nay-sayer and couldn't resist the concerted pressure for a good-news budget. Still, Reisman was credited with having defeated Lalonde's and Health and Welfare's attempts to introduce a guaranteed annual income by changing the income tax system. At the time he made no public complaints but bent his head to serve his political masters, muttering darkly all the while.)

During the campaign that followed, Simon Reisman suffered the ignominy of being directly, and he felt unfairly, blamed for the government's economic direction. Robert Stanfield, the Conservative leader, said in his speeches on the hustings over and over that, once in office, he would fire the officials in Finance and seek new and better advice. The shame of this was doubly difficult to bear since Reisman knew such a thing had never happened to Bob Bryce; Bryce had really been able to control the country's financial management but had not been singled out for Opposition attack. Now Reisman was being called a powerhouse when he wasn't powerful, a klutz when he wasn't a klutz at all. He was a victim of the times.

Then, in the autumn, after a brief feeling of reprieve when the Liberals won the election in July, Reisman suffered additional affronts that proved too much to bear. Jack Austin, the new principal secretary to the Prime Minister, who had begun convening regular meetings of a group of economists from the private sector to give the PM "additional advice", decided to hire a young government economist, Joel Bell, who had written the nationalist Gray Report, as a full-time adviser in the PMO. Reisman could see Bell turning into the new Ivan Head and his own job diminished the way the under-secretary's in External had been. Turner complained bitterly to Trudeau, but despite reassuring statements from the PM, Reisman figured the writing was on the wall. Even worse, Pitfield was appointed Clerk, a sign that the cabinet committee system with its continuing challenge to Finance's authority would be cranked up once more. Reisman was wild; he noisily declared to his friends that he was quitting the government service at the tender age of fifty-five, and four other senior deputy ministers — James Grandy, Sydney Williams, Herb Balls, and Elgin Armstrong — eventually announced that they would retire early with him at the end of the year.

Rumours flew in Ottawa. There was going to be a deputies' revolt. Bob Bryce was to be brought back from Washington, where he was working for the International Monetary Fund, to mediate the crisis. Gordon Robertson, the retiring Clerk who was staying on in the Privy Council Office to take charge of federal-provincial affairs, would retain the Clerk's traditional function of advising the Prime Minister on public service appointments so that Pitfield wouldn't be involved in personnel work. Only the last rumour proved true. Within months of the announcement of Pitfield's appointment, the last "great men" deputy ministers as Pitfield called them were gone: Ed Ritchie had had a serious heart attack (he later recovered sufficiently to become ambassador to Ireland); Al Johnson was appointed president of the CBC; and Simon Reisman was in the consulting business with his old friend Jim Grandy.

THE UPROAR caused by the departure of so many older deputy ministers didn't affect Michael Pitfield's serene belief in the superiority of his system. He came back to Ottawa in January of 1975 from a term spent teaching and studying at Harvard University to start his job as Clerk, convinced in his own mind that he had been right and would now be proven so. The trouble with the old mandarins was that they had been suffering the pain of their own obsolescence. Government would now be orderly, given the proper will and the proper managers in charge.

In his morning meetings with Trudeau, Pitfield reinforced Trudeau's own belief that economic policy-making had to be expanded beyond the narrow confines of the Department of Finance. (Early in the first Trudeau régime, Walter Gordon had said to the new Prime Minister that he should be careful about upsetting his officials in Finance, that they were the linchpin of the governmental system, and Trudeau replied that Finance had to be upset, its power defused, "Otherwise the minister there would be as powerful as I am.")

The man chosen to replace Reisman was Tommy Shoyama, who was known to be amenable to collegial decision-making and interventionist government, having cut his bureaucratic teeth in the CCF administration of Tommy Douglas in Saskatchewan. (A more likely choice for the job, Al Johnson, who had been the deputy provincial treasurer of Saskatchewan and Douglas's much admired financial wizard before coming to Ottawa in 1964, and then proven himself exceptionally able as an assistant deputy in Finance, the secretary of the Treasury Board, and the deputy minister in Welfare, was seen as too much of a spender to be acceptable to John Turner's connections in the business community. Johnson did not want the job in any case. He had been offered it by Trudeau in 1970 before it was given to Reisman.) Pitfield began attending an ad hoc committee of top economic officials, which was chaired by Shoyama and charged with seeking solutions to what was now, in early 1975, becoming double-digit inflation.

While the officials pondered the options they could present to the ministry, Turner set out across the country to try to persuade industries and unions to practise voluntary wage-and-price restraints. Surely this was government as it was meant to be. Pitfield believed the problems of the economy were in hand. After all, they were modern problems that would yield to Pitfield's modern governmental techniques.

Of course they didn't yield, and what ensued in Pitfield's fateful first year as Clerk was decision-making chaos. The public first realized the extent of this internal governmental turmoil on Thanksgiving night in 1975, when Pierre Trudeau appeared on television wearing his heavy-duty navy-blue crisis suit to tell the populace they were going to have to mend their spendthrift ways and comply with the anti-inflation measures his government meant to impose. The country was experiencing its worst economic difficulties in forty years, he said gravely, and wage-and-price controls were the only solution. The announcement hit the nation like a hurricane; fifteen months before in his winning election campaign Trudeau had insisted wage-and-price controls were not a solution at all.

The roots of this astonishing decision to contradict himself went back several months to May, when Turner's consultation exercises with labour and business floundered and, among the government's economic experts, hopes for voluntary restraints on wages and prices to bring inflation under control were dissipating to the point that even officials in the Department of Finance began to urge Turner to adopt interventionist measures. They had been working on a contingency controls plan in their ad hoc committee and had heeded the advice of a task force housed in the Department of Consumer and Corporate Affairs whose existence went back three years to the shutdown of the Prices and Incomes Commission. When Turner raised in cabinet the possibilities his officials were suggesting to him, he couldn't get support for tough measures from any of his colleagues. They didn't exactly laugh him out of the Privy Council chamber but anti-interventionist feeling still ran strong, particularly with Trudeau.

Chagrined but not yet exasperated, Turner, who was quite naturally worried about what controls would do to his political image, went back to his department and had his officials prepare a let's-not-do-much-at-this-time budget that was brought down in June. It was an obvious diversion that pleased neither the public nor the Department of Finance officials, who felt they weren't being allowed to express their views and at the same time weren't getting direction from cabinet so they could produce alternative programs. All the budget really did was buy the government time and store up trouble down the road. The ad hoc interdepartmental committee of top officials from the economic departments was then given a mandate for the summer: to draft position papers on possible solutions to combat the country's continuing economic difficulties for consideration in September in case the fuse of two-digit inflation was still burning then.

It was still burning on September 8 when the bureaucrats brought their contingency plan document to the cabinet's Priorities and Planning Committee. In appropriate Pitfieldian style, they came bearing options saying in effect that (a) the politicians could continue doing nothing until the inevitable explosion occurred or (b) they could reach for a fire extinguisher in the form of some kind of direct government intervention in the economy: freeze with mandatory controls; freeze, then selective controls; no freeze but selective controls.

In their view fiscal and monetary fine-tuning was no longer effective: direct intervention was necessary. But of course it was for the ministers to decide, in their wisdom and at their leisure. A beginning on the decision-making was to be made at a meeting planned for the following week at Meach Lake; it was both the annual cabinet autumn think-in and the first time the ministers would meet as a committee of the whole after a six-week summer hiatus. No one realized that just two days later John Turner would turn this stylized policy-making process upside down.

All summer long Turner had been stewing. Caught between his colleagues and his ambitions on the one hand (both of them saying controls of any kind were unacceptable) and his conscience and his officials in Finance on the other (both of them saying controls were essential), he had apparently decided his job as finance minister really was intolerable. His discontent went further than his unhappiness with the government's management of the economy. After thirteen years in Ottawa, he had begun to feel that his political career had passed its zenith and that in the current situation he had nowhere to go but down. He decided to express these feelings to Trudeau.

The day was September 10. The scene was Trudeau's elegant Centre Block office. The dramatis personae: two wilful, proud men who'd been open opponents at the leadership convention of 1968 and outwardly amiable but privately mistrustful of each other ever since. Trudeau knew that Turner was thought of everywhere as his obvious successor and that in some factions of the Liberal Party it was hoped that the succession day wouldn't be far in the future. Turner was smarting under long-suppressed anger at Trudeau's indifference to his feelings and inability to give praise, a response to the leader that was not confined to Turner but permeated the cabinet, where by this time bruised egos and buttoned lips among the survivors were the norm.

Turner explained that his position was very difficult and he felt he would have to resign, expecting in his heart of hearts that Trudeau would brush the offer aside, saying that he would use the power of his office to back him on the tough economic decisions ahead or that he would give him another prestige-laden but less damaging portfolio (preferably External Affairs) and that, after all, I won't be here forever and your time will come. Turner had a memory for Liberal history and Liberal myths that was second to no one's, not even Pickersgill's or Coutts's. He knew that this was what King had said to St. Laurent and St. Laurent had said to Pearson and Pearson had said to Trudeau and, frankly, he needed the hype.

Instead, Trudeau, ever the rationalist, chose to think that Turner meant precisely what he said about resigning, murmured that this was all very unfortunate, then offered Turner a place on the Supreme Court bench and, when he saw Turner's face freeze, tendered another blandishment. How about a seat in the Senate? For an ambitious politician of forty-six, with a political following that outweighed Trudeau's own in English Canada, and an unbroken record as a winner, this was like a slap in the face with a gauntlet. Tempers rose, sharp words were exchanged, and at the end of the interview Turner emerged without a job, facing a life crisis, while Trudeau was without a finance minister, facing an economic crisis.

By the time the full cabinet met the next morning in an emergency session, everybody around the table knew that the inflation situation, left smouldering far too long, was about to explode into a political uproar of a kind the Trudeau government had never met before. The October Crisis of 1970 had been an external problem. This was internal. The Liberal Party's most powerful and most visible member next to the PM himself had deserted. Parliament was to meet within a month, the party's own convention would sit in judgment within two months, and the press was baying at the ministers' doors, calling them economic incompetents who were twiddling while the country burned. They had to find a finance minister and they had to conjure up an inflation policy and they had to do both things quickly. And they did, in the Liberal way — which meant mobilizing to save their political skins. The right man answered the party's need, the cabinet rallied to their leader, and they all bit the policy bullet within the course of eight days.

For Trudeau the problem was not so much in selecting the right man for the Finance portfolio as in getting him to comply. Donald Macdonald was the obvious choice from a front bench mostly made up of men who were weak, tired, disenchanted, old, or a combination of all four. Macdonald was a Trudeau supporter from before 1968; he had served him loyally in various taxing roles and was now struggling valiantly with the Energy, Mines and Resources portfolio. He was an anglophone (it was agreed that to follow Turner with a francophone would have been a disaster in English Canada) and no prima donna (he performed extremely well in cabinet committees); he was acceptable to the financial community and had never drawn the distrust from his close colleagues that always clung to Turner's glossy ambition like flies to sticky paper.

The big difficulty was that Macdonald had already stated in public that he was tired of politics and meant to get out before the end of the year. In the several meetings they had over the few days following Turner's resignation, Trudeau reiterated two things: that Macdonald was desperately needed and ought to do his duty but that if he accepted the portfolio he would have to face the need for direct control measures. The irony was clear to both of them: Trudeau and Macdonald had both been more firmly anti-interventionist than the rest of the cabinet, and it had been their opposition that prevented other, more timid ministers from supporting Turner in his tough-measures stance months before.

The prime-ministerial appeal for help which had so rarely been expressed by Trudeau, coupled with the promise of support that had not been forthcoming for Turner, worked its magic on Macdonald. By September 19 he had agreed to take on the job — as one of his daughters nonchalantly told her Rockcliffe Park schoolmates days before the news was announced. In the meantime, the cabinet ministers had met at Meach Lake and talked themselves into believing in interventionism as a political necessity. The Liberal Party line, which only days before had still been "Let the free market do it", was now "The government must step in".

All this time an expanded version of the ad hoc committee of bureaucrats continued conferring. Representatives of various departments who had been attending these meetings in a desultory fashion, leaving the real work to Finance, Treasury Board, and Consumer and Corporate Affairs, were now in constant attendance, and Pitfield — as well as Jim Coutts, who had just arrived in the PMO — turned up regularly to facilitate communications between the committee and the Prime Minister and cabinet.

The permutations of the possible variables, political as well as economic, kept proliferating. The Meach Lake meeting had given the bureaucrats a political strategy direction. It was now up to them to sketch the tactical road map. What Tommy Shoyama wanted was a control system of a classic kind: a six-month, across-the-economy freeze for psychological and political reasons, to be followed by select controls, the apparatus for administering them to be worked out in the breathing-space provided by the freeze. Sylvia Ostry, now deputy minister at Consumer and Corporate Affairs, opposed controls. For her, strategic flexibility was crucial — the most she wanted was stand-by legislation to empower the government to intervene in cases of a clearly unacceptable wage settlement or price increase.

But for the cabinet, controls were in, though a short-term freeze was out because Liberals, though they'll blithely take over NDP ideas, rarely steal Conservative policy, even in desperate need. The directive came straight from the Prime Minister: I recognize the problem, I accept your analysis, but I won't accept a freeze. So design me a program that doesn't involve a temporary freeze or comprehensive controls but will be effective.

The cabinet met in committee and as a whole nearly as often if not as lengthily to receive their proposals and send them back for amendment. Controls were to be long-term — possibly three years — but only to include larger corporations. A new structure would be set up. Space was designated for the Anti-Inflation Secretariat and the Anti-Inflation Board. Jean-Luc Pepin was recruited to head up the Anti-Inflation Board in company with Beryl Plumptre, who had been the highly visible, consumer-champion chairman of the now defunct Food Prices Review Board.

Michael Pitfield wrote to all the deputy ministers in the government and told them they would be required to release anyone in their departments for seconding to the anti-inflation cause on twenty-four hours' notice. The premiers of the provinces were notified during an urgent meeting they were summoned to on Thanksgiving Day. Trudeau's speech to the nation was written, polished, and tested out before delivery with Keith Davey and James Coutts. In brief, the operation had about it all the excitement of the start of a lovely war.

With his eye on the glories of the Liberal past, when the bureaucracy and the party had been so mutually supportive, Jim Coutts started to say optimistically to Michael Pitfield that the inflation crisis would give the public service a new *esprit de corps* and turn the deputies into a close-knit group in the way the Second World War and the reconstruction afterwards had done with the old mandarinate. But the frantic nature of the wages-and-prices-control decision — so far from the stately, rational process Pitfield's system was supposed to produce — presaged something else: a protracted nervous breakdown in the government decision-making system as it affected the economy that was to last for the next several years.

ONE RATIONALIZATION FOR CONTROLS had been that they would provide a breathing-space while the government figured out what to do in the long term. The breathing-space never came. Stagflation continued. Prices climbed ever upwards — though at a somewhat reduced rate — as the consumer price index revealed to a gloomy populace month after month. Unemployment was near to Depression proportions. In the OECD figures comparing per-capita income, Canada — which had once been second only to the United States — had now fallen to eighth on the world scale. The Canadian dollar dropped below ninety cents U.S. in the autumn of 1977 and continued on down, as the international money markets responded to the economy's difficulties: the record strikes and low productivity in the work force and the serious balance-of-payments problem in the nation's current account reflecting and exacerbating the country's long-term reliance on foreign capital.

The way in which the Liberal government sought to deal with these difficulties took on a pattern described by one of the most important public service officials involved as "endless Pitfieldian seminars that sapped the officials' energies and went nowhere, interrupted by crises that blew up in our faces and that were followed in turn by frantic cosmetics meant to cover up the general confusion. It was as though no one was in charge. Finance wasn't — that would have been a regression in Pitfield's eyes. The various deputy ministers' committees couldn't be because there was so little direction given them and so much internal disagreement. The PMO was supposed to be — but the PMO didn't know what it wanted other than to win the coming election. It was a mess."

The next indication of the "mess" came just weeks after controls were imposed when Trudeau gave his famous New Year's Eve television interview saying perhaps the free market wasn't working any more, a remark that sent the business community into high hysteria and the academic community into deep pondering. How come the Prime Minister was talking like John Kenneth

233

Galbraith and leaning towards crypto-socialist liberalism while
Gerald Bouey, the Governor of the Bank of Canada, was sounding
like Milton Friedman and pursuing monetarism, as were all central bankers everywhere? What was going on?

Those questions were still unanswered almost a year later
when the old ad hoc committee of economic officials (now called
DM-10) which had been meeting in the ''endless seminars''
produced *The Way Ahead*, outlining the economic and social directions the government intended to take after controls, a much
criticized and soon forgotten pamphlet written by Ian Stewart, a
PCO official who was now, since Jim Coutts had reorganized the
PMO, the chief economic adviser to Trudeau. The authorship of
this document fell to Stewart mainly because, according to several
of the deputies who took part in the meetings, he was the only
one who understood what Pitfield wanted the group to say — or at
least, said one of them nastily, ''He had to understand, the poor
guy. Pitfield was his boss.'' Two of the most practical and experienced participants in the DM-10 ponderings, both of them trained
economists, Tommy Shoyama and Sylvia Ostry, had opposing
views on many matters but they were in accordance on this one:
an undirected group without a political mandate was an impossible forum for producing practical policy.

The next year Donald Macdonald, who had been valiantly
holding the fort as minister of Finance, decided he couldn't take it
any more and resigned to practise law in Toronto. Trudeau
stubbornly chose Jean Chrétien, who had served as his minister
of Indian and Northern Affairs and as president of the Treasury
Board, to be his successor. It was the fulfilment of a long-held
dream, the appointment of a French Canadian to the most important economic portfolio in the ministry. Trudeau knew the ancient
prejudices in English Canada; he had heard the Ottawa legends
about the token Quebecker who messed up in practical matters.

Among the most famous of these stories was a tale that had
delighted the old mandarinate. During the deliberations of the
famous Rowell-Sirois commission, N. W. Rowell, the English-
Canadian commissioner, had fallen ill, leaving Joseph Sirois, the
French Canadian, in charge. Sandy Skelton, the son of O. D. himself and a brilliant economist employed by the Bank of Canada,

had been charged with helping Sirois finish the report. Every Friday, the story went, Skelton and Sirois would come to an agreement on certain ideas to be included; every weekend Sirois would go home to Quebec, and every Monday he would come back again and renege on the previous week's accord. Finally help was sought from Louis St. Laurent, the commission's legal counsel. St. Laurent discovered that Sirois's priest had ideas of his own on the economy and what the Rowell-Sirois report would mean to Quebec, which he was stuffing into Sirois's head in the confessional on Saturday nights. St. Laurent was then supposed to have gone to see the bishop, who had the priest quietly transferred to another post, and had another, less opinionated, confessor installed; and all went swimmingly thereafter.

Apocryphal or not, this was the archetypal old anglophone story about francophones. That the attitude it expressed no longer held true — that Finance now for instance was desperately seeking qualified French Canadians as assistant deputies in the department — did not matter. Trudeau was determined to redress the old insults, to show once more that Quebeckers could succeed in Ottawa.

"It was a terrible situation for Chrétien to come into," one of the men who worked with him closely in Finance said afterwards. "An election was coming, preparations had to be made for controls to come off, the government deficit was very high, the current account imbalance was worsening and here he was — supposed to produce a miracle, to become a landmark figure in Canadian history. I don't know who could have managed in that situation, French or English Canadian. Certainly Chrétien didn't no matter how hard he tried and that was very hard indeed."

Under pressure to give the economy a fillip for an early summer election in 1978, Chrétien brought down a budget in April. It proposed to compensate the provinces for an across-the-board reduction in their retail sales taxes for six months. This short-term stimulus to the economy would cost the federal government eight hundred million dollars in subsidies to the provinces but would directly affect voters in every province except Alberta, which had no sales tax. Although it earned cautious approval from the financial community in Toronto and in the petroleum industry in the West, the budget precipitated a new round in the

Ottawa-Quebec fight. Jacques Parizeau, the Parti Québécois finance minister, rejected this federal interference in his economic planning and announced his own tax cuts, suspending Quebec's eight-per-cent sales tax on textiles, clothing, shoes, and furniture for a year and permanently removing the sales tax on hotel rooms — measures that were specifically aimed at stimulating industries located mainly in Quebec. This much-publicized fiscal feuding between French Canadians offset the budget's effect in English Canada, took further wind out of the federal Liberals' election sails (which weren't exactly billowing anyway given the polls that spring), and badly damaged Chrétien's reputation, since Parizeau was seen to have bested him at his own game.

A worse blow for Chrétien came that summer, this time dealt by his own leader, the very man who had been so anxious for him to triumph. By the end of the parliamentary session Trudeau was in a petulant mood. He was sick of the contradictory advice on the economy that was swirling around his head. He was sick of being told he had to do something about it before he could win an election. In July he went to West Germany to a world leaders' economic summit meeting and was impressed by the confident arguments put forward by Helmut Schmidt, that country's confident chancellor, to the effect that the indispensable element in controlling inflation was to cut government spending. Trudeau then returned home to deliver a hastily conceived speech on television incorporating the German line, a speech that became famous as his "Canadians-are-fed-up" talk and that prompted the rejoinder, "Yeah, fed up with you."

In Ottawa this spectacle was seen as the ultimate ironic comment on the Trudeau government's decision-making reforms which had preoccupied and so often infuriated the capital's officials for so many years. "It was, as far as we could tell, an impulsive gesture made out of pique and political expedience," said an experienced public servant. "Only Pitfield and Coutts seemed to have known about it in advance. It completely by-passed the consultative process Pitfield and Trudeau had been pushing at us for a decade. It made the French-Canadian finance minister look foolish when he was asked specific questions about the spending cuts and obviously didn't know the answers. It bewildered officials in Finance itself, who were obviously supposed to pick up the pieces.

"Tommy [Shoyama, the deputy minister] was working in his garden when he heard the news. If he had only known in advance he could have at least prepared a framework for the speech; cuts had been considered for months in the department — it wasn't as though Finance was completely ignorant of the Germans' ideas. Anyway a public commitment to restraint on public expenditures had been made at the federal-provincial First Ministers' Conference in February. The August speech didn't make Trudeau look decisive as he and Coutts and Pitfield thought it would; it made him look disoriented. It was a disaster — the antithesis of rational planning, really the antithesis of what Trudeau was supposed to stand for."

One thing the episode left no doubt about was that the old caste was broken; certainly no mandarin was dictating financial policy to the politicians. But at the same time it revealed a demoralized, misdirected senior civil service. Outside the offices of the PMO-PCO the man who had conceived so much of the new system, Michael Pitfield, had few defenders. Because of his close association with Coutts and Trudeau in policy-making, he was seen to have been politicized without becoming practical. "The old mandarins may have been great talkers but they were also admirable doers," one of the deputies said later. "Pitfield had only the first qualification. He was a spinner of beautiful theories but a dreadful administrator. He shut his door and refused to answer his phone when the going got rough. Even those who previously had been fiercely critical of the old mandarins started to long for their strength of character, their ingenuity under stress. What we wouldn't have given for a Bob Bryce in those years. My Lord, thinking about him was enough to make you weep."

The post-Bonn speech was followed by a number of other measures meant to jack up the economy — another budget in November and the establishment of a Board of Economic Development Ministers under the chairmanship of Bob Andras, the president of the Treasury Board, amid much talk of structural changes in the economy and the desperate need for an industrial strategy, which had been discussed without being formulated for most of the decade.

But the government's image of being clownishly inept in the face of the economic challenge of the 1970s was by this time beyond repair. Out in the country, everywhere that known members of the Liberal Party went, they were confronted with the complaints of their business colleagues, their neighbours, and their friends, complaints that made them in turn furious at Trudeau and at Davey, Coutts, and Pitfield, his advisers, who were blamed for the government's economic-policy performance. In the end the Liberals had to call the long-postponed election, vulnerable to their political opponents who were gleefully pointing out that the party's reputation for competence had vanished with the boom. For the first time in fifty years, Liberal times were bad times. The unthinkable had happened. *The Liberals couldn't cope.* This is where they stood then in the desperate spring of 1979 — facing a sullen electorate, with an unhappy, reluctant leader and an embittered party behind him — at what many people were calling the crossroads of modern Liberalism.

PART FIVE

JOHN TURNER, MARC LALONDE, AND THE CRISIS OF LIBERALISM

AFTER THE FORMALITIES of dissolving Parliament had been dealt with on the night of March 26, 1979, Pierre Trudeau appeared on television just before ten o'clock to tell the nation with something less than joyous anticipation that he was calling an election for May 22. Out in the country, most Grits were as startled by this news as the rest of populace. The election had been expected for many months but the party's English-Canadian stalwarts had thought that the Prime Minister, having waited so long, would wait a few weeks longer and set the date for early July "when the corn is high", as Jerry Grafstein, the Toronto lawyer, put it — the reasoning being that by early summer the economy might be on the upturn and the weather, and the public mood along with it, would have improved.

Liberals everywhere knew the party was in trouble. The press had been grinding the government for two years, summing up its ineptitudes, listing the scandals and near-scandals its members had perpetrated, making much of every candidate who had defected during the long period of waiting for the election call. When party adherents were asked in the bleak winter preceding the election's call to analyse the causes of the Liberals' difficulties, almost to a man they would begin by citing the decision in 1975 of John Turner, the former Minister of Finance, to abandon politics for the practice of corporate law.

It wasn't that the Grits all loved John; he had vociferous critics in the party as well as ardent admirers. It was just that as a collective, Liberals recognized his symbolic importance. For years, Turner had epitomized in his person the alliance for power that had held the party together for as long as most of them could remember. Sitting in his elegant law office on the thirty-eighth floor of the Royal Bank Tower in downtown Toronto that winter — sitting there in the diffused golden light with the pale velvet broadloom under his polished shoes and the portrait of Sir Wilfrid Laurier behind his handsome silver head — Turner knew this too. Everywhere he went — in the boardrooms of the major corporations where he held directorships, in the expensive clamour of Winston's restaurant at noon, on the tennis courts at the Queen's Club, even in the elevators of downtown towers and in the line-ups at airport check-in counters, people kept coming up to Turner to tell him, their eyes alive with longing, that if only he would become the prime minister — as though all it took was an act of will — then *everything* (i.e., the economy, the federation, the whole body politic) would be set to rights. Turner would always deal with these earnest entreaties, no matter how often he heard them, with a flash of empathetic charm, that blend of smiling modesty and deep confidence in the listener's judgment that made him the perfect political man. He was the prince-in-exile, the once and future contender for the Liberal crown.

Turner had grown up in the old Liberal establishment's midst and almost everything he had done in his life had fitted that establishment's mores. His mother, Phyllis Gregory Turner, had been a miner's daughter from Rossland, B.C., who had the brains and gumption to study economics and political science at the University of British Columbia in the 1920s. Her academic prowess won her a fellowship for post-graduate study at Bryn Mawr College in the United States and a further fellowship to the London School of Economics. In England she had married a journalist, Leonard Turner, and they had two children, Brenda and John. After her husband died in 1931, when John was two, she then brought the children to Ottawa to raise them alone on a government economist's salary, working first for Hector MacKinnon at the Tariff Board and then during the Second World War as the oil-and-fats administrator of the Wartime Prices and Trade Board under the formidable Donald Gordon.

Turner always resented the widespread idea that he had been born rich. "What my mother was able to give me," he liked to say, "was a good education [at Ashbury College, an Ottawa private school Turner attended until he was twelve, and St. Patrick's College, a Roman Catholic secondary school] and a real sense of the excitement of public service." When John was five, the Turner family had a summer cottage next to Mike and Maryon Pearson's place at Kirk's Ferry in the Gatineau Hills, and when he was a pre-adolescent during the early years of the war, he used to wake up in bed at night and hear important public figures of the day, people like C. D. Howe and Robert Fowler, arguing and laughing with his mother in the living room. Sometimes when he was out walking his dog in the Ottawa twilight, he would encounter Mackenzie King with his own dog, Pat. "No guff," he said later, when describing this childhood experience. "The old guy himself! In the flesh!" (As an adult Turner had two modes of talking — a precise officialese that was tailor-made for meetings with bureaucrats or businessmen and a gutsy, slangy rat-a-tat-tat manner he used on political platforms or in private conversations. He could move from one to the other with a facility that often left his listeners startled. One minute he would be sitting stiff as a magistrate in a dark-blue suit, discussing "an inflationary period when what must be avoided at all costs is an attack on the fiscus," and the next he would be waving his arms, flashing his eyes, and talking like a ski pro.)

Phyllis Turner was remembered in Ottawa as a glamorous woman, both formidably intelligent and formidably ambitious. ("Sort of early Women's Lib," Turner said zestily in describing her after the women's movement became fashionable. "You dig?") She demanded excellence of her son and excellence is what she got. By the time she remarried in 1945 and moved on to become a powerful figure in British Columbia society as the wife of the Vancouver industrialist Frank Ross, Turner was sixteen and ready for college. He spent four febrile years at the University of British Columbia as a student of political science, fraternity man, track-and-field star, sports-writer on the student paper, and jive-talking big man on campus. ("Hey there, snappy pair of kicks, who ya' featurin' tonight?" he was supposed to have said to another undergraduate when he was trying to find out the name of his date for a dance.) When he won a Rhodes Scholarship in 1949, the student paper sent him on his way with an editorial that said he had been the most popular student on the campus.

At Oxford, he studied jurisprudence and civil law. Years later a fellow student who became a senior public servant remembered that Turner was "never brilliant but he was a social and academic success by dint of unflagging effort. He always seemed to be filled with some kind of terrible dread of doing or saying the wrong thing. He would turn up in my rooms for lunch every month or so and we would spend a couple of amiable hours together. But after he went into public life, I tried to recall what he stood for and it might have been anything for all I could remember — plus-fours-for-golf or build-a-causeway-to-Calais. He just wouldn't say anything he thought might offend. It was as if his eye was on the future and the great career that was expected of him even then.''

From Oxford Turner went on to Paris for a year to improve his French, and then returned to Canada, first to read law and then to practise in Montreal with the firm of Stikeman, Elliott. For much of the next decade while he learned his profession he was the very model of a socially acceptable bachelor, the sexiest thing on the squash courts, the handsomest man at the balls, escorting the prettiest and most eligible girls, belonging to the Junior Bar of Quebec, of which he eventually became president, and getting himself into the headlines in 1958 as the man who danced with Princess Margaret at a party given in her honour by his stepfather, Frank Ross, who was then lieutenant-governor of British Columbia. For the next eighteen months, British and Canadian papers tried hard to turn this into a romance, reporting that Margaret had ''summoned Turner to her table'' at later parties on her Canadian tour, that he was ''a secret caller at Clarence House'', and even that he was the subject of ''formal discussions with the Queen''. He *was* the only non-official Canadian guest invited to her wedding and the whole Margaret episode, which Turner remembered as ''a lotta fun — a real gas, you know what I mean?'' gave him a glittery air when he went to the Liberals' Kingston Conference in 1960 to present a careful paper on legal aid. After that, he was marked by senior Liberals as a ''comer'' — Phyllis Ross's boy grown into an impressive young man — and asked to the party's 1961 policy convention. A year later, he was talked into contesting the Liberal nomination in the Montreal riding of St. Lawrence–St. George during one long lunch at the Reform Club. In the eyes of Keith Davey he was the very model of a new Liberal, handsome, articulate, and progressive.

Turner reinforced this view by running a model campaign in the 1962 election. His supporters always used it as a starting-point when they were contrasting his experience in the Liberal Party with Pierre Trudeau's. The nomination was a five-way fight, which Turner won on the first ballot, and the election that followed was a tough one against Egan Chambers, the capable incumbent Tory. Turner drew his workers from a non-partisan crowd, all the bright young English-speaking Montrealers from his own milieu, and they proved so good at political organizing that the candidate was able to turn out a crowd of ten thousand for a rally at Peel and Sherbrooke streets when Lester Pearson came to town. The campaign went by in a blur of debates, apartment blitzes, stylish liberalism, pretty girls, outdoor parties, striped marquees, balloons, and vigour, and ended, of course, in victory. Turner was re-elected in March the following year, fully expecting that Pearson would make him a member of his new government's cabinet. But in Ottawa Turner soon found out that while the newspapermen and the voters might have been dazzled by him, the professional governors were wary. The attitudes that had been endearing in a young lawyer were thought to be pushy in a freshman MP. In the capital's grey corridors, all that glittered was suspect.

"I had a rough time," Turner remembered. "Mr. Pearson had this sort of avuncular attitude towards me. He had known me nearly all my life and he felt I was too impatient, that I needed to understand the administrative process, to be in what he called 'the kitchen of government' for a while. It turned out to be a big plus." For five years Turner served an apprenticeship to power, as a backbencher, a parliamentary secretary, a minister without portfolio with "special responsibilities" to Jack Pickersgill, then briefly as registrar general, and finally as a full-fledged minister in the new portfolio of consumer and corporate affairs, a post he was given in 1967 in the same cabinet shuffle that saw Pierre Trudeau become the minister of justice.

"If Turner had been nothing more than the pretty boy the backbiters said he was," Keith Davey said later, "he would have buckled in the early sixties. But he didn't buckle. He learned. How to be a politician. How to roll and punch and roll again. How to be a winner." And, it might be added, how to build a power base within the Liberal Party.

Turner became familiar with the party regulars in those years through travelling the country constantly, speaking at riding association gatherings, in church halls, and at by-election rallies, fund-raising dinners, and nomination meetings. No favour was too big to ask of him. No crowd too small for him to address. ("I mean, so you only get eight guys out to a union hall in Northern Ontario in a snowstorm — what the hell, you can turn it into something good and they never forget you, those eight guys, and they've all got wives and mothers and buddies. That's a lotta votes.") Turner liked to quote admiringly a remark he had heard made about Nelson Rockefeller, the former governor of New York and vice-president of the United States, that he stepped into a room full of people as though it were a warm bath. Through his own ardour for the minor political arts, Turner quickly built a solid party network that stuck with him when he was a contender at the 1968 leadership convention. "That convention was the last glimpse anybody ever had of the young John Turner," said John de B. Payne, a Montreal public relations man, Liberal Party stalwart, and for many years Turner's grey eminence. "It was a crucible. He saw how the deals were made, how power is traded. It was a toughening experience."

It was also an experience that created a certain coolness between Turner and Trudeau, although no one in either man's entourage admitted this for years. It was Turner who lost the most when Trudeau decided to run for the leadership a month after Turner himself declared. He lost his appeal as the youth candidate, he lost support he had counted on in Quebec, and he lost the old Liberal establishment vote, which he had hoped would be his. When Turner went to see Lester Pearson to sound out his reaction to his candidature, Pearson told him that he wasn't going to throw his support to anyone, that Turner wouldn't win in any case, but that a well-run race would put him in line for the next time, and furthermore that he should try to cultivate the calmness of maturity to go with his energy and drive — advice that was not exactly what Turner wanted to hear but that was given with a great deal of avuncular warmth, from an old careerist to a young one. What Turner gained from the 1968 convention was a reputation as a fighter and a certain grudging respect from the Trudeauites when, refusing to release his delegates, he had hung on tight-lipped until the last ballot, which saw him come third after Trudeau and Robert Winters.

"The PM knew that Turner held on only to show that his power base was firm. If he had thrown his votes to Trudeau, it wouldn't have been such a cliffhanger. Trudeau resented this at the time and he never forgot it," said a public servant who worked closely with both men. "There was always an underlying mistrust between them from that day on."

Ten years after the convention Turner could still recite the precise number of votes the candidates had won on each of the four ballots and speculate how it might have gone differently if only certain people had delivered to him the delegates they had promised on the first or second ballots. But, at the time, he quickly submerged his disappointment, and when Trudeau appointed him minister of justice in his first cabinet he was determined to turn the department into a place where he could take a tough public stand, consolidating his position in the party and burnishing his reputation in the country at the same time. He was acutely conscious of the difficulty of following in the footsteps of Trudeau, who had used the justice department to superb effect, and he decided to become a zealous and genuine reformer on his own account. He announced that he would revamp the old pork-barrel system of appointing judges, and set up a complicated process for reforming and reviewing the law on a continuing basis, and he instructed his department to prepare several solid bills on bail and arrest, expropriation, wire-tapping, and legal aid, the main thrust of which, he was at pains to point out in the many speeches he gave on law reform, was to balance the citizen's rights against those of the state.

His energetic behaviour and his increasing visibility in the press and at meetings of the English-Canadian wing of the party brought out the carpers. "I tell you," one backbencher told a journalist in 1971, "this guy has been programmed to be Prime Minister since he was twelve. If he figures the smart politics of the moment calls for a reformer, then a reformer is what he'll be. I once said to him that people would like him better if he would be more spontaneous and he looked at me with those blazing blue eyes and I got the feeling he was going to punch out 'Be more spontaneous' on a piece of cardboard and feed it into a slot in his gorgeous middle."

Turner turned aside the carping and went right on building

his reputation inside and outside the party. He was popular in the House of Commons and observed its rules punctiliously. He was scrupulously courteous to the lawyers and judges his job required him to meet. ("I'm talking about thirty thousand legal eagles, kid, and they all know me.") He cultivated supporters in the cabinet, especially Ron Basford, the Minister of Consumer and Corporate Affairs from British Columbia, who had been active in his leadership campaign in 1968, and James Richardson, the Minister of Supply and Services from Manitoba, whose affiliations added strength to his own connections in the West. He talked on a systematic basis to the Liberals who belonged to his 195 Club, named after the number of delegates who had voted for him on the last ballot at the leadership convention; they were his hard-core supporters. He had always been judicious in his choice of executive assistants, hiring the brightest young men he could find. David Smith and Jerry Grafstein from Toronto, Lloyd Axworthy from Winnipeg, Irwin Cotler from Montreal, and Dick Hayes, Michael Hunter, and John Swift from Vancouver worked for him during his decade as a minister. Every one of them, other than Cotler — who as a reform-minded lawyer had a strong base in the Jewish communities in Montreal and Toronto — was a prominent Liberal with his own wide connections in the party network.

Most mornings before his working day began, Turner was in contact by telephone with people in law firms and corporations across the country to find out "what the boys are thinking". He had the precise memory all good pols cultivate. Seemingly without effort he could start off a conversation, even with people he hadn't expected to meet, by bringing up some detail of the last time he and his listener had talked together, a practice that proclaimed, "I care about your opinions, your problems, your solutions. You're my kind of guy." Even if the listener was sophisticated enough to suspect this behaviour was part of a cultivated technique, he was very often charmed all the same. Turner was just so adept at every-thing he tried, so much the model man that ambitious careerists of the seventies were meant to emulate, that he seemed too good to be true.

At the same time as he was building his great career, he was able to maintain an enviable family life. His wife, whom he had met when she worked on his 1962 campaign, was the daughter of David Kilgour, the president of the Great-West Life Assurance Company in Winnipeg, and if ever a model man had a model wife, Geills Turner was it. She was good-looking, athletic, well-connected, well-educated, and quick-witted. She had done post-graduate studies at Harvard and had worked in Montreal as a financial analyst. But after her marriage she devoted herself to Turner's career, learning the intricacies of the political process, sitting in the House of Commons' gallery during question periods, keeping up with policy directions and political manoeuvring, while bearing four children in quick succession and running an impeccable Rockcliffe household at the same time. The Turners were stars on the Liberal circuit, beautiful people with dazzling smiles.

In short, during his first decade in politics, Turner seemed to do everything right. His method was to work feverishly on all fronts, covering all contingencies, cultivating all connections, and never getting into trouble. He survived the October Crisis of 1970 with his reputation intact despite the fact that his was the department directly concerned with imposing the War Measures Act, and the Public Order Act that followed it. When he was constantly bombarded in the House of Commons by Opposition questions, he stood up to the attack well, attempting to make himself seem sympathetic to those who were concerned with the curtailment of basic liberties implicit in the legislation, while gravely insisting on its inevitability at the same time. Had the nation itself been less in favour of the government's Draconian actions during the FLQ crisis, Turner might have been attacked more vigorously, but at the time his deftness was generally admired.

In commenting on this skill, Brian Mulroney, the Montreal lawyer and one of the Conservative Party's most important organizers in Quebec, said in wonderment not long before the 1972 campaign, "Turner's so smooth, he's never made a mistake anybody can pin on him. He's the Liberal dream in motion." What Mulroney didn't know — and neither did anyone else — was that the Liberal dream would soon go awry, and with it, John Turner's political career.

AS THE CRISIS OF LIBERALISM DEEPENED in the 1970s, thoughtful Grits — and John Turner numbered himself among them — began to reflect on Liberal history, sifting through the myths that were part of the party's folk memory in the hope that they might uncover palliatives to ease their discontents. The party's roots were traceable to the pre-Confederation era, when politicians in the British North American colonies could be divided roughly into two main groupings: conservatives who wanted to preserve the English oligarchic system along with their own privileges as its chief beneficiaries, and reformists who were pressing for a more egalitarian society in which they would have a fairer share of the wealth and a greater voice in government.

What late-twentieth-century Liberals chose to remember of their early-nineteenth-century forerunners was their adherence to the reform side of the political balance scales. But the truth about the party's antecedents was more complex than that. There were many political splinter parties in the two groupings, with the Tories and their frequent allies from French Canada, *les Bleus*, usually ranged on one side of issues, and Brownites, Liberals, Clear Grits, *les Rouges*, and William Lyon Mackenzie — the rebel of 1837 back from exile in the United States and now forming his own party of one — on the other. In the years leading up to Confederation these splinter parties divided, combined, and divided again and again over the thorny questions involved in forming the new dominion, crossing the conservative/reform boundary lines frequently.

John A. Macdonald, Canada's first prime minister, was of course an avowed Conservative, but the group he led at the time of Confederation was a coalition which took in politicians from both the conservative and reform groups, plus a variety of "loose fish", local politicians from the various regions who were ready to combine with whoever offered them and their supporters the best deals in tariffs and patronage, roads and railways.

The chief opposition to Macdonald came from two recalcitrant reform groups: *les Rouges* of Lower Canada, a group of French-speaking radicals whose chief target was the Roman Catholic Church, and the Clear Grits, originally an assemblage of discontented Presbyterian and Methodist farmers from the area southwest of Toronto that George Brown, a bloody-minded radical newspaperman who had immigrated to Upper Canada from Scotland and founded the Toronto *Globe*, was able to weld into the main element of his post-Confederation reform alliance. (The Clear Grits had been named after the kind of first-grade sand the Scottish stonemasons of Upper Canada liked to use in making mortar. One of the pre-Confederation reform leaders, David Christie, was reported to have said that he wanted the reform movement to attract only followers who were "clear grit". The Grits disappeared as an entity in the 1870s, but the term clung to Liberals and was still widely used a century later — admiringly by Grits themselves and pejoratively by Tories — especially in country places in the Maritimes and Ontario, where memories for party affiliations were long and partisanship was bitter.) Both Grits and *Rouges* had a republican strain in their ideologies, but at first they were unable to unite successfully because of religious and racial antipathies. Gradually, over the Confederation and post-Confederation period, taking in allies from the Maritimes, they drew together and began to use the word liberal as a synonym for reform. Alexander Mackenzie, a Scottish stonemason who had been Brown's faithful friend and advocate for many years, became the first Liberal prime minister, suffering through four difficult years in office until the voters turfed him out in 1878 and brought Sir John A. back again. Mackenzie was replaced by Edward Blake, a Toronto lawyer who directed the party doggedly but unsuccessfully from 1880 to 1887, the only federal Liberal Party leader in Canadian history never to become prime minister.

When they got into late-night discussions over drinks about the party's glorious past, modern Grits gave Mackenzie and Blake scant attention. "Liberals are leery of losers," Gordon Dryden, the Toronto lawyer, often said sagaciously. Instead, they preferred to focus on Sir Wilfrid Laurier as the real founder of their party. Laurier was an attractive man, an elegantly handsome lawyer from a Quebec country town, eloquent, ambitious, and sensitive. Early in his political life, as one of the young leaders of *les Rouges*, he had realized that, if his confrères were ever to gain office, they would have to form an alliance with the English and at the same time soften their anticlerical image by identifying themselves with a political program acceptable to the Roman Catholic Church.

Laurier proselytized that these goals could be reached through stressing the liberalism of his party, demanding the separation of religion and politics, and at the same time denying its old republican and anticlerical dogmas. What he was saying to both races was that *les Rouges* could take a moderate approach compatible with the philosophy of Mackenzie and Blake. He emphasized compromise and admiration for the liberal reform ideals that were then being articulated by William Gladstone in England and that were to have a hold on the imaginations of Canadian Liberals for decades to come. Laurier's wonderful voice and serene exterior soothed the bigots and excited the practical among the English-speaking reformers in Canada, and his views were instrumental in the accommodation reached between the Grits and *les Rouges*. But even so, when he was chosen leader by the Liberal caucus in 1887, it was less because the party really wanted him than because his predecessor, Edward Blake, insisted he was the man the party needed.

Laurier's successes during his four terms as prime minister from 1896 to 1911 taught the Liberals several of their most enduring truths, including the pre-eminent one — the importance of reaching and maintaining an accommodation between the French and the English. They realized he was able to win the 1896 election because the Tories had lost sight of this basic fact of the Canadian federation. Sir John A. Macdonald's own great coalition which kept the Tories in power for most of the first thirty years of Canada's history had been destroyed. The Tories had lost the support of many of *les Bleus*, the Quebeckers who had originally combined with Macdonald's group, for two main reasons: in 1885 the Tories had hanged Louis Riel, the rebellious French-speaking Métis leader, turning him into a racial martyr, and they had condoned the Manitoba School Act of 1890, which contravened the French-language rights agreed to in the incorporation of Manitoba into Confederation. When the Tories fell to fighting among themselves in a prolonged succession crisis that saw four men in as many years attempt to fill Sir John A.'s shoes as prime minister following his death in 1891, their support in the rest of the country began to soften, and without their Quebec base they floundered. Taking as his own Macdonald's old role as conciliator between the founding races, Laurier swept into office in 1896, promoting racial accommodation all the way.

For Liberals, the lessons of Laurier's leadership went far beyond the French-English entente. He buried dogmatism, abandoning the ideological rigidities that had plagued *les Rouges* and the Clear Grits. He built his electoral strength on the organizational backs of Liberal provincial premiers, Oliver Mowat of Ontario, William Stevens Fielding of Nova Scotia, and Andrew George Blair of New Brunswick, whom he brought into his cabinet as power-brokers for their regions. He embarked on the building of a second transcontinental railroad and sought support from the business community, modifying his party's commitment to free trade in order to propitiate the country's new industrialists. He supported the aggressive, open-immigration policy of his minister of the interior, Sir Clifford Sifton, whose purpose was the settlement of the West, and he talked optimistically about the glorious future of Canada.

Laurier's successes were turned into precepts the Liberals followed for decades. But his failures became fixed in the Liberal folk wisdom as well. By returning to the old Clear Grit nostrum of reciprocity with the United States as a cure for the young Dominion's economic woes towards the end of his fourth term as prime minister, he alienated his business support and lost the election of 1911. That disaster was recounted often afterwards in order to remind Liberals that any move to continentalism needed to be approached cautiously and disguised in patriotic rhetoric to be acceptable to the electorate.

Despite the unpopularity in Quebec of his decision to send Canadian troops to aid the Empire in the Boer War, and his naval bill of 1910, which committed Canada to building ships that could be placed at the disposal of the Royal Navy — both actions that cost him crucial support in his home province in that same election of 1911 — Laurier on the whole skilfully walked the French-English tightrope throughout his years in office, balancing French

Canada's racial fears and English Canada's imperialist passions. When he was out of power during the First World War, his skill at managing the accommodation between the founding peoples faltered. By 1917, when he himself was old, sick, and suffering from the vicissitudes of six years in opposition, the Liberal Party nearly destroyed itself over the racially charged issue of military conscription. That year the Military Service Act was brought in by Sir Robert Borden's Conservative-Nationalist coalition to ensure the availability of fresh troops to fight with the British in the Great War which had been raging for three years and had already cost tens of thousands of Canadian lives. Military conscription was anathema in Quebec, and Laurier had no choice but to oppose it. One by one, English-Canadian Liberals deserted him to support conscription and Borden was able to attract enough of them to form a Union Government.

One of Laurier's former ministers, William Lyon Mackenzie King — wily Willy as he was to prove himself during the course of his long and illustrious life in politics — viewed this schism with dismay. King was the grandson of the "little rebel" of Upper Canada, William Lyon Mackenzie, the most colourful of the pre-Confederation reformists, and from childhood he had felt himself destined for a great career. Isabel Grace Mackenzie King, his sappy sainted mother, drove him on to glory in order to vindicate her own disappointments with the other men in her life, her father and her husband. King's ineffectual, debt-ridden father, John King, was a Liberal lawyer from Berlin, Ontario, who moved his young family to Toronto in the vain hope of bettering his prospects; he always counselled young Willy to get in with the best social set wherever he found himself to ensure his rise in the world, and as a young man, King did just as father urged, ingratiating himself with the rich and powerful at home and abroad. The elder Kings were model parents for a political leader. Their thwarted hopes and sad manipulations created in their eldest offspring just the right neuroses every megalomaniacal man of destiny must possess.

In 1900, with three university degrees behind his name, including an M.A. in economics from Harvard, King had arrived in Ottawa to join the Department of Labour as a civil servant working under his Liberal patron, Sir William Mulock, an old family friend. King was able and hard-working even though he was ridden with angst and ambition. Shall I marry or burn? Shall I devote myself to public service or move on to greater things? Does Sir Wilfrid love me or does he not? These were the anguished questions he addressed privately in the pages of his remarkable diary. In public, he was all efficiency, rapidly becoming his department's deputy minister and accumulating some impressive successes as a negotiator in labour disputes in the process. But the bureaucracy was to prove only a way station on the road to his real destiny as a politician.

After much persistence in seeking a suitable seat, he was finally elected to the House of Commons from North Waterloo in 1908 and appointed minister of labour by Laurier, who seems to have found him exasperating and at the same time useful. In a prophecy dazzling in its understatement, Laurier told King, "You will take a great part from the start. You have the instinct for politics." After this splendid beginning, King to his dismay lost his seat in the election debacle of 1911 and spent the next few years viewing the party from outside Parliament, working as a labour negotiator for the Rockefeller family in the United States and experiencing great frustration at being out of the political mainstream for part of that time.

Whether he was at the centre or the periphery of Canadian politics, King in those years of his young adulthood and early middle age was busily absorbing the important lessons of Laurier's political life, among them the disastrous effects of internal dissent on a party's prospects. During the conscription crisis of the First World War, he skilfully concocted one of the many schemes of his long career that by its ingenious ambiguity made him appear to be on both sides of an issue at once. In the 1917 election, he managed to decline Laurier's invitations to stump the country on his behalf over the contentious conscription issue, though, as a good Grit, he firmly rejected the Unionist call and ran under the Liberal banner in the Ontario riding of North York — reiterating his loyalty to his leader while standing four-square at the same time for vigorous pursuit of the war effort.

Two years later, in 1919, King won the Liberal leadership

with the support of four-fifths of the Quebec delegates to the convention, most of them French Canadians who couldn't tolerate W. S. Fielding, King's chief rival and the ex-minister of finance, because he had deserted Laurier over conscription. They saw Fielding as a traitor and King as a loyalist, particularly after he made a fervent speech eulogizing Laurier the night before the balloting. These Quebec votes were the decisive factor in King's victory, the factor he never forgot.

The party King inherited was unhappy and faction-ridden. It had been reduced in the election of 1917 to the status of a French-Canadian rump: of the eighty-two seats the Liberals held in Parliament, sixty-two were from Quebec. Racial bitterness between Laurier Liberals and the Liberal Unionists who had gone over to Borden still festered. Western Liberals who favoured free trade resented Eastern Liberals of both races because they were seen as favouring high tariffs. Farmers in Ontario and the Prairies, many of whom had been traditionally Liberal, were in revolt against party politics in any form and were trying to form their own movement.

It was King's mission to build a political alliance out of these unlikely elements and he set out to do so with a sureness of purpose and a shrewdness of instinct about the nature of Canada unmatched by any other politician of his own or any other time. Without him and his single-minded vision, it is possible the Liberal Party might have disappeared as an entity in the 1920s and become one with the Tories on the right side of the political spectrum, with a farmer-labour alliance on the left. King's task took many years and many twists of fate to accomplish, but before he was through he had created the modern Liberal Party, a shifting coalition of as many of the country's interest groups as he could charm, coerce, bribe, or otherwise bend to his purposes.

He turned the Liberal partnership between French and English, initiated by Laurier, into an explicit and inviolable alliance. As an Ontario Presbyterian, he knew very little about Quebec. "I don't think you could ever say Mackenzie King really understood the aspirations of French Canadians," Jack Pickersgill said later. "Knowing Laurier gave him a kind of insight into French Canada. He could read French and speak a little bit. But French civilization had no particular appeal to him; it was just that he understood the French Canadians' place in Canada. No one was grounded in the myths of Canadian history the way King was. Going back a hundred years his family had been intimately associated with those myths.''

In the early stages of his leadership, King found managing the province of Quebec a thorny problem. He had to contend not only with his own fractious Quebec caucus but with the power of the provincial government under Premier L. A. Taschereau, with the political influence of the Roman Catholic Church, and with the economic suasion of the protectionist elements in the Montreal business community. But King soon made common cause with a Quebecker who suited him both ideologically and temperamentally, Ernest Lapointe, the member for Quebec East, who was first his minister of marine and fisheries and later his minister of justice. Over the years, Lapointe evolved into a Quebec lieutenant on whose judgment in matters affecting French Canada King could rely implicitly.

King gave Lapointe real power in cabinet, beyond that of any other regional representative, made him a trusted confidant outside cabinet, and saw in him "the most loyal and truest of [all my] colleagues and friends''. When Lapointe died in 1941, King went to great lengths to make sure the best replacement for him was found, finally selecting Louis St. Laurent and then treating his opinions with the same respect he had accorded Lapointe's — though his affection for him was of a different order.

Not content to lead a centrist party, King sought alliances in the West almost from the time he took office in 1921. "I want the West to think I'm its friend," he wrote to his brother. He diligently wooed members of the Progressives, the agrarian reform movement formed by the prairie farmers who had bolted the Liberal Party in disgust. He paid close heed to the advice of Charles Dunning and J. G. Gardiner, provincial Liberal leaders in Saskatchewan, and to J. W. Dafoe, editor of the *Winnipeg Free Press*, recognizing his power as a Liberal force in Manitoba and to a lesser degree throughout the West. Eventually, Dunning, Gardiner, and T. A. Crerar, one of the Progressives' leaders and a former Liberal who had been a minister in Borden's Unionist government, joined his federal cabinet. King brought in stalwarts from other regions as well, Ian Mackenzie from British Columbia and J. L. Ralston and J. L. Ilsley from the Maritimes among them, taking care to give their views the respect they were due — the more votes a stalwart could command, the more respect he was given.

This carefully spun web of connections formed the basis of King's electoral support: he wanted to be able to count on Quebec, important pockets of Western Canada, the traditional Liberal areas of the Maritimes, and the old Clear Grit vote in southwestern Ontario. He was never sure of support in the rest of Ontario, and Tory Toronto was his despair.

The business communities in both that city and Montreal disliked him personally, but he cultivated an entente with them over the decades through wooing such leading figures in the financial world as Sir Lomer Gouin, the former premier of Quebec and a favourite of Montreal businessmen, whom he brought into his first cabinet; Herbert Marler, a Montrealer with extensive business interests who was made a minister without portfolio shortly before the election of 1925; Vincent Massey, the liberal scion of the aggressive Toronto farm-implement manufacturing family whom King rewarded for his efforts on behalf of the party with appointments first in the Canadian legation in Washington and later in the Canadian High Commission in London, where, as chief of the delegation, Massey was able at last to satisfy his Anglomania; Charles Dunning, who went from prairie politics into the pulp-and-paper industry and then became King's minister of finance in 1935; and in later years C. D. Howe, the engineer from Port Arthur whom the Liberals sought out eagerly as a candidate for the 1935 election because of his widely known reputation for vigorously surmounting obstacles and his popularity with businessmen.

At the same time as he was cultivating business, King continued to see himself as a friend of labour. His early successes as a negotiator between management and labour left him with the lifelong view that he himself would be a better minister of labour than anybody he could appoint to that post in his various cabinets. He often undertook personal consultations with union leaders and he recognized the value of the *Toronto Daily Star* in holding the labour vote in central Ontario, and cultivated the paper assiduously.

It was usually forgotten by Liberals later but when he was elected leader in 1919, King was seen as a progressive young man because of his relative youth (he was forty-four) compared to his grey-beard opponents, and because of his thinking on industrial relations as outlined in his book *Industry and Humanity*, published the year before. At that leadership convention, he wrote for the party platform a boldly progressive statement on social security. *Realpolitik* kept him from realizing the ideas contained in that platform for many years, but he continued to regard himself as a reformer and was crafty enough to try systematically to head off any threat from the left, such as that posed by the farmers' movements of the 1920s and the Co-operative Commonwealth Federation, the social democratic party founded in 1933. He did this by talking a convoluted language of social reform when necessary and, if actually pressed to the wall, introducing social legislation he thought appropriate and acceptable to the other factions in his alliance. It was King who established the foundations of the Canadian social security system — old age pensions in the 1920s, a form of unemployment insurance in the 1930s, and family allowances in the 1940s — that have allowed Liberals ever since to boast about being a reform party.

In brief, King dealt with Canada as though it were what the political theorists call a "consociational democracy" — a federation of regions and special interests held together at the centre by an alliance of its various elites. King was far from beloved or charismatic as a politician. He lost his own seat several times and under his leadership the Liberals were often unpopular. (In 1943 the Liberals registered lower on the Gallup poll — only twenty-eight per cent of the decided voters were pro-Liberal — than at any time in the next thirty-five years, though in 1958 and again in 1976 they fell to twenty-nine per cent.)

The Tories were always infuriated by the King myth; they felt he was not so much a brilliant politician as a conniving and above all a lucky one. Certainly King was lucky in his Tory opponents. In his lifetime the Conservatives never really recovered from their folly in choosing the arch-imperialist Arthur Meighen to succeed Borden, thereby consolidating Quebec's animosity to their party. After King destroyed Meighen, they continued to pick leaders — R. B. Bennett, R. J. Manion, John Bracken, and George Drew — who by ineptitude or ill fortune alienated important segments of English Canada as well. King was also lucky in his timing. He managed to lead a party that was out of office during the worst years of the Depression and in office during the best years of the boom. He was a superbly able wartime leader, keeping his fractious alliance going by invoking God and country in public and the ghosts of his mother and his mentor, Sir Wilfrid, in private.

How much of his success was due to luck and how much to cunning will probably always be debated in Canada. What's beyond debate is that King had a formula for success — conciliate and conquer — which he clung to tenaciously and which suited the Canadian situation and the Canadian temperament of the time. The formula kept the Liberal Party in power for all but five years from 1921 to 1957, twenty-two years under King himself and nine more under Louis St. Laurent, who inherited his alliance.

What Louis St. Laurent added to King's formula was the famous Liberal gloss — that aura made up of equal parts competence and arrogance — an addition that was to prove a mixed blessing. All the elites loved "Uncle Louis". The business community worked easily and happily with him. He was a corporation lawyer, after all, who had gained his reputation as a legal counsellor to American investors in the pulp-and-paper industry. This made him very much their kind of prime minister. His cabinet was dominated by men who had important business connections, C. D. Howe, Douglas Abbott, James Sinclair, and Walter Harris. His bureaucrats were entranced by him. Even the press and the academics were respectful. But despite the huge majorities the party achieved under his leadership in the boom-time elections of 1949 and 1953, St. Laurent's taste for electoral politics, never very strong, grew weaker in office. He paid far too much heed to his bureaucrats and to the least politically astute members of his cabinet, especially C. D. Howe, whose political judgment King had always questioned. Eventually the electorate was alienated — not so much by Louis St. Laurent himself as by his government's propensity for conducting the country's affairs as though

Canada were a corporation and it was an all-knowing board of directors charged with "maximizing" its profit picture. Nobody ever said of Uncle Louis, as they had of Mackenzie King, that he was "a crazy little s.o.b.". But then nobody ever accused King of thinking he was entitled to power by virtue of belonging to the "government party". In commenting on Liberal arrogance, A. G. S. Griffin, a Toronto businessman who had been a member of the Wartime Prices and Trade Board and later of the Department of External Affairs in the 1940s, once wrote, "It is a curious phenomenon of Canadian political life, this predisposition to insolence and disdain . . . which the Liberal party can't seem to avoid, a sickness which requires only an electoral victory to get it started. . . . Where does it come from? Mackenzie King? Oddly, although I think it does, he himself never contracted it — like a 'carrier' he only bestowed it on his disciples. He himself continually warned them about neglecting the grass roots."

His own contemporaries laughed at King. They knew him as a "fussy old fart", as one of them inelegantly described him, an eccentric who loved his mother and his dogs more than he was ever able to love anybody else, a seemingly puritanical bachelor who engaged in odd practices — consorting with and trying to reform prostitutes in his youth, and communing with spirits from the nether world in his maturity through ouija boards and batty spiritualists in three countries who acted as his mediums. But latter-day Liberals recognized that King had defined, refined, and codified into a kind of holy writ the basic tenets of Canadian Liberalism.

Unity within the party — which meant keeping Quebec happy — was his first goal. Only through Liberal unity could Canadian unity be achieved because the Liberal Party was the only truly national party. Therefore, for a Liberal to be disloyal to the party or its leader was tantamount to treason. Divisive issues were to be avoided, and all policies — including those affecting international affairs — were judged first in terms of their viability on the hustings. Strong ministers were chosen, because it was expected they would have coat-tails in their own regions, and, once in place, ministers were allowed considerable power in running their own departments and their own fiefdoms. Liberals were clearly

distinct from Tories in King's view. The Liberals belonged to the
party devoted to social egalitarianism; they were the inheritors of
the reform tradition. The Tories were the party of the big interests
and hence the enemy.

That King himself loved the company of the rich and powerful
didn't seem to trouble him. He was much sought after as an employee by two of the great marauding American capitalists, John
D. Rockefeller and Andrew Carnegie. He courted big business
carefully in Canada and accepted donations from rich friends that
gave him creature comforts (holidays in Bermuda, the means to
refurbish the house in Ottawa he had inherited from Lady Laurier,
a handsome retirement fund for himself). He was distinctly non-
egalitarian in his treatment of those of his social inferiors unfortunate enough to work for him. None of these ambiguities
seemed strange to him. As a Christian idealist who believed in
democratic capitalism, his view was that business and labour had
to be partners, social equality could be achieved by the conciliation
of the interests of the rich and the poor, and the Liberals were the
party to accomplish this feat. The socialists couldn't do it because
they believed in confrontation rather than conciliation — and only
conciliation would work in a country as diverse as Canada.

King really believed, as he wrote to his brother, that "Destiny
[intended me] to carry on the fight which grandfather commenced
so bravely on behalf of the common people in their struggle against
autocratic power." He was, as his biographer MacGregor Dawson
put it, "an opportunist with principles" — which was the way
most English-Canadian Liberals who followed after him liked to
think of themselves.

No one ever wrote King's political maxims down in a little
red book for Grits; instead they were passed from Liberal to Liberal
after his death in a tribalistic oral tradition. The chief interpreter
of King's ideas was Jack Pickersgill, who had laboured loyally
in his service, but other younger Liberals — particularly Gordon
Dryden, Jerry Grafstein, Jim Coutts, and Tom Axworthy, a
political scientist from Winnipeg who came to work in the PMO
as a policy adviser in 1975 — knew the King maxims intimately
and quoted them frequently.

None of them was any more devoted to Liberal orthodoxy

than John Turner, who had absorbed it in his childhood. When Turner formally became a Liberal in 1962, it was the party of King and St. Laurent — the "know-how" party, as Grattan O'Leary liked to call it — with which he was allying himself. Throughout his early career, it was the King–St. Laurent mode of governing Canada through an alliance of its elites that was always the basis of Turner's political thinking.

It didn't become evident until after the 1972 election that the party Turner thought he belonged to — the party he had grown up with and joined — really did not exist any more. In the great crisis of Liberalism in the 1970s it seemed that Turner was not the harbinger of a new Liberal era of prosperity as his supporters hoped; he was the reflection of an old one — a perfectly preserved specimen of the King–St. Laurent Liberal born twenty years too late.

III

THE OLD LIBERAL ALLIANCE had really begun to crumble before Lester Pearson took office. "It was like a Roman wall," Michael Pitfield once remarked. "You only realized how well it had been built in the first place when you saw it in ruins." Pearson's engaging personality and conciliatory style helped disguise the basic fact that the alliance couldn't be easily repaired and so did the number of Liberals left over from the St. Laurent régime who were influential in his cabinet, particularly Pickersgill, Chevrier, and Martin, who stood by their leader during the dark years in opposition, as well as Mitchell Sharp and Bud Drury, who had been bureaucrats under St. Laurent and became Liberal ministers in 1963.

But Pearson's prime energies as party leader were necessarily expended on Quebec, and while he was engrossed in the arduous pursuit of the ever-elusive solution to the province's discontents, two other vital bases of the King–St. Laurent Liberal alliance were eroding: the West and the business community.

Western discontents with the federal government were already rumbling in the 1950s; the rage shown at C. D. Howe during the 1957 campaign was a public reflection of them. But Walter Gordon's centralization of the federal party apparatus at its Ottawa headquarters in the 1960s caused a direct confrontation with Liberals in the West at a time when Diefenbaker's visceral appeal to regional hatred of central Canada was at its zenith. Gordon became the personification of Toronto's power over the hinterland. If there was anything Westerners hated it was the kind of easy eastern superiority his pin-striped suits and imperturbable manner represented in their minds. From the outset Western Liberals were sure that his ideas about managerial efficiency would undermine the historical prerogatives of their provincial party barons. Their model was Jimmy Gardiner, the Minister of Agriculture under King and St. Laurent, dispensing patronage, and sometimes justice, to his supporters on selected Saturday mornings in a suite upstairs in the hotel on the main street of Melville, Saskatchewan, and looking after Western interests in Ottawa the rest of the time. This was the kind of messy politicking that didn't fit into an efficiency chart, and Gordon's misunderstanding of it infuriated Gardiner's political heirs.

It didn't help much when Gordon sent Keith Davey, who was even more of a Toronto man than he was, into the West in the early sixties to recruit new adherents for the party and to soothe the feelings of old loyalists. Gordon and Davey had already made their fateful decision to concentrate their limited resources of financial and organizational power on holding Quebec and making gains in the cities of Ontario and British Columbia. This was where their social reform policies could be most effectively communicated by mass media advertising. This was where their polling showed the message would be most warmly received.

What the polling couldn't show was how angry this scheme would make Ross Thatcher, the Liberal leader in Saskatchewan, the Western province with the best record of electing Liberals provincially and federally. When Davey moseyed into Thatcher's territory seeking a new Saskatchewan provincial chairman to be part of his central campaign committee, they had a meeting that became a classic tale in the Liberal anecdotal repertoire.

Davey had been advised to confer with Thatcher out of courtesy on his choice of chairman, and he was relieved when the Westerner responded unctuously to his preliminary remarks by saying, "Well, I can get along with any Liberal in the province." But when Davey went on with his prepared speech, adding that he and Mr. Gordon had been thinking about appointing to the job Otto Lang, a young law professor at the University of Saskatchewan, Thatcher shot back furiously, "Except that son of a bitch!" Long before he met Davey, Thatcher had been angry at the federal Liberals because they hadn't responded well to his request for financial support in his first election campaign against Tommy Douglas in 1960. Now he felt his chances of overthrowing the socialists in Regina were going to be diminished by the leftist ideas that were emanating from Pearson's office in Ottawa.

Later, when Gordon's economic nationalism was revealed in the first Pearson régime, other Western Liberals began to agree with Thatcher, though few of them were as vehement in their dislike of Gordon and Davey as he was. The Westerners were reacting to the passing of an era. Part of Mackenzie King's formula for holding the West had been to try to make sure that the irreconcilable differences between the free-trading Westerners and the protectionist central Canadian Liberals were blurred. But with Gordon in the Department of Finance, clouding the issue was impossible.

What was less predictable than Western rage at the Liberals — and what turned into one of the ironies of the Pearson period — was that Gordon, the offspring of the Toronto business establishment, should prove a prime cause of the alienation between the Liberal Party and big business that marked the 1960s and 1970s. Gordon's program to restrict the inflow of American capital and reverse the pattern of direct foreign ownership in the most advanced sectors of the economy threatened to change the shape of Canadian continental capitalism. The reaction of business to this prospect was vicious, even in the sheltered industries of banking and publishing. Businessmen recognized Gordon as the most dangerous kind of enemy — the enemy within — responding much as American businessmen had reacted in the 1930s to Franklin Delano Roosevelt's New Deal.

From the time of Laurier until the advent of Gordon, Liberal leaders had sought accommodations with businessmen, though they were consistently more successful in Montreal than in Toronto. To overcome the radical anti-establishment reputation of the old reform alliance, Laurier had wooed what the historian Donald Creighton called ''the new plutocracy'' — the emerging bourgeoisie of the century's first boom, made up of bankers, engineers, corporation lawyers, railway-builders, mining promoters, pulp-and-paper producers, and public-utility men. But in 1911 he lost their support along with the election because of his adoption of reciprocity as his platform, and the traditional alliance of businessmen with the Conservative Party was reinforced. Over the next quarter-century, as successive Conservative leaders bungled their stewardships, business began to question the federal Tories' capabilities and to look favourably on the Liberal Party. King's continuing efforts to ingratiate himself with business paid off in 1935, thanks to R. B. Bennett's extraordinary last-minute effort to save his government by putting forward the proposals for social relief generally known as Bennett's New Deal, proposals that sounded suspiciously socialistic in businessmen's ears. While Bennett was behaving so uncharacteristically, King was busy recruiting C. D. Howe and convincing businessmen of his belief, as the historian J. L. Granatstein has described it, that the role of government was "to keep taxes low, to reduce government spending to the minimum, and to facilitate the flow of trade within the country and abroad". Big business showered the Liberals with donations in that election, apparently accepting the Liberal Party's campaign slogan "King or chaos". From that time on, younger businessmen in Toronto and the West were increasingly comfortable with what had become "the Government Party". As a result of their experience with government during and after the Second World War, they formed a cosy alliance with the Liberals through cabinet ministers who belonged to their generation and consulted them respectfully before major policy changes were introduced.

The Grits still managed to brand the Tories with the reputation of being the party of Bay Street, and their task was made easier by the fact that many members of the older generation of Toronto businessmen — the fathers and uncles of the dollar-a-year men — remained staunch Conservatives. Walter Gordon's father, for instance, switched parties to vote Liberal for the first time in his life when his son ran for election in 1962. The Colonel was then eighty-eight years old and, like most of the businessmen he talked to downtown, was so appalled by the populism and inefficiencies of John Diefenbaker that he was able to look with favour on Lester Pearson, expecting that when he came to power the old St. Laurent efficiency in government would be restored.

Reassured by the presence in Liberal ranks of such reliable figures as Bruce Matthews, the president of Excelsior Life, John Connolly, the Ottawa lawyer and Liberal Party president, and William Wilder, the young vice-president of Wood, Gundy, the most important securities firm in the country, businessmen were more than willing to come to the Liberals' aid financially in order to turn Diefenbaker out of office. Even J. A. "Bud" McDougald, the doyen of the old Toronto Club business clique, undertook to raise money for Pearson. "Of course, that was before I found out

he was pink,'' McDougald told an interviewer in 1974, only to
have his wife, ''Jimmy'', lean forward to contradict him. ''You
know he wasn't just pink, Bud,'' she said querulously from
the depth of a pink chaise longue. ''He was *red!*'' What Mrs.
McDougald was expressing hyperbolically was the business community's rage at having been fooled into believing in Pearson in
the first place. They were angered, once Pearson got into office,
not just by Gordon's economic nationalism but by the general
left-liberal policies of the government, which had been articulated
first by Tom Kent and Maurice Lamontagne and had attracted to
the party a new political type in English Canada: a group of well-
educated, progressively inclined, upwardly mobile professionals
who called themselves small-l liberals, people like Edgar Benson,
Mark MacGuigan, Herb Gray, Jerry Grafstein, Ian Wahn, and
Allen Linden in Ontario, Richard Cashin and Ed Roberts in
Newfoundland, and the Axworthy brothers, Tom and Lloyd, in
Manitoba.

After Gordon lost his hold on the party in 1965, the old
guard attempted to reassert itself through the competent and persistent pressure of Sharp, Drury, and Robert Winters, who had
become president of Rio Algom Mines after 1957, when he was
defeated, until his re-election in 1965, when he came back into
the cabinet expecting to restore single-handedly the old intimacy
between big business and government by turning himself into the
new C. D. Howe. Pearson dealt with the party's increasingly obvious left-right schisms by doing what James Eayrs, the political
scientist, called his ''sunny-side up'' act, mediating, flattering,
and procrastinating his way from crisis to crisis.

John Turner straddled the two camps, cultivating contacts
among younger left Liberals while maintaining his bona fides as a
promising young man with the older men on the right. He had
won the nomination in St. Lawrence–St. George in 1962 as a
proponent of the new politics and remained a friend of Keith
Davey's, though he was always wary of Walter Gordon. He had
connections in the West among the old Dafoe-style Liberals, connections in the Vancouver business elite, and in English Montreal,
and he knew how to talk like a progressive, a free-trader, a
reformer, and a capitalist all at once. In the early Trudeau years,

he was able to continue this King-like balancing act. In this ambivalence, Turner was the reincarnation of the old-style Liberal conciliator. But as the Trudeau years wore on, the question of what Liberalism stood for began to be asked in all segments of society with an increasing urgency, and Turner got caught on the question's horns.

Although Trudeau had come to power with an unsettling left-wing image, the fears of business had been relieved at first by the continuing eclipse of Walter Gordon and by the comforting presence in Trudeau's first cabinet of Mitchell Sharp and Bud Drury. In 1969, Edgar Benson, Trudeau's first minister of finance, disturbed businessmen both big and small with his White Paper on tax reforms, but after a prolonged storm of hysterical protest and many months of high-priced lobbying, most of the proposals were softened. Later Benson was eased into the defence department and then left politics altogether to become chairman of the Canadian Transport Commission. When Turner followed him into Finance in 1972, it was generally believed that the business community would be mollified. They were being given the most important English-speaking minister to deal with the economy, a man they liked and could trust.

Turner had qualms about accepting the portfolio; it had been the graveyard of many an ambitious politician's hopes. The economic and political climate turned the job into a far worse ordeal than he had feared. In the period from 1972 to 1974, he was caught between the business community, which was suffering paroxysms of fear owing to Nixonomics and the OPEC crisis, and the PMO, which was deeply engaged in its appeasement of the NDP. Turner had been weaned on the old Liberal notion that social legislation was admirable as long as the economy could bear it — the Liberalism of the balanced budget. Now he had to work desperately to try to stave off plans for a guaranteed annual income taking shape under the aegis of Marc Lalonde and his deputy, Al Johnson, in the Department of Health and Welfare without appearing reactionary; to listen to a cacophony of complaints from businessmen about government overspending at the same time; and to try to continue to pay his dues to the party according to the sacred Liberal precept of unquestioning solidarity with the Leader.

Turner was able to make it known throughout this ordeal that he was unshakably loyal. When Keith Davey, who had been his friend for years, spoke to Turner in early 1973 about his own decision to seek the job of campaign co-chairman for Trudeau, he told Turner he realized that if Trudeau won the next election, this might mean that Turner would never be prime minister. Turner set his handsome jaw into its man-of-destiny position and told Davey that he had to do it anyway, for the sake of the team, and that he in turn meant to give his all to the party. And no minister did more to ensure the Liberal victory in 1974 than Turner. In that election he was running for the third time in the Ottawa riding of Carleton, his old seat in Montreal having disappeared through redistribution, and because of the superior organization he had in place, he was able to travel the country tirelessly on the party's behalf. Turner would get up on platforms night after night throughout Ontario and the West and make speeches for local Liberal candidates, and the audiences would palpitate with excitement. Liberals began to say Turner was not just loyal, he was heroic.

But after that election Turner found it increasingly difficult to maintain the heroism. Both his personal ambitions and the kind of Liberalism he believed in were approaching a crisis. In the election's aftermath, Turner's mother, Phyllis Ross, was having lunch with him at Le Cercle Universitaire in Ottawa when she spied Senator Grattan O'Leary, who had been an acquaintance of hers for years. "Grattan," she asked him plaintively, after they finished discussing the election's outcome, "what are we going to *do*? This man [Pierre Trudeau] is staying far too long. If he doesn't go soon, John will never be prime minister." She was articulating, much to O'Leary's amusement, what all Ottawa was saying *sotto voce* — that Trudeau had shrewdly cornered Turner, his one important rival for support among the party faithful, in the unenviable portfolio of finance, and it was turning into a trap from which there was no escape.

By the time Turner had endured another year as Trudeau's minister of finance after the 1974 election, a year that brought the resignation of Simon Reisman as his deputy, the failure of the attempt to talk business and labour into voluntary restraints in order to hold back inflation, and the prospect of wage-and-price controls, he had had enough. He was a proud man and much sought after. For thirteen years he had seen himself as the Liberal dauphin; he had been called one of the best cabinet ministers in Canadian history and the most ardent Grit of his generation, and when he went to Trudeau's office to offer his resignation in September 1975, it was almost as though he was trying to force Trudeau into a recognition of what he stood for in the annals of Liberalism. When Trudeau refused him that recognition and accepted his resignation, it caused a furor throughout English Canada. Bruce Hutchison, the newspaperman, protégé of John Dafoe, biographer of Mackenzie King, and the old Liberalism's most lyrical voice, told Turner that by this act Trudeau showed he didn't understand the nature of the Canadian duality.

The truth was, of course, that Trudeau understood the nature of the duality very well and had set out to alter it radically ten years before. In that mission, he had benefited from the zealous support of a politician who had been born in the same year as John Turner, was a citizen of the same country and a member of the same party, but was a world apart from him in demeanour and philosophy, a man who represented the new Liberalism in much the same way that Turner represented the old. His name was Marc Lalonde.

WHEN JOHN TURNER was a little boy in Ottawa in the 1930s, setting off for Ashbury College in his blazer and his knee-pants to be trained in the ways of the Canadian ruling caste, Marc Lalonde was a little boy on Ile Perrot, a farming community southwest of Montreal, setting off for the local one-room school to be trained for a life on the land. The Lalondes had lived in the same district and farmed the same acreage "forever" as he said, which meant for at least five generations, herding cattle, growing feed, harvesting the sugar bush season after season, and his brothers were expected to follow in their ancestors' footsteps. But Marc was different. He was clever, perhaps brilliant, the only one of his contemporaries to finish primary school in a community where most children dropped out after the fourth grade to help on the farms.

It was decided when he was twelve that he should be allowed to do something no one else in his family had ever managed — to leave Ile Perrot and study at a classical college at Ville St. Laurent run by the Fathers of the Holy Cross, who were less fashionable than the Jesuits and more populist in their outlook. When he got there, young Marc was terribly lonely among the town boys who seemed to him sophisticated. He had never played tennis or baseball the way the other boys had. They were the children of the bourgeoisie. They even talked in a different way. He was tall and ungainly, and to compound his woes, his mother had bought him knickers to wear when everybody else was in long pants. School life was hard and rigorously religious. Up at 5:45, mass at 6:15, seven days a week. Holidays centred on the religious festivals: All Saints' Day, Christmas, Easter, St. Jean-Baptiste Day. Summer on the farm. Work. Study. Pray.

As compensation for his awkwardness and his loneliness, Lalonde made sure he was the best student in his class. He did so well he was advanced a grade, and then stood first again. He became involved with the college's theatre group, playing leading roles in Molière comedies. The priests approved of him, and when he was in his middle teens he became very involved in Jeunesse Etudiante Catholique, the youth arm of L'Action Catholique, a movement begun in the 1930s, whose philosophical basis lay in the reformist encyclicals of Pope Pius XI and their interpretation for the French-speaking world by Emmanuel Mounier and Jacques Maritain. What it preached was stark and affecting: to be a Christian was to make a social commitment; the true Catholic must involve himself with the things of this world. It had a slogan: *Voir, juger, agir.* Define a problem, judge it on a Christian basis, act on that judgment. The slogan was to guide Lalonde's whole life. L'Action Catholique attracted a number of remarkable Quebeckers in the late 1930s and 1940s, including Gérard Pelletier, Claude Ryan, and Pierre Juneau, as well as Marc Lalonde.

As a student, he knew little about the world outside Quebec. His parents were *bleu*, voting provincially for the Conservatives and then the Union Nationale. His teacher-priests read only *Le Devoir*, and Henri Bourassa, the paper's founding editor, was a far larger figure in their students' lives than Mackenzie King or even Ernest Lapointe, whose names were rarely mentioned. The Second World War raged in Europe; it was largely ignored. L'Action Catholique taught that party politics was a carbuncle on society; it was society as a whole that had to be changed first and governments would then adjust to the new social order. Duplessis was a superficial element. St. Laurent was a nice old gentleman, a good Catholic, and when he became prime minister, everyone said, better to have him than the English, and that was that.

When Lalonde left the college laden with academic honours in the spring of 1950 he was twenty years old and uncertain about what to do next. He knew he wanted to be some kind of *animateur social*, so he took a stopgap job working for Jeunesse Etudiante Catholique, which meant living in a *jéciste* house in downtown Montreal and organizing for L'Action Catholique in schools and classical colleges for fifteen dollars a week. He was asked to serve at the same time as the executive secretary of the Canadian Association of Youth Movements. His new life was a revelation. He began to travel outside Quebec for the first time, to meet English Canadians as well as Europeans and Americans, and to engage in political discussion, mostly about world affairs. The international youth rallies he was invited to attend were a cold war phenomenon, anti-communist in their inspiration, mostly financed by the U.S. government under the Marshall Plan or indirectly through the budget of the Central Intelligence Agency. There was a fervour about these gatherings that suited Lalonde's nature, but after two years he decided he must pursue a definite career.

He hesitated about choosing between doing post-graduate work in the social sciences and studying law. He sought the advice of Gérard Pelletier, who had been secretary-general himself of Jeunesse Etudiante Catholique ten years earlier and was sympathetic to Lalonde's involvement with personalism, since it was a movement that had had a deep effect on him and on Trudeau. Pelletier sent him to see Trudeau, who was just winding up his job in the PCO in Ottawa. Trudeau told him that he should choose the law; it would give him a specific career and a stricter intellectual discipline. Lalonde enrolled at the Université de Montréal and over the next three years he was politicized. He had been reading *Cité libre* since its inception, and Trudeau's writing particularly aroused him against Duplessis. He spent a summer working on a study of ''Politics and Christian Involvement'' in collaboration with a young sociologist named Maurice Pinard. He spent another summer in the combines branch of the federal justice department in Ottawa, and yet another in India on a World University Service seminar, where he encountered the horrendous poverty of the third world for the first time. All these experiences led him to believe that the state was important, despite the teachings of the Holy Cross priests, and that the true Christian had to be involved in its direction.

His law professors disapproved. You have a brilliant future, Lalonde, they told him. Don't spoil it by getting yourself entangled in politics. That's for the opportunists, petty men looking for petty gratifications. Lalonde didn't believe them. Only in the province of Quebec was politics for the petty; in other places the most intelligent were involved. Mounier was writing in *Esprit* that a Catholic could rise above politics and at the same time accept an active political role in order to counter communism and existentialism. He won a Rotary Club scholarship to Oxford and he set out to get a degree in Modern Greats (philosophy, politics, and economics), "working like a horse" as he described it to overcome his problems with English. He had married a girl he had met at the Université de Montréal, Claire Tétreau, a sweetly shy young woman, pretty as a flower, given to nodding while he talked. After he finished his Oxford degree, his old university in Montreal offered him a teaching job at $5000 a year, and he took it, having decided he didn't want to practise "*la loi du bumper*", the petty law open to French Canadians of his class.

The next year, Davie Fulton, the Minister of Justice in Diefenbaker's government, was looking for a French-speaking assistant and one of his neighbours on Clemow Avenue in Ottawa, Douglas Fullerton, an ADM in the Department of Finance, mentioned having met this bright young Quebecker named Lalonde at a conference. Lalonde was interviewed for a job with Fulton on the same day as Michael Pitfield and they both came to Ottawa to work in 1959, eager to learn and ambitious to succeed. They admired Fulton with his lofty attitudes and his beautiful manners. They learned some important lessons about the government process by observing his cabinet preparations and his relationship with his bureaucrats; they learned some hard politics by watching his assistant from British Columbia, Ian Pyper, who knew his way around the Conservative Party. They competed intellectually, sparking ideas from each other's experience. They were an unlikely duo, very different men from very different milieus and their friendship was oddly touching.

At night, they took courses in administrative law together at the Université d'Ottawa towards a *diplôme d'études supérieures*. In June of 1960, when they went to the degree-granting ceremony held by the university, Davie Fulton was sitting on the platform waiting to accept an honorary doctorate. Pitfield and Lalonde hadn't told him about their studies and when they stepped forward to be handed their diplomas, the minister's jaw dropped in astonishment. Where had they found the time and the energy?

Before the ceremony, Michael Pitfield's mother, Grace Pitfield, had given a lunch in honour of the two young men to celebrate their accomplishments. Sitting regally at the head of a table in the Bytown Inn, she talked to the assembled party. About

her old friends, Georges and Pauline Vanier, the viceregal couple
ensconced now at Government House. Did Mr. Lalonde know
them? No, alas. About the changes she had seen in Quebec in her
lifetime. About her fears for the future since Duplessis's death
the year before. Nothing was the same any more. McGill, where
she served on the board of governors, was being attacked by
Quebec nationalists who resented its dominant academic position,
its Englishness. The city of Montreal was encroaching on her land.
The Pitfields and their friends used to be able to ride for miles
through open country from the stables at Saraguay. Now Saraguay
was surrounded — surrounded by the developers, by the Jews, by
the French Canadians . . . Where would it all end? She talked on
and on, chanting the litany that the English in Quebec were to
recite again and again in the years to come. Lalonde sat across the
table, his face impervious, watching her.

He was always watchful in those days. *Voir, juger, agir.* "I
come from a long line of Norman farmers," he would say, in
arguing with Pitfield over some esoteric theory. "It's like being
from Missouri. You've got to show me." There was something
very old in his attitude although he was barely thirty. Smiling the
wonderful smile that so often wreathed his big face, making it
almost beatific, he exuded paternalism, as though he felt responsible
for the people he came into contact with, a responsibility based
on a knowledge superior to theirs.

During the eighteen months he spent in Fulton's office,
Lalonde cast off forever any residual ideas from his early education about the banality of politics. Political involvement was crucial if change was to be effected. He admired Fulton but was
appalled by Diefenbaker and by the calibre of the French-Canadian
Conservatives who had come to Ottawa in the sweep of 1958.
"That was a tragedy for the Conservative Party," he said later.
"Dief went to Duplessis and more or less said, 'Give me your
slate.' Duplessis gave him a number of old cronies he didn't want
himself. What a missed opportunity! It could have made Quebec
a two-party province federally."

Later, when Lalonde became a Liberal, snide comments were
made that he was a turncoat, interested in power rather than ideology. The truth was something different. Lalonde was never a

Tory, or, for that matter, a Grit. But he was profoundly involved with an ideology, his own rendering of the ideology of personalism. To put it to work he reached the conclusion that he had to join a party that had federal power. He toyed briefly with the Conservatives, but he knew the Liberal Party was the only practical possibility, proving once more the truth of Frank Underhill's succinct statement, "Quebec politicians have never been either Liberal or Conservative. They have always been simply and wholeheartedly French."

When Lalonde formally became a Liberal in 1966, it was with a specific purpose: he wanted to see a French Canadian succeed Lester Pearson as Liberal leader. He had been practising law in Montreal since leaving Fulton's office in 1960, coming up to Ottawa regularly to work on royal commissions and government inquiries — the Norris commission on Great Lakes shipping, the Carter commission on taxation, and the Fowler commission on broadcasting — and eventually to work as an adviser in Pearson's office. By now he was deeply involved in the politics of the Quiet Revolution, having worked for the provincial Liberals in 1962. But when the Lesage Liberals began to pander to nationalistic feelings in Quebec, Lalonde threw his lot in with federalism. He joined the board of *Cité libre* and put together the study group that produced the Manifesto of 1964, which he signed along with Trudeau and five others.

Trudeau had been influencing his thinking for years. They had both come into contact through their post-graduate studies abroad with the intoxicating ideas then prevalent in the Western world that peace and progress could be brought about by the new internationalism. They were both ardent Catholics, drawn to the ideas of personalism, though Trudeau was always much more private about his religious responses than Lalonde was. They both despised parochialism of any kind, the attitude which in Quebec showed itself in nationalist rhetoric and parish-priest hostility to the disturbing threats of the outside world. They shared the opinion that French Canadians had to "come out of the wigwam" and "abandon the euphoria of all-embracing ideologies", as Trudeau put it, to be pragmatic about taking part in Canadian society.

Pragmatic is what Lalonde became, pragmatic some said to

the point of ruthlessness. He was meeting regularly with the new-guard Quebeckers in Pearson's government, Marchand, Pelletier, and Trudeau, plus Maurice Sauvé, Maurice Lamontagne, and Jean-Pierre Goyer, to discuss both separatism and the Liberal leadership succession. In Lalonde's mind, Trudeau was the man for the job from the beginning and in retrospect it almost looked as though Lalonde had willed him to it, encouraging him to run for Parliament in the first place in 1965, figuring out the master plan in his leadership race, pressuring Pearson to help Trudeau, overcoming as many of the obstacles in Trudeau's path as he possibly could. After Trudeau became prime minister and Lalonde was serving as his principal secretary, a man who worked for him in the PMO said, "The more I watch them together, the more I have the uncanny feeling that everybody has it wrong. Trudeau didn't choose Lalonde to be his alter ego, Lalonde chose Trudeau. It was as if Lalonde, out of all that seeing, judging, and acting he'd done, all those endless conversations he held with Pitfield in the early sixties, constructed the perfect model government for a bilingual federal Christian democratic state and put in place the guy who seemed the perfect model leader."

In the end, who chose whom really didn't matter: Lalonde's interests melded with Trudeau's like Bismarck's with the Kaiser's. In many ways, Lalonde was the embodiment of all the hard-headed, hard-working, pious farmers in Trudeau's ancestry. The Lalonde farm was only thirty miles, as the crow flies, from the land the Trudeaus worked, the place where the young Pierre went for holidays with his grandmother and his cousins. Lalonde's pietism seemed to strike an important chord with Trudeau, though his relationship with him was nevertheless very different from Marchand's and Pelletier's. The three older men were comrades-in-arms, and in the worst vicissitudes of the Trudeau era, when one or other of them was in personal difficulty, they expressed a tenderness for each other that was palpable, the result of a long friendship between equals.

Trudeau's wealth, his education, his ease in English, his sophistication, had made him the obvious front man for the Quebec federalists' purposes, the leader who could match the English at their own games. Lalonde himself expressed his feelings about

The Liberal Alliance of the Seventies

Grits gambolled in the garden at 24 Sussex Drive during a victory celebration in July 1974 when a new Liberal alliance was formed between the remaining Pearsonians and the surviving Trudeauites.

The Reigning Heroes

On the night in June 1975 when Turner presented his last budget as Trudeau's finance minister, the alliance still held. Three months later, Turner resigned and the Liberal Party's traumatic years began.

The Lasting Influence

CP Photo

CP Photo

Lalonde met the press with Turner in 1973, just before the new
Liberalism swamped the old, and faced the music with René Lévesque
in 1979, as federalism did battle with separatism for the recognition
of the visiting prime minister of France.

The Soldiers of Misfortune

Simon Reisman (*opposite, top*) and T. K. Shoyama (*below*, with Jean Chrétien) were the deputies in the Department of Finance who did battle with the economic impossibilities of the 1970s.

Pitfield as Protégé, Pitfield as Power

CP Photo

Two views of Michael Pitfield: as a cadet at West Point when he was eighteen and already a Bachelor of Arts, and as Clerk of the Privy Council when he was thirty-seven and the most powerful bureaucrat in Ottawa.

Liberal Party of Canada

Trudeau emotes for the party faithful at a policy convention in 1978
and confers with the party powerful at a breakfast at 24 Sussex that
same year when the Liberal machine was readying for battle.

The Private
Liberal Leader

Trudeau, as complete
strategist, confers with
Jim Coutts, his principal
secretary, in a party aircraft coming back from an
electoral foray; as complete
bureaucrat, he scrutinizes
the papers of state in his
office on Parliament Hill.

The Saleable Liberal Leader

Weekend Magazine / D. Montgomery

Trudeau as gunslinger and sloganeer, the ''leader who must be a leader'' that the Liberal Party set out to sell to the electorate one more time in the spring of 1979.

the inferior position Quebeckers had suffered from within the Canadian duality when he said, "To understand French Canadians you have to understand our frustration, humiliation, and fear — and on the other hand, our pride and hope. You might ask why should I talk this way? I taught in a university. I was a successful lawyer. I have achieved in politics. Nevertheless, I feel this strongly."

Lalonde saw Trudeau as the standard-bearer of French-Canadian pride and hope. He respected him. He was loyal to him beyond question. But he always gave the impression that his fierce devotion was not to the man, Trudeau, but to their cause. It was as though Trudeau was the outward and visible sign of that cause and Lalonde was its inward and spiritual grace.

As soon as he took up the role of principal secretary when Trudeau became prime minister in 1968, Lalonde set about Trudeau's work, organizing the new PMO, co-ordinating the promised policy reviews, working fifteen-hour days, living in a small apartment, seeing his family in Montreal only on weekends. He was a relentlessly efficient and cold disciplinarian and those who could not accept his fierce authoritarianism soon left the PMO. Within the first year, both Pierre Levasseur and Eddie Rubin, young men who had been close to Trudeau before his elevation to the leadership and who were policy-oriented, creative, and lively, abandoned Ottawa, taking their irreverent laughter and their stimulating ideas with them. Lalonde didn't encourage unconventional policy approaches from anyone. Ministers and members who had theories they wanted to "bounce off" the Prime Minister were diverted to the regional desks or cabinet committees so that "input" could be "streamed appropriately". Lalonde believed implicitly in the rigorously formalized system of policy-making Trudeau had embarked on as soon as he became prime minister. His job was to defend Trudeau's ideas, guard his door, reward his supporters, and flay his enemies.

During the first autumn of the first Trudeau régime, a journalist who had known both Lalonde and Trudeau for years wrote an article about Trudeau's distaste for the press, which was already marked despite the Trudeaumania the newspapers had reflected during his leadership race; the article suggested mildly that this distaste was a bad augury to those who had hoped for an open government under Trudeau, the participatory democracy he had been promising. Lalonde immediately fired off a stiff note to the writer — one of the many such letters to newspapers and magazines that were forthcoming from his various offices in the next decade — saying the article betrayed an ignorance of Trudeau's essence and of his very real concern for freedom. Later, in a conversation enlarging on the letter, he gave his own coldly rational assessment of that essence, saying that Trudeau was brilliant, the right man in the right place, but on some occasions a little erratic. One had to recognize, he went on with the air of a father confessor resigned to a human frailty, that's what Pierre was like. Every few months or so he could be expected to blow his cork, especially when he was harassed by journalists whom he didn't think were well informed. Remember when Lalonde had arranged for him to give the keynote speech to the Canadian Bar Association [in September of 1967]? It was crucial to his plan for Trudeau's bid for the Liberal leadership and Trudeau delivered the speech well but ended up at a press conference after it using French vulgarisms in response to a reporter's question that insulted half the Quebec population as well as the reporter himself. He pushed back when the press pushed him. Trudeau couldn't resist being outrageous occasionally. It was a flaw, but not an important one.

What was important in Lalonde's eyes was Trudeau's strength on the Quebec question. Lalonde would brook no suggestion that Trudeau might be wrong in any way about what was good for Quebec, either then or later. Federalism was the true belief, separatism was heresy. Anybody who could not see that, who urged flexibility or compromise, who talked of "special status" or a "third way" between federalism and separatism, was a miscreant or a fool. This attitude reached a high point in the autumn of 1970.

While the Quebec federalists had been busy taking over the Liberal Party and the government of Canada in the late 1960s, they had been contending at the same time with an intensified display of nationalist feeling in their home province. Lesage had been defeated in his third campaign of 1966 by the Union Nationale and replaced as premier, first by Daniel Johnson and then by

Jean-Jacques Bertrand, who mouthed radical slogans about "equality or independence" while invoking the old nationalist memory of Maurice Duplessis. The same period had seen a marked increase in the extremist activities of a group of avowed terrorists called the Front de Libération du Québec and modelled on the Front de Libération Nationale which had actually won independence from France for Algeria. Even more significant was the establishment in 1968 by René Lévesque, the former minister in Lesage's Liberal government, of the Parti Québécois as a coalition of moderate, left- and right-wing nationalists who dedicated themselves to achieving the goal of independence for Quebec but by parliamentary, not violent, means. Lévesque, the *Cité libristes*'s ally of a decade before, now vilified the Three Wise Men and their federalist caucus as *vendus* and Trudeau himself as a "museum piece" and *un roi nègre en veston sport*. The evidence of a gathering momentum behind the separatist movement increasingly concerned the federalists, who engaged the counter-espionage branch of the RCMP in their fight against what they tarred as political subversion. For a few months they were able to take heart from a victory of sorts in early 1970. In January that year, Robert Bourassa, a well-educated, well-connected young lawyer, had been installed, with Jean Marchand's support, as the Quebec Liberal Party's new leader, and in April he had become the province's premier, having won a whirlwind campaign promising 100,000 jobs. Trudeau called Bourassa's election victory "a vote of confidence in Canada". But in the wake of the election, Quebec nationalists began to publicize widely their view, backed up by statistical analysis, that Bourassa had won only because English-speaking voters had been solidly behind him and that the poor showing of Lévesque's Péquistes in terms of numbers of seats in the legislature did not reflect the fact that their vote among French-speaking Quebeckers was nearly as high as the Liberals'.

English Canada scoffed at this reasoning and at the subsequent increase of terrorist activities by the FLQ — robberies and repeated bomb plants in post offices, trust companies, and banks. Then, on October 5, an FLQ cell abducted the British trade commissioner, James Cross, and issued a communiqué listing their conditions for his release. The scoffing stopped. Five days later, another FLQ group kidnapped Pierre Laporte, the journalist who had been part of the early *Cité libre* group and was now a minister in Bourassa's cabinet. The events that followed these kidnappings — which came to be called the October Crisis — have been the subject of endless dissension in articles, books, and judicial inquiries, both federal and provincial.

Certain facts about the period are incontestable. In the wake of the kidnappings, the federal government invoked the War Measures Act, citing an apprehended insurrection in Quebec as their reason for calling out the army and endowing the government with emergency powers to preserve public order. Under the Act, the Quebec provincial police rounded up more than four hundred people whom they suspected, mostly on the flimsiest of grounds, of FLQ connections and put them in jail, detaining some without laying charges for several weeks. Pierre Laporte was murdered. James Cross was released, and the kidnappers were allowed safe passage to Cuba.

On October 23, during the height of the crisis, two English-Canadian journalists went to see Lalonde in his Ottawa office to discuss the situation. For a week, government spokesmen had been saying that the cabinet possessed secret knowledge which justified the emergency measures. Now Lalonde talked gravely for nearly an hour about the situation, particularly about what came to be called "the provisional government plot". Rumours had been spreading wildly in Ottawa and Montreal that the cabinet's secret knowledge involved a group of prominent Quebeckers who were planning to replace the provincial government of Robert Bourassa with a committee of public safety. Figuring prominently in the rumours as participants in the so-called plot were René Lévesque and the Péquiste economist Jacques Parizeau, Marcel Pépin, the trade unionist, and Claude Ryan, the publisher and chief editorialist of *Le Devoir*, a man whose opinions carried great moral force in both French and English Canada.

Ryan had been the general secretary of L'Action Catholique for seventeen years before joining *Le Devoir*, but despite their common background, Lalonde had never been able to rely on Ryan's editorial support for Trudeau. Always independent of mind, Ryan had supported first Mitchell Sharp and then Paul Hellyer for the Liberal leadership in 1968. Ever since Trudeau became prime minister, he had subjected his actions to relentless scrutiny and had been particularly irritating to the federalists in some of his statements about Lévesque in his new role as Péquiste leader, writing that he had given the separatist cause respectability. Nevertheless, Ryan had supported Bourassa in the April election and had given the Trudeauites approval when he thought they merited it.

The rumours of his involvement with a takeover plot that amounted to a coup d'état seemed improbable to both journalists. Lalonde assured them these rumours were being taken seriously in Ottawa. Nothing less than democracy in Quebec was at stake, he said, reiterating Trudeau's view that democracy was a fragile flower in the province at the best of times. He suggested that one of the journalists, Peter C. Newman, who was then the editor-in-chief of the *Toronto Star*, should speak to Trudeau himself to confirm that he shared Lalonde's apprehensions about the possibility of such a plot and arranged for Trudeau and Newman to talk on the telephone later in the afternoon.

(Trudeau did confirm with Newman the seriousness with which the rumoured plot was being regarded in Ottawa, but Claude Ryan, when contacted two days later about the rumours by Beland Honderich, publisher of the *Star*, denied them emphatically. No real proof of the plot's existence was ever offered.)

Before saying farewell to his interviewers, Lalonde hunched his shoulders and murmured in sepulchral tones, "Pray for us." His visitors stared at him briefly in bewilderment, not so much at the admonition itself but at its reflection of the intense emotion expressed in the previous hour by the normally controlled Lalonde. In response to their startled silence, he snapped, "Well, I don't suppose *you* pray, anyway." Hard is the lot of the believer in the land of the infidel.

Lalonde's dramatic demeanour was characteristic of the behaviour of French-Canadian federalists in the capital during the October Crisis. The next day the provisional-government plot was the chief topic of conversation at a large party held by Bernard and Sylvia Ostry at Five Oaks, their baronial house on the Aylmer Road.

The Ostrys were both federal public servants in 1970, just

beginning the decade of their greatest importance in Ottawa. A formidable pair, intellectual and stylish, they had both grown up in Winnipeg, studied at the University of Manitoba, and gone on to do post-graduate work in England, he at the London School of Economics and she at Cambridge. They were old friends of Pierre Trudeau, a fact that was much mentioned in Ottawa as their careers thrived in the 1970s. But Trudeau was only one of the Ostrys' many important connections. A list of their acquaintances was like a roll-call of the Canadian intellectual, political, and bureaucratic elites. For several years, starting in the mid-1960s, they held an annual party in the autumn, the Ostry National Day reception as it came to be known in a city where national days were constantly celebrated by the diplomatic corps with cocktail parties. It was usually such a glittering event that the Ostrys' friends travelled from all over the country to be there. But the atmosphere at Five Oaks on that particular October Saturday in 1970 was so unforgettably overwrought that the gathering was referred to ever afterwards in Ottawa as the famous Ostry crisisfest. There were soldiers in the hall, their young faces strained, guns over their shoulders, while the dignitaries they were meant to guard were whispering in the corners of the reception rooms. Little knots of English Canadians gathered to hear "the real story" from the French Canadians present — Paul Desmarais, the chairman of Power Corporation, who was said to be packing his own gun; Maurice Sauvé, former Liberal cabinet minister and now the vice-president of Consolidated Bathurst, and his wife, Jeanne, the Montreal journalist; Alex Pelletier, the film-maker and wife of Gérard Pelletier, and Jean-Luc Pepin, the Minister of Industry, Trade and Commerce, whose personal bodyguard was among the soldiers in the hall. The real story was the story of the provisional government, repeated with variations, that the takeover was scheduled for this very weekend, that only the army could prevent it, and so on. David Anderson, the Toronto Liberal lawyer and Cell 13 stalwart, came out of one such huddle and said dazedly to a friend, "Good Lord, these people are terrified — and if you question what they are saying or ask them if they genuinely believe an insurrection is in the offing, they act like you're a traitor, or a closet separatist or something."

What Anderson was expressing vividly was the kind of tense misapprehensions that palpitated between the Liberal French and the Liberal English in party circles that fall. In the early stages of the crisis, the English Canadians were at first disbelieving and then alarmed by the French Canadians' fear and the air of high drama which characterized their every utterance about the FLQ kidnappings. By the time Trudeau evoked the War Measures Act, the English Canadians' liberalism fell before the intensity of the francophones' concern, with only a group of NDPers voting against the Act in the Commons.

John Turner, who piloted the War Measures legislation through the House, remembered Trudeau's toughness throughout the crisis period with admiration. "That's the closest I ever felt to him. We were like buddies in combat. I mean, when you stand beside a guy who's eyeball-to-eyeball with danger and he doesn't blink, you can't help but feel admiration." Bryce Mackasey, the Minister of Labour, whose ardour as a reform Liberal was as well known as his stage-Irishman mannerisms, supported the emergency legislation, his eyes glistening with tears, and urged dissenting NDP MPs "to read between the lines of it". Even Walter Gordon, who was gravely concerned about the implications for civil liberties of the government's action on the day the War Measures Act was evoked, was soon mollified. He spoke to Edgar Benson and Donald Macdonald, his friends in the cabinet, and was sufficiently convinced by them of the seriousness of the "apprehended insurrection" that he was able to meet a group from the Canadian Civil Liberties Association and tell them that when the full details were known, they too would be convinced that the situation was as grave as a war.

All these prominent Liberals clearly believed that the jailing of suspected separatist sympathizers was justified and so was calling out the army. Their old friend Keith Davey didn't entirely agree. When the government brought down its Public Order (Temporary) Measures Act — the bill that replaced the stopgap War Measures Act — one of whose clauses made membership in the FLQ retroactively a crime, Davey stood up in the Senate to vote against it in a move that startled acquaintances familiar with his arch-loyalty to the party. "I don't have any long-winded intellectual position on this," he told people who inquired. "I just think it's wrong. It doesn't seem to me to be a Liberal thing to do." When Marc Lalonde heard about the objections of people like Davey to the government's actions, he just set his lips in a tight line. Such people were lightweights who didn't understand Quebec. Trudeau understood Quebec. Trudeau was right.

Discussions about whether the use of the War Measures legislation was justified in the FLQ crisis continued for the next decade. Gérard Pelletier said the Act's invocation caused him severe anguish. Jean Marchand, who had played a central part along with Lalonde and Trudeau in managing the crisis, remarked ruefully that had the Montreal police given the federal cabinet the right information, the Act might never have been invoked. Trudeau himself in an interview with George Radwanski recalled his qualms and apprehensions, which had never been entirely assuaged. Only Lalonde remained adamant, saying that the toughness of the War Measures legislation had probably kept Canada free of terrorism for the next decade.

Lalonde never wavered in his devotion to federalism, remaining at Trudeau's side long after Pelletier and Marchand had withdrawn to less taxing roles in the diplomatic corps and the Senate. Whatever Trudeau needed done, he did. He ran for office in the Montreal riding of Dollard in 1972, to shore up the French-Canadian contingent in the cabinet, and then took on the formidable portfolio of health and welfare because Trudeau wanted him to oversee a review of the social security system. In the wake of the PQ victory in 1976, he became minister of federal-provincial relations, shouldering the difficult and inglorious job of coordinating the federalist forces against separatism. But the most taxing of the jobs he undertook for Trudeau in the 1970s was that of Quebec leader. It was in this crucial role that the zealotry in his nature was most clearly evident.

THE QUEBEC LEADER'S POSITION has always been unique in the Liberal Party. It reflects both the special nature of Quebec politics — always a drama unfolding, replete with warring factions, personal vendettas, and escalating crises — and the special importance of Quebec seats to the Liberal Party's prospects of governing. In the 1960s most of the French-Canadian federalists had despised the role as it had been played in the past. They saw the Quebec leader as a kind of collaborator. When Trudeau became prime minister, he wanted to abolish the job, saying Quebeckers didn't need a pro-consul any more since they were no longer a captive province but an equal partner in Confederation. Jean Marchand, who had served as the last and best of Lester Pearson's Quebec lieutenants, didn't agree. Obviously, Trudeau didn't require a Quebec lieutenant to interpret the province, but there was another part of the job that couldn't be done away with so readily. From Marchand's own experience, it was clear that Quebec Liberals would need to consult a cabinet minister about organizational questions, just as Liberals in other provinces would want to consult their own senior ministers. Surely Trudeau himself would be too busy with affairs of state to deal with such trivial, if essential, matters as patronage appointments and riding nominations, and, given the hierarchical nature of Quebec society, the minister in charge of these details should still have an official title. Trudeau agreed with this reasoning and when Marchand was confirmed in the role of Quebec leader, there were widespread expectations that he would be able to continue the reforms of the Quebec wing of the party begun in the Pearson era. In that period, one of the Quebeckers who made the loudest fuss about the need to clean up the party's political practices was Maurice Sauvé. Sauvé was an economist who was director of a world youth organization in Europe in the 1950s before coming home to work first for Marchand's union organization, then with the Gordon commission, and later as an organizer for Lesage in the triumphal Quebec election of 1960. Sauvé then turned to the federal arena and got himself elected as the MP for Iles-de-la-Madeleine in 1962, against the wishes of some of the old-guard party bosses.

Sauvé had an aggressive manner that irritated his peers in Quebec and Ottawa. He was rambunctious, ambitious, and opinionated, but he was also lively, expansive, and intelligent enough to be able to make connections in English Canada with journalists and the new-guard Ontario Liberals from Cell 13 who liked his flamboyant idealism and bicultural charm. At one point he was widely talked of in left-Liberal circles there as the best possible Quebec leader, even though he held only a minor post in Pearson's cabinet as minister of forestry. He and his executive assistant, Claude Frenette, wanted to reform the Quebec wing of the federal party in the same way the provincial party had been reformed, and they agitated constantly to this effect in Ottawa and Montreal. Since Guy Favreau, Pearson's Quebec leader, was too distracted by problems in the capital to even think about the need for open ridings and democratic conventions, Sauvé and Frenette were concerned that the federal Liberal Party in Quebec would continue in its old corrupt ways and that all young and idealistic Quebeckers would pour their energies into the Quiet Revolution. For years they flailed away at old-guard Liberals, demanding reform, demands they afterwards believed made possible the entrance into federal politics of the Three Wise Men. (Sauvé's own political career was eventually destroyed by party in-fighting and his own intractibility. He quit politics forever after losing the election of 1968. His original riding had been swallowed up in a redistribution and no other safe seat was made available to him by Marchand, who made no bones about disliking him, partly because he had refused to support Trudeau for the leadership. Sauvé quickly became vice-president of Consolidated Bathurst Incorporated, a company controlled by the conglomerate Power Corporation, itself a Liberal bastion in the business world, and his political activities after 1968 were confined to advising his wife, Jeanne Sauvé, who was elected MP for the Montreal riding of Ahuntsic in 1972. She was appointed to the cabinet immediately as minister of state for science and technology.)

Claude Frenette, the man who had played Tonto to Sauvé's Lone Ranger in the struggle to democratize the Quebec Liberal

Party, became Quebec president of the federal party in early 1968. By that time the federal and provincial wings had been split and the new federal organization had adopted the same formally democratic structures as the provincial organization, with riding associations open to public membership, regular conventions scheduled to discuss party policy, and a central executive elected by delegates from the ridings.

After Trudeau became prime minister, Frenette as party president and Marchand as Quebec leader worked together to make the reformed party structure a success. For a couple of heady years it seemed as though the bad old days of bossism were over. Party membership rose from 10,000 to close to 80,000. Frenette had weekly consultations with Marchand and André Ouellet, the Quebec caucus leader, to give them the party's views on government appointments and policy-making. Marchand was dynamic in his determination, attending meetings faithfully, lending the strength of his personality and his personal suasion with Trudeau to the reform cause. But gradually the democratic thrust dissipated. As principal secretary at the time, Marc Lalonde was hostile to policy-making outside the PMO and eventually Marchand went along with him on this, saying that the elected wing of the party was more accountable and therefore more important than the grassroots structure. Party stalwarts in Quebec, like Robert Fowler, the lawyer and veteran of royal commissions, and John Payne, the public relations executive, who had been giving Liberal ministers shrewd advice for years, were cut out of policy discussions entirely.

In Ottawa, Marchand was under intense pressure trying to administer the new Department of Regional Economic Expansion and he slowly lost interest in the party structure, finding less and less time to take the painstaking care necessary for the fostering of greater democracy within it. He began to leave the day-to-day management of the Quebec political machine to Senator Louis Giguère.

"Bob" Giguère had been on the fringes of the Liberal reform movement in Quebec throughout the 1960s. He was the founding secretary of the Institut Canadien des Affaires Publiques, at whose meetings he had met Trudeau, Lalonde, Pitfield, and other Quebec intellectuals. He had been a Liberal campaign official in 1962 and 1963, served as Quebec campaign chairman in 1965, and raised money for the Trudeau leadership effort in 1968. Further-more, his daughter, Diane Giguère, the novelist and broadcaster, was an old friend of Trudeau's. Even so, when Trudeau appointed Giguère to the Senate in September 1968, some of the reform Liberals were dismayed. They already saw him as an old-style politician decked out in a new guise, "a chameleon looking for the best power colouration", as one of them described him. Giguère had always been employed in minor jobs in trade or labour organizations, or held political appointments on various govern-ment commissions, but after his appointment to the Senate, he rapidly turned into *un homme d'affaires* in the business commu-nity, becoming a director of several companies, including the Campeau Corporation, a firm of Ottawa developers. It wasn't long before reform Liberals began to mutter about Giguère's grow-ing prosperity. How come he's so rich? they kept asking each other. Giguère was living well in a luxurious Montreal apartment and travelling frequently to Florida, where he was a member of the St. Andrew's Club near Delray Beach, in company with a crowd of people with fortunes in the twenty- to thirty-million-dollar range.

By now he was cynical in his conversations about democra-tizing Quebec politics. He told a reform Liberal dismissively that he could put a pig up as a Liberal candidate and get him elected when objections were made about the quality of some of the can-didates he was recruiting for the 1972 campaign. Whispers about Giguère's business activities continued in Liberal circles and fi-nally, in 1976, he was charged with influence-peddling in what was known as the Sky Shops affair. He was acquitted of the charges in 1979 after a long, complex trial, at which evidence was given that he had made a $95,000 profit within six months out of the sale of shares he had bought in Sky Shops, a company that held airport concessions granted by the federal Department of Transport, and that he had been given a $100,000 interest in Publicor, a holding company of Canadian Advertising Limited, which was awarded federal government advertising contracts. His response to questions about these deals was, "What's wrong with a senator doing a little business?"

Giguère's behaviour angered French-Canadian reform Liberals. But the deterioration of Jean Marchand's performance as a cabinet minister saddened them. By the mid-1970s, when he was serving as minister of transport, Marchand was greatly altered. The bluntly honest, humane, witty cavalier had all but disappeared. He had become exhausted physically and intellectually by his pressured life as a cabinet minister, a life which had damaged so many "men of heart" as he called them. He was suffering from high blood pressure, had been charged in court with leaving the scene of a car accident, and was being taunted by the Opposition for his erratic performance in the House and in the Department of Transport. At one point he had publicly admitted the department was "in a mess"; at another, he had cried out emotionally across the Commons floor at the Opposition benches, "You are trying to kill me." In early 1975 he was eased out of the Quebec leader's role in favour of Lalonde, and the next year he resigned from the transport portfolio in protest over Trudeau's response to the bilingualism-in-the-air dispute. He served briefly as minister without portfolio, then as minister of the environment, then quit his seat in the Commons to campaign against separatism in Quebec, ostensibly to shore up the doomed Bourassa government in the provincial election of November 1976.

Despite the great affection in which Marchand was held, his public performance had deteriorated so badly that when Lalonde replaced him as Quebec leader, there was a collective sigh of relief in Liberal ranks. Lalonde had no instinctive talent and no particular taste for so crassly political a job, and he had an awkward baptism in the role. When Gérard Pelletier left the cabinet in 1975 to become ambassador to Paris, the Liberals decided to parachute into his riding of Hochelaga Pierre Juneau, the highly capable chairman of the Canadian Radio-Television Commission, in order to strengthen the French-Canadian contingent in cabinet. In the twenty-two elections since the Laurier victory in 1896, Hochelaga had gone Liberal all but twice — in 1911 and 1917 — and it was thought to be one of the safest Liberal seats in the country. To the astonishment of most observers, a local Conservative nonentity named Jacques Lavoie topped Juneau at the polls, forcing him to give up the communications portfolio to which Trudeau had prematurely appointed him before the by-election.

Lalonde, determined never to suffer such ignominy again, quickly became the most efficient Quebec political boss since Lapointe. He was relentless in his partisanship, running the Quebec caucus with an iron hand, rewarding the faithful and freezing out the dissidents, scaring the Tories and squeezing the Socreds, with all the self-confident piety of the worker priest he might have become.

The key to his authority stemmed from the absolute trust that Trudeau placed in him and from the detailed knowledge of the labyrinth of Quebec politics that he had begun to acquire when he was principal secretary. At first he pursued reform, particularly in the realm of party financing, putting pressure early in 1975 on individual riding associations to raise money from small donors rather than relying on contributions from large corporations. He was also convinced of the need to give a more important role to women in political life and to bring about a *relève* in the Liberal caucus — a fresh team of modern MPs to replace the old and tired — that had been talked about since 1972 and that he determined would now be achieved. Towards these ends, he promoted the careers of such young Liberals as Monique Bégin, a sociologist who had been secretary of the Royal Commission on the Status of Women and who was elected as MP in 1972, appointed first a parliamentary secretary and later Lalonde's successor as minister of health and welfare; and Francis Fox, a Rhodes Scholar and Montreal lawyer who had worked in the PMO under Lalonde and was made solicitor general in 1976.

Despite these reform efforts, after Lalonde had held his job for a little more than a year party members began to say that he was so tough in his demands, so rigid in his adherence to structures he had set up, that instead of behaving like a democrat, he was acting like a throwback to a very old-style leader indeed. He kept track of every riding and every member of the Quebec caucus, "animating the limp" as he put it and "channelling the energies of the strong". Quebec Liberals had always felt the need to speak with one voice if they were to advance their interests vis-à-vis the demands of their anglophone allies. Lalonde was fond of saying that the Quebec Liberals had "*l'habitude du pouvoir*" and that this habit was the basis of the discipline within their ranks.

His critics responded that the discipline was determined instead by other habits, those of docility and greed. "When you enter the Quebec Liberal Party," one of them remarked, "you enter a career — there are a series of steps you have to go through, a *cursus honorum*, and your success is assured. If anything, Lalonde has strengthened this tradition. The Quebec members are not as dumb as they used to be in the days of Lapointe and St. Laurent. Lalonde's sense of racial pride, his rivalry with the English, demands that his MPs have university degrees. But they are just as docile. They aren't intellectuals. Such people go to the PQ. And they're not the smart careerists. Those people are busy making money in the brokerage houses or in the middle-management of English [Canadian] companies like Eaton's, where the owners are scared now not to have French Canadians. Instead, Lalonde gets mediocrities, grown-up good boys who want sure careers. Belonging to such a huge caucus, they can see that they don't have much chance at a cabinet seat. But they know if they serve three or four terms and vote with the party, they'll get their rewards — an appointment to a board, a small-time consulate abroad, government business for their law practice. Very few Quebec Liberals go without their share of the patronage pie."

Certainly those members of the Quebec caucus who agreed with Lalonde did well under his leadership. Yvon Pinard, for instance, was rapidly advanced. A lawyer from Drummondville who was elected in that riding in 1974, Pinard heartily approved of Lalonde's disciplined approach to caucus business, saying, "We are so large a family [in the Quebec caucus], we need a father to guide us." Pinard's academic background was parochial — he had studied law at the University of Sherbrooke — as was his law practice. But his political credentials were as impeccable as his precisely combed hair. (His cousin had been a provincial Liberal cabinet minister; Pinard himself had worked tirelessly in election campaigns both for the cousin and for Jean-Luc Pepin in the Drummondville riding; and furthermore he was an old friend of André Ouellet's, the caucus leader and Lalonde's organizational right-hand man.) Pinard demonstrated an active concern for the niceties of parliamentary procedure. Lalonde saw to it that he was appointed to a House procedural reform committee, sent to an international gathering of parliamentarians, and eventually made parliamentary secretary to Allan MacEachen, the president of the Privy Council and House Leader.

Pinard's steady progress was in striking contrast to what happened to Serge Joyal, the member for the Montreal riding of Maisonneuve-Rosemont, another young lawyer elected in 1974. Joyal had been active in radical student movements in the 1960s and had studied constitutional law at Oxford and administrative law in France before earning a doctorate at the London School of Economics. As soon as he came to Ottawa he displayed for the world to see on television, in the House, in the press, his brilliance, his resolute independence of mind, and his self-confident opinion that despite his youth (he was twenty-nine), he was cabinet material. Marchand liked Joyal, who had been his executive assistant, and enjoyed his bravura manner. Lalonde did not.

When Joyal refused to become parliamentary secretary to either Otto Lang or John Roberts, the normal training route to advancement, his refusals were accepted grudgingly as proof of his obstinate independence. But when he publicly opposed the party line on such crucial matters as the bilingualism-in-the-air dispute of 1976 and the sales tax dispute with Quebec in 1978, and spoke out against the Liberals' "panic" as he called it in the face of the PQ victory, he was warned of his folly and then ostracized. Joyal was sure Lalonde was making a deliberate effort to cut him off from two other dissenters in the Quebec party, Pierre de Bané and Louis Duclos, lest the trio form a contentious core around whom disaffected party members could rally. It didn't matter who Lalonde sent to chastise him — his former mentor, Marchand, and the two most important Quebec ministers after Lalonde, Chrétien and Ouellet, all did so — Joyal remained scornful of "Lalonde's chapel", as he called the Quebec MPs who accepted preordained progress in exchange for obedience. Ironically, it was a scorn not unlike Lalonde's own for the campus politicians he met as a student, those small-time lawyers who were going to take part in the small-time politics his professors warned him about in order to better their lot in life. Lalonde had long since put that scorn behind him, and he called Joyal's protest against his iron rule "the mewlings of a cry-baby".

Lalonde was as adept at confounding, neutralizing, frightening, or absorbing his party's political enemies as he was at controlling his own caucus. In dealing with the Créditistes, the mainly rural members of the Quebec Social Credit party, he used a variety of outflanking techniques in his attempt to hasten the downfall of that party, whose decline had been steady since its great successes of the early 1960s and had accelerated after the resignation of its dynamic leader, Réal Caouette, in 1975. His tactics with Quebec Conservatives were slightly different. He always "invoked the racial imperative", as Lowell Murray, the Progressive Conservative campaign chairman, described it. This involved openly calling up tribal fears about the Tories as the party of English supremacy, fears that were deeply imbedded in the Quebec folk memory. From the 1920s to the 1950s, conscription was the wicked word; in the 1960s and 1970s, it was "Diefenbaker" and his perceived racial antagonism as displayed in the flag debate and his scornful denunciation of French-Canadian ministers involved in the scandals of the 1960s. André Ouellet, the Minister of Public Works, Lalonde's chief liaison man with local Quebec Liberals, would get up at nomination meetings in rural ridings and say about the Tories, *"Ils mangent les Canadiens français"*, and then go on to offer as proof of this contention the sorry careers of Léon Balcer under Diefenbaker and Claude Wagner under Joe Clark.

Lalonde was not entirely above this kind of tactic himself. Once Lowell Murray went to a party on Parliament Hill in the company of a Quebec Tory organizer named Bernard Flynn. Despite his Irish name, Flynn was a French Canadian, and when Lalonde overheard him speaking in accented English he drew him aside to hiss, "What are you, a French Canadian, doing with these guys?" implying, as Murray put it, that Flynn was consorting with the devil. Usually Lalonde's methods of neutralizing Tories were more subtle, as in the case of Jacques Lavoie, the unilingual Conservative who had defeated Pierre Juneau in Hochelaga. After he came to Ottawa, Lavoie felt isolated in the Conservative caucus as the only one of the four Conservatives from Quebec who couldn't speak any English. According to the Tories, Lalonde made sure sympathy was freely expressed to Lavoie by Liberal MPs, notably Ouellet, in the members' lounge of the Commons;

Lavoie soon crossed the floor and Lalonde had revenge for his loss in Hochelaga.

Jean-Pierre Côté's appointment as lieutenant-governor of Quebec in the spring of 1978 was a perfect example of Lalonde's use of the power of appointment in demoralizing the Opposition. Côté, a former Liberal postmaster general of no particular distinction, had been appointed to the Senate in 1972 to clear his riding of Longueuil for a candidate the Liberals wanted. Now he was being shifted to the lieutenant-governor's job to make way for the appointment to the Senate of Claude Wagner, the heavyweight MP from the riding of St. Hyacinthe, who was desperately unhappy in the Conservative Party after he lost the leadership to Joe Clark, and whose defection was calculated to do the Tory cause grave harm not just in Quebec but in the country at large.

This technique didn't always work. The Liberals twice tried to neutralize Heward Grafftey, the Tory member for Brome-Missisquoi, who had won seven consecutive elections there. First, Grafftey was offered the job of associate commissioner of official languages; then, during the long countdown to the 1979 election Jean Marchand met Grafftey in the parliamentary cafeteria and asked him if he would like a Senate appointment. Grafftey refused both offers, furious at the suggestion he could be bought.

A far bigger Tory fish that the Liberals tried to hook in the same period was Brian Mulroney, the Montreal lawyer and president of Iron Ore. Mulroney had been a Tory since his childhood in Baie Comeau, a pulp-and-paper mill town on Quebec's north shore, and throughout his rise to his position as one of the darlings of the country's business elite, he had worked tirelessly for the Conservatives as an organizer and a fund-raiser in Quebec. After he was defeated for the Conservative leadership in 1976 by Joe Clark, Mulroney took to sulking in his Sherbrooke Street office and in the Oyster Bar of the Ritz, and Lalonde tried to captivate him with promises of the Liberal nomination in Westmount (the seat Bud Drury had held since 1963 and was willing to give up as soon as it was needed) and a place in the Liberal cabinet. He could play the role of representative of the English-Canadian business class in Montreal, the role Doug Abbott had played in the 1940s. Mulroney turned down the offer and the seat went to Don Johnston, a Montreal tax lawyer and friend of Pierre Trudeau.

In describing the episode, Mulroney talked of Lalonde with a bemused combination of despair and admiration. "He's tough, he's smart, he's a big winner among the big winners — and a Tory in this province might as well commit suicide as come up against the likes of that guy, expecting to outwit him." Mulroney didn't commit suicide, of course; he went back to fund-raising for the Tories and to keeping his *bona fides* in order by trying to attract important candidates to his party.

One night in March 1979 he was summoned to the house of Louis Desmarais, a Montreal businessman and the brother of Paul Desmarais of Power Corporation. Louis had been wooed for months by Mulroney and was thought to be a sure Conservative candidate in the coming election. Desmarais started to explain, somewhat abashedly, that he thought he would change his mind and run for the Liberals instead. Over Desmarais's shoulder, Mulroney could see Desmarais's image on the television screen as he made the same announcement, only in more definite terms, to the news cameras. He found the situation infuriating, hilarious, and prototypical. All the Tories could promise Desmarais was that if he ran for them and lost, as he very well might since safe Conservative seats in Quebec were rare even in the late 1970s when the tide was running so strongly in the Tories' favour elsewhere, they would put him in the Senate and appoint him to the cabinet when (or if) they won office. The Liberals, on the other hand, could offer Desmarais a sure nomination and a sure victory in the riding of Dollard, which had been the bailiwick of Jean-Pierre Goyer, a cabinet minister now retiring from politics, and which was duly bestowed on Desmarais despite objections from many members of the riding's constituency association who had wanted another candidate from their own ranks.

In general, Lalonde was less able to place candidates easily than his predecessors in the Quebec leader's job because of the constituency reforms instituted in the 1960s, but very few ridings put forward nominees he disapproved of and suitable ridings for candidates he particularly wanted to see elected could generally be found by retiring to other positions the appropriate incumbent

MP. "The party," said Jeanne Sauvé, in 1979, "is still by no means a pure instrument in Quebec. This doesn't have to do so much with the nature of its leadership — it has to do with the nature of the province's politics."

With his disciplined caucus behind him, Lalonde could deal with anglophone Liberals firmly, voicing his troops' opinions in the national caucus, constantly reminding his cabinet colleagues of Quebec's interests and priorities. He would say to the Minister of Agriculture when a new policy was being discussed, "This is Quebec's position — we expect you to take heed," or advise the Minister of Finance, engaged in making budgetary changes in the tax structure, changes that might affect Quebec industries such as shoe- and clothing-manufacturing, "We still need the tariff that will inhibit the importation of cheap foreign goods."

Lalonde never showed any sign of feeling squeamish about the seamier aspects of party politics. His pragmatism was quite consistent with his old L'Action Catholique precept of *voir, juger, agir.* One dealt with certain aspects of society as one found them in order to achieve a larger mission, the retention of a resurgent Quebec in a more equitable confederation. To that end he had struggled mightily for more than a decade. As much as anyone he had been responsible for making sure suitable French Canadians were given important appointments at the top levels of the civil service and in the cabinet.

The Ottawa he had come to in 1959 had been unfriendly territory, almost an enemy camp, a resolutely English town. French Canadians were the men who ran the creaky elevators in the gloomy government buildings and filled the petty patronage jobs at the Queen's Printer across the river in Hull or in the post office building near the railway station downtown. They were the women who typed the letters in the bilingual MPs' offices in the Centre Block or lugged the heavy trays in the parliamentary restaurant, moving among the powerful on rubber-soled shoes, remembering that this one liked his steak *bleu* and that one devoured all the Oka on the cheeseboard and threw a minor tantrum if he didn't get an alcove table. There were still only a few token French Canadians in the upper-middle reaches of the public service, mostly men from the genteel Quebec families who could afford to send them abroad for at least part of their educations. Even at that, the top jobs were rarely available to them and they were forced to endure the exhaustion of always working in their second language. Bilingual government cheques were a great concession to the duality, and the House of Commons didn't have a translation system. When Georges Vanier was appointed governor general in 1959, he arranged for the Government House gates to carry for the first time the legend "Résidence du Gouverneur Général" and for his own proclamations to be signed "Georges" in the French manner, having during most of a lifetime spent in the Canadian army and the Canadian diplomatic corps used the English "George".

In the twenty years since then, Ottawa had changed dramatically and Lalonde had been instrumental in that change. In 1969, the year the Official Languages Act was passed, guaranteeing Canadian citizens the right to deal with the federal government, its agencies and Crown corporations, in either English or French, only ten per cent of public servants employed in the so-called officer categories (i.e., the good jobs) had been francophone. By 1979, nearly a quarter of the officer-category jobs were held by francophones. Furthermore, the jobs French Canadians had been appointed to in government departments and government agencies were among the most important: deputy-ministerships in health and welfare (Maurice LeClair), in secretary of state (André Fortier), in external affairs (Marcel Cadieux), in transport (Sylvain Cloutier), in justice (Roger Tasse); the presidencies of the Canadian Broadcasting Corporation (Laurent Picard) and of the Canadian International Development Agency (Paul Gérin-Lajoie); chairmanships of the Canada Council (Charles Lussier), of Air Canada (Yves Pratte), of the Canadian Radio-television and Telecommunications Commission (Pierre Juneau), and of the National Capital Commission (again Pierre Juneau); the ambassadorships to France (Gérard Pelletier), to UNESCO (Jean-Louis Gagnon), and to Belgium (Lucien Lamoureux). French Canadians held the four key posts in the cabinet: Trudeau was Prime Minister, Lalonde was Minister of Federal-Provincial Relations and then of Justice, Jean Chrétien was in charge of the Department of Finance, and Monique Bégin headed the Department of Health and Welfare.

French was in use everywhere — at cabinet committees and deputy ministers' meetings, at official dinners and in departmental publications and by switchboard operators all over town who spent their days gabbling into phones *Office of the Minister, Bonjour,* ... *Bureau du Ministre, Good morning,* ... whether the politician they were working for was called Roberts or Chrétien. It was a minor revolution.

But even as Lalonde had altered Ottawa, Ottawa had altered him; the sweetness that had tempered his single-mindedness in the sixties had vanished. Beset by a series of scandals and misfortunes involving Quebec and Quebeckers, which were given prominent space in the anglophone press — among them the Trudeaus' spectacular marriage breakdown; the Giguère Sky Shops uproar; the so-called Judge's Affair, in which André Ouellet had tangled with Mr. Justice Kenneth Mackay of the Quebec Superior Court over a judgment in a price-fixing case involving sugar refineries and had been forced to resign the cabinet for several months as a consequence; the revelation of break-ins carried out by the RCMP and aimed at undermining the legally constituted Parti Québécois — Lalonde grew steadily more morose in his outlook. "One of the worst moments came over the Francis Fox episode," said an aide in his office. "Francis was such a white hope, a new generation of federalist and a particular protégé of Marc's. [Fox was the young lawyer from Montreal who, having made an impressive ministerial beginning as solicitor general responding to Opposition attacks on the government's relationship with the RCMP, fell victim to public abuse early in 1978 when it was discovered he had signed another man's name to a hospital document in order to obtain an abortion for a married woman friend.] When we got the terrible news of what had happened to him, Marc just sat slumped on a chair with his big farmer's hands hanging down beside him and stared at the floor. He was depressed for days."

However discouraged he became, Lalonde never yielded in his determination. His conversational style by the end of the decade had become scornful, his face hard and set. He seemed obsessed with the notion that English Canadians could not or would not understand what had happened in Quebec in the previous decade — how fierce the fight had been to hold the province in Confederation, and would continue to be. "In English Canada you may have to convince people there is a national-unity problem," he told an acquaintance in April of 1979. "In Quebec, you don't need to convince anybody. It's part of the whole fabric of our lives." He said this with the frustrated fury of a man who had always until now been able to beat every opponent and master every obstacle — the town boys at the *collège classique*, the law students at university later on, the tutorial system at Oxford, the mandarin system in Ottawa, *les Bleus*, *les Créditistes* — everybody and everything, except the separatists and the English Canadians' intransigent ignorance of the importance of the Quebec question. The English Canadians didn't seem to understand how much French-Canadian federalists had suffered at the hands of their intellectual peers in Quebec, most of whom were separatists and who were given regularly to calling the Trudeauites sell-outs and to saying that the Liberal Party was still dominated by the English despite the Trudeauites' best efforts to take it over.

With Lalonde, as with Pierre Trudeau himself in the late 1970s, one had the sense that they were weary of English Canadians, that they were like bored partners in a sour marriage of convenience. They had explored the English Canadians' essential mysteries and they were sick of what they saw. The English Canadians' political concerns were petty, the politics of polls and image-making, of interminable squabbles over freight rates and oil prices, of regional rivalries and personal ambition.

Quebec politics was, in contrast, the politics of the world's mainstream, involving the large questions of the century — the issue of national self-determination, the role of the federal state in the destiny of multi-ethnic societies. For fourteen years they had been major players in the epic struggle between the forces of federalism and the advocates of separatism that had spasmodically torn Quebec society since the conquest of 1759. In the late 1970s, as Victor-Lévy Beaulieu wrote, "Two branches of the great Quebec family are locked in Homeric combat under the nose of English Canada which is present in the simple role of spectator." The whole struggle was coming to a climax now that René Lévesque had become premier of Quebec.

IN MANY WAYS, the Trudeau-Lévesque confrontation had about it a mythic aura. Each man represented a tradition rooted in Quebec's history. Lévesque had emerged from the nationalist tradition of Papineau, Bourassa, Taschereau, and Duplessis, based on tribalism and emotion. Trudeau came out of the pragmatic, federalist-constitutionalist tradition of Lafontaine, Cartier, Laurier, Lapointe, and St. Laurent, focused on the accommodation of the French Canadians to the finality of the conquest and based on reason and a more abstract concept of brotherhood beyond blood ties. Trudeau and Lévesque were the same age but their styles were very different. By now Trudeau was remote and aristocratic in his solitude, while Lévesque was accessible and lovable. Lévesque projected an image of a Chaplinesque "little man", standing chain-smoking in front of audiences in working-class districts, clad in an ill-fitting suit like something a factory foreman would wear to mass on Sunday, making promises, lifting hopes, and speaking, as he kept saying, *"au fond de mon coeur"*. On the surface, anyway, it looked as though Trudeau was sure to lose the referendum on whether or not Quebec should remain with Canada, which Lévesque had promised to hold as part of his election platform in 1976.

Since the early 1970s, the federalists' strategy for holding Quebec had been frustrated by the fact that their provincial Liberal allies were balky and unreliable as advocates of federalism. From 1970 to 1976 they had had to contend with the weaknesses of the provincial Liberal premier, Robert Bourassa. Since 1978, they had been forced to deal with the obduracies of the new leader, Claude Ryan.

Even though Lévesque continually put down Robert Bourassa as the federalists' hand-picked puppet, the relationship between the Trudeauites and the Premier of Quebec was not as co-operative as their common Liberal label might have led the innocent to suppose. In part this was because Bourassa had been seen to panic under the pressure of the October Crisis in 1970. The fear seemed to turn into a paranoia from which he never recovered. The fortress-like atmosphere of the Premier's Office building in Quebec — it communicated with the National Assembly by an underground passage, it contained the cabinet's meeting rooms in bomb-proof calm, it housed the Premier's apartment with access to a helicopter pad on the roof and was known locally as the Bunker — symbolized the mood that emanated from the Bourassa government. After the conference of federal and provincial premiers held in Victoria in 1971, Bourassa blackened his reputation with the Trudeauites for good by reneging on his initial agreement to endorse the unanimous acceptance of the ''Victoria formula'' for amending the constitution after repatriation. Under pressure from Claude Ryan, who wrote in *Le Devoir* that no repatriation should be tolerated without a prior agreement on the redistribution of federal powers, Bourassa withdrew the Quebec government's support, torpedoing in one stroke three years of Trudeau's efforts to reform the constitution. In part the problem was that no premier of Quebec could be as federalist as the Trudeauites and hope to remain in office.

Defending provincial rights was one thing; overt anti-federalism was another, and Bourassa's notorious Bill 22, adopted in 1974, with the purpose of making French the sole official language of Quebec, directly challenged Trudeau's Official Languages Act of 1969. Bourassa talked in his speeches about *le fédéralisme rentable*, implying that he was only a Canadian because federalism was more profitable than separation. He avoided the word ''Canadian'' and wrote about Quebec as a ''French-speaking state within a Canadian economic common market''. Furthermore, the provincial government's bungling (outrageous overspending on the Olympic Games of 1976), hints of corruption (links of some Liberal deputies with organized crime were established in a justice department report), and ineptness (provocative handling of civil servants' trade-union claims that triggered prolonged and bitter strikes in the hospitals and schools), all suggested that Bourassa had become such a liability that he could blow his enormous electoral majority and let the Parti Québécois slip into power.

When Lévesque and his separatist team did indeed take over in November 1976, despite the desperate attempts of federal stars like Jean Marchand and Bryce Mackasey to shore up Bourassa's campaign with a clearly federalist message, the Trudeauites' problems became simpler and starker. The Péquistes's number one project had been the introduction of Bill 101, which went far further than the Bourassa Liberals had in attempting to turn Quebec into a unilingual French state in the courts, the schools, and the business world. For the federalists, it presaged a return to the wigwam from which the Trudeauites had struggled so hard to drag Quebeckers for the previous quarter-century. In the referendum the Péquistes were promising, Quebeckers were going to be asked if they wanted to remain in Canada or not. In response to this coming battle, the Privy Council Office's federal-provincial relations secretariat had been reinforced under the direction of career public servant Paul Tellier and raised to the status of a ministry when Marc Lalonde himself moved in to direct the fight against separatism, mainly through renewed efforts to bring about the changes in the Canadian constitution that Trudeau had been seeking for more than a decade. But adding another draft constitution to the many proposals already in existence for replacing the British North America Act was an exasperatingly blunt weapon in the struggle with Quebec. Both the federal document *A Time for Action* that was published over Pierre Trudeau's signature in 1978 and the government's proposed legislation, Bill C-60, which Marc Lalonde defended before the Joint Parliamentary Committee in the summer of 1978, were objected to as much by English-speaking premiers as by Lévesque.

Apart from shadow-boxing — introducing a bill to allow for federal referendums; establishing a Task Force on Canadian Unity chaired by John Robarts, the former premier of Ontario, and Jean-Luc Pepin, the former federal minister of industry, trade and commerce; publishing documents to prove the federal case that separation would cause Quebec a severe loss of jobs; skirmishing on the finance minister's temporary sales tax; offering grants to the pro-Canada groups who were girding their loins for the debate on the still-undefined referendum question — there was little that the Trudeauites could do other than pray for a renewal of the provincial Liberal Party.

When Claude Ryan finally threw his hat into the ring and

announced he would seek the leadership of the Liberal Party that had been vacant ever since Bourassa's defeat, it was not obvious to the Trudeauites whether the St. George who was offering himself was that much better for their purposes than the separatist dragon he proposed to slay. The Pope of St. Sacrement, as the eminent publisher of Quebec's most important paper was now called in reference both to his piety and to the name of the street where *Le Devoir* has its offices, had long espoused a version of Quebec nationalism that steered a third path between the dogmatic federalism of Trudeau and Lalonde and the evangelical separatism of Lévesque, Claude Morin, and Jacques Parizeau. For years Ryan had campaigned in his writings and speeches for what was unacceptable to Trudeau, a special status for Quebec that recognized the Québécois as one of Canada's two equal founding nations. Though Ryan had remained a thorn in the Trudeauites' flesh — at the 1968 federal leadership convention, in the October Crisis of 1970, at the Victoria negotiations over the constitution, during the unhappy episode of the air controllers' strike in 1976 over the use of French in air traffic — as the Quebec leadership race in 1978 wore on, it became obvious he had the moral strength, personal integrity, and political potential to challenge the Parti Québécois on its own ground. When Ryan won an overwhelming victory on the first ballot at the party's convention in Quebec City on April 15, 1978, it began to look as though the Trudeauites might soon become close to irrelevant in the long-drawn-out war against separatism.

They knew the referendum on Quebec's future could not be delayed much longer. That was the important battle; the upcoming federal election was a nuisance that had to be faced. But in reviewing their federal election strategy, in the endless campaign discussions that continued all spring and summer that year, the Trudeauites realized to their chagrin that their anglophone Liberal colleagues were indifferent to the separatist scare which they said was now boring English Canada and was not an issue on which an election could be fought. "That stuff just won't play in the country any more," Keith Davey kept saying at the campaign strategy meetings he co-chaired with Lalonde, dismissing the key issue of the Trudeauites' political lives. "What's on people's minds is the economy, inflation, and the decline of the Canadian dollar.'' Each time Davey made this audacious statement, Lalonde set his mouth in a hard line. Quebec's future would have to be an issue. If Trudeau went down to defeat, he would go down fighting for what he believed and Lalonde would go down with him. *Invictus!*

As the Liberals headed into the 1979 campaign, it was obvious that Lalonde and Trudeau had altered the old Liberal alliance they had both so despised. They had forged a new Liberal Party with a different kind of French-English balance. They were now the stable-masters instead of the trained donkeys. The trouble was that the herd they commanded was fractious with discontent.

IN THEIR DISPARATE PERSONS, John Turner and Marc Lalonde were almost too perfectly representative of the old Liberalism and the new — one of them the golden-boy politician turned into a silver fox at fifty, a corporate lawyer with an important reputation among corporate men; the other, the disdainful pietist with the face as long as Lent, the technocrat intellectual turned into a political boss, the believer who would never give up his faith in federalism. Their interests, their conversations, their friends, their mannerisms, their hopes, and their fears were very different. And yet they were locked together in the Liberal Party, personifying two strains of a political alliance that was now so shaky that its enemies fully expected its centre would not hold. The Liberals were going into the desperate campaign of 1979 as members of a party that had been drastically altered over the previous twenty years. The balance of power had changed fundamentally, a change that had caused deep resentment among English-Canadian Liberals of the old school, Liberals who were being called in party circles that winter "the Turnerites".

It was an indication of John Turner's remarkable political appeal that although he had been out of active politics for more than three years, his presence still had magic. He still turned heads wherever he went. He still made headlines in the press and attracted the television cameras at any Liberal gathering he attended. As a partner in the Toronto law firm of McMillan, Binch, Turner was constantly deflecting questions about his future. Publicly, he disclaimed any interest in returning to the political world. Privately, the story was different.

The truth was that Turner loathed the new Liberalism of the Trudeauites — the Liberalism of the cabinet committee system, of big government, of obsessive involvement with the problems of Quebec. The new Liberalism was keeping him from what should have been rightfully his by now: the leadership, the prime-ministership, a front-rank place in history. He had bucked the new Liberalism while he was a member of the Trudeau cabinet, at

307

first subtly and then more openly as the years wore on. Now that
he was out of government, he was devastatingly effective in private
conversation at analysing its defects.

Turner saw himself as the natural inheritor of the mantle of
C. D. Howe, whose memory he revered as a hero of the Liberal
past. He believed that if Howe had left politics in 1953 — before
the pipeline debate and the election of 1957, when his heedless
arrogance had been revealed — he would have been remembered as
the greatest Liberal of them all, the arch doer, the giant among
pygmies. When Howe was an old man retired from politics and
living in Montreal, Turner had done his personal legal work, and
the lessons he had learned as a young boy in Ottawa in the 1930s
and 1940s when Howe was in his prime were rekindled in his
mind. It was from the Howe–St. Laurent perspective of the
Liberal Party as a three-way managerial combine of elites from
business, the bureaucracy, and politics that Turner always launched
his critique of the Trudeauites.

He would bound out into the reception area of McMillan,
Binch on the thirty-eighth floor of the Royal Bank Tower in downtown Toronto, the ultimate corporate law office of the 1970s, the
kind of place where all the symbols of the old Toronto establishment law firm (the copies of *Punch* on mahogany highboys, the
Bartlett prints, the dark-green leather club chairs) had been
replaced by all the symbols of the new Toronto establishment law
firm (the modified-Bauhaus chrome-and-leather furniture, with
the copies of *Fortune* on the glass-topped tables and the internal
winding staircase to the firm's other offices on the thirty-seventh
floor). He would stand there for a moment, as handsome as a
mother's dream, great suit, thick hair, tennis tan, still projecting
the jolting energy that demanded of his visitor, approve! approve!
Barely would the door of his own office close behind him than his
guard would go down and he would begin to talk politics. His
conversation was sprinkled now with a lot of corporate-insider
jokes and mild locker-room cursing ("Christ! I'm talking about a
hell of a guy, a guy who's a really big hitter in this town, ya'
know what I mean?") lest his analyses of political and economic
problems seem too soberly theoretical for consumption by "the
boys" — the term Turner used to describe the captains of industry

he had been moving closer to since he had entered the world of big business.

The trouble with Trudeau, he would say, is that he doesn't understand other men and he doesn't understand English Canada. Trudeau had never travelled west of Toronto before he became prime minister; the only people he knew were some academics, and damn few of them. As a consequence, he didn't have "the feel" of the business community. He was so theoretical in his knowledge of economics — all he had was a couple of courses at Harvard behind him — he never stopped to consider that the economy had to be able to bear the government's social security programs. What's more, he had wrecked the bureaucracy and ruined the cabinet's workings. Strong personalities couldn't thrive under him in either of those arenas. Turner had refused to tie himself up in the endless discussions of the cabinet committees. He had sent an assistant deputy minister or in important cases his deputy, Simon Reisman, though Reisman hated the whole thing as much as he did. He himself went only to meetings of the priorities and planning committee, where decisions were actually taken. Even at that, the system slowed up decision-making. He could have dealt better with economic problems in Finance if the department hadn't been undermined by the Trudeauites with their unbridled big spending that had produced huge deficits. If government were a business, it would have gone broke in the 1970s. Trudeau had wrecked the Liberals' old alliance with business. The English-Canadian ministers who had any serious connections with that world had left his cabinet: Bob Winters had refused to join it at all in 1968 after he had been defeated at the leadership convention. The boys remembered that. Bud Drury was gone; so were Mitchell Sharp and James Richardson. Bob Andras, Tony Abbott, and Alastair Gillespie, the only businessmen left, were pussy-cats from the small-business world. Trudeau hadn't even been able to keep Don Macdonald, one of his original backers for the leadership, who had followed Turner as finance minister and was now practising corporate law as a partner in McCarthy & McCarthy, another big law firm a couple of bank towers away. Businessmen had even quit the Senate as a consequence of Trudeau's indifference to their opinions. John Nichol had resigned; he had been at university with Turner, and was key in the B.C. business community. John Aird had quit. He had been on a dozen big boards; he had establishment connections that ran back, through his father, Sir John Aird, to the time of Borden and Laurier. He was upset about the Trudeauites' curtailment of Canada's defence capabilities, but the PM didn't care and Aird was lost to the party as an effective mediator with business, though he was kept from being vocally critical by his appointment to the chairmanship of the Institute for Research on Public Policy. Trudeau had alienated the West, ignoring its new economic power, so much so that nobody out there of much stature business-wise would think of becoming a Liberal. Turner had family connections in Vancouver and the Kootenays; his wife, Geills, had family connections in Winnipeg and Calgary; they knew what Western businessmen thought of Trudeau. The criticisms would roll on, most of them rooted in Turner's detailed knowledge of Canadian history and of the Liberal Party's place in it, all of them nourished by what he was hearing day after day at board meetings and in the offices of his corporate clients.

In 1979, Turner was already a member of nine corporate boards and at their meetings he connected with the boys who really mattered — in the banking world (W. Earle McLaughlin, chairman of the board of the Royal Bank, and Arnold Hart, former chairman of the Bank of Montreal); in the insurance companies (J. Page Wadsworth, chairman of Confederation Life and former chairman of the Canadian Imperial Bank of Commerce, and Hal Jackman, chairman of Empire Life); in the transportation industry (Ian Sinclair, chairman and chief executive officer of Canadian Pacific, Robert Bandeen, president of Canadian National Railways); as well as in the newspaper business (Gordon Fisher, president of Southam Incorporated); and in mining (Stephen Roman, chairman and chief executive officer of Denison Mines Limited).

What he brought these men was the glamour of access. He could drop the really big names: ''David'' for David Rockefeller, chairman of the Chase Manhattan Bank in the United States, ''Giscard'' for Valéry Giscard d'Estaing, president of the French Republic, ''Helmut'' for Helmut Schmidt, the chancellor of the Federal Republic of Germany, all of whom he had known when he was finance minister. Turner was lively, coherent, and above all adept at making five-minute boardroom speeches that were reflective of businessmen's prejudices and sympathetic to their woes.

When these woes were sifted, they seemed to come down to two: big businessmen hated big government because it rivalled their supremacy and they disliked Pierre Trudeau because he didn't understand the business viewpoint. Not only had Trudeau never cultivated a network of contacts in the business world; he wasn't bound by any emotional ties to the mystiques of business despite the fact that his financial independence was due to his father's entrepreneurial success. On the contrary, his personal wealth freed him of the obligations that his Liberal predecessors had felt towards the business community. For Trudeau, business was just another interest group. His staff had tried hard in recent years to remedy this situation. Jim Coutts enjoyed good connections through the upper and middle reaches of the management world and he had tried to develop a warmer relationship between the PM and businessmen by arranging breakfasts in Toronto, lunches in Montreal, and dinners at Sussex Drive, from which corporate presidents returned to their boardrooms with tales to tell about the man himself and his wife, Margaret, who had a penchant for calling from upstairs, her plaintive cries of "Pierre, could you come up here?" drifting down the stair-well through the cigar smoke into the dining room while her husband, the Prime Minister, was doing his best to listen gravely to their talk. But despite these gatherings, the distance was never bridged. Lurking in the back of the collective business mind was the unsettling knowledge that Trudeau was an intellectual, that he had been a radical, that he did not believe in what they believed in. He was always questioning the most sacred tenets of capitalism's Darwinian creed: hard work, straight deals, maximized profits, minimized government interference, big is beautiful, the race is to the swift, and all's right with the capitalist world. *It made him so goddamn hard to talk to.*

Business suspicion wasn't so much a result of not getting what it wanted from the Trudeau government. It generally did. But in the 1970s it prevailed only after having to fight back efforts by the Trudeau government to contain it, to regulate it, to tax it in ways that had never been tried in the days of Pearson, of St. Laurent, or even of that anti-big-interests maverick from the hinterland, John Diefenbaker. Business was already scared enough by the changes it faced in the world economy and it gained little reassurance from Ottawa. Accelerating inflation combined with stagnating growth was bothering corporate managers, who called for government to set an example by forceful measures to reverse the rate of growth of public deficits. Trudeau's dramatic introduction of wage-and-price controls was not exactly what businessmen had had in mind. Limiting the escalating wage settlements demanded by the powerful trade unions was fine, of course, but the complicated measures worked out by the Anti-Inflation Board to roll back price increases if a company's profits were too high were the kind of inappropriate, ineffective, and time-wasting bureaucratic imbroglio that typified the private sector's complaints about the evils of big government. Businessmen were worried about the falling value of the Canadian dollar, but they no longer had down-to-earth mandarins to reassure them over lunch at the Rideau Club. The upper level of the financial bureaucracy was now staffed by theorists. Tommy Shoyama, the Deputy Minister of Finance, was a former socialist from Tommy Douglas's CCF government in Saskatchewan. Ian Stewart, the main economist in the Privy Council Office, was an academic manqué. So was Sylvia Ostry, who in 1978 had become chairman of the Economic Council, which was nothing but a haven for professors who wanted to publish their research without the bother of having to teach students. Trudeau himself spouted J. K. Galbraith's wacky notions periodically — as he had in his famous New Year's interview with Bruce Phillips on CTV at the end of 1975 when he started speculating about the failure of the free market economy and scared the pants off every chief executive officer in the country. That speech really blew the boys' minds, Turner told his friends.

The Trudeauites found these charges ridiculous. Business still had clout with government, they contended. Its major organizations, like the Canadian Chamber of Commerce, the Business Council on National Issues, and the Canadian Manufacturers' Association, could still command a hearing in ministers' offices. The Conference Board of Canada and the Canadian-American

Committee, now called the C. D. Howe Research Institute, still published analyses and reports which expressed the concerns of continental business strongly and clearly. Besides, business had maintained its powerful voice within the formal institutions of government.

The Senate of Canada had originally been established in 1867 as the protector of the interests of the propertied in Canada. The power of appointment to the Red Chamber had remained ever since in the hands of the country's prime ministers, who had been free over the decades (within the bounds of the constitution's requirement for regional representation) to use the office as a patronage payoff. Despite the appointment of the occasional maverick, like the committed social reformer David Croll or the ebullient constitutional expert Eugene Forsey, the bulk of senatorial appointments had gone to men (and the rare woman) for one of three reasons: their direct service to the Liberal Party (the last five presidents of the party had been made senators); their attainment (and then loss) of high public office (former premiers like Ernest Manning of Alberta, Duff Roblin of Manitoba, or Louis Robichaud of New Brunswick); their important personal standings in the business community (Hartland Molson, Salter Hayden) and proven ability as fund-raisers to extract from businessmen monetary expressions of their confidence in the two-party system (Maurice Riel, the Liberal fund-raiser from Montreal, John Godfrey, his counterpart in Toronto). Whether they came directly from the business world or not, most senators, once appointed, were quickly invited onto corporate boards so that their ability to represent business views in Ottawa could be enhanced.

In the 1970s representing business was no longer just a matter of senators talking to cabinet ministers in parliamentary corridors, as it had been even in Lester Pearson's time. Senators now used well-staffed committees to monitor the legislation that was passing through Parliament and to try to adapt new laws to fit the business community's viewpoint. Apart from playing the leading role in emasculating the government's white paper on tax reform, the Senate had consistently and successfully neutered bills proposed by the government to regulate, in the interests of the Canadian consumer, the performance of companies, the production of hazardous products, the chartering of banks. When a bill affecting business was published, corporate boards considered its implications and thought through the alterations they wanted. Members of a senator's law firm might help draft the desired amendments in appropriate legalese. The senator would approach the relevant minister to get his co-operation, talk to the senior civil servants to inform them of the problem, take his case to the Commons committee hearings, and then set to work in the committee on banking, trade and commerce or the national finance committee to block or change the bill in question.

In 1976, when the Senate finance committee started a study of the federal government's practice of renting office space, eight senators held directorships on twelve private corporations involved in the real estate business. Of these, three were on the finance committee, including Bob Giguère, who was a director of Campeau Corporation which was earning $10.1 million in federal government rentals alone. Other Senate committees put forward the policy views of big business publicly: the Senate committee studying Canadian-American relations, for instance, called for North American free trade. Senator Croll's inquiry into poverty and Senator Davey's report on the domination of the mass media by newspaper chains, both completed in the 1970s, were anomalies. The Senate's usual work was direct mediation between business and the government process. "Without us," one forthright senator told an inquiring scholar, "the cabinet and the bureaucracy would never get the type of co-operation out of the private sector which is needed to make the [capitalist] system run."

Despite the part-time services of senators paid from the public purse with salaries and pension plans indexed to the cost of living, despite the full-time services of consultants and lobbyists hired to press their companies' cases directly within the bureaucracy, despite the reassuring sentiments expressed about the state of Canadian business by the one-man royal commission on corporate concentration that Robert Bryce had chaired in the mid-1970s, despite all these conduits of corporate concern leading into the guts of government, big business was still distressed with Trudeau's administration.

First, there had been the Benson white paper on tax reform.

Later there was the long battle to establish a competition policy which business had fought vigorously ever since Ron Basford had introduced his Competition Act in 1971. Basford's successors as ministers of consumer and corporate affairs had been revising and reintroducing the Act ever since, without getting it through the House. Then there was the period of minority government from 1972 to 1974 when the NDP had managed to extract as the price of its support for the Liberals a number of measures that challenged the core ideas of business life.

The NDP was able to take the credit (or the blame, depending on the point of view) for most of the measures initiated during this period, but Trudeau's government did not set them aside when they regained a majority in 1974. The Foreign Investment Review Agency, a new institution that promised to give the cabinet permanent discretionary power to intervene in the big-time game of foreign corporate mergers, was brought to life in 1974. In tackling the problem of foreign takeovers it presaged more delays, more paperwork, and more frustration for business. Petro-Canada, a new Crown corporation that would give government a privileged position in the energy industries, was set up under the presidency of Maurice Strong, a self-made Canadian entrepreneur and international bureaucrat, with whom conventional businessmen felt uneasy.

The inquiry into the proposed gas pipeline down the Mackenzie River Valley, headed by Mr. Justice Thomas Berger, a former NDP politician, was another sign of the Trudeauites' dangerous tendencies to buck business. Its hearings delayed for years the plans of Canadian Arctic Gas, the consortium of major continental oil firms, to push through the biggest construction project since the building of the CPR. When the judge's report was finally made public in the spring of 1976, the National Energy Board ruled against the Canadian Arctic Gas application, and Trudeau went along with their findings, the worst suspicions of the eastern business community were confirmed. Businessmen went around Toronto and Montreal saying to each other, "Look at what happened to poor Bill Wilder."

They were referring to the fact that the Canadian Arctic Gas consortium was headed by William Wilder, one of the eastern

Canadian corporate elite's biggest stars. Wilder had been president
of Wood, Gundy Limited, the country's largest investment firm,
where his father had been a vice-president before him. He was an
Upper Canada College boy and a Harvard man. He had married
Judith Ryrie Bickle, the daughter of another powerful broker, and
he belonged to all the right clubs — the York, the Toronto, the St.
James's, the Tadenac Fishing. At Wood, Gundy he had acquired
a matchless reputation for being able to bring off intricate financial arrangements involving both the public and the private sector.
Furthermore, he was a Liberal. He had deserted the Tories, the
party of his father and his father-in-law, and had worked on
Mitchell Sharp's campaigns in Toronto-Eglinton. One of his best
friends was Alastair Gillespie, the Minister of Energy, Mines and
Resources, and it was his department that was ostensibly responsible
for the pipeline decision. Wilder knew Coutts well, so his influence was supposed to extend into the PMO. He had been lobbying
Ottawa for years on this pipeline. He believed the majority of the
cabinet was in favour of his application. But then Trudeau said
no. *Clearly, you couldn't make a deal with this guy no matter
who you were.*

This was the point of view that businessmen had been
expressing to John Turner ever since he had started to practise law
in Toronto. For three years he had been under constant pressure.
Publicly he had to present himself as a private citizen who loved
practising law and was glad to have retired from public life. At
the same time he needed to keep his political profile high through
criticisms of government policies that were effective enough to
make a noise in the press without alienating his Liberal allies, who
believed in the party's ancient maxim: "Never ever bad-mouth
the leader — at least not when anybody can pin it on you." His
early speeches after leaving government were innocuous enough
to satisfy these strictures, but in the autumn of 1976 he made his
first error. In the wake of the Parti Québécois victory in November,
he spoke to a large meeting at the Primrose Club in Toronto. The
Toronto Star headlined the story as "Turner hammers PM: Hasn't
done enough to rescue Quebec". Turner claimed the *Star* had
misrepresented his sentiments, saying angrily, "That was just a
lousy heading; I couldn't get Marty Goodman [then the *Star*'s

editor-in-chief] to change it.'' He was amazed at the angry reactions of old Liberal friends; the party closed ranks behind the leader. Coutts said to an inquirer, ''John knows better than that — I don't know what's got into him.'' Thereafter Turner was painstakingly circumspect for a while, refusing interviews, choosing his public appearances carefully, showing himself willing to serve as chairman of Liberal fund-raising events, turning up at Liberal conventions to smile the dazzling smile, flash the piercing blue eyes, and toss the princely head.

Then, in the autumn of 1978, the façade of loyalty to leader and party cracked. First Global television and then the *Toronto Star* carried stories about the fact that Turner and one of his law partners, a highly astute, disaffected Liberal named William A. Macdonald, had been providing a regular ''newsletter'' for a group of corporate clients ''on request''. These documents were, according to the press, candid in the extreme, drawing on Turner's intelligence system inside the government to describe the performances of cabinet ministers and bureaucrats as they were viewed from the inside. Jean Chrétien had ''lost leverage'' as finance minister; Alastair Gillespie, the minister of energy, lacked the confidence of the prime minister; Jack Horner, the trade and commerce minister, was spending ninety-five per cent of his time away from his office. And then, oh heresy, oh sin, Turner and Macdonald suggested: *The Liberals were probably going to lose the next election.*

Turner denied that the documents were ''newsletters''; they were nothing but legal services, providing businessmen with briefings of the kind that cabinet ministers received from their advisers. He wrote letters to the cabinet ministers involved to apologize for ''getting personal''. But the press wouldn't let up: the feud between the Trudeauites and the Turnerites which had been covert for so long was now out in the open.

There had been rumours in party circles for months that Trudeau wouldn't go anywhere the Turners were expected, that he had called the American Embassy to check that the Turners hadn't been invited to a party he meant to attend, though on the rare occasions when they did meet, courtesies were observed. The previous spring, Trudeau had come to Toronto to a large dinner at the York Club and had perfunctorily kissed Geills Turner on the cheek when he spied the Turners in the crush. She turned away from him, eyes bright with emotion, and immediately whispered to a woman behind her, "He always does that — he always *pretends* to be glad to see us."

Now there was no pretending. After the newsletters were made public, in an interview with Peter Desbarats of CTV, Trudeau responded to a question about the possibility of his retirement by saying, "If I were resigning it would be because I thought that I was no longer the best man to lead the Party and then I would really rely on the Party choosing who the best man to succeed me is. Just as Mr. Pearson did back in '68. . . . You say the obvious man is Mr. Turner. I understand he's been the obvious [choice] . . . what for six or eight years, perhaps ten?" Oh unkind cut!

For the next six months the Turnerites and the Trudeauites went on sniping at each other in private with an occasional minor public eruption that reverberated throughout the Liberal Party. The party regulars' nerves were raw. They had been preparing for an election more or less seriously since the summer of 1977 when Coutts and Davey had tried unsuccessfully to talk Trudeau into riding to a renewed and even larger Liberal victory at the polls on his personal popularity, which was momentarily inflated by the separatist scare after the PQ victory in Quebec and by his dignified response to his marital troubles. The polls had been falling ever since, with Liberal support wasting away everywhere outside Quebec. In 1978, the year a general election would normally have been called, the Liberals had to back away first from setting a spring date, then from setting an autumn one. They were forced to call fifteen by-elections in seven provinces in October 1978 to fill vacancies in the Commons brought about mostly by the resignations of MPs under the expectation that a general election was imminent. The irony was that of the fifteen vacancies, ten were created by the government itself, which had given patronage appointments to both Liberal and Conservative MPs, in order to clear seats for new candidates and to reward old faithfuls ready for retirement. Two other vacancies were caused by the premature retirement of Liberals who could have held their seats until a general election. Only three, in other words, were vacancies created by factors beyond the Liberals' control. That their plight was to a large extent of their leader's making didn't sweeten Liberal tempers, and the mood within the ranks during the campaign for the 1978 by-elections was even more irascible than it had been during the sullen election of 1972.

When the votes were counted, the Liberals had lost in thirteen of the fifteen ridings, that is, every contested seat in English Canada, including St. Boniface in Manitoba, where there was a large francophone vote and which had gone Liberal with only one exception since it was created in 1925. "After that disaster, we were like surfers waiting for the perfect wave," said Brian Flemming, the Halifax lawyer who served as a policy adviser in the PMO from 1976 to 1979. "It never came and we knew we were going to have to get on the surf-boards and try to ride in under conditions so bad it took more guts than brains to attempt it."

The news got worse and worse for the Liberals in the press that fall and winter of 1978–79. The party reverberated with rumours that Trudeau would be asked to step down to make way for Turner, and that Turner had reactivated his 195 Club and was renting office space for a leadership race. In November at a party national executive meeting, Marc Lalonde lambasted the English-Canadian Liberals present in the wake of the dismal by-election results. You let us down, he told the assembled company, pointing his long finger of scorn. We won our seats in Quebec this time, we won them last time [in 1977 when the Liberals had been victorious in four out of five by-elections held in Quebec]. What's the matter with you? One of the Liberals present, in reporting this afterwards, said the obvious, though unstated, response was, "You're what's the matter with us, you and your goddamn obsession with separatism." Then, in December, the *Toronto Star* published the results of a specially commissioned Gallup poll which showed that with John Turner as leader, the Liberals could win the coming general election in both English and French Canada.

At official campaign committee meetings across the country, and over drinks and dinner afterwards, Liberals began to argue incessantly about what policies should be stressed in the campaign to come. The French Canadians still wanted to run on the question

of Canadian unity, using a promise to patriate the constitution as
an electoral plank. The federal-provincial relations experts in the
PMO had been working feverishly on constitutional reviews for
two years. There was another first ministers' conference scheduled
for February 1979 to discuss patriation and to try to reach an
agreement on how to bring it about. It could be 1968 all over
again, they argued, with Trudeau seen as the saviour of the country. The English Canadians continued to be sceptical about this
approach, especially after the Pepin-Robarts Task Force on Canadian Unity report, which was published in January, questioned
the Trudeauites' ideas on federalism. Then, the February first
ministers' conference on the constitution ended in confusion. The
premiers could not agree among themselves on patriation, let alone
with Trudeau, who made concession after concession to them in
an attempt to achieve his goal.

The English Canadians repeated what they had been saying
for months. They wanted policies that would deal with the economic issues, a policy promising government aid to home owners
suffering from high mortgage rates, for instance, which would
attract middle-class voters and consolidate Liberal votes among
the working class, who were in danger of defecting to the Tories
or the NDP. The remnants of the old Liberal left, what was called
the new guard in Pearson's time, surfaced and began to complain
that the party was losing ground because it had abandoned its
liberalism. Turner didn't really speak for them, they insisted. He
had become infected with the right-wing notions of the American
multinational executives he was consorting with, people who were
entranced with the simplistic economic theories put forward by
Ronald Reagan, the former governor of California now manoeuvring
for the Republican presidential nomination — theories that didn't
apply in Canada in any case, since it had always been a mixed
economy where publicly owned corporations and government
subsidies to business had been the rule since the beginning. By
attempting to pander to right-wing sentiment, the Liberals would
lose their sustaining principles of the past, their progressive approach to social welfare, the balance they had struck between the
needs of business and labour, their belief in individual liberties. If
the Turnerites prevailed — or if the Trudeauites tried to fend them

off by adopting their conservatism in modified form — the Liberal era really would be over.

Throughout that bad winter Keith Davey and Jim Coutts, the old soft-shoe team who had been seen as political wizards only five years before, were suffering a particularly difficult ordeal. As chief political advisers to the Prime Minister, they had to back off from Turner, who had been a comrade-in-arms for seventeen years. They had to answer to Trudeau and for Trudeau to the English-Canadian members of the party, who were increasingly angry with him. Several important new candidates Coutts and Davey had gone to considerable trouble to recruit in 1977 and 1978 were now declining to stand in the general election. John Evans, the ex-president of the University of Toronto, Maurice Strong, the business star, Bruce McLeod, a former United Church moderator, and Doris Anderson, the one-time editor of *Chatelaine* magazine, had all bowed out. Less well-known candidates, both old and new, were grumbling incessantly that the long wait was costing them alternative jobs, lost incomes, prestige in their communities, all things Liberals hold dear.

In the face of these complaints, Coutts and Davey had to hold the party apparatus together somehow so the election could be fought as efficiently as possible, to keep on pretending optimism and fostering the belief that the Liberals were still one big happy family. But all the time they knew very well that in 1979 the Grits were internally divided into factions that they had to weld together into an electoral machine whose one purpose was the retention of power.

PART SIX

THE POWER MACHINE AND THE POLITICS OF DESPERATION
The Liberal Party in 1979

BEFORE THEY WENT WEARILY BACK to their Ottawa hotel rooms on the night of March 26, 1979, Keith Davey and Jim Coutts, the chief Liberal strategists for the election that was just getting under way, met for an hour in Coutts's office to watch the Prime Minister on television and to go over for what seemed like the thousandth time the main details of the campaign to come.

The slogan they had decided on — A Leader Must Be A Leader — said all anybody needed to know about their overall strategy. Trudeau was what they were stuck with and Trudeau was what had to be sold. One of Davey's many political maxims, memorized nearly twenty years before, was "Lead to your strength, not your weakness". Just how the Prime Minister's controversial public persona fitted that maxim at the moment was a question whose answer he couldn't quite articulate, since Trudeau seemed to be as much the Liberals' weakness in English Canada as he was their strength in the province of Quebec. "Let's be brassy," Coutts and Davey had said in trying to still their qualms. "Let's let it all hang out. This is *our* guy and we're for him."

It wasn't that Coutts and Davey loved Trudeau as they had loved Pearson fifteen years before. They were too old now for hero worship and Trudeau was too remote, too unpredictable, too different from them in any case. Their feelings for him seemed to be a mixture of respect, fear, a superstitious regard for the Liberal axiom that you support the leader come thick or come thin, and a hard-headed acceptance of the political realities of the 1970s. They knew they were living in an era of leadership politics, at the pinnacle of what was one of the most leader-dominated parties in the democratic world. Whatever power they had was dependent on their relationship with this intellectual statesman they called "our guy". (In the same sporty style, the press had taken to describing Coutts and Davey as "Trudeau's handlers", a phrase that kindled the Prime Minister's ire. "It makes me sound like some kind of prize-fighter," he complained at a PMO staff meeting. "I don't know what *he's* croaking about," Coutts said afterwards to Tom

325

Axworthy, one of his assistant principal secretaries. "It makes *us* sound like those sweaty guys who sit in the corner of the boxing ring behind the water buckets, holding the fighter's teeth and his satin bathrobe.")

In the months before the election's call — as one poll result after another came in showing the Liberals trailing behind the Tories — the mood in the Prime Minister's Office had been for the most part grim but resolute. Coutts saw to that. If despair was expressed at how bad the situation looked for the party, it was done ironically and out of earshot of anybody who might do the Liberals harm. When Axworthy wrote a letter to a friend in Paris he began his description of the Grits' predicament with the line "Greetings from Custer's Last Stand!" (The friend was Bob Murdoch, who had been Trudeau's executive assistant before he escaped to a job with Lafarge Cement's French operation in the summer of 1978 when so many Liberals with political jobs were trying to find permanent work before the election debacle that was expected.)

Axworthy was the Manitoban charged with liaison work for the Prime Minister among Liberals in the West. In his mind the General Custer pressing on to certain slaughter was, of course, Pierre Trudeau, though the Prime Minister himself, drawing on a different set of cultural ikons, talked instead of the plight of Napoleon in 1815 or of Laurier a century later when English-Canadian Liberals were deserting him by the thousands over the conscription crisis of the First World War.

Trudeau had said to his national campaign committee after one of the many meetings they held to discuss the need to wait for the most propitious moment at which to call the election, "The troops will need nerves of steel." In repeating this sentence afterwards, a Liberal who had been present remarked, "He means nerves like his." Outwardly, Trudeau was facing his sea of troubles with a self-containment that even his detractors in the party found remarkable, and that his partisans, who seemed to be dwindling in number every day, said was magnificent even when they were only talking among themselves.

The five years since he had joined forces with the Toronto Grits to win the election of 1974 had brought Trudeau one defeat after another in his public and personal lives. He still flashed the old arrogance in the House of Commons and in skirmishes with the bitterly hostile press. But in private he seemed far from arrogant. He knew he was likely to lose the coming election and had known it since the previous spring. He had come to the prime-ministership with three specific ambitions: the streamlining and democratization of the governmental process; the creation of a bilingual federal public service that would ensure equality for French Canadians within the bureaucratic system; and the patriation of the constitution with an entrenched bill of rights that would guarantee linguistic equality in the country as a whole. The first ambition had resulted in a travesty; the second was only partly realized; and after the last failed constitutional conference in February, the third looked unattainable. So much of what Trudeau had worked towards had never been and perhaps never would be achieved. In personal conversation, he gave the impression of being distracted and weary, aware of the need to put on the bold face that Coutts insisted was imperative, but despising it at the same time.

At a farewell party held just before the election's call for Richard O'Hagan, his communications consultant, who was leaving the PMO to become a vice-president of the Bank of Montreal, Trudeau spoke to an old acquaintance, a professor who had been asking to see him to discuss an academic study of participatory democracy. Trudeau promised they would talk at length after the election was over, and then added in a voice laden with rueful self-deprecation, "That's if you still want to see me after I've lost." As he moved on through the crowd, a Liberal who had overheard him said in hoarse desperation, "I wish to God he would stop acting like a Christian martyr about to kiss his scourge." Trudeau was at the nadir of his career that winter, and to those who had known him earlier in his life he seemed desperately alienated and alone.

II

THE OBVIOUS LONELINESS had to do with his broken marriage and the fact that Trudeau had been living for two years in a blaze of publicity that his estranged wife, Margaret, kept fanning compulsively, talking out loud to whoever would listen about her personal ambitions and her sexual energies. There was something that went beyond irony in the situation that this man who had lived a life so free of ordinary intimacies and encumbrances until he was over fifty should have the details of his private life bandied about in the newspapers, poked at, and analysed by people whom he had never met and who in reality knew very little about him. "I mean," said one of the Toronto Grits in a remark that owed more to perspicacity than to delicacy, "the poor guy's walking around with his fly open."

When it became apparent that Mrs. Trudeau's memoirs were to be published that spring in a ghost-written book called *Beyond Reason*, just when the Liberals' mandate was expiring and the election could no longer be postponed, one of the Prime Minister's old friends from the 1950s said bitterly, "I'm sick to death of stories about Margaret Trudeau. But every time she opens her mouth, I can't help think that she is a kind of monstrous metaphor for what happened to Pierre — how power inflated his ego, trivialized his ideas, and cut him off from his roots."

This man hadn't talked to Trudeau alone or at length for many years. The sentence "I never see him any more" ran like a refrain through the conversations of most of Trudeau's old friends and acquaintances. In part, Trudeau was the victim of the alienation from the ordinary that afflicts all political leaders even in so small and unpompous a nation as Canada. Mackenzie King's diaries reveal that the longer he was in power, the lonelier he became, a loneliness that wasn't alleviated even when he had stepped down from the leadership. Joan Patteson, the bank manager's wife who was King's last, best confidante, remembered that on the night of the 1949 election, when Louis St. Laurent won his first great victory — a victory made possible in large measure because of the political alliance King had painstakingly put together and handed on to St. Laurent intact the year before — King listened to the returns on the radio alone with her, then went sadly off to bed without any important Liberals bothering to telephone to discuss the party's triumph with him.

In Trudeau's case, the loneliness of high office took on a special poignancy because of his isolation from his home province and from the touchstone ideas and relationships of his past. In some ways, he was like a man in exile. His mother, who had been ill for many years, had died in 1973. His sister and brother, who were both by nature reticent, rarely came to Ottawa and never appeared in public with him. His sons, Justin, Sacha, and Michel, were still very young and he complained sadly that he couldn't get them to speak French to him. They were the offspring of Rockcliffe, pupils at local nursery and elementary schools, under the care of housekeepers and nannies, watched over by RCMP security officers, scrutinized by the press. The life Trudeau had lived in the exciting intellectual climate of the Montreal of the 1950s must have seemed very far away.

In truth, the Quebec of the first half of the century, the backward province that had formed Trudeau's outlook and stimulated in him the fierce desire to transcend its parochialism, no longer existed. It had been altered by the revolution he and the other intellectuals of his generation had helped foment. To many young Quebeckers in the Cégeps and the universities, who had grown up in the new Quebec, the ideas of the *Cité libristes* were almost quaint. "C'est un vieux," a young girl was heard to say dismissively after he gave a federalist speech at a college in Montreal early in 1979. Trudeau was seen by her generation as an anachronism, much as St. Laurent had been viewed by Trudeau's friends twenty-five years before.

The Quebeckers who actively supported Trudeau now were for the most part people he would have scorned or ignored as a young man: businessmen fearful of what an independent Quebec would do to their profit pictures, careerist lawyers with an interest in federal government contracts or judicial appointments, older people in rural districts whose families had been *rouges* since the time of Laurier. The huge Quebec Liberal caucus was loyal to him beyond question, as was the entire Quebec party machine. But he was uncomfortable with the role of Le Chef, and in any case he was a very different kind of man from the usual French-Canadian Liberal politician. He had left the management of the machine first to Marchand and then to Lalonde and he attended caucus meetings like some grand seigneur, appearing among his people to hear their complaints, hopes, and fears. When Marchand resigned his House of Commons seat in 1976, there was a great outpouring of regret in a Quebec federal caucus meeting. Trudeau said after it was over, "They need that kind of emotional release; it's a catharsis for them." The man to whom this remark was addressed found it oddly paternalistic and distant, since it ignored Trudeau's own loss of a close comrade.

Trudeau had never been given to open expression of his feelings. Easy conversation of any kind was usually possible for him only among intellectuals he knew well, and other than Pitfield, there was no such man in his entourage now. The old *Cité libristes* had long since scattered. Roger Rolland and Jean LeMoyne had left his office. Others who had been appointed to federal government jobs (Charles Lussier, Pierre Juneau, and the rest) now crossed paths only rarely with Trudeau, meeting him mostly on official occasions in a crush of people.

Jean Marchand, having lost his bid for election to the Quebec legislature, was by now underemployed in the Senate, discredited as a political force in Quebec, frequently ill and depressed. He remarked sadly, "Pierre has changed so much now. He has been traumatized by the events of his private disaster [his marriage]. I hardly ever see him any more." Even Gérard Pelletier and Jacques Hébert, Trudeau's closest friends, were reachable much of the time only by long-distance telephone. Hébert was busy travelling the country and the globe, administering the national and international youth programs which he had founded, and engrossing himself in the problems of the third world. Pelletier's duties as Canadian ambassador to France kept him in Paris for most of the year.

Another of Trudeau's old friends and intellectual allies, Madeleine Gobeil, was also in Paris, working as a cultural officer at UNESCO. Although Trudeau never discussed his relationships with women — not even with his wife, according to her account — a variety of female friends surfaced in Ottawa and Montreal after he became prime minister, telling enigmatic stories of little trysts and memorable moments spent in the company of Pierre. (For a while it was a running joke in some Montreal circles to say, "My God, Trudeau seems to have slept with as many women as Norman Bethune," Bethune having become a legend after his death for his sexual adventuring.) But as far as their mutual friends knew, Madeleine Gobeil had been the most enduring romantic relationship of Trudeau's life.

Gobeil, who grew up in Ottawa as one of the nine children of a minor federal civil servant, had been a prize-winning pupil of the Grey Nuns and the recipient of an important scholarship that enabled her to go to university. As a student, out of a joyous naïveté and an intense intellectual hunger that the parochialism of her environment could not satisfy, she had sent letters to various writers whose ideas interested her. Two of these notes had resulted in close friendships of many years' duration — one with the formidable French intellectual Simone de Beauvoir, and the other with Gérard and Alex Pelletier. The Pelletiers were nearly twenty years older than Gobeil but they encouraged her career from the time she first wrote to them in the early 1950s. When she was a nineteen-year-old university student, they introduced her to Trudeau. More than a decade later, after he became the Liberal leader and began his public flirtations with so many other women, from Jennifer Rae, the diplomat's daughter who had worked on his leadership campaign, to Barbra Streisand, the American actress whom he had met in London early in 1969, his continuing friendship with Gobeil was a matter of some fascination to the people in Ottawa who knew them both.

For Gobeil herself the model was the relationship between her great friend Beauvoir and Jean-Paul Sartre, a sustained closeness between two free people. During most of the time that Trudeau had been in federal politics, Gobeil had been teaching French literature at Carleton University. She also travelled extensively in Europe as well as in Africa and the Middle East. When she was in Paris, she would meet Beauvoir often for a late lunch and they would sit together in some bistro near Beauvoir's apart-

ment in the 14th arrondissement, talking about everything from
the impact of *The Second Sex* on the new feminists to Sartre's
attraction to the extremist attitudes of the French student movements.

Gobeil was widely read beyond her own discipline, she was
perceptive, and she was sensitive. ("I treasure in myself," she
once wrote, "this strange combination . . . a fierce desire for life
as well as a lucid perception of its ultimate futility.") She was
also beautiful. Her younger sister, Charlotte Gobeil, who became
a CBC television star, resembled her enough that they seemed like
two aspects of one personality when they were together: Madeleine
introverted, gentle, solicitous of others, Charlotte extroverted, deliberately outrageous, witty. Once at a summer picnic in the
Gatineau Hills with a group of Ottawa friends, a woman watched
the Gobeils talking together, both wearing long, drifty dresses
and beribboned straw hats, and said, "They are like something
from Colette. All you need to do is to look at them to believe in
the persistence of the French fact in North America."

What was probably as important to Trudeau as Gobeil's other
qualities was that she was also independent, loyal, and discreet.
Even after he was ensconced at 24 Sussex they continued their
long-standing habit of spending one or two evenings a week in
each other's company when they were both in the same city. During
the October Crisis of 1970, Gobeil set aside time each day to be
with Trudeau as a support in agonizing times. Yet when Trudeau
married in the spring of 1971, Gobeil heard about the wedding
through a newspaperman who called her for a comment. Trudeau
had told Gobeil he was in love with Margaret Sinclair and she had
asked him for old times' sake to let her know when he was getting
married so she could escape Ottawa beforehand in order to avoid
the questions of the curious and the solicitude of the kindly. On
the night before his wedding, Trudeau had prevailed upon his old
friend Pelletier to take their mutual friend, Gobeil, out for dinner
to break the news. ("It was so typical of Pierre to do this," another friend said. "He is unable to bear other people's pain. He
never seems to understand that hurt can also be inflicted by
avoidance. It reduces one to nothing.") Pelletier could not bring
himself to tell Gobeil about Trudeau's still-secret plans and talked

awkwardly about the difficulties the future might bring. In the middle of the next night Gobeil realized what had been wrong with Pelletier when a desk man from the *Toronto Star* woke her to yell questions about Trudeau's marriage down the telephone, trying to gauge the nature of her surprise or pain or disinterest from whatever comment he could jolt out of her.

As soon as the university year was over, Gobeil left Ottawa to live in Paris permanently, first to finish a doctorate at the Sorbonne and then to work at UNESCO. Trudeau asked about her often afterwards when he saw her sister, Charlotte, or when he was coming to Paris to stay at the Canadian Embassy after the Pelletiers were in residence there. To his puzzlement, she never wanted to see him, and they didn't meet again for years.

The world that Gobeil represented — the world of ideas, of long, intense discussions between friends, of unencumbered travel and intellectual quests — was lost to Trudeau long before their friendship was broken. His life had altered considerably as soon as he became prime minister. But it was also true that in the years of his marriage and his separation — which coincided in part with his rapprochement with the Toronto Liberals — it altered even more. In those years, Trudeau seemed to many old acquaintances to become almost a different person, changed drastically by the office he had sought in order to put his ideas into effect. It was as though power had inflated him at first, blown his ego up like a balloon, and now, after the vicissitudes of the last few years, had deflated him, turned him in on himself.

His old comrades hadn't been replaced. In English Canada, the intellectual community's view of Trudeau had steadily deteriorated. His name was a rude joke in common rooms and at learned society meetings, a synonym for sellout. When the statement was made that Trudeau was a brilliant thinker — as it was so often throughout his public career by politicians of all parties and journalists of many different persuasions — the usual response among academics was some variation of "By what standards? You certainly can't say he is *original.*" Partly this attitude seemed to be plain envy, masked by the civilized mannerisms and impressive vocabularies that were still the identifying marks of the don, even in the high-tech, low-budget world of Canadian universities in the 1970s. Ramsay Cook, who had known Trudeau for several years before his sudden celebrity and remained one of his few champions in academe after the War Measures invocation, expressed this view elegantly when he wrote, "On the [scornful] attitude of many intellectuals in Canada to Trudeau, I remain puzzled. But I think there is a clue to the answer in the last few sentences of George Orwell's marvellous essay on Charles Dickens, sentences that read in part, 'In Dickens, I see . . . the face of a man who is always fighting against something, but who fights in the open and is not frightened, the face of a man who is generously angry, in other words of a nineteenth century liberal, a free intelligence, a type hated with equal hatred by all the smelly little orthodoxies which are contending for our souls.'"

In response to Cook's view, a bureaucrat who had spent many years in academe before coming to work in Trudeau's Ottawa as an administrator and policy-maker remarked, "Envy and fear of a free spirit may have been behind the dislike for Trudeau expressed by many Canadian intellectuals in the early days. But I think there is more to it than that. There is something about him that stifles other people's creativity. He never encourages discussion of his ideas from outsiders or indeed insiders. He suffers from what the Americans call 'the Chomsky syndrome' [after the academic polymath Noam Chomsky of the Massachusetts Institute of Technology]. Because he knows so much in one field, he thinks he knows everything. In Trudeau's case, his field is Quebec and the constitution and on that subject he is unassailable. But in so many other areas, particularly economic policy, there were people he should have heeded, whose brains and experience he should have bowed to. Instead, able and original thinkers were turned off by his contentious attitudes. For all his love of dialectic, he had trouble accepting others' ideas when they clashed with his. If you weren't a brilliant performer, he disdained you. If you were, he had to savage you to show his superiority. In the end, he kept returning to ideas he had formulated himself twenty and thirty years before. It was a tragedy. The most intellectual prime minister in our history cut off from his own kind. The people he was left with were the process-minded, managers not thinkers, political fixers who couldn't see beyond the next opinion poll."

Whatever the reasons for Trudeau's isolation from the comrades of his past and the counsel of his peers, as the 1979 election began he found himself in a curious position. The intellectual loner who had despised the Liberal Party machine was now entangled in its toils. Although he was in control of the party, he was also the party's captive.

For many months he had been forced to travel constantly on party business, fulfilling obligations and attending functions he clearly found distasteful and tolerated solely because his political advisers told him they were crucial to the survival of the Liberal alliance. He would get up at a meeting of Liberals and read a speech about the Liberal past and the Liberal future containing ideas of dubious validity (viz. "The Liberal Party is the party of the radical middle") from a text prepared in his office. If his mood were good he would sometimes do it brilliantly, memorizing the lines beforehand, referring only rarely to his notes, sounding as though these ideas came straight out of his own being instead of straight out of the nimble minds of Jim Coutts, or his assistant, Tom Axworthy. But if Trudeau was in one of his periodic lows as a consequence of his wife's behaviour or as a result of a disturbing turn of events in Quebec, or for some other reason his staff could not fathom, he would read the same sort of speech mechanically, almost uncomprehendingly, displaying once more his lack of "a gut feeling for politics", as the English-Canadian Liberals persisted in describing the cultural and intellectual differences inherent in his attitudes to party affairs.

A systematic study of how Trudeau spent his prime-ministerial time, conducted by Michael Pitfield's staff in the mid-seventies, showed that twenty per cent of it was devoted to political activity, and that's the way Trudeau preferred to think of party politicking — as an element in his job. For Trudeau, as he told a writer not long before the election's call, the Liberal Party was "an important instrument in the Canadian reality" with which he had achieved a symbiosis. "I did get into the political game [after the near-defeat of 1972] and I felt I could learn a lot from what you might call the ward-heeling pols," he explained carefully. "Some of my amusement with and affection for Keith Davey is because he is a professional pol. . . . I had a lot of fun in the 1968 to 1972 period but the difference [afterwards] was that I was a bit closer to the pros. Their schemes amuse me. Coutts's foxiness, for instance, I like to see it working, in the same sense as I like to see Allan MacEachen in the House [of Commons] with his deft knowledge of that world. Politics is a great game and you try to outfox people. Resourcefulness is something I have pleasure in observing and using.''

This dispassionate attitude had always been a source of chagrin to the Grits who had joined forces with Trudeau in 1973. They were constantly trying to chivvy him into loving politics, not just observing it, into spending more time shoring up the morale of the troops, improving his image in the press, using the government policy-making machinery to political advantage, learning how to be ''a real Liberal'' as they described it.

''When we first knew him, you just couldn't tell what he would do next,'' one of them remembered. Once at a dinner meeting of key party people in Toronto, a Scarborough Liberal started talking to him about inflation. He had friends who needed to buy a house on the crazily inflated Toronto market, he explained to Trudeau, but they were worried about high mortgage rates and always wanted to talk about how these rates were linked to the government's economic policy. What should this guy tell them? ''Move to Regina,'' Trudeau had said promptly, to the horror of the dinner's organizer, who told him afterwards that this was definitely not the way to win the loyalty of the troops.

Ever since then, the Toronto Grits had laboured mightily to help Trudeau understand the party's workings, to show him how to play the great game they found so much more engrossing than he did. In the period just before the 1973 party convention, for instance, Gordon Dryden, the original founder of Cell 13, had realized that, in the wake of Trudeau's poor showing at the 1972 election, he was going to need an overwhelming display of approval from the delegates when they came to vote on whether to hold a leadership convention, now a required procedure at the first post-election assembly. Dryden concocted a scheme whose express purpose was lobbying the vote without appearing to do so.

He decided to do four things: to get Jean Marchand to brief the large Quebec delegation beforehand, telling them that they must "vote right" since much of English Canada had rejected Trudeau at the polls and it was vital to show now that the Liberal Party, the only federal party that really made a place for French Canadians, was behind him; to make sure there was a full complement of Newfoundlanders in attendance because they were still amenable to control by a party boss and could be directed to vote for Trudeau; to guarantee as far as possible that all privy councillors and senators hale enough to move were planning to attend the convention since they had automatic voting rights and understood the rules of Liberal loyalty sufficiently to do their duty, and thereby offset the votes of the unruly; and finally, to devise a complicated system of punching holes in delegates' tags so the anti-Trudeauites could be readily identified and a team of pro-Trudeauites could invite them out for drinks and discussions while the voting was in progress.

Dryden's tactics worked. The leader pulled more than ninety per cent of the delegates' votes, and when Dryden told Trudeau afterwards how it had been done he was both intrigued and amused, asking to have details repeated as though he were listening to an anthropologist's description of the strange rites of some hitherto unstudied tribe.

But in the two-year-long countdown to this election, after several dozen such strategies and their accompanying tactics had been unfolded, Trudeau gave the impression that the activities he had to undertake and the attitudes he had to assume on the Liberal Party's behalf were no longer either amusing or intriguing. Instead, they had turned into exhausting all-too-familiar chores that frequently violated his privacy and sometimes contradicted his stated principles.

He had always said that citizens should serve a political party only if such activities fitted into the overall patterns of their own lives; persuading people to come to his aid was anathema to him. Now he held meeting after meeting with Liberals who were either old faithfuls or new hopefuls, displaying a knowledge of their backgrounds and an interest in their ideas derived from the briefings that Coutts and his staff provided for him and that were calculated to win their allegiance. When he came to Toronto to make a speech or attend a function, for instance, Coutts would invite down to his hotel suite for a pre-meeting chat Liberals such as David Smith, say, or Jim Peterson, lawyers in their late thirties who were thinking of standing for federal office to help provide the renewal in the ranks the party needed. These meetings were often successful and party members would come away saying the PM had been far easier to get along with than they had heard, that he had shown real respect for their views and real interest in their careers.

At other times, Trudeau couldn't keep himself under control. Sometimes the musings of possible candidates would cause his eyes to grow opaque with boredom or his murderous competitiveness to surface. When John Evans finally was convinced that his duty to his country demanded that he give up his job as president of the University of Toronto — along with offers from Cornell and Yale to stand for their presidencies — Trudeau dutifully appeared at his nomination meeting in April of 1978 and then came back in the autumn to campaign with him before the October by-elections. Evans was being hailed in the press as a possible prime minister and the finest flower of the English-Canadian establishment — which indeed he was — and he had been described, because of his work on the Task Force on Canadian Unity, as even more adept than Trudeau himself in his ability to sum up clearly a complex discussion. When the glowing possibilities of Evans's political future were mentioned by a Toronto businessman at one of the lunches his staff had arranged for the Prime Minister, Trudeau said with a shrug, "Well, he'll have to get himself elected first." Later, when he and Evans were out door-knocking and hand-shaking together in downtown Toronto, at the southern end of the Rosedale constituency, Trudeau was openly jubilant when Evans proved awkward at hustling votes. "He certainly doesn't know how to handle this kind of situation, does he?" the Prime Minister said to the staff man at his side. "Everybody is crowding around *me* instead of him. He keeps getting stuck in long conversations instead of working through the crowd." After Evans was trounced in the election by David Crombie, the Tory candidate, he was publicly critical of Trudeau at an Ontario party meeting and refused to run again in the upcoming general election, saying privately that his candidacy had been one of the worst experiences of his life.

In much the same vein, even though Trudeau had never made any bones about his dislike for the press and his need for privacy, he had been persuaded by his staff to give regular news conferences, to meet publishers and journalists over breakfast, lunch, and dinner, to submit to interviews with television personalities, and to refrain from showing his disdain for what he regarded as their ineptitudes. "Okay, so these aren't journalists of the calibre of those who work for *Le Monde* or the London *Times*," Richard O'Hagan, who had been charged with improving Trudeau's press relations, would say to him. "This is the press you have to deal with and it's necessary to respond to their needs at their level."

O'Hagan had tried to get Trudeau to address by name the important columnists, Allan Fotheringham, Richard Gwyn, Charles Lynch, Douglas Fisher, Bill Wilson, Geoffrey Stevens, and Dalton Camp. Trudeau wouldn't do it. He couldn't even be relied on to remember the Christian name of George Radwanski, his biographer, though he had admired Radwanski's lucid interviewing style during their conversations for the book.

At the time of the Trudeau marital separation, O'Hagan had conducted a mock interview with the Prime Minister, throwing out the nastiest questions he could think of so Trudeau would be ready for the onslaught of press inquiries about the activities of his wife. Later, he had convinced Trudeau to travel by cross-country train on a summer holiday with his young sons through the Rockies to Prince Rupert in British Columbia in order to provide poignant evidence of his bravery as a single parent and to display at the same time his new-found "gut feeling" for the West. He had even extracted from Trudeau an agreement to submit to a television interview in April of 1978 at 24 Sussex with the children present, conducted for the CTV network by Stephanie McLuhan, one of the daughters of Marshall McLuhan whom Trudeau knew and liked. (This interview had been planned in response to Liberal advisers from three Toronto advertising agencies, Terry O'Malley of Vickers & Benson, Hank Karpus from Ronalds-Reynolds, and Jerry Goodis of MacLaren's, who had been invited to the prime-ministerial residence for dinner the previous summer along with Jerry Grafstein, Martin Goldfarb, and Keith Davey. The ad men had been so enchanted with the sight of the Prime Minister crawling under the piano chasing after his sons, who were kibitzing with him before bedtime, "they were practically salivating trying to figure out how to get that image across on television," said Keith Davey, who had arranged the dinner. On camera, the actual interview was less than enchanting; Trudeau was wooden with discomfort, the children edgy.)

Trudeau had even been patient with his advisers when they repeated ad nauseam that he must stop giving the impression of being obsessed with Quebec by making appearances and concocting policies that would win him votes in two areas that were unfriendly to him, the Western provinces, where the party's strength was now at an all-time low, and Ontario, where the voters were volatile and Liberal popularity had "gone soft", in their jargon. ("Trudeau doesn't identify with Toronto or the West," one of his staff members said solemnly in explaining the need to repeat these suggestions to him. "He identifies with Quebec," a statement that seemed akin to saying of Charles de Gaulle, "He identifies with France.")

Some of the things Trudeau was willing to do to win votes in Ontario and the Western provinces were straightforward image-making: attending a hockey playoff in Toronto or the Commonwealth Games in Edmonton; riding a horse at the Calgary Stampede or having lunch at the Courtyard Café in Toronto with a Liberal candidate and then walking down Yonge Street to look at the city's marvels; travelling to each of the Western provincial capitals to speak personally to individual premiers in preparation for a federal-provincial conference on the economy or holding the first-ever full-scale cabinet meeting in the West; giving a big dinner in Toronto for the President of Italy and inviting ethnic community leaders and newspaper editors by the score to sew up the ethnic vote; throwing a huge reception in Ottawa for Walter Mondale, the U.S. vice-president, who was also a close friend of Richard O'Hagan's, and inviting most of the important Liberals in the country to attend; or taking up a long-standing invitation to speak to the Economic Club of New York just before the election's call was planned, in order to create a splash in the newspapers that would remind Canadians that Trudeau was a world-class statesman. All these actions were standard practice: the kind of tricks a party in office can play as part of the game of outfoxing its opponents.

But some of the things Trudeau did to win votes were neither standard nor, in the end, image-enhancing. To many ordinary Canadians they seemed basely cynical. One such act was Trudeau's decision to invite into his cabinet the dissident right-wing Tory from Alberta, Jack Horner, who as one of the noisiest of the Diefenbaker "cowboys" had been crudely opposed to the Official Languages Act that was a cornerstone of Trudeau's federalism. Another was Trudeau's long delay in responding to repeated Opposition and press charges of abuses of civil liberties by the RCMP in their surveillance activities in Quebec and elsewhere, a delay that was finally ended with his decision to appoint Judge David McDonald, a former Liberal from Alberta, to head up a commission of inquiry which Trudeau no doubt hoped could conveniently defuse the controversial issue of the Mounties' allegedly illegal behaviour until after the next election. A third was his curiously ambiguous statements about the possibility of holding a referendum on the reinstatement of the death penalty, which appeared to pay more heed to a Gallup poll that showed a majority of Canadians favoured hanging than it did to Trudeau's own passionate abolitionist stance. A fourth was his surprise appointment of Edward Schreyer, the one-time premier of Manitoba, as governor general, a job that had been promised to George Ignatieff, a distinguished former diplomat who was as clearly suited to the role as Schreyer was not.

In 1963, when Trudeau had been furious at Lester Pearson for reversing his stand on the acceptance of nuclear warheads to arm missiles already installed on Canadian territory, he had written in *Cité libre*, "The philosophy of the Liberal Party is very simple — say anything, think anything, or better still, do not think at all, but put us in power because it is we who can govern you best." Sixteen years later he still may not have seemed like a "real Liberal" to the Toronto Grits, but by his own definition he appeared to some of his old friends to have become one.

When his statement on the possibility of restoring the death penalty was made public, one such old friend said, "Sometimes I get the feeling that if he were told it was necessary to shoot in the leg every tenth person crossing the corner of Wellington and O'Connor, he'd do it. Why does he think it's worth it?" The answer was obvious. In order to fulfil his aims for Quebec, Trudeau needed to retain power. To retain power he needed the Liberal machine, and to that end he was willing to bend his iron will to the party's needs.

TO QUITE A REMARKABLE DEGREE, as the seventies drew to a close these needs were interpreted for Trudeau by a few men who were usually called in Liberal circles "the PMO in-group" or "the Coutts 'n' Davey gang". It was tacitly considered to consist of eight people, two of whom weren't Liberals at all. Besides Coutts and Davey, there were Coutts's assistants, Tom Axworthy and Colin Kenny, plus Davey's closest cronies in Toronto, Jerry Grafstein, the lawyer, who was an expert in communications, and Martin Goldfarb, the pollster, who was officially a non-partisan interpreter of voter behaviour since he had accepted contracts in the past for Conservative provincial parties. Then there was Richard O'Hagan, the Prime Minister's media consultant, whose opinions had been heeded by Coutts and Davey for nearly twenty years and would once again be germane in this campaign, even though he had resigned from the PMO a month before; and Michael Pitfield, the Clerk of the Privy Council, who would have been appalled at the very idea of being identified as a Grit but who undoubtedly had more influence on the Leader's thinking about the political process than any other English Canadian, Liberal or otherwise. Coutts, Davey, and O'Hagan operated on the premise that if you could convince Pitfield of the importance of a certain action, then it would be much easier to convince Trudeau. A ninth man, Marc Lalonde, didn't belong to the group at all but his actions had to be closely monitored by it for two reasons: as Quebec leader and francophone co-chairman of the Liberal Party of Canada campaign committee, he was the key figure in managing the largest bloc of sure Liberal votes in the country, and as Trudeau's unwavering loyalist in cabinet, he could be counted on to look after the Prime Minister's interests in and out of the Privy Council chamber.

The small size of the PMO group was all the more remarkable in light of the fact that it was made up of the remnants of two successive waves of political reformers — the Pearsonian New Guard and the Just Society Trudeauites — who had entered politics in order to democratize the Liberal Party, to make it more open to what the Pearsonians had called "the grass roots" and the Trudeauites "the people".

In the previous twenty years, there was no doubt that the Liberal Party had changed from the old King–St. Laurent male club reeking of whisky and cigar smoke, with its hints of electoral skulduggery, campaign funds allotted by party bosses, parachuted candidates, big donations from big business, and powerful cabinet ministers lording it over their regions, with a party membership held together by patronage and ancestral memories. On paper, it had been democratized. It now had a more open formal structure. A national executive, elected by the party membership rather than appointed by the leader, met regularly. Delegates from the constituencies gathered in convention every two years (in contrast with the King–St. Laurent era when the party met only three times, in 1919, 1948, and 1958, and then only to choose a leader). The party's elected president and appointed national director were invited to take part in the political planning committee, the group of ministers and officials from the Prime Minister's Office who met once a week, and in the deliberations of the national campaign committee whenever it convened.

Despite these changes, and others of their ilk, haggled over in party committees and enshrined in party documents, despite the rhetoric of participation and leader accountability, of membership renewal and policy consultation, despite the open nomination meetings in the constituencies and the reform of fund-raising practices, the party was in essential ways no more powerful than it had been under King and St. Laurent. In fact, some political scientists argued that it was slightly less so, since King had been dependent on the good will of the party's regional elites — if not its grass roots — in order to hold the various factions of his alliance together and had altered his policies to suit their demands, as expressed by regional cabinet ministers, in effect sharing decision-making with them. Now that the party's elites were dependent on the leader's ability to swing the electorate's votes rather than the other way around, and cabinet ministers were engrossed in the management of their departments, the party was often described by both its adherents and its opponents as little more than a leader's machine driven by a small cadre on his behalf, with policy made by a government bureaucracy far from the party's sight. To many Canadians, it seemed as though the Liberal Party had gone from oligarchy to oligarchy in one generation.

The most publicized participants in the new oligarchy, Jim Coutts and Keith Davey, were talked of by journalists and other politicians as though they had grabbed power for themselves out of insatiable ambition and unmatchable cunning. But they knew that whatever power they possessed was ephemeral, that it was derived entirely from their relationship to Trudeau and the control over the party and the government that his office bestowed on him.

Grattan O'Leary, who had been a close observer of the Canadian political process for more than sixty years, once remarked, "It would be plainly foolish for anybody trying to fathom how Canada works not to come to grips with the power of the prime minister. It has always been an office of enormous weight in this country. Ministers are servile to him because of his control over their careers and his party caucus even more so. The senior civil servants are dependent on his favour; the judiciary is appointed through him, as is the Senate. Success at the top of the governmental hierarchy depends on catching the prime minister's interest and currying his favour. If the Canadian power structure is a pyramid, there is absolutely no doubt who is on top. And in the Trudeau era, because of the tenor of the times and the personality of the man himself, this power has become self-evident to all who have the wits to see."

O'Leary made these statements without real rancour just as the man he had hoped would occupy the top of the pyramid, Robert Stanfield, was preparing to bow out as Conservative Opposition leader, after losing a third election to Pierre Trudeau in 1974. It was O'Leary's view that the prime minister's importance would have grown inexorably as government had expanded over the previous ten years, no matter who occupied the office. Other observers were less sanguine. It had been repeatedly charged that Trudeau had wilfully "presidentialized" the prime-ministership at the expense of the parliamentary system. No matter how many arguments were raised by Trudeau's defenders about the limits on prime-ministerial power that had been devised or refined during

the Trudeau era (the collegial cabinet system, the reformed committee system in the House of Commons, the caucus consultation
process, the efforts at participatory decision-making within the
Liberal Party) or the limits that the Canadian political system itself had always imposed (Parliament with its emphasis on the
Opposition's right to question and to obstruct and the even more
constraining division of powers between the federal and provincial
governments), his opponents' view of Trudeau remained fixed.
He was seen as the most powerful political leader in Canadian
history, a man whose mastery of the techniques of modern leadership politics — the deployment of an expert staff whose loyalties and energies were devoted to him personally, the use of polls
in the reading of public opinion and of television in manipulating
it — was the secret of his strength. Reflecting on this phenomenon, O'Leary observed, "I have always wanted to amend Lord
Acton's formula. Power doesn't necessarily corrupt but in my experience, it almost invariably accrues. If people think you possess it, they endow you with more by acceding to your demands."
    This was a maxim that Jim Coutts understood implicitly. For
nearly four years he had resolutely used the powers, both real and
projected, that accrued to the Prime Minister's Office to try to
keep the Liberal Party in line, the Opposition buffaloed, the press
at bay. Though they were still commonly described as a team, he
and Keith Davey were no longer equals. Coutts had the constant
access to the Prime Minister that kept him at the centre of the
political process. He involved himself in policy-making, conferring with Pitfield and other public servants on what could possibly
be produced by the vast bureaucratic machine that would enhance
the government's image or devastate its opposition. Davey, by
contrast, no longer saw Trudeau alone on a regular basis as he
had before Coutts became principal secretary, and he had never
wanted to be involved in policy-making, mostly because he felt
intellectually inadequate to do so. For that reason, he had declined
the cabinet position Trudeau had offered him in 1974. All he was
interested in was what he called "fine-tuning" policy, that is,
giving advice on what he thought would grab newspaper headlines or make the top stories on the radio and television news-
casts. In brief, the Senator had been relegated to the secondary

role of heeding the rumbles emanating from the party and the public outside the PMO, of discussing with Coutts what he heard, reaching a mutual conclusion on what to do about it, and then getting done out there what Coutts thought was "do-able".

It could be argued — and frequently was among Liberals — that Coutts had been the Prime Minister's de facto English lieutenant ever since the autumn of 1977 when the party had gone on a kind of permanent election alert and Donald Macdonald, the remaining English-Canadian cabinet minister who possessed both a substantial national reputation and the respect of Pierre Trudeau, had retired from active politics. Certainly Coutts was by design the Prime Minister's chief agent in running the Liberal Party. Instead of pleasing Liberals — who previously had complained that the PMO was too remote from the party when it had been staffed by non-party people such as Marc Lalonde and Ivan Head — Coutts's power seemed to make them uneasy. Their distrust was due to the fact that they believed Coutts had become too close to Pitfield, that he was no longer "one of us" but had become "one of them".

From the beginning of his tenure as principal secretary, Coutts had involved himself with the workings of the public service, not only through his conversations with Pitfield, with whom he had always been close, but through his attendance at interdepartmental meetings and through personal contact at lunches or in their offices with the key deputy ministers of the era. Coutts had let the senior bureaucrats know immediately on his arrival in Ottawa that he was speaking to them as a politician, that he understood the role of the civil service and did not expect them to be partisan Liberals. What he did expect was that they would be supportive of the government they served and that they would not involve themselves in any futile "Who's in charge here?" arguments but would work toward meshing the political and bureaucratic systems. However straightforward Coutts's original aims were, by the end of the seventies the PMO was generally perceived in Ottawa as being entangled with the bureaucracy to an unhealthy degree. Politicians said that Coutts had been bureaucratized and bureaucrats claimed that the public service had been politicized.

"I don't know how you sort that one out, or indeed whether

you need to," said a public servant who had worked closely with
three prime ministers, including Trudeau. "The public servant
must always have a close relationship with those who are in power
if he is to fulfil his role as policy co-ordinator. The problem seems
to have been something else. Coutts came to the principal secretary's job with only the skills of a political manager at his command, unlike his predecessors who had policy skills as well.
Lalonde had shown substance on social welfare and on the constitution. Austin had substance on energy matters. At issue in Coutts's
time was the economy, which really demanded a policy person of
substance in that area, which he didn't possess. When you added
his superficiality on economic matters to the impracticality of
Trudeau and Pitfield, neither of whom had any experience in the
world outside the intellectual hothouse they had set up together,
you got a vacuum at the centre. When we went to economic summit
meetings and saw the kind of practical economists, tough-minded
men with experience in the financial world who surrounded Helmut
Schmidt, say, we realized how ill-served our government was. In
Ottawa, the bureaucrats flailed around the edges of the PMO-PCO
operation, trying to figure out what the politicians wanted them to
do. Coutts never had any serious impact on how the government
acted; he was concerned with how it *appeared*."

Just as important to Coutts as trying to make the government
look good was making sure no one else made it look bad. Sylvia
Ostry, the chairman of the Economic Council, ran into this problem
when she scheduled a press conference in the autumn of 1978 in
order to unveil a study completed by her staff which showed that
a government proposal for a new contract to settle the demands of
fractious postal employees would set a dangerously inflationary
precedent. Coutts got wind of the study and reacted angrily. Didn't
she know the government was in the midst of the by-election
campaigns and such statements would be harmful to its image?
He called her to complain and had urged both Robert Andras, the
Secretary of the Treasury Board, and Tommy Shoyama, the Deputy Minister of Finance, to call her as well to suggest she cancel
the conference entirely or at least postpone it until after voting
day. Ostry refused, and when news of the collegial squeeze put
on her ran around the senior levels of the bureaucracy, it inspired

considerable sympathy. At the weekly lunch meeting of deputy ministers, Gordon Robertson, the former clerk of the Privy Council, came up to Ostry to escort her to the buffet as a show of solidarity with her position, saying, ''I hear you've been given a rough time.''

Ostry's experience was far from an isolated incident. Under the pressure he was sustaining in trying to make Trudeau look good, Coutts had changed noticeably, becoming overbearing with politicians as well as bureaucrats. When Liberals told him the party's diminishing popularity was making them nervous, or voiced complaints about the government's policies, he would cut them off with a fierce ''If you know what's good for you, you'll stop that.'' He took to opening casual conversations with the statement ''I hear you've been saying nasty things about me.'' Since many people, alarmed by the change in his character and the obvious growth of his power, *had* been saying nasty things about him — and even those who had not were so nonplussed by this ploy they were hard-pressed not to look guilty — the most common response was a weak laugh and a residual resentment.

Coutts's chastisement of Liberals who deviated from the party line extended even to those who had august reputations of their own. During the government constitutional reform push in the summer and autumn of 1978, Eugene Forsey, the austere and scholarly senator who had been until then one of Trudeau's most ardent supporters, took a strong public stance against the Liberals' latest constitutional-amendment proposals. Since Forsey was the country's best-known expert in this field, his opposition was doubly damaging. Coutts spied him crossing the floor in the gloom of the Chateau Grill one day at lunch-time and beckoned him over to his table to ask imperiously, ''Why are you doing this to *us*?'' Forsey, who at the age of seventy-four wasn't used to being either beckoned or intimidated, responded, ''Why are you doing this to the country?'' Few Liberals had Forsey's independent reputation or his fortitude, and having once been called to account for their actions, they were loath to cross Coutts again.

Coutts still occasionally turned on his considerable charm, cajoling, flattering, and tantalizing Grits with promises of future glory, taking care to show he remembered people's vanities and dreams. He got away with what one of his colleagues called this "soft-soap routine" with Liberals he saw only rarely, since they usually wanted to believe he admired them, to think that he was still just little Jimmy, the guy who did the hilarious imitation of Paul Martin, the endearing figure in the *Mr. Pearson* film, who only seemed to be thrusting himself forward because the camera crews had camped out in his office.

People whose jobs brought them into contact regularly with Coutts were not as susceptible to his blandishments. They thought he had made the PMO into "a walled-off Cathay . . . with the same view of the outside world that prevailed among Kublai Khan's Chinese: anybody who is not inside . . . and subject to its peculiar discipline and ideology . . . is an outsider and therefore a subject for manipulation. . . ."

The essence of the PMO style was what Coutts continued to call professionalism. Professionalism demanded that his colleagues do their jobs competently no matter how bad or good the day and that they maintain their public loyalty to the leader and the party line, no matter how much they might privately disagree. All his training — in Pearson's office, at the Harvard Business School, in the management consulting business — had taught him that you have to hang on and hang in; you have to present the confident face, the offhand "beats-me" answers to the difficult questions, the optimistic view in face of the pessimistic forecast. In important ways, Coutts had modelled himself on the Kennedy brothers of Boston, Mass., and Washington, D.C. But instead of giving his loyalty to "the Family", as they did, he gave it to "the Party", by which he meant a little band of brothers who thought about Liberalism as he did.

"Do you want to know what the Grits' idea of pig heaven is?" a Tory strategist who had ample cause and the good sense to fear the Liberals' political skills once asked rhetorically. "It's to be in Washington scrubbing Ted Kennedy's back in Ethel Kennedy's swimming pool in plain view of all the little Vassar-graduate groupies shrieking over their banana daiquiris at the water's edge."

Coutts would have resented that description, since he denied having been formed by mentors either Canadian or American, saying instead that he had "learned a little from a lot of people rather than a lot from anyone." Still, in his role as principal secretary, he had put together a team of Liberal professionals uncannily like the new frontiersmen Bobby Kennedy had recruited first for his brother Jack, and then for himself, in the sixties and that Teddy Kennedy was recruiting still for his Senate office on Capitol Hill in the seventies, men who thought that politics should be practised by quality people with vitality and an acute sense of craftsmanship.Disillusionment with the Kennedys may have been widespread elsewhere, but among the Liberal Party professionals they were still revered.

Coutts's closest colleagues were Tom Axworthy and Colin Kenny, who were official policy advisers and liaison officers in the West and Ontario respectively. More important, they bolstered Coutts on a daily basis in his role as chief strategist and tactician for what had become a kind of perpetual election campaign. Axworthy was the more amiable and more popular Liberal of the pair. He had the kind of warmth that Keith Davey had projected in the Pearson years, coupled with a solid academic background. Axworthy had grown up in North Winnipeg, in the only WASP family living on a tough city block that housed mostly working-class immigrants whose offspring warred in ethnic gangs. He liked to say he was too fat to run from these kids and too myopic to fight so he had to learn to talk. His interest in politics was kindled when he was an undergraduate at the University of Manitoba in the sixties by the rhetoric of the Kennedys and of the American New Left. Later, he was even more affected by the economic and social policy ideas of Walter Gordon, and worked in Ottawa as a researcher with the task force on the structure of Canadian industry that Gordon put together in 1967. He then completed an M.A. thesis at Queen's University that analysed Gordon's impact on the Liberal Party, studied for a period at Oxford, began work on his doctorate, served as an advance man on the 1974 federal campaign, then as a special assistant to Ron Basford,and ended up working for Coutts's management consulting firm in Toronto before joining him as an assistant in the PMO in 1975. Axworthy was Coutts's resident expert on Liberal history, his left-Liberal nationalist conscience, the best anglophone speech-writer on the staff, and a master of the kind of witty line or quick quip that could be used to open speeches or to repulse a nosy newspaperman. He had studied voting patterns at Queen's and was able to analyse the bases of Liberal strength in every part of the country. As a combination acolyte-apprentice, Axworthy was busy learning the ways of power as promising young men had done in Liberal prime ministers' offices for more than half a century.

Kenny was a different kind of professional. He was interested in process rather than policy and had developed an efficiency as an organizer that was remarkable considering his relative youth. He had gone straight into Liberal organizing from being a student, first at Bishop's College School in Quebec, at Norwich University, and then at Dartmouth College in New Hampshire where he had completed an M.B.A. After working first for the party in Ontario, he joined the PMO in Marc Lalonde's time. He had devised a ministerial riding reporting system which placed under each cabinet minister's control several ridings adjacent to his own. The minister's constituency assistant was supposed to attend the ridings' meetings and prepare a report to be sent to Kenny describing their election readiness. MPs and ministers both claimed that this scheme had turned into a spy system; Turner refused to take part at all and Sharp insisted on sending his reports directly to the Prime Minister rather than to one of his minions. Coutts had meant to get rid of Kenny because of his unpopularity — he was called "Colonel Klinck" by party workers who resented his habit of barking out orders at them as though he was a Teutonic army officer and they were in the ranks — but he decided Kenny was "pure political gold" because of his encyclopedic knowledge of Ontario constituencies and his superlative ability at directing operations and "advancing" an election campaign. This ability to plot a leader's tour for maximum effectiveness was based on techniques Kenny learned from an intensive study of the Kennedys' campaigning style as described in a book by their chief advance man, Jerry Bruno, and adapted to suit Canadian conditions.

Both Kenny and Axworthy admired Coutts's wit, his mastery of the Ottawa system, his cool-headed ability to deal with any problem that came his way, his wide acquaintance among important Canadians, his willingness "to take the heat" from the leader when he was irascible, from cabinet ministers who were angered by what they saw as Coutts's usurpation of their influence, or from Liberal MPs who were convinced that Trudeau's indifference to their requests for personal interviews was due to Coutts's refusal to help them. (Conservatives in Ottawa liked to joke that Liberal discipline in the late seventies meant that Grits had to say, "When Trudeau's right, he's very, very right but when he's wrong he's Jim Coutts.") In brief, Kenny and Axworthy as well as Coutts were advocates of Bobby Kennedy's belief that professionalism in politics demanded hustling hard, politicking constantly, and displaying a toughness of mind that stopped just short of ruthlessness.

KEITH DAVEY WENT ALONG WITH the theory behind Coutts's passion for professionalism — after all, he loved the Kennedys, too — but its practice made him uneasy. The Senator still had about him a quality that might best be described as kindliness and he treated his political contacts in much the same way as he had treated the entire Liberal organization when he was the national director fifteen years before. He still thought the best in people could be activated by optimism and camaraderie. "Coutts specializes in the beautiful people and the big ideas," he still liked to say. "I talk to ordinary guys and find out their ordinary concerns."

This was one way to characterize Davey's interlocking roles as co-chairman of both the national campaign committee and the political planning committee. Another would be to describe him as the party's chief cosmetician. He still talked to what he called "key Liberals" daily, but the days when he had known every Liberal constituency president in the country, and every Liberal candidate as well, were long gone. Now he said he saw the party's role "realistically" and what he was interested in was the country's mood and the ways to read it. This was what he called "understanding the political process" — that is, the engineering of public approval for government actions through the use of polls and the management of information.

His official political duties ostensibly were crammed into the three days he spent in Ottawa each week. He flew up from Toronto via Air Canada on the 7:30 flight every Tuesday morning and went straight to Parliament Hill in a cab, clutching a briefcase that contained his continuing-priorities file folder and his schedule for the week. The first thing on that scrupulously kept schedule was the political planning committee which met in the Centre Block of the Parliament Buildings from nine to ten o'clock and was co-chaired by Davey and Marc Lalonde.

Coutts and Davey had put together this committee in 1976 as the most important single instrument for keeping the leader and the cabinet in touch with the party and the party in touch with the government's policy thrusts. It was meant to replace what had formerly been called "political cabinet" and its purpose was to relieve the already overloaded cabinet agenda of some of the burden of purely political discussions and to allow for a more intense focus by a smaller group on the party's problems and plans. The committee's agenda was set by Coutts. It was staffed by PMO officials and attended by Coutts himself, as well as by the same cabinet ministers who belonged to the Priorities and Planning committee of the cabinet — Marc Lalonde, Don Jamieson, Roméo LeBlanc, Judd Buchanan, Jean Chrétien, Otto Lang, and Ray Perrault — plus two MPs, Peter Stollery, the chairman of the Liberal caucus, and Jim Fleming, who represented the party's communications committee which Coutts had set up to make sure members were kept informed of the party's views on developing issues, plus two party people other than Davey, Gerry Robinson, the national director, and Al Graham, the national president.

The opening item of business every Tuesday was "emerging issues" and any member could speak to any subject, from what was bugging people in the West (and there was always something bugging them) to alarming developments in Quebec (and there was always something Lalonde found alarming) to which MPs or ministers were doing the party's image a disservice by performing ineptly in the Commons or talking too selfishly to the press (and there was always somebody who needed a kick in his collegial conscience). Sometimes the talk would focus on a specific problem, such as the televising of House of Commons proceedings, which had begun in 1977 and had proven disturbing ever since. Joe Clark and Ed Broadbent, the Opposition leaders, had continued to look better than expected because of their grasp of the niceties of the Commons style and their ability within the structured setting of the Question Period to damage the Liberals through the adroit use of the intensive briefings on issues provided by their increasingly skilful staffs; and the Prime Minister had continued to look worse than he usually did on television because of his general boredom with House proceedings and his occasional harsh or contemptuous responses to questions. The situation was particularly galling to the Liberals since it had been their parliamentary reforms that had provided the increased funds for the Opposition research staffs and their confident belief that televising the Commons procedures, which brought the House into the nation's living rooms, would result in good publicity rather than bad. Suggested remedies for this problem had progressed from the simple (let's tell the PM to put pancake makeup on the hollows under his eyes and to stop wearing light-coloured suits) to the more difficult (my God, how can he be persuaded from sneering quite so openly?).

Relationships within the political planning group were not always entirely amiable. Lalonde might, for instance, pick up in the opening chitchat the fact that Keith Davey had attended a Toronto Blue Jays baseball game at which there had been open booing while "O Canada" was being sung in French and then proceed to berate Davey as though he was personally responsible for this outrage. Or Davey might raise his doubts about a measure in Chrétien's budget that closed tax loopholes for professionals such as doctors, lawyers, and accountants, pointing out that this action was damaging to thousands of Canadians whose support the Liberals needed. But however conflictual the discussions might prove, by the time the hour was over, a consensus had generally been pounded out and committee members would leave knowing what the Liberal Party position was on a given situation — i.e., what they should say in order to provide a united front. ("The Liberal Party has no dogma," Michael Pitfield once said. "Its creed is unity — national unity and party unity.")

When the political planning committee broke up, Davey walked over to the Senate to make phone calls and then went on to have his regularly scheduled lunch with Judd Buchanan, the Minister of Public Works and the Senior Minister for Ontario, a grandiloquent title that meant he was charged with keeping the other ministers and members for the province united and happy, partly through his co-ordination of government patronage for the area. Buchanan and Davey would fill each other's ears with the grit of party politics: who wanted what and how these needs could be satisfied expediently.

The patronage system was one of the aspects of party politics that Davey had most ardently wanted to see abolished when he was a young and eager reformer. But he had long since come to terms with it, as had most of his fellow members of Cell 13.

(Besides Davey, three lawyers from that group, Royce Frith, Dan Lang, and Richard Stanbury, had become senators, and two others, David Anderson and Joe Potts, had been appointed directors on the most prestigious government boards, Potts at the Bank of Canada and Anderson with Air Canada.) Out of power, party politicians — reform or otherwise, Liberal, Conservative, New Democrat, Socred, or Péquiste — tend to talk disparagingly about patronage. Once in power, they speak instead of the right of the people's elected representatives to make appointments to sensitive government jobs and boards, leaning on the argument that if the politicians don't make such appointments, then the civil servants would have to, giving them greater power though they have less accountability. To federal Liberals, particularly, when newspapers ran headlines saying "Opposition Accuses Government of Patronage", it was about as meaningful as proclaiming "Opposition Accuses Government of Governing". To them patronage was an essential part of the governmental process.

All the same, the whole question of appointments continued to make Davey uncomfortable, partly because of the difficulties he had undergone over his own senatorship in 1966. When Gordon and Davey were blamed for Pearson's failure to win a majority in the 1965 election, and Gordon offered his resignation, Pearson had told him that Davey would have to resign as well. To Davey's face, Pearson had been gentler, suggesting it might be time for him to pursue his interest in broadcasting through an appointment to the Board of Broadcast Governors or the CBC. Davey had responded with a forthright, "No, sir, I want the Senate," and Pearson had reluctantly agreed. Then on the very day that Davey was making his farewell speech to a Liberal executive meeting, Pearson telephoned him to say he had changed his mind, he wanted Davey to forget about the Senate and to stay on as national director until he was ready to call a convention to choose a new leader. Gordon advised Davey that this course would be madness and that he had to squeeze Pearson now. Pearson was very upset by Davey's stubbornness and left him dangling for a month ("the toughest time of my whole life," Davey remembered) until he finally did name him as the youngest senator appointed up to that time.

Since then the system of making appointments had become much more coherent if not less secretive or nerve-wracking for the would-be appointees. Now there was an order-in-council appointments officer in the PMO — a job held first by Francis Fox before he ran for office in 1972 and then by Marie-Hélène Fox, his sister — who kept track of which jobs were coming up and prepared a regular list for the senior ministers from each region, as well as compiling lists of suitable candidates for such jobs. (In addition to Buchanan, who was responsible for patronage in Ontario after Donald Macdonald left the cabinet, the senior ministers were: Ray Perrault for B.C., replacing Ron Basford, Jack Horner for Alberta, replacing Senator Earl Hastings, Otto Lang for Saskatchewan, Joe Guay for Manitoba until he was appointed to the Senate in 1978, Allan MacEachen for Nova Scotia, Roméo LeBlanc for New Brunswick, Don Jamieson for Newfoundland, Daniel Macdonald for P.E.I., and, of course, Marc Lalonde for Quebec.) The senior ministers in turn were supposed to discuss possible candidates for those jobs at a meeting of fellow ministers from their regions and then bring the results of their consensus to the weekly meeting of the full cabinet, where the names would be discussed once more, and the appointments agreed on, and made by the Prime Minister.

This was the theory. The practice was something far messier and far more important in party life than a bloodless recounting of the system would indicate. There were something in excess of three hundred and fifty full-time appointments that by tradition and by statute belonged to the prime minister, a figure that included deputy ministers, ambassadors, the heads of important agencies such as the St. Lawrence Seaway Authority and the Canadian Radio-television and Telecommunications Commission, and so on. Then there were between a thousand and twelve hundred full- or part-time positions on advisory councils and boards that came under ministers, over five hundred judicial appointments to be made through the Department of Justice, plus jobs with over four hundred crown agencies, all of which had appointed boards. Below that level, there was contract work for Liberal lawyers from the Department of Justice (as special prosecutors in every town across the country large enough to boast a court) or the

Canada Mortgage and Housing Corporation (whose legal contractual costs were estimated to amount to several million dollars a year in the 1970s), and for architects and engineers through other government departments whenever contracts were let for more than $25,000. (Contracts under $25,000 a year were at the discretion of the deputy minister.) In addition, ministers were influential in the distribution of government grants such as those that came under DREE or LIP, and various academic studies showed these grants usually went disproportionately to Liberal ridings. All of these important jobs or contracts had come to be called metropolitan patronage. The old petty patronage that had so disgusted Davey and his friends in Ontario, and Trudeau and his friends in Quebec, was no longer thought to be of much importance, except in rural areas, particularly in the Maritimes and Quebec, where people still cared passionately about who did the enumerating for the census or drove the road-graders for the Department of Transport or acted as district returning officers, or which filling station was privileged to pump gas for RCMP cruisers. To federal Conservatives, hungry after sixteen years on the Opposition benches, all this looked like an embarrassment of patronage riches, but the Liberal senior ministers found that their special assistants were bombarded by supplicants and that there were never enough jobs to go around. The designation "senior minister" brought them considerable authority but it also meant continuing headaches.

The headaches were what Buchanan usually wanted to discuss with Davey at their weekly lunches. Few experienced Liberals were intrepid or self-important enough to ask ministers directly for appointments in the first rank, those to the Senate or the diplomatic corps, which were relatively rare and guarded by the Prime Minister as his own.* (Probably the only Canadian who ever publicly said he should be made a senator was Larry Zolf, the writer, broadcaster, historian, and wit from Winnipeg, who for years had been conducting a satirical campaign to get himself appointed to the Red Chamber.) It was the appointments below that level — to the citizenship courts, the Immigration Appeal Board, the boards of Air Canada, the Canadian National Railways,

*For a list of senators in 1979, and the monetary value of their appointments, see Appendix, page 407.

the Canadian Transport Commission, and so on — that devoted party workers wanted, and if they were given on either a non-partisan or an otherwise unfair basis (that is, if they went to insufficiently worthy Liberals), anger ran through the party ranks. Liberals wanted recognition for what they had done for the party; they wanted their friends to see that their efforts were appreciated by the bigwigs in Ottawa, that they were politically astute and loyal enough for the party to look after them out of gratitude. Often this desire for recognition had little to do with monetary gain; a middle-aged big-city lawyer would far sooner have an appointment to an important board than government legal work.

As a consequence of party members' preoccupation with appointments, there was intensive horse-trading done on patronage matters at the ministers' regional meetings. A minister might be trying to get his former campaign manager appointed to the Immigration Appeal Board, for instance, and would end his pitch on her behalf by promising that he wouldn't ask for another appointment at this level for six months, that he wouldn't press on the county court appointment coming up, and so on. Some ministers were very adept at the process. John Munro was famous in party ranks for looking after his own. Alastair Gillespie, who as a gentleman and a Rhodes Scholar was more fastidious, was seen by his workers as an ingrate.

Keith Davey himself would often be asked for help in getting jobs for Liberals, and if he knew them well, he might put their case to the senior ministers involved or even to Jim Coutts, who could occasionally be persuaded to slip a word into the Prime Minister's ear before a cabinet meeting on behalf of some particularly deserving somebody. In the protracted election-alert period, when scores of appointments were made to the government's advantage — to clear ridings of tired-out Liberal MPs or of Conservatives whose seats might be taken by a Liberal next time around — the patronage discussions at all levels were particularly fraught. In the period from 1977 to 1979, the Liberals picked off six Tory MPs: Jacques Lavoie of Hochelaga and Jack Horner of Crowfoot, who were persuaded to cross the floor and, it was said, promised appointments if as turncoat Liberals they weren't re-elected; Jack Marshall of Humber–St. George's–St. Barbe and Claude Wagner of St. Hyacinthe–Bagot, who were appointed to the Senate; Robert McCleave of Halifax East–Hants, who went to the bench; and Gordon Fairweather, the long-time member for Fundy-Royal, who was named chief commissioner of the newly formed Canadian Human Rights Commission. Despite Fairweather's impeccable reputation as a parliamentarian and civil libertarian and his eminent suitability for the job, this announcement caused anger among both Grits and Tories. Liberals felt that an equally illustrious Liberal could have been found for the job — a standard party response to suggestions that appointments should be less partisan — and Tories thought Fairweather was being disloyal. In New Brunswick, his home province, the Tory premier Richard Hatfield issued a statement supportive of Fairweather, saying with the acerbic wit that made him a unique practitioner of his calling, "After all, Gordon deserves it. He's been in politics for twenty-five years and you only get twenty for murder."

Other seats cleared and appointments made in the same period were those of Joseph Flynn of Kitchener, who was persuaded to step aside (although his appointment to the Canadian Pension Commission was delayed by a press outcry), and of John Gilbert, the NDP member for Broadview, and Hugh Poulin, the member for Ottawa Centre, both of whom were named to the Ontario County Court. In addition, three former cabinet ministers resigned their seats, and received important appointments — Bud Drury as chairman of the National Capital Commission, Stanley Haidasz as a senator, and Mitchell Sharp as commissioner of the Northern Pipeline Agency.

When these appointments — and a slew of others to lesser jobs — were revealed through order-in-council announcements, the press and the Opposition attacked the Liberals relentlessly. But the appointment that made Liberals themselves angry was the one bestowed on Bryce Mackasey in December 1978. Mackasey was "a mouthy mick", as Brian Mulroney, himself a loquacious Irish Catholic, called him, who had represented the Quebec riding of Verdun from 1962 to 1976. He had enjoyed great public popularity as minister of labour in the first Trudeau régime but had been seriously criticized after the election of 1972 for the changes in the unemployment insurance legislation that were perpetrated under his aegis, and his career since then had been chequered. He was named postmaster general and then minister of consumer and corporate affairs, both jobs he was considered to have discharged indifferently, resigned in a fit of pique from the cabinet in 1976, and was elected to the Quebec legislature. When he tried to return to federal politics by standing for election in Ottawa Centre in October 1978, he lost to Robert de Cotret, an economist who was an important addition to Tory ranks.

Two months later, Mackasey was named chairman of Air Canada, the kind of job that dozens of high-powered Liberals in the country wanted. The response was immediate and furious. Keith Davey, who had always been a booster of Mackasey's because of his broad public appeal, and who was said to have convinced him to run in Ottawa Centre, was blamed for getting him an appointment that was thought to be beyond his capabilities or his just deserts.

Mackasey didn't help matters much when he turned up at his first Air Canada board meeting exuding political bonhomie. Lorna Marsden, a vice-president of the party and a sociologist from the University of Toronto, who had a doctorate from Princeton, an intense interest in policy-making, and a reputation as one of the Liberals' brightest new hopes, was mortified when, in the course of being introduced around the table, Mackasey, on being told her name, responded in his broadest brogue. "Ah, yes, Lorna," he said with the smile that had warmed the cockles of a hundred hearts at a score of parish bingoes. "Dear Lorna. Many's the brave political battle we've fought side by side." Until that moment, Marsden had never met Mackasey in her life.

Keith Davey hated being blamed for Mackasey's appointment. He hated having Dorothy Petrie's job described disparagingly in the press. (Following her job as the Ontario campaign committee chairman in 1974, the future Mrs. Davey had been appointed to the Immigration Appeal Board in 1976 for a twenty-one-year term at a salary close to $40,000, which brought their combined incomes from government-appointment jobs to more than $70,000 a year.) He also hated being asked for jobs by people he knew were deserving or needy and not being able to do anything for them, since he himself was reliant on making supplications to the senior ministers or the Prime Minister. As a consequence, he was always glad when his Tuesday conversations with Buchanan turned to other matters, the work of the Ontario campaign committee, for instance, in trying to find suitable candidates to stand in Ontario ridings now that so many of the big names had fallen by the wayside, or the curious fact that the polls Goldfarb was running for him showed Toronto voters were blaming the federal government for the actions of the municipal government in restricting the height of downtown buildings, yet another indication that Trudeau was like a lightning rod for the electorate's complaints.

The next regularly scheduled event on Davey's weekly program was the Ontario caucus gathering at 9:30 on Wednesday morning, followed by the national caucus at 10:30, two meetings held in the Centre Block, where he would sit quietly in the back corner of the room and take in what Liberal senators and MPs had to say in this brief period when they had direct access to the leader. At nearly every caucus he was struck by the same paradox: MPs who were able, in their offices or at tables in the parliamentary restaurant over the Gaspé salmon and the Oka cheese, to articulate a series of bitter complaints — about the decline of the importance of Parliament under Trudeau's régime, their own relegation as individuals to being little more than ombudsmen for their constituents' pension complaints, passport problems, immigration difficulties, and tax troubles — would turn into tame tigers at the prospect of fearlessly facing up to the Prime Minister. Those who did speak in caucus were given a fair hearing by Trudeau, but his relentless logic and superior oratory kept many of them silent.

On Wednesday evening Davey would usually dine with Jim Coutts at the Four Seasons Hotel, where the Senator stayed when he was in the capital, and their talk would range broadly, covering every conceivable political subject that might have come up in the planning committee or over lunch with Buchanan or during the caucuses, plus half a dozen other matters of mutual concern, ranging from the mood of the Liberal MPs (which was up and down, depending on whether Joe Clark, whom they called "the wimp", was behaving sufficiently wimpishly) to the state of

Coutts's love life (which was also up and down, though usually
more up than not, power having proven the ultimate aphrodisiac
for Coutts as well as for Henry Kissinger), to the condition of
Davey's consultancy business (always so-so since Davey had never
shown much talent for money-making and was always happier
politicking. The party didn't pay him beyond his Senate salary,
except for expenses during the actual eight weeks of an election
campaign, and his Toronto friends were always worrying about
his finances, particularly after his divorce, when part of his Senate
salary was gobbled up by alimony payments).

No matter what else went on in their conversations, Coutts
and Davey's most intense discussions were always about Trudeau,
since he was the centre of their political lives. They often talked
about what they called his negativism, his unhappy tendency to
air his mind in public, which would be a problem for any image
manager but was a particular source of chagrin for Coutts and
Davey, neither of whom could countenance pessimism or would
ever admit to spiritual despair. They would seek remedies for the
Prime Minister's latest "display of excessive candour", as they
gingerly described his outbursts (the same displays a novelist friend
of Trudeau's called "the moments when he just can't keep the
mask in place any more and his soul jumps out and screams").
Perhaps Trudeau might have lectured the populace once more like
a stern-faced paterfamilias on its need to tighten its collective belt
rather than inflate its expectations in the face of economic duress,
or he may have slipped into his intellectual discussant's guise at a
meeting of students in Calgary that they had painstakingly put
together in order to improve his press in the West. (Student to
Trudeau: "I am an anarchist and I'd like to know whether you
will join us against economic and educational elitism or are you
afraid of an educated electorate?" Trudeau to student: "The first
rule of an anarchist is to demand nothing of the state he wants to
abolish." Davey to Coutts: "What's that supposed to mean?")

Before their dinner was over, they would generally decide
that Coutts should tell Trudeau the next morning at their regular
meeting that he must be more positive and more popular in his
pronouncements, and if that admonition didn't have an effect,
then Davey would seek one of his now rare appointments with

him and "lay it right on the line". Even after they had reached this conclusion and followed it through for the hundredth time without any appreciable long-term effect on Trudeau, Coutts and Davey still continued to bluster for each other's benefit. When they got particularly discouraged, Davey would say to Coutts, "Do we hate Tories?" and Coutts would reply "Yes! Yes!" sounding the sibilants in a kind of joke cheerleader's yell meant to keep themselves going in hard times.

The next morning, with the stratagems he and Coutts had agreed on the night before in mind, Davey would meet Gerry Robinson, the national director of the Liberal Party, for their regular talk about the state of the party machinery. Robinson's role was very different from the one Davey himself had played in the 1960s when he held the same title. Robinson was considered to be a factotum — as were the three other national directors who had succeeded Davey: Allan O'Brien, Torrance Wylie, and Blair Williams — charged mainly with running the party's central office, now located on Bank Street, and with co-ordinating the meetings of its national executive, its policy conventions, and its communications with party members through mailings on party events and policies, notably a highly professional magazine called *Dialogue* that was edited by Audrey Gill, a former journalist. Davey had chosen Robinson for the job and got along well with him, but his own relationship with the formal party structure (that is, the national executive, which was elected by constituency delegates at national conventions every two years) was uneasy. Having been the arch party man, he was now unmistakably a leader's man. The trouble had surfaced at the 1975 national convention, when Trudeau had wanted Davey to run for president of the party to replace Gil Molgat, whom he found inadequate. Davey had reluctantly agreed to do so, and then realized that he was in for a tough fight with Alasdair Graham, a senator from Nova Scotia, and had withdrawn from the race at the last moment. It wasn't that Graham was more popular than Davey; the problem was that Davey had become a focus for party anger at Trudeau over Turner's resignation and the imposition of wage-and-price controls. But ever since, the relationship between Graham and Davey had been touchy. Nominal courtesies were observed. Davey was invited to

all national executive meetings and Graham was invited to all
national campaign committee and political planning committee
meetings, and much ego-stroking was indulged in on both sides.
("He's a great Canadian," Liberals were always saying about
each other, teeth set in sunny smiles.)

"Of all the meetings involving the party, only the political
planning committee really mattered," said a PMO official in 1979.
"The rest were window-dressing, keeping the party thinking it
was more than just an election machine, whose chief purpose was
to raise money and provide campaign workers and cheering crowds
at policy conventions as a backdrop for the leader's speeches.
Davey and Coutts would tell Graham and Robinson about big
changes a few days or at most a week or so before they happened,
just so they could appear to be on the inside. But the important
decisions came out of the PMO the way they always had; the party
has never had real power over the leader's decisions having once
elected him except the power to call for a leadership review."

Davey's Thursday-morning conversation with Robinson represented the last of his regularly scheduled Ottawa appointments.
But around those fixed engagements he would fit in occasional
meetings of the national campaign committee and brief visits to
the Senate, where he would sit for a quarter-hour or so at a time
while one of his more important colleagues would harangue a
half-filled chamber; or he would arrange to have lunch with a
journalist or an MP or to have dinner with a cabinet minister who
wanted his advice on how to improve his image in the party and
the press. In the months before the election, this advice was sought
frequently by Otto Lang, who had served as minister of transport
and of justice, and was widely perceived to "have coat-tails in
Saskatchewan", meaning his reputation could garner votes beyond
his own constituency. Lang and Davey might each bring two or
three other people to their dinners for a brainstorming session
whose express purpose, as Davey described it, was "the political
rehabilitation of Otto Lang".

Lang had been a friend of Davey's ever since the early sixties
when he had been appointed as the party's Saskatchewan campaign chairman in spite of the opposition of Ross Thatcher, the
Premier. But that was ancient history now. And so was the fact

that Lang had been a brilliant law professor with an incisive intellect that made him one of the few remaining ministers for whom Trudeau felt a kinship. What mattered now was that Lang had a public reputation for arrogance and self-indulgence in a country that still wanted its politicians to be humble and Calvinistic. He had been a voracious user of government jets for private purposes (travelling to his riding with his seven children in tow, attempting to send their young nanny home to Scotland for a holiday without paying her fare), and had employed his attractive wife, Adrian, in his ministerial office as a press assistant, excesses that created an image that had to be fixed. If it wasn't, Lang would no longer have coat-tails and the Liberals would lose even more of their remaining slender support in the West.

Whether his Thursday dinner in Ottawa was with Lang or someone else, Davey would try to wrap it up in time to board the 10:50 flight back to Toronto in order to stop in on Dorothy Petrie before going home to his bleak townhouse on the city's northern outskirts, where all he did was sleep and talk on the phone. The main change in Davey's life after December 1978, when he and Petrie were married, was that he went straight to the house they had bought together in lower Forest Hill. He still spent an inordinate amount of time on the phone, a habit the second Mrs. Davey fondly condoned. As a former Liberal activist herself, she knew very well that talking on the phone is the politician's disease and that Davey had contracted a chronic case in his twenties. On any day he was in Ottawa, Davey calculated he received twenty-five phone calls either at the Senate or at the Four Seasons and placed nearly that many more. From Thursday night to Tuesday morning, when he was in Toronto, ostensibly conducting his consulting business but usually fulfilling Liberal commitments rising out of his Ottawa meetings, the calls were not quite so frequent. They just lasted longer.

The most important of these calls were usually to Davey's closest political colleagues in Toronto, Jerry Grafstein and Martin Goldfarb, who were his chief aides in what was now his most important political role: the interpretation of public behaviour so that voters could be politically influenced, the role that in the United States was described as "political consultant" and involved

vast sums of money paid by candidates to experts they hired to
get them elected.

As a trio, Davey, Grafstein, and Goldfarb didn't earn vast
sums from their political consulting. (Goldfarb made the major
part of his income from commercial accounts such as Hiram
Walker or Ford of Canada and sometimes encountered difficulties
getting paid when Liberal coffers were low; Grafstein's law partners were frequently exasperated by the amount of unchargeable
time he spent on political activity.) They didn't get rich from
politics but they were fascinated with its practice. Grafstein and
Goldfarb were both Jews with intellectual interests who might
have been academics if other imperatives in their lives hadn't
driven them into professions where there was more money to be
made. Davey was their idea of a mensch, a real liberal, a guy
with heart.

Goldfarb was a paid expert but Grafstein was a volunteer,
still as emotionally attached to the Liberal Party as he had been
when he first joined it after leaving law school in the early sixties.
He had formed close friendships among the Pearsonian new guard,
including reformers in Quebec such as the young lawyers Jean
David and Michel Robert, as well as Claude Frenette, Maurice
Sauvé's assistant. He had edited a magazine called *The Journal
of Liberal Thought* and as a result of that, and several innovative
papers on law reform published in professional journals, Trudeau
had asked him to become an assistant deputy minister in the
Department of Justice when he was minister in 1967. Grafstein
had declined, deciding to serve as an executive assistant to John
Turner instead. But he was one of the rare Liberals in the network
who still tried to influence Trudeau on policy matters and would
write him copious letters of advice, to which Trudeau generally
replied with courtesy.

The job Grafstein undertook for the party during elections
was to direct Red Leaf, the advertising agency without walls
as he called it, which the Liberals had set up for the duration of
the 1974 campaign, drawing on the best talents from the best
agencies (who coincidentally tended to get the best advertising
accounts from the most important government departments). Red
Leaf was to be reactivated for the 1979 campaign with a slightly

different group of ad men, among whom Terry O'Malley of Vickers & Benson, Hank Karpus of Ronalds-Reynolds, and David Harrison of MacLaren's were the most important. Its purpose was to be the same: to formulate a sophisticated advertising response to what the opinion polls were telling Davey was on the public mind.

The man who conducted those polls was Goldfarb, and in Davey's view he was without parallel in Canada and probably in the United States. Goldfarb had taken academic degrees in anthropology and sociology and saw himself as being fundamentally a professional student of human behaviour, a calling he regarded as close to an art that he was set on perfecting. Davey had hired him in 1974 to replace the American pollsters the Liberals had formerly used and Goldfarb had proven uncannily accurate in his interpretations of what was on the English-speaking electorate's inner agenda over the last five years.

Davey's regular conversations with Grafstein and Goldfarb, which were conducted sometimes on the phone, sometimes face to face, were squeezed into frenetic days that involved him in hours of non-stop talk at meetings, lunches, dinners, and parties, talk that went on over Sanka and eggs Benedict, steaks and strawberry pie, salads and tins of Tab, talk so incessant and so intense, one would think Davey's throat would constrict, his ears buzz, and his optimism falter. But they never did, because all this talk was an essential part of Davey's lifelong effort to keep up his Liberal network.

THE CONCEPT OF KEEPING UP your network was essential to the style of the contemporary Liberal Party. "He has a reliable network," one Grit would say admiringly of another, meaning he knows a lot of people and can call in many favours. "I'll get Joe to m.c. my fund-raising dinner. He owes me one," a Liberal would remark. Or, "I'll ask David to speak to Don and Ron about a judgeship for Stephen/to come with me for lunch at Le Mascaron when I have another go at talking Turner into running in Eglinton/to canvass a poll for John to show everybody's behind him."

What the English-Canadian Liberal Party had become in 1979 — other than the "important instrument in the Canadian reality" that its leader so coolly described — was the crucial "network", the one that had Keith Davey and Jim Coutts sitting at the centre with the rest of the leader's cadre, reaching out to a huge circle of friends who comprised the party elite, though that was a word they themselves would never use. They liked to talk about "insiders", "networks", "activists", and "the grass roots", instead of the cadre, the elite, the campaign workers, and the committed supporters the political scientists described. Grits preferred to think that any member of the grass roots could become part of the network and then get to be an insider if only he worked hard enough.

Keith Davey estimated that there were ten thousand Liberal activists. "Twenty-five hundred come to party conventions," he said, "and there are three more like them at home," with about two hundred and fifty of those intensely involved as insiders. Then there were another 240,000 committed Liberals who identified themselves as supporters of the party, the people who had to be mobilized in a campaign, to staff candidates' offices, to stuff the voters' mailboxes with literature, to give coffee parties, to be taken in busloads to large rallies, or to drive voters to the polls. To win a majority of the available parliamentary seats in English Canada, eighty to ninety per cent of these Liberals had to be motivated to vote, or so Colin Kenny, who made a career of studying these matters, believed. Mobilizing all those "gut Grits" was the purpose of the marked voters' lists kept in the ridings in the hands of the experienced poll captains.

The purpose of all the rest of the party's hard-learned professional campaigning techniques — the expensive opinion-polling and the even more expensive television and print advertising, the superlative speeches written by the high-priced help to be delivered by the leader at the huge rallies with the orchestrated crowds, the massive efforts to get the right headlines in the press and the right stories on the television news — the purpose of all that was to win the floating vote. It wasn't the Liberal grass roots that occupied the minds of the insiders as the campaign drew near. They had been given their due: the visits from the leader at nomination meetings, the trips to the policy conventions for their association presidents, the mailings from headquarters cheering them on to the Liberal nirvana in the future. It was the uncommitted voters that the insiders talked about with so much anxiety in the winter of 1979, to the frustration of their law partners, lovers, wives, children, aged parents, or any other dependants they might be harbouring.

"To be a real insider, you have to think the Liberal Party is the most important thing in the world," remarked Mimi Fullerton, a young Toronto businesswoman who was herself an admired party "comer". "You have to talk about the party all the time and to keep your career revolving around it. That's why law is the best profession." Jerry Grafstein, who was both a lawyer and an insider, agreed: "You have to decide the party is vitally important to your life and to give a lot to it. If you do, it encapsulates you. And if you ever leave it, you have terrible withdrawal symptoms."

The insiders addicted to Liberalism in the late 1970s were described as being composed of "Cell-13 . . . plus" by David Smith, a Toronto alderman, an insider who meant to seek a federal seat or the city's mayoralty, he wasn't sure which. His description was correct in that the network had its beginnings with the Pearsonian reformers, though the people Smith described as "plus", by which he meant younger Liberals, were taking over now. In early 1978, when the Grits still believed they could win another big victory for Trudeau, Grafstein had wanted to write a book to be called *The Last Campaign*, describing the magnificent

ultimate effort the old Pearsonian loyalists would make under Keith
Davey's leadership before they went on to far, far better things.
"Once more unto the breach, dear friends," he would say, and
Davey would laugh at his romanticism while recognizing the reality
of the situation that inspired it.

There were now two distinct branches to the central Liberal
network — Coutts's branch and Davey's. Some people, like
Grafstein and Smith, who had worked for Davey at party headquarters in 1961 while he was still an undergraduate at Carleton
University, could claim to belong to both. But most Liberals by
age and type were clearly in one or the other. Davey's connections were mostly among Liberals who had been born in the late
1920s or early 1930s, just before or just after the beginning of the
Great Depression, and Coutts's were mainly among those who
were born just before, during, or just after the Second World War.

In Davey's group, still active twenty years after they had
founded Cell 13, were Gordon Dryden, who was the party's
treasurer; Gordon Edick, who had been persuaded to run Tony
Abbott's campaign in Mississauga in 1974 and had been credited
with winning him the seat and was expected to help him win
again this time; Boyd Upper, who had given up the practice of
medicine to build medical complexes and was still active behind
the scenes; and Royce Frith, the lawyer to whom Davey had
entrusted the crucial Ontario campaign chairmanship for this election after first getting him a Senate appointment, making Frith
"the only Grit in history to receive his reward *before* he delivered," as the party scuttlebutt had it. Other old friends from
Cell 13 were less active now. Dan Lang and Richard Stanbury
were engaged in practising law and sitting in the Senate; Robert
Stanbury had resigned his seat in Parliament to become a corporation lawyer; Joe Potts had run John Evans's losing campaign in
Rosedale and was mooted to be a prime contender for the next
available Ontario Senate seat, or, failing that, a judgeship; David
Anderson was practising law and going to crown corporation board
meetings; Phil Givens had been mayor of Toronto, an MP, and an
MPP but had given up Liberal politics to become the Metro Toronto
police commissioner; James Service had become a wealthy real
estate developer after serving as the mayor of North York; James

Trotter had been an Ontario MPP and then was appointed a judge; and so it went.

But there were dozens of other Liberals Davey had made common bond with years before who were still active: Bryce Mackasey, Eugene Whelan, Otto Lang, and Barney Danson, the privy councillors who supposedly had the "roots" or the "coattails" Davey admired; Joe Cruden, who had contested York West for the party and served on the Etobicoke school board while working in middle management at Bell Telephone, and was now crucial to the party's fund-raising operation in Ontario; Torrance Wylie, who had been at the Cooper Street headquarters as a summer student while Davey was national director, became national director himself, and was now chairman of the Federal Liberal Agency, the official responsible for party funds under the new Election Expenses Act. There were dozens more who were not so active but who could still be persuaded to do a job on the party's behalf: Izzy Asper, the former leader in Manitoba; Charles McElman, a senator from New Brunswick, who had served on Davey's media committee; John Connolly, another senator and the one-time national party president, who had an office next door to Davey's on Parliament Hill; and William Macdonald, John Turner's law partner, who had one of the shrewdest minds in the party and was sitting this election out but was still warmly disposed to Davey despite his role as Trudeau's man. In a class by himself among Davey's connections was Walter Gordon. Even though Gordon had stopped supporting the party, Davey still saw him regularly and quoted him often.

Jim Coutts was emphatic in his belief that his Liberal connections were not all that different from Davey's, since they were both composed of "basically the same kind of people, the upwardly mobile middle class", which meant that Coutts, of course, recognized that the Liberal Party had been the party of the middle in terms of class as well as policy for most of the previous century.

Members of the upper class, that thin layer at the top of the heaving Canadian mosaic, the people with the inherited money, the old-family names, and the international connections, had rarely engaged directly in politics and even more rarely in Liberal politics.

They preferred to contribute to the campaign funds of the middle-class men who had the time, the techniques, the ability, and the ambition to do the governing. (The ultimate expression of this lack of interest in political engagement was that of the late J. A. McDougald, the chairman of the Argus Corporation, who in 1974 had explained his lifelong disinclination to stand for office by saying, "Obviously one wouldn't want to pat all those little children on the head and go to all those awful straaaw-burry festivals," apparently unaware that in the 1970s, strawberry festivals were largely the projects of dedicated folklorists, and little children were more often than not at home munching Fritos and watching *Mork and Mindy* while their parents were at political meetings.)

Walter Gordon was always an anomaly in the Liberal Party and so was Vincent Massey before him. Both of them were drawn to it, as Alison Grant Ignatieff — who was Massey's niece and one of Gordon's closest friends — once remarked, "Because they wanted power and not just influence. In Walter's case, as in Mike Pearson's, it was the power to put his ideas into effect." Mrs. Ignatieff's father was W. L. "Choppy" Grant, the famous principal of Upper Canada College, who would say nothing of his political affiliation save that he always "voted his conscience"; her grandfather was George M. Grant, the distinguished principal of Queen's University, who was a friend of Sir John A. Macdonald's; her brother, George Grant, had become, with the publication of his books *Lament for a Nation* and *Technology and Empire*, one of the country's pre-eminent thinkers and its chief conservative philosopher. Another of her uncles was the Honourable J. M. Macdonnell, the president of National Trust, who had cut a splendid figure as a Conservative MP off and on from 1945 to 1962, standing up in the Commons in his later years, bone thin and ramrod straight, to orate in the manner of the Rhodes Scholar, recipient of the Military Cross and the Croix de Guerre, and son-in-law of a baronet that he so plainly was. Another uncle's wife, Louise Parkin, became secretary of the socialist League for Social Reconstruction and a member of the CCF, despite the fact that her husband, Raleigh Parkin, was an investment counsellor in Montreal. In brief, there weren't many Liberals among the Grants' connections. Principal Grant always said that Mackenzie King looked to him distressingly like a butler, and even Vincent Massey, who had cleverly used King in his long, long climb to the Canadian High Commission in London and to Rideau Hall in Ottawa, described him as a man of "watery sentimentality".

If the one clearly upper-class man in Keith Davey's Liberal circle was Walter Gordon, the one in Coutts's was John Aird, whose father had been a Conservative; Aird had been attracted to the Liberal Party by C. D. Howe, who took him on as a fund-raiser, a role that the rich and well-connected never seemed to mind playing on behalf of either party. Another such man, John Godfrey, who was the son of a judge and himself a distinguished Toronto lawyer, took over from Aird as the party's chief fund-raiser, though he belonged to no one's network but his own. (Godfrey was crusty, handsome in the manner of an R.A.F. fighter pilot, and inordinately proud of his ability to toddle around to the offices of the corporate mighty and squeeze out of their denizens large sums for democracy's own sweet sake.)

The differences between the people in Davey's Liberal circle and those in Coutts's may have been slight, but what differences there were indicated certain important changes the middle class had undergone in Canada in half a generation. Coutts's friends were the beneficiaries of the Canadian postwar boom; none of them was from a rich family but many had been abroad to study at the great American and European universities and most of them practised their professions in a manner and cultivated their pretensions in a style that Davey's network did not. Typical of Coutts's Liberal connections were John Roberts, the Secretary of State, who had studied at Oxford, had been married first to a Belgian countess and then to a fashion photographer, and found his holiday pleasures in Mexico and the south of France; Ed Roberts, the former Liberal leader in Newfoundland, who had been educated far from his native province at Upper Canadian institutions and was given to discussing the merits of malt whiskies or the importance of copper salmon-poachers; or Jim Peterson, the candidate in Willowdale, who had studied at Columbia, the Sorbonne, and the Academy of International Law in the Hague, and practised law in John Turner's firm; or Roy MacLaren, a for-

mer diplomat, who had left External Affairs in the late 1960s
for a series of impressive titles in the business world: director of
public affairs at Massey-Ferguson, chairman of Ogilvy and Mather
(Canada) Limited, publisher of *Canadian Business*. Many of these
people had known each other before they met Coutts and Davey.
John Roberts and Roy MacLaren had been members of the Department of External Affairs together; Jim Peterson had been an
executive assistant to Paul Martin, while John Roberts was an
executive assistant to Maurice Sauvé. (To be an executive assistant to a minister had always been a good route into the Liberal
centre; an even better one was to be an assistant in the Prime
Minister's Office, as Coutts had been in the past and Geoff O'Brian
and Alan Lufty were now. Another route was through involvement
with Liberal associations, training grounds that had produced
Davey and Dryden in the 1940s, and where fresh talent like David
Chong, Janny Vincent, Vince Borg, and Peter Donolo had been
surfacing in the 1970s.)

Most of these insiders were Anglo-Saxon or Anglo-Celt in
background though there were a few prominent Liberals who were
Jews. The other "ethnics", such as Charles Caccia, the Italian-
Canadian MP for Davenport, or Stanley Haidasz, the Polish-
Canadian senator and former MP for Parkdale, ran separate networks of their own among the party's grass roots and related to
the centre when necessary through Davey. Fifteen years before,
the Cell 13 crowd had been very close to Maurice Sauvé and
Claude Frenette and their associates in Quebec, but now the connections there were minimal, even among English-speaking
Quebeckers.

In fact, very few of the insiders came from outside Ontario,
a reflection of both the ancestral politics that was practised still in
the Atlantic provinces and the sorry state of Liberalism in the
West, where Keith Davey was usually hard-pressed to choose campaign chairmen outside of Saskatchewan. There, Davey Steuart,
the senator who had been a close colleague of Thatcher's, ran
things along with Otto Lang and his brother-in-law Tony Merchant. In British Columbia, the organizing had previously been
done by Art Laing, a member of the Pearsonian old guard and no
friend of Davey's; in recent years there were so few Liberals left

in B.C., the party's organizing and fund-raising chores were shared by George Van Roggen, Ray Perrault, Larry Jolivet, Paul Plante, and Gordon Gibson, the recently retired Liberal leader who meant to seek a federal seat in 1979. Pat McGeer, who had been the provincial leader earlier, had bolted the party to become a Social Credit cabinet minister. He still talked brilliantly and bitterly about the death of Liberalism in the West, slipping occasionally by saying "we should have . . .", meaning "we Liberals should have . . .". McGeer came from a distinguished Liberal family and was internationally acclaimed for his research in neurology. His loss was felt acutely among the few remaining B.C. loyalists, as was that of Ron Basford, who had quit the cabinet, and his former assistant, Tex Enemark, who had abandoned the party to become a provincial public servant.

Because of his own Alberta background and his close association with Tom Axworthy, Coutts had slightly better Western connections. He talked frequently to Lloyd Axworthy, Tom's brother and the Liberal leader in Manitoba, and occasionally to his campaign manager, David Walker, a young and feisty political scientist; and with Keith Mitchell, Mike Hunter, and John Swift, young lawyers practising in Vancouver; and of course with Harry Hays, now a senator and fund-raiser from Calgary, whom Coutts had shepherded into the House of Commons in 1963. Otherwise, Alberta was a network wasteland. Even the doggedly activist Liberals there, people as diverse as Michael Webb, an urbane South African liberal who had become a Calgary lawyer and served on the national executive, and Nick Taylor, the talkative oil man who was the maverick provincial Liberal leader, were deeply alienated from the Coutts and Davey group. For a campaign chairman in the province this time the Liberals had to rely on an Edmonton lawyer named Branny Schepanovich, a former classmate of Coutts's at the University of Alberta, who had the unhappy task of trying to keep his candidates' hopes up when the majority of them were likely to lose their deposits.

Even more striking than the paucity of Westerners among the insiders was the absence of women. "Coutts knows there should be women in the network," Grafstein said. "Take Lorna Marsden. She isn't an insider yet but she's got the right stuff and

Coutts can relate to her. Or Dale Godsoe [a Halifax Liberal activist who was as politically important in the Maritimes as her husband, Gerald Godsoe, a lawyer who had been a policy adviser to
Gerald Regan, the former Liberal premier]. Or Kathy Robinson is
coming along. Or Joyce Fairbairn, the PM's legislative assistant;
she's out of another network, she's buddies with Bud Drury and
Allan MacEachen, but she has feelers out on the Hill and Coutts
respects that.''

For most of the women close enough to the central group to
see it functioning, and educated enough to understand its importance, this kind of talk was small comfort. There were women
executive assistants and special assistants on the Hill in the late
seventies, Penny Lipsett, who worked for Judd Buchanan, or
Patrice Merrin, who worked for Marc Lalonde, or Sandra Severn,
who had worked for John Turner, James Richardson, and then
Alasdair Graham, for instance, who were just as able as the best
of the male assistants such as Ted Johnson or Eddie Goldenberg.
But the women didn't have the men's entrée to the PMO or their
expectations of advancement.

Most women in the party realized how hard it was for women
to climb the Liberal pyramid. They knew the stories about the
male prejudices the women cabinet ministers — Judy LaMarsh in
the Pearson era — and Iona Campagnolo, Monique Bégin, and
Jeanne Sauvé now, had to do battle with, even though Bégin had
Lalonde's protection as one of his protégés, Sauvé had her husband's cabinet experience to draw on for support, and Campagnolo
had both exceptional beauty and a toughness born out of fending
for herself as a divorcée in a northern B.C. town.

Women knew the Liberal network was a male combine of
the kind Lionel Tiger had written about in his book *Men in Groups*,
where men bond together, choosing each other, as Tiger wrote,
''in processes analogous to sexual selection . . . [so that] the bond
established generates considerable emotion. . . . Males derive important satisfactions from male bonds that they cannot get from
male-female bonds.'' In other words, outside of sexual partner-
ships — and there were plenty of those in party life — women
Liberals were still mainly thought of as understudies or back-up
troops, secretaries, special assistants, even campaign chairmen

and candidates, though rarely in the choice ridings. (There were 21 women running in this election as against 261 men; even at a proportion of one in twelve, it was an unusually high number.) Women were increasingly useful to the Liberal Party. But they were not yet central to the network.

Liberal male insiders liked to get together at political conventions or to watch election-night returns or candidates' debates on television. It didn't matter whose, Tory, NDP, Péquiste, Republican, Democrat, provincial or federal, Canadian or American. They also liked to tell each other political anecdotes that illustrated their professionalism. They would describe for the benefit of younger men the time Keith Davey had talked an NDPer, a history teacher named Rod Stewart, into defecting to the Liberal Party for a 1964 by-election in the riding of Waterloo South. The social democrats in the riding were angry at Stewart and one morning he woke to find that T U R N C O A T had been painted in four-foot-high dark letters on the side of his white house. This vandalism won him considerable sympathy and, presumably, some votes in his riding, though not the by-election. Grits who had been undergraduates at the University of Toronto with Keith Davey always thought he had hired the painter himself. They remembered that when he was a student politician, trying to rouse college spirit before a crucial intra-mural football game between Victoria, his own college, and St. Michael's, the Catholic college in the university, he and a friend had broken into a field house, commandeered a can of white lime meant for the officials to mark the yard lines on the football field, and crept about under cover of darkness writing SMC in huge letters all over the buildings around the Vic quad. Next day, an unusually large and spirited crowd of Vic undergraduates turned out to cheer their team to victory. The day after that, two priests from St. Mike's came over to Vic in a delegation to apologize for their own students' prankish vandalism. Davey thanked them graciously and with a resolutely straight face.

When he heard this story, or the Stewart-the-Turncoat one, Coutts would say, "Listen, you guys, that one's okay. But never tell an anecdote more than two prime ministers old. It makes you sound like a fogey." Coutts, of course, was no fogey. He was sleek, urbane, and technically proficient, the professional's professional. He hadn't forgotten the fact that not all Liberals wore suits from bespoke tailors or kept three kinds of mineral water, French, German, and Italian, chilling in the refrigerator, as he did in his Yorkville house. He knew there were lots of Grits out there with paunches resting on their silver belt buckles, out-of-date sideburns, checked pants, and a propensity to say Kwee-beck. He even liked to tell stories about those people and their collective wisdom. But they didn't belong to the bund, any more than women did; or people who were too earnest, like Martin O'Connell, the MP, or Michel Rochon, the former policy adviser in the PMO, who were both seriously concerned with participatory policy-making; or too self-centred in their ambitions, like Brian Flemming, the Halifax lawyer, who had impeccable qualifications on paper but was too independent of mind and too given to airing his acute perceptions for the benefit of the press to really fit into the network.

"The Liberal Party is like a high-powered fraternity," said Wilson Parasiuk, an NDP MLA in Manitoba, who had worked for the federal government as a public servant and observed the Liberals intently. "It rushes the most promising young men in every generation. And then it demands their absolute loyalty."

The famous Liberal Party loyalty showed itself in many ways and was expressed in several favourite aphorisms. The most vivid of them was a remark that Colin Kenny liked to repeat, "Ya' dance with them that brought ya'!" This sentiment was otherwise voiced as "You must always look after your own," meaning you share the risks and the rewards, you stick together in good times and bad, and you never do the party harm if you can possibly help it. After John Turner resigned from the cabinet in September of 1975, in the midst of an Ontario provincial campaign when Bob Nixon, the Ontario Liberal leader, seemed closer to winning power than any Liberal had come since Mitch Hepburn was defeated in 1943, Jack Pickersgill — watching the drama from his retirement house in Rockcliffe — got on the phone to Turner almost immediately. "You've done poor Bob Nixon harm," said Pick, or words to that effect. "You had better hie yourself down to the airport when he comes through Ottawa today and show your support." Sure enough, Turner, smarting badly from the biggest shock of his political life, was right there on the tarmac at Uplands to put his arm around Nixon's shoulders, smiling for the boys in the press corps, beating the drum for Liberalism.

Disloyalties, no matter how large or small, were generally dealt with promptly by the party. A Toronto Liberal who was close to the Coutts and Davey group during the period in 1973 when they were formulating their approach to Trudeau was having a love affair at the same time with an executive assistant to a cabinet minister, and indiscreetly confided some of the group's secrets in an abandoned moment. The assistant couldn't resist repeating the group's tactics to the cabinet minister, the minister mentioned them to Keith Davey, and the indiscreet Liberal was told off and cut off until it was proven, after many, many months of trial, that no secret would ever slip out from that source again, even if it was only told to a non-network Liberal.

For out-and-out defectors from the party the treatment was more stringent. Paul Hellyer, who had been an original member of the Cell 13 group and had been supported for the leadership in 1968 by many of its members, quit the cabinet in anger at Trudeau in 1969 and made a run for the Conservative leadership in 1976. He was effectively ostracized thereafter. Once while passengers were boarding an Air Canada plane bound from Ottawa to Toronto, as Hellyer filed down the aisle he caught a glimpse of John Munro, a former colleague. Munro called out so the handful of Liberals on the plane, who were coming home from a party function, could hear him plainly, "Where are you sitting, Paul?" Hellyer, who'd obviously been through this treatment before, responded, "Okay, John, I know the next line. You just want to know so you can be sure you don't have to sit near me." Hellyer had been flagrantly disloyal, so good Liberals quite naturally disdained him.

The historical basis for this ritualistic Liberal loyalty was in the lesson King had learned from the devastation wrought on the Laurier Liberals by the conscription quarrel of the First World War. In brief, minor Liberal loyalties were derived from the major Liberal shibboleth: you stick with Quebec no matter what, and should you quarrel with French-Canadian Liberals, never do so in public. Jeanne Sauvé said in 1979 that the private differences then between the two groups of Liberals, the French and the English, were worse than she had ever seen them, a situation she found to be a mystery and a sorrow. "For myself, I don't care so much, I've made my life, I could live until I die in Quebec. But for my son, I do care. I don't want him cut off from the larger Canada. And if he, and thousands like him, aren't to be cut off, this entente just has to hold."

And hold it did, of course. No matter how fierce the infighting got — in the national executive where some of the English Canadians were accused by some of the French Canadians of siding with Turner against Trudeau, or on the national campaign committee where there were disagreements about how much money from the fund-raising drives should go to Quebec or how many days of the leader's time should be spent in the province when he was needed elsewhere — no hint of these disaffections was revealed in public. Rare Liberals like James Richardson, who had quit the cabinet in 1976 over the Prime Minister's bilingualism policies and had given public voice to French-English tensions, were called bigots or right-wingers.

To be called right wing in the Liberal Party was to be beyond the pale. No matter how prosperous, power-hungry, or self-engrossed Liberals became, they always liked to think they were progressive. "Progressive" meant looking after the interests of the "little people", the dispossessed and the disadvantaged. Tom Axworthy described his brother Lloyd Axworthy as having put together a "classic Liberal alliance of the middle class, the working people, and the poor" in his Manitoba provincial constituency of Fort Rouge. Even in his new incarnation as a big-business lawyer, John Turner talked of the need for "compassionate capitalism".

These ideas also derived from Mackenzie King and his espousal of the Christian idealism of the early twentieth century, that middle-class response to Marxism in which progressive liberals set out to enfranchise the working class, to "uplift" them, draw them into the bourgeoisie, convince them that either they or — and this was crucially important — their children could be upwardly mobile too.

For the 1978 policy convention, Coutts and Axworthy had written Trudeau a speech expressing their view of Liberalism which said, in part, "The Liberal tradition has two parts to it. On the one hand, we have to protect the individual against the State so that the individual may remain free, master [of his] own destiny. But on the other hand, and this of course is an aspect of equal importance from the point of view of Liberal ideology, the State has to intervene to protect the weak members of society, minorities, those who need protection from the State against stronger forces than themselves. And these two traditions we have always seen within the history of the Liberal Party of Canada. I have no need to recall to those of you present the history of our social policies from unemployment insurance up to health insurance, from old age pensions up to baby bonuses. And this tradition which has marked previous legislation, has also marked us [in the Trudeau era] in making individuals freer among themselves, in making different parts of Canada freer . . . DREE for example, the goal of which is precisely to create a greater degree of equality of chance in the different parts of the country.''

None of this was thought to be mere rhetoric or historical wool-gathering among mainstream modern Liberals. It was just horse sense. Liberals knew their bedrock vote was a coalition of minorities who tended to see themselves as ''outs'' but wanted to be ''ins'': French Canadians, of course, outside Quebec as well as within, ethnics of all stripes in the English-speaking cities, Catholics both urban and rural (except in Newfoundland, where they had historically voted Conservative), plus small pockets of the so-called genetic Liberals who lived in rural areas in Ontario and the Atlantic provinces where their ancestors had lived and voted for decades the way they still voted in the 1970s. (Maurice Careless, the University of Toronto historian and expert on the Confederation era, once remarked that more than a century after 1867 there were still places in small-town Ontario where he had heard older people saying they always voted Reform.) These minority groups were welded together by the party's leaders, who came in overwhelming numbers from the professional middle class — the lawyers, doctors, architects, and accountants whose numbers were disproportionately large in the Liberal ranks.

Allan Gregg, a public-opinion-polling expert the Conservatives had hired for this campaign, found that when he was sampling voter attitudes and asked Canadians what a Liberal looked like, they would say, "Like Art Phillips." (Phillips was the lawyer and former city mayor running for the Liberals in Vancouver Centre who had married Carole Taylor, a glossy television star, and was so smoothly handsome himself the couple were called "the Ken and Barbie dolls" by the B.C. press.) When Gregg asked the same voters what a Tory looked like, they usually answered, "A big-businessman. Old, fat, and a WASP." And an NDPer? "A professor with a lot of frizzy hair and the kind of glasses your grandfather wore."

Absurd as these caricatures were — and they drove Tories and NDPers wild with frustrated anger at their simplicities — many Liberals liked them. They wanted to think that the Tories were "Bay Street" like George Drew on the one hand, or loony incompetents who couldn't administer a hotdog stand, like John Diefenbaker on the other. The New Democrats gave them more trouble conceptually. For thirty-five years, since King was frightened by the CCF surge in Ontario in 1943, the Liberals had been trying to contain the social democratic party by adapting its ideas, trying to form coalitions with its leaders, and appealing to its members to support them in crucial votes. The NDPers were just too smart and too much inclined to give voice to more vivid expressions of the kind of "progressivism" so many Liberals had espoused in their youths for Grits to be comfortable with them. This uneasiness extended even unto Trudeau himself, who had hated to be attacked by David Lewis during his leadership of the NDP when he displayed his marvellous intellectual and oratorical gifts, bolstered by his moral certitude, for all the House to see in the daily Question Periods.

The Grits of Mackenzie King's era had called CCFers like Lewis "Liberals in a hurry"; contemporary Liberals liked to think they were impractical dreamers who didn't have enough sense to join the party where your ideas could be put into effect. When it was pointed out that in the 1970s the NDP, under the leadership of Ed Broadbent, a lucid if low-key professor with solid support in the labour movement, was attracting young people who might formerly have been Liberal types — such as Robert Rae, the golden offspring of a mandarin family, who had been elected MP for Toronto-Broadview in October 1978 and was proving a highly effective finance critic in the Commons; or Marc Eliesen, the research director for the NDP federal caucus, who had been employed by the Department of Finance when he was fresh out of McGill and, hating the Liberal-bureaucratic combine he saw there, put his talents to work for the NDP governments in Manitoba and British Columbia before coming back to Ottawa; or Alexa McDonagh, a candidate in Nova Scotia running against Brian Flemming, who was a dramatically eloquent social worker, the wife of a Liberal lawyer, and the sister of a Liberal adviser to Gerald Regan — when these names and reputations were described to Liberals, they just shrugged. "It's the League for Social Reconstruction all over again," they would say. "Those people will get sick of it, always sitting there on the Opposition benches yelling across the floor. There's a limit to altruism. If you can't win, you can't get any policies effected, no matter how high-minded or well-meaning they are."

In those sentiments were expressed the last, if not the least, of the Liberal maxims. Winning matters. The Grits were willing to stick with Pierre Trudeau in 1979 because he believed in and indeed epitomized the French-English entente, because he was "progressive", but, above all, because he was a winner.

"I can't believe they're going to run this election without any strong new policies and with only Trudeau as their platform," said Lowell Murray, who was the Tory campaign chairman and Joe Clark's one-man brains trust. Murray was a highly intelligent, seasoned politician in his early forties, as technically proficient as Coutts and Davey themselves. He had worked for Davie Fulton, the gentleman Tory from B.C., and with Dalton Camp and Eddie Goodman, the smooth Tories from Toronto, and for Robert Stanfield, the sterling Tory from Nova Scotia, and Richard Hatfield, the witty, winning Tory from New Brunswick, and he knew a thing or six about elections. Now he was backing Clark with a campaign team drawn from across the country, made up of young people who were devoted to him.

"What the Grits should be doing is running the Liberal Party, running a Liberal team," said Murray. "The party's a tough old bird with a strong residual pull on the affections of Canadians, and they're ignoring that at their peril. If the leader hasn't got any new policies, they should steal some from us or from the NDP. They've done that often enough before. Trudeau's a spent force in English Canada. But Liberalism is a long, long way from finished.''

SITTING TOGETHER IN THE PMO on the night of March 26, 1979, watching Trudeau deliver the television announcement that he had called an election for May 22, Coutts and Davey didn't know what Murray had been saying about their plans and prospects in his office at Conservative headquarters a few blocks away. Even if they had known, they wouldn't have paid any heed. They recognized even more clearly than he did the difficulties they faced in the coming campaign. Goldfarb had told them the winning numbers just weren't there for the Liberals and that in his view elections were always won or lost on the day that they were called. What they were practising now was the politics of desperation.

But in a sea of uncertainties they clung to an idea that had formerly stood them in good stead: they had made a game plan and they meant to stick to it. Coutts and Davey both believed that you never run to lose. If Trudeau couldn't win a majority, then they had to keep Clark from getting one. They had to deny him the victory that would put him in office and keep them from power for the next four years. Buried in the bad news that Goldfarb had been bringing them was a glimmer of good.

The electorate was highly volatile, Goldfarb claimed, because it was in a state of insecurity. The economic situation had frightened the public in a way in which most voters, who had been watching the good times roll in Canada all their adult lives, had never been frightened before. The opinion samplings had shown that Canadians were furious at Trudeau for not rescuing them from this fix. People thought he was indifferent to their troubles and arrogant because of his wealth, the privileged playboy husband of a silly, privileged playgirl. ("In my riding," Lloyd Axworthy said when this piece of Goldfarbian wisdom was revealed, "they figure Margaret Trudeau is the new Marie Antoinette. What she's telling us is 'Let them sniff coke.'")

Angry as the voters were at Trudeau, though, they still harboured the paradoxical belief that he was the better leader —

the smarter, stronger, tougher, and certainly the more tried and
true. Somehow Joe Clark made the uneasy feel uneasier. "Inexperienced", "awkward", "fumbling and bumbling", "weak
maybe", "just too young" were the words and phrases the voters
kept voicing haltingly as they sat in their living rooms talking to
Goldfarb's sympathetic teams of interviewers about their unnamed
insecurities and their unaccustomed fears.

In the next few weeks Coutts and Davey hoped to reinforce
these attitudes through every campaign technique they knew and
a few they had never tried before. Presenting Trudeau as a strong
leader was their strategy. Their tactics were more complex. One
of their favourite campaign techniques involved the judicious use
of surprise, and a surprise is what they had been able to pull off in
the timing of the election's call. For several weeks they had known
when the moment was expected, but they had held their last tactical
planning meetings during the lengthening March afternoons so
they wouldn't have to keep the PMO lights burning late into the
night and thereby rouse suspicions in the Press Gallery and give
the Opposition an edge. Tonight, after Trudeau finished his address to the nation, they had the satisfaction of seeing Clark thrown
off balance trying to respond extemporaneously to television
reporters' questions in a dimly lit hall in Regina, where he had
travelled on Conservative business, little suspecting the election
would be called. Making Clark look like a hesitant bumbler: that
was their goal.

They also planned to let it be known that the Liberals in
Quebec were running scared because the Créditistes were planning
to choose as their new federal leader Fabien Roy, a member of the
provincial legislature from the Beauce, whose supposed charisma, enhanced by the Péquistes's planned intervention in the federal campaign, might cost them many seats unless they went to
the country immediately. (Lalonde claimed privately that Roy
didn't scare him much, that he was a fabrication of the media.
But putting the fear of the Lord into the Liberal troops and the
hope of their failure into the anti-Liberal press had never done the
party's prospects any harm.)

In addition, the Liberals had in mind yet another series of
patronage appointments. These would be announced after the writs

were issued and would free more seats in Quebec and the Maritimes for new candidates, a plan that sprang from the recognition that every riding Lalonde could keep from the Créditistes and that the Atlantic bosses could wrest from the Tories would count in their overall plan.

Coutts and Davey had also put together the most expert campaign staff that they could muster: the best advance men to fan out ahead of the leader and make sure that the crowds, the bands, and the backdrops were exactly what was needed to look good on the television news; the best press officers to travel on the campaign plane and neutralize, since they couldn't hope to captivate, the media; the best speech-writers to stay behind in the PMO and come up with the fresh phrases that would bolster the wobbledy policies that were all they had been able to come up with given the economic situation; the most expert image-making team to work with Grafstein in Toronto and churn out the cleverest ads.

All these people would be kept happy by the weekly meetings, daily briefings, wacky slogans, inside jokes, and optimistic prophecies that had been Davey's specialty for nearly twenty years and that as campaign co-ordinator he meant to practise just one more time using his crowded Senate office as his headquarters. He had phones hooked up there directly to the party's Ottawa offices and into the PMO and could talk all day long to his campaign chairmen out in the provinces, and to Coutts as he hopped out of the Prime Minister's plane for the speech stops in the boondocks.

They had even figured out how Coutts's constant presence on the plane could be used to keep the leader from depression (make him promise not to read Margaret's book and see to it that he doesn't get the newspapers carrying the excerpts); or from the fatigue that made him snappish (pace his schedule well, keeping the early engagements to a minimum and making sure the advance men insist that in every hotel room he sleeps in the windows open wide so he can get the fresh air he needs); or from turning into his sarcastic, Socratic self while lecturing audiences (let him talk about the constitution since he insists, but he will have to wait until the last three weeks, when he can hold forth for audiences of Liberal insiders who still know how to look animated when they feel enervated and when to cheer the leader during an appropriate pause).

As they reviewed these and several other of the hundreds of tactical details that made up their intricate plan, Coutts and Davey decided that the campaign they had come up with was as technically proficient as anyone could make it and that when he was "on", the politician who had to front it was as gifted a platform performer as either of them had ever seen. Now all they could do was to hope he was "on" oftener than "off" and to run full-out themselves.

It was with a certain sober satisfaction then that they turned out the lights in Coutts's office and walked out into the Ottawa cold. No matter what Goldfarb says, maybe we can squeeze a minority, Coutts thought to himself. Maybe our luck will hold.

What neither he nor Davey realized, as they went their separate ways, was that the campaign they were beginning that March night would last not eight weeks but forty-eight, that it would involve not one election but two, and that surprise after surprise would emanate from the Liberal Party and its unlikely leader in the months and years to come.

TO BE CONTINUED

AFTERWORD

WHEN IT WAS FIRST PLANNED, *Grits* was intended to encompass the election of 1979, and Pierre Elliott Trudeau's subsequent resignation as Liberal leader. Events played havoc with this plan, as they did with those of many others. As the research was extended and the files and the manuscript grew, it became clear there were two distinct books involved. Now a second volume is projected under the working title *The Liberal Party in the Eighties: The End of the Trudeau Era*. It will include descriptions and analyses of the 1979 and 1980 federal elections when the party, having reached a low point on March 26, 1979, began its ascent towards a new apogee; the Liberals' relationship to their pollsters, fund-raisers, advertising agencies, and the national media as revealed in those two elections; the brief period in between when the Progressive Conservatives under Prime Minister Joe Clark held office and the Liberals in opposition prepared the strategies and policies that helped them regain the treasury benches, bringing into sharp focus once more their ideological adaptability and their acute sense of how power works in Canada; the Quebec referendum and the federal-provincial negotiations that resulted in the patriation of the constitution in 1982 and the partial realization of Pierre Trudeau's political goals; the new nationalism of the National Energy Program and its effect on Canadian-American relations and on regional antagonisms; the changing role of women within the party's councils; the worsening economic situation and the Liberals' attempts to salvage it; the party membership's continuing discussions of how Pierre Trudeau had altered Liberalism and its fascination with the long-distance race to succeed him.

I will leave the speculation on its date of publication to people more clairvoyant than myself.

ACKNOWLEDGEMENTS

DURING THE FIVE YEARS it took to research and write this book, I had the unflagging intellectual and emotional support of Stephen Clarkson, who was first my friend and then my husband. He held hundreds of discussions with me on everything from the implications for contemporary Liberalism of Mackenzie King's Christian idealism to the best kind of file folders to use in organizing a mass of research material. His broad knowledge of politics and his specific expertise on the Liberal Party were always freely shared with me; he has the true teacher's gift of demanding and encouraging at one and the same moment. As I look through the manuscript for the last time before it goes to the printers, I realize again with inexpressible gratitude that his intelligence and integrity light up every part of the work, as they do every day of my life.

Many other people were generous beyond expectation in the help they gave me. Because so much of the book deals with contemporary events, I was reliant on extensive interviews with many of the principals involved, most of whose names appear in the listing at the back of the book.

In addition to the authors of the published works listed in the Bibliography, and cited in the Notes, I would like to thank several people who gave me the benefit of advice in their special areas of interest, particularly Professor John Bossons of the Institute of Policy Analysis and Professor Peter Russell of the Department of Political Economy, both of the University of Toronto, as well as Michael Adams, president of National Polling Trends, and Bob Vincent, president of the B. J. Vincent Company Limited, who was endlessly patient with the complications involved in preparing the table on Liberal appointees to the Senate included as an appendix. During the period when he was a graduate student at the University of Toronto, David Trick gave me expert research help on several specific questions and prepared with great dispatch the Chronology. Kathleen Finlay also helped with occasional research and Elizabeth Reicker and Lloyd Heaslip of the Library of Parliament responded with alacrity to my requests for information.

In the academic year 1977–78, I enjoyed the luxury of a Southam Fellowship at Massey College in the University of Toronto where I began the book; the Canada Council gave me a generous grant under its Explorations program which enabled me to travel the country in 1978 and 1979, and to go to Ottawa on many occasions; and the Ontario Arts

Council gave me a grant under their program offering aid to writers with works-in-progress.

My colleagues at *Saturday Night* magazine, Robert Fulford and Bernadette Sulgit, remained encouraging to me throughout the project, displaying the acutely sympathetic awareness of the miseries and pleasures of the writer's life that has made them as celebrated as they are unusual in the Canadian publishing world. For twenty years Fulford has been sharing with me his perceptions of Canadian society. He asked me to write about Ottawa when he was a young editor on the old, much lamented, bi-weekly *Maclean's* and I was first living in the capital and observing its workings with amazement. Later, I was his Ottawa editor when he began his editorship of *Saturday Night*, and I have worked for him and his magazine off and on ever since. In the mid-1970s, Richard Doyle and Clark Davey of the Toronto *Globe and Mail* gave me free rein to write about politics in that paper's pages, an experience that added substantially to my knowledge of this country and to my interest in the subject. That interest was first kindled by my father, Christopher McCall, a Presbyterian of dour demeanour, who was as fascinated with Mackenzie King and Louis St. Laurent, and as pitying of John Bracken and George Drew, as if he had been a clear Grit and not a true-blue Tory.

Mary Harrison, a colleague and friend of several seasons, expertly typed my notes, letters, and manuscript, and managed to make the work seem, in her inimitable way, always more than a duty and very often a pleasure. At various stages in the editing of the manuscript, Ivon Owen, Norman Williams, Jane and Martin Lynch, Jan Walter, Eleanor Sinclair, Anne Holloway, and, of course, Douglas Gibson, the publisher of Macmillan of Canada, were very helpful. Barbara Czarnecki dealt meticulously with the difficult job of preparing the index.

Many friends were warmly encouraging: Robert Collison, Jean Crowe, Maria Costa, Shirley Gibson, Elizabeth Gordon, Gwenyth Grube, Jane Jacobs, Merrijoy Kellner, Allan King, Martin Knelman, Wanda O'Hagan, Alan Powell, Patricia Watson, and Helen Dacey Wilson, among them. At various times and for varying periods I was offered a room of my own in which to work by Orlie McCall and Lynda Miller in their house, Max and Madeleine Clarkson at Glen Lea Farm, Bob and Orlie Vincent in their offices, and John Macfarlane, the publisher of *Saturday Night*, in the magazine's premises on Bond Street.

I would like to mention in particular two other people: Ethel Teitelbaum, whose insight into human behaviour and gift for friendship are unique in my experience; and James Reed, who is himself in search of wisdom and unusually talented in imparting understanding and evoking strength. In their disparate ways, they both flagged me onwards, especially on those occasions when I would sooner have given up than not.

Having begun these acknowledgements thanking my husband, I would like to end them by thanking our children, Ashley, Kyra, and Blaise. Ashley's warmth and acuity have made me hopeful all her life and Kyra and Blaise have shown me many kindnesses — their father's grace — in the four years we have lived together as a family. All three joined in my excitement on the good days, hugged me on the bad, filled our house with laughter, and, in the practical help they offered, gave me glimpses time and time again of the forthright and loving women I know they will become.

Christina McCall-Newman

Massey College, September 1977 —
70 Bond Street, Toronto, July 1982.

CHRONOLOGY

1957

June 10   General election. Progressive Conservatives win minority government with 112 seats (Liberals 105, CCF 25, Social Credit 19, others 4).

Oct. 15   Cell 13, group of progressive Toronto Liberals, founded by Gordon Dryden.

1958

Jan. 14–16   Liberal leadership convention elects Lester Pearson as party leader.

March 31   General election. Progressive Conservatives win majority government with 208 seats (Liberals 49, CCF 8).

May 12   Final report of the (Gordon) royal commission on Canada's economic prospects warns of dangers of foreign control of Canadian economy.

Gallup poll puts Liberal popularity at 29 per cent.

1959

Sept. 1   Marc Lalonde and Michael Pitfield come to Ottawa as aides to justice minister Davie Fulton.

Progressive Conservatives win P.E.I. general election, leaving Newfoundland as only province with a Liberal government.

Sept. 7   Quebec premier Maurice Duplessis dies.

Nov. 5   Walter Gordon, in report to Pearson, urges reorganization of Liberal Party.

1960

Feb. 15   Leader's advisory committee established by Gordon to increase central control over party.

June 22   Quebec general election. Union Nationale government defeated by Jean Lesage's Liberals.

Sept. 6–10   Liberal study conference on national problems held in Kingston.

Sept. 16   Prime Minister John Diefenbaker appoints (O'Leary) royal commission on publications, with Pitfield as secretary.

1961

Jan. 9–11   National rally of Liberal Party held in Ottawa.

May 1   Davey becomes national organizer of Liberal Party.

July 31–   T. C. Douglas elected national leader at founding
Aug. 4   convention of New Democratic Party.

1962

April   Trudeau's "New Treason of the Intellectuals" published in *Cité libre*.

June 18   General election. Progressive Conservatives reduced to minority government with 116 seats (Liberals 100, Social Credit 30, NDP 19). Walter Gordon and John Turner elected for first time. James Coutts defeated.

Sept. 6   First volume of the report of the (Glassco) royal commission on government organization is published, recommending modernization and streamlining of federal government.

Sept. 25   Diefenbaker appoints (Carter) royal commission on taxation, with Pitfield as secretary.

Dec. 17   Pearson delivers speech calling for royal commission on bilingualism and biculturalism.

1963

Jan. 12   Pearson delivers speech favouring presence of nuclear missiles in Canada.

April 8   General election. Liberals win minority government with 129 seats (PCs 95, Social Credit 24, NDP 17).

April 22   Pearson government sworn in, with Gordon as finance minister.

May 1   Coutts named appointments secretary to Pearson.

            Pearson names Turner parliamentary secretary to Minister of Northern Affairs and Natural Resources.

June 13   Finance minister Gordon brings down first budget.

July 1   Gordon Robertson appointed clerk of Privy Council, replacing Robert Bryce, who becomes deputy minister of finance.

July 22   Pearson appoints royal commission on bilingualism and biculturalism.

1964

May   Trudeau, Lalonde, and colleagues publish "An Appeal for Reason in Canadian Politics" in *Cité libre* and *Canadian Forum*.

Oct. 7-10   Queen's visit to Quebec marked by separatist demonstrations.

Dec. 15   House of Commons approves design of new Canadian flag.

1965

March 29   House of Commons passes Canada pension plan.

April 2   Pearson criticizes U.S. Vietnam policy in speech at Temple University.

April 15   Pitfield joins Privy Council Office.

Sept. 10   Trudeau, Gérard Pelletier, and Jean Marchand announce they will run as Liberals in general election.

Oct. 5   Gallup poll puts Liberal popularity at 48 per cent — the Pearson government's all-time high.

Nov. 8   General election. Liberals retain minority government with 131 seats (PCs 97, NDP 21, Social Credit 14, others 2). Trudeau elected for first time.

Nov. 11   Gordon resigns from cabinet. Davey resigns as national organizer of party.

Dec. 18   Cabinet shuffle. Turner enters cabinet as minister without portfolio, Marchand as minister of citizenship and immigration.

1966

Jan. 9   Trudeau becomes parliamentary secretary to Pearson.

Feb. 24   Pearson appoints Davey to Senate.

May 1   Coutts leaves Prime Minister's Office for Harvard Business School.

Dec. 8   House of Commons passes bill creating medicare.

1967

Jan. 4   Pearson announces that Gordon will rejoin cabinet as minister without portfolio.

Feb. 3   Pearson appoints royal commission on the status of women.

March 14   Lalonde becomes chief policy adviser to Pearson, replacing Tom Kent.

April 14   Cabinet shuffle. Trudeau enters cabinet as justice minister. Gordon named president of Privy Council.

Sept. 9   Progressive Conservative leadership convention elects Robert Stanfield as national leader.

Dec. 14   Pearson announces that he will retire.

Dec. 21   Turner named minister of consumer and corporate affairs.

Dec. 21   Justice minister Trudeau announces proposals for reform of criminal code.

Dec. 24–31   Trudeau meets Margaret Sinclair in Tahiti.

1968

Jan. 18   Turner declares candidacy for Liberal leadership.

Feb. 5–7   Federal-provincial conference on constitution leads to confrontation between Trudeau and Quebec premier Daniel Johnson.

Feb. 15   Watkins report on foreign ownership of Canadian industry is published.

Feb. 16   Trudeau declares candidacy for Liberal leadership.

Feb. 29   House of Commons passes amendments to Unemployment Insurance Act, extending coverage and raising benefit levels.

March 11   Gordon resigns from cabinet.

April 4–6   Liberal leadership convention elects Trudeau as national leader.

April 9   Secretary of State Judy LaMarsh resigns from cabinet.

April 20   Trudeau government is sworn in, with Turner as solicitor general and Pelletier as minister without portfolio.

June 25   General election. Liberals win majority government with 155 seats (PCs, 72, NDP 22, Social Credit 14, others 1).

July 5   Cabinet shuffle. Turner named minister of justice.

July 31   Trudeau names Lalonde principal secretary in Prime Minister's Office.

Oct. 11–14   Parti Québécois founded, with René Lévesque as leader.

December   Gallup poll puts Liberal popularity at 52 per cent.

1969

April 1	Department of Regional Economic Expansion created, with Marchand as minister.
April 24	Transport minister Paul Hellyer resigns from cabinet in dispute with Trudeau.
July 7	House of Commons passes Official Languages Act.
Nov. 7	Finance minister Edgar Benson brings down white paper on tax reform.
Nov. 20–3	Liberals hold policy conference at Harrison Hot Springs, B.C.

1970

Oct. 5	October Crisis begins with abduction of British trade commissioner James Cross.
Oct. 13	Liberals win Nova Scotia general election, bringing number of Liberal provincial governments to a peak of six.
Oct. 16	War Measures Act proclaimed.
Oct. 17	Quebec labour minister Pierre Laporte found murdered.
November	Gallup poll puts Liberal popularity at 59 per cent — their highest ever.
Nov. 20–2	Liberal policy convention held in Ottawa.
Dec. 3	James Cross released unharmed.
Dec. 9	Report of the Senate committee on mass media (chaired by Davey) warns of increased concentration of media ownership.

1971

March 4	Trudeau marries Margaret Sinclair.
April 24	NDP leadership convention elects David Lewis as national leader.

April 29 Communications minister Eric Kierans resigns from cabinet in dispute with Trudeau.

June 14–16 Victoria Conference on constitutional reform produces Victoria Charter, which Quebec and Saskatchewan later reject.

June 29 Consumer and corporate affairs minister Ron Basford introduces Bill C-256, the first of a series of efforts to amend Combines Act.

1972

Jan. 28 Cabinet shuffle. Turner named minister of finance.

May 2 Gray report on foreign investment published.

Oct. 30 General election. Liberals reduced to minority government with 109 seats (PCs 107, NDP 31, Social Credit 15, others 2). Lalonde elected for first time.

Nov. 15 Martin O'Connell replaces Lalonde as principal secretary in Prime Minister's Office.

Nov. 27 Cabinet shuffle. Lalonde named minister of national health and welfare.

Dec. 27 Lester Pearson dies.

1973

Jan. 9 RCMP break into Montreal office of Parti Québécois to obtain party membership lists.

Feb. 19 Finance minister Turner introduces indexation of income tax deductions.

March 1 Pitfield leaves Privy Council Office to become deputy minister of consumer and corporate affairs.

April 27 Consumer and corporate affairs minister Herb Gray announces creation of food prices review board.

Aug. 1 Trudeau announces that Davey will co-chair Liberal 1974 campaign committee.

Nov. 26   House of Commons passes Foreign Investment Review Act.

Dec. 6   Trudeau announces government will introduce legislation to create Petro-Canada.

1974

March 22   Mr. Justice Thomas Berger named to head inquiry into Mackenzie Valley pipeline.

May 8   Liberals defeated on confidence motion in House of Commons.

May 15   Jack Austin replaces O'Connell as principal secretary in Prime Minister's Office.

July 8   General election. Liberals win majority government with 141 seats (PCs 95, NDP 16, Social Credit 11, others 1).

July 30   Quebec National Assembly passes Bill 22, making French the sole official language of Quebec.

Oct. 4   Trudeau appoints Pitfield as clerk of Privy Council, replacing Gordon Robertson.

Dec. 3–4   Four deputy ministers — Simon Reisman, James Grandy, Sydney Williams, and Herb Balls — announce their early retirement. A fifth, Elgin Armstrong, joins them Dec. 16.

1975

July 4–7   NDP leadership convention elects Ed Broadbent as national leader.

Aug. 19   Coutts named principal secretary in Prime Minister's Office, replacing Jack Austin.

Aug. 28   Pelletier resigns from House of Commons to become ambassador to Paris.

Sept. 10   Turner resigns from cabinet.

Oct. 13   Trudeau announces imposition of wage and income controls.

Oct. 14   Communications minister Pierre Juneau loses Hochelaga by-election.

Dec. 28   Trudeau questions viability of free-market economy in CTV interview.

1976

Feb. 22   Progressive Conservative leadership convention elects Joe Clark as national leader.

Feb. 25   House of Commons passes bill to remove tax deduction for advertisers in *Time* Canada.

March 16   Consumer and corporate affairs minister André Ouellet resigns from cabinet after being found in contempt of court in sugar price-fixing case.

April 20   Senator Louis Giguère charged with influence-peddling in Sky Shops affair.

June 20-8   Anglophone air traffic controllers strike over use of French.

June 30   Marchand resigns from cabinet over air traffic controllers strike.

September   Gallup poll puts Liberal popularity at 29 per cent — their lowest since 1943, 20 points behind PCs.

Sept. 14   Cabinet shuffle. Bud Drury, Bryce Mackasey, and Mitchell Sharp retire from cabinet.

Oct. 13   Defence minister James Richardson resigns from cabinet over bilingualism policies.

Nov. 15   Quebec general election. Robert Bourassa's Liberals lose to Parti Québécois under René Lévesque.

1977

April 20	Jack Horner crosses floor of House of Commons to join Liberals; appointed minister without portfolio the following day.
May 24	Liberals win 5 of 6 by-elections in Quebec and P.E.I.
May 27	Pierre and Margaret Trudeau formally separated.
July 6	Solicitor General Francis Fox announces (McDonald) royal commission to investigate RCMP wrongdoing.
July 13	Gallup poll puts Liberal popularity at 51 per cent, 24 points ahead of PCs.
Aug. 26	Quebec National Assembly passes Bill 101, strengthening the predominance of French in Quebec.
Sept. 6	Finance minister Donald Macdonald resigns from cabinet.
Sept. 16	Cabinet shuffle. Lalonde named minister for federal-provincial relations.

1978

Jan. 30	Solicitor General Francis Fox resigns from cabinet after admitting he signed another man's name on a hospital order form in order to obtain an abortion for a woman who was not his wife.
April 10	Finance minister Jean Chrétien brings down budget, beginning Ottawa-Quebec dispute over sales tax.
April 15	Quebec Liberal leadership convention elects Claude Ryan as provincial leader, replacing Robert Bourassa.
April 21	Trudeau appoints Claude Wagner to Senate.
June 20	Trudeau introduces Bill C-60, proposals to reform the constitution.
June 29	Giguère acquitted in Sky Shops affair.

Aug. 1	Trudeau returns from Bonn summit to announce shift in economic policy towards government restraint.
Sept. 8	Labour minister John Munro resigns from cabinet after admitting he phoned a judge on behalf of a constituent.
Oct. 16	Liberals lose 13 of 15 by-elections.
Nov. 24	Trudeau establishes Board of Economic Development Ministers under Treasury Board president Robert Andras.
December	Gallup poll puts Liberal popularity at 35 per cent, 10 points behind PCs.
Dec. 7	Trudeau announces appointment of former Manitoba premier Edward Schreyer as governor general.
Dec. 14	Trudeau announces appointment of Bryce Mackasey as chairman of the board of Air Canada.

1979

Jan. 25	Report of the (Pepin-Robarts) task force on Canadian unity questions Trudeau's concept of federalism.
Feb. 5–6	First ministers' conference on constitution ends without agreement.
Feb. 23	Parti Québécois issues manifesto on sovereignty-association.
March 26	Parliament dissolved. General election called for May 22.
March 30	Margaret Trudeau's autobiography, *Beyond Reason*, is published.
April 23	Liberal government of P.E.I. defeated in general election, leaving Liberals without a single provincial government.

May 22   General election. Progressive Conservatives win
              minority government with 136 seats (Liberals 114,
              NDP 26, Social Credit 6).

June 4   Trudeau resigns as prime minister.

APPENDIX

LIBERAL SENATORS: TABLE OF REMUNERATION

	Province or territory represented	1. Accumulated Remuneration as of Dec. 31, 1979*	2. Expected Future Remuneration to Date of Retirement†	3. Yearly Pension at 75‡	4. Actual Value of Pension at Retirement§	5. Total Value of Senatorship at Retirement ‖
Willie Adams Born (b.) June 21, 1934; appointment date (app.) April 5, 1977; retirement date (ret.) June 21, 2009. First Eskimo in Senate; an electrician at Rankin Inlet on Hudson Bay; named to board of Panarctic Oils Ltd., government-sponsored consortium.	Northwest Territories	$88,600	$3,381,100	$134,356	$1,152,477	$4,622,177
Margaret Anderson b. August 7, 1915; app. March 23, 1978; ret. August 7, 1990. Liberal Party worker; daughter of W. S. Anderson, Newcastle lumberman and onetime cabinet minister in a N.B. Liberal government	New Brunswick	$56,900	$558,742	$18,546	$164,738	$780,380
Hazen Argue b. January 6, 1921; app. February 24, 1966; ret. January 6, 1996. A CCF MP, he switched to Liberals after losing in a bid for the NDP leadership and was defeated as a Liberal candidate in Assiniboia in 1963 and 1965.	Saskatchewan	$318,250	$1,041,656	$54,049	$463,620	$1,823,526

Note: For references noted by symbols in column headings, see page 428.

LIBERAL SENATORS: TABLE OF REMUNERATION

	Province or territory represented	1. Accumulated Remuneration as of Dec. 31, 1979*	2. Expected Future Remuneration to Date of Retirement†	3. Yearly Pension at 75‡	4. Actual Value of Pension at Retirement§	5. Total Value of Senatorship at Retirement ‖
Jack Austin b. March 2, 1932; app. August 19, 1975; ret. March 2, 2007. Arthur Laing protégé; lawyer for Vancouver mining interests; deputy minister, Energy, Mines and Resources, and principal secretary to Trudeau. In 1979 became chairman of GM Resources Ltd., controlled by Cemp Investments Ltd. (Charles and Edgar Bronfman).	British Columbia	$140,500	$2,816,404	$114,971	$986,201	$3,943,105
Irvine Barrow b. February 15, 1913; app. May 8, 1974; ret. February 15, 1988. Halifax accountant and businessman (cable TV); sometime president of N.S. Liberal Association. One of three administrators of private trust fund for N.S. Liberal leader Gerald Regan, later N.S. premier.	Nova Scotia	$174,050	$390,467	$17,461	$149,780	$714,297
Nancy Bell b. May 26, 1924; app. October 7, 1970; ret. May 26, 1999. Former president of B.C. Women's Liberal Association; daughter of Charles Bowman, long-time editor of the Liberal-leaning Ottawa *Citizen*.	British Columbia	$249,500	$1,447,173	$67,969	$603,731	$2,300,404

William Benidickson b. April 8, 1911; app. July 8, 1965; ret. April 8, 1986. Lawyer; Liberal MP for Kenora-Rainy River for twenty years; brother-in-law of James Richardson, ex-Liberal and ex-Minister of Defence, of the Winnipeg family of grain merchants.	Ontario	$328,250	$281,530	$23,204	$199,039	$808,819
Florence **Bird** b. January 15, 1908; app. March 23, 1978; ret. January 15, 1983. Journalist, author, broadcaster under name Anne Francis; born in Philadelphia; educated at Bryn Mawr; wife of late newspaper correspondent John Bird; chairman of Royal Commission on Status of Women in Canada, 1967–70.	Ontario	$56,900	$121,580	$4,324	$38,407	$216,887
Lorne **Bonnell** b. January 4, 1923; app. November 15, 1971; ret. January 4, 1998. Doctor; Liberal MLA in P.E.I. for twenty years and acting Liberal leader in province.	Prince Edward Island	$230,000	$1,269,147	$61,858	$530,606	$2,029,753
Peter **Bosa** b. May 2, 1927; app. April 5, 1977; ret. May 2, 2002. Italian-born insurance agent; a leader of Toronto's Italian community; special assistant to Minister of Citizenship and Immigration, 1963–64.	Ontario	$91,200	$1,882,200	$82,903	$711,121	$2,684,521

LIBERAL SENATORS: TABLE OF REMUNERATION

	Province or territory represented	1. Accumulated Remuneration as of Dec. 31, 1979*	2. Expected Future Remuner- ation to Date of Retirement†	3. Yearly Pension at 75‡	4. Actual Value of Pension at Retirement§	5. Total Value of Senatorship at Retirement ‖
Sidney Buckwold b. November 3, 1916; app. November 4, 1971; ret. November 3, 1991. Businessman; ex-mayor of Saskatoon; twice unsuccessful Liberal candidate for federal seat; director of Bank of Montreal and other companies.	Saskatchewan	$230,850	$654,229	$32,595	$279,594	$1,164,673
Eric Cook b. July 26, 1909; app. February 14, 1964; ret. July 26, 1984. Retired lawyer; a son of Sir Tasker Cook, mayor of St. John's and government leader in the Legislative Council of Newfoundland; was president of the Newfoundland Liberal Association.	Newfoundland	$348,850	$192,935	$26,828	$205,038	$746,823
Ernest Cottreau b. January 28, 1914; app. May 8, 1974; ret. January 28, 1989. School principal; past president of Yarmouth County Liberal Association; representative of the Acadians of western Nova Scotia.	Nova Scotia	$176,150	$451,602	$19,898	$170,685	$798,437

Name	Province					
David Croll b. March 12, 1900; app. July 28, 1955; life appointment. Mayor of Windsor; cabinet minister in Mitchell Hepburn's Liberal government in Ontario; MP for Spadina riding in Toronto; first Jewish provincial cabinet minister and first Jewish senator; chairman of financial company in the group headed by Samuel Belzberg.	Ontario	$438,700	$322,795	—	—	$761,495
Keith Davey b. April 21, 1926; app. February 24, 1966; ret. April 21, 2001. National organizer of Liberals, 1961–66; national campaign director, elections of 1962, 1963, 1965; co-chairman, national campaign committee, in elections of 1974 and 1979; chairman of Senate committee on mass media, 1969–72.	Ontario	$318,250	$1,719,558	$77,320	$663,231	$2,701,039
Azellus Denis b. March 26, 1907; app. February 7, 1964; life appointment. Montreal lawyer; MP for St. Denis from 1935 to 1964; succeeded his brother Dr. J. A. Denis, who held seat from 1921 to his death in 1934.	Quebec	$349,500	$533,956	—	—	$883,456
Jean-Paul Deschatelets b. October 9, 1912; app. February 24, 1966; ret. October 9, 1987. Lawyer; MP for Maisonneuve-Rosemont, 1953–65; Minister of Public Works, 1963–65; assistant government leader in Senate, 1966–68; Speaker, 1968–72.	Quebec	$372,450	$368,645	$26,762	$229,558	$970,653

LIBERAL SENATORS: TABLE OF REMUNERATION

	Province or territory represented	1. Accumulated Remuneration as of Dec. 31, 1979*	2. Expected Future Remuneration to Date of Retirement†	3. Yearly Pension at 75‡	4. Actual Value of Pension at Retirement§	5. Total Value of Senatorship at Retirement ‖
Paul Desruisseaux b. May 1, 1905; app. July 8, 1966; ret. May 1, 1980. Sherbrooke and Montreal lawyer and entrepreneur (publishing, broadcasting); formerly a director of major companies.	Quebec	$313,250	$12,154	$10,338	$88,678	$414,082
Raymond Eudes b. October 10, 1912; app. April 8, 1968; ret. October 10, 1987. Montreal lawyer; MP for Hochelaga from 1940 to 1965, when he stepped aside for Gérard Pelletier, one of the Liberals' Three Wise Men.	Quebec	$287,000	$368,809	$24,148	$207,139	$862,948
Douglas Everett b. August 12, 1927; app. November 8, 1966; ret. August 12, 2002. Chairman and C.E.O., Royal Canadian Securities, Winnipeg; Liberal fundraiser in Manitoba.	Manitoba	$308,250	$1,927,869	$84,470	$724,569	$2,960,688
Michel Fournier b. September 29, 1905; app. December 9, 1971; ret. September 29, 1980. Farmer; Liberal MLA in N.B. from 1945 to 1963 (Minister of Industry and Development, 1960–63).	New Brunswick	$229,050	$27,526	$6,776	$58,124	$314,700

	Province					
Royce Frith b. November 12, 1923; app. April 5, 1977; ret. November 12, 1998. Lawyer, formerly of Toronto; broadcaster; unsuccessful Liberal candidate in 1954 Ontario election; president, Ontario Liberal Association, 1961–62; member of Royal Commission on Bilingualism and Biculturalism, 1963–69; Liberal campaign chairman for Ontario, 1979.	Ontario	$91,200	$1,376,570	$56,639	$485,835	$1,953,605
Louis (Bob) Giguère b. December 18, 1911; app. September 10, 1968; ret. December 18, 1986. Liberal organizer and fundraiser in Quebec; fundraiser for Trudeau in 1968 leadership race; sat on board of Campeau Corporation and other companies.	Quebec	$280,750	$320,619	$21,412	$183,663	$785,032
John Godfrey b. June 28, 1912; app. October 1, 1973; ret. June 28, 1987. Toronto lawyer; son of an Ontario Supreme Court judge; Liberals' chief fundraiser in the early Trudeau years; director of Montreal Trust Co.	Ontario	$188,750	$351,737	$16,691	$143,173	$683,660
H. Carl Goldenberg b. October 20, 1907; app. November 4, 1971; ret. October 20, 1982. Montreal lawyer; McGill gold medallist in economics and political science (1928) and in law (1932); arbitrator in major labour disputes; served on royal commissions of all kinds; special counsel to Trudeau on the constitution, 1968–71.	Quebec	$230,950	$111,189	$9,692	$83,134	$425,273

413

LIBERAL SENATORS: TABLE OF REMUNERATION

	Province or territory represented	1. Accumulated Remuneration as of Dec. 31, 1979*	2. Expected Future Remuneration to Date of Retirement†	3. Yearly Pension at 75‡	4. Actual Value of Pension at Retirement§	5. Total Value of Senatorship at Retirement ‖
Alasdair Graham b. May 21, 1929; app. April 27, 1972; ret. May 21, 2004. Cape Breton journalist and broadcaster; sometime ministerial assistant and defeated Liberal candidate; became president of Liberal Party of Canada in 1975.	Nova Scotia	$219,950	$2,241,714	$95,244	$816,981	$3,278,645
Joseph Guay b. October 4, 1915; app. March 23, 1978; ret. October 4, 1990. St. Boniface shoe-store owner, mayor, and Liberal MP; joined Trudeau cabinet as Manitoba representative after resignation of James Richardson; elevated to the Senate to clear seat in 1978.	Manitoba	$56,900	$570,518	$18,987	$162,865	$790,283
Stanley Haidasz b. March 4, 1923; app. March 23, 1978; ret. March 4, 1998. Doctor; leader of Polish community in Toronto; MP, 1957–58 and 1962–78; five times a parliamentary secretary before getting a cabinet post (Minister of State for Multiculturalism in 1972); boosted into Senate to make way for new blood in 1978.	Ontario	$56,900	$1,289,582	$49,920	$428,202	$1,774,684

Earl Hastings b. January 7, 1924; app. February 24, 1966; ret. January 7, 1999. Sometime petroleum landman; lifelong Liberal campaigner in Saskatchewan and Alberta; named Trudeau's ambassador to Alberta after 1974 election (the second time the Liberals were blanked in the province in the Trudeau years).	Alberta	$318,250	$1,396,340	$66,224	$568,058	$2,282,648
Salter Hayden b. May 31, 1896; app. February 9, 1940; life appointment. Toronto lawyer (McCarthy & McCarthy); dean of the Senate (jointly with Norman Paterson); onetime Liberal fundraiser.	Ontario	$526,200	$247,047	—	—	$773,247
Henry Hicks b. March 5, 1915; app. April 27, 1972; ret. March 5, 1990. Rhodes scholar; lawyer; president of Dalhousie University; member of N.S. Legislature, 1945–60; Premier, 1954–56; Leader of Opposition, 1956–60. One of three administrators of private trust fund for N.S. Liberal leader Gerald Regan.	Nova Scotia	$219,950	$528,012	$26,009	$223,102	$971,064
Elsie Inman b. December 5, 1891; app. July 28, 1955; life appointment. Married in 1910 to George Strong Inman, a Liberal lawyer who became a judge, Mrs. Inman served as president of the Women's Liberal Association of P.E.I. and organized women's Liberal clubs.	Prince Edward Island	$438,700	$281,560	—	—	$720,260

415

LIBERAL SENATORS: TABLE OF REMUNERATION

	Province or territory represented	1. Accumulated Remuneration as of Dec. 31, 1979*	2. Expected Future Remuneration to Date of Retirement†	3. Yearly Pension at 75‡	4. Actual Value of Pension at Retirement§	5. Total Value of Senatorship at Retirement ‖
Paul Lafond b. July 12, 1919; app. October 7, 1970; ret. July 12, 1994. Hull career Liberal; wartime RCAF officer (he won the DFC in 1944); executive secretary, National Liberal Federation, from 1948 to 1968.	Quebec	$249,500	$891,256	$46,468	$398,593	$1,539,349
Keith Laird b. January 12, 1907; app. April 6, 1967; ret. January 12, 1982. Windsor lawyer; onetime law partner of and campaign manager for Liberal cabinet minister Paul Martin; father of Bruce Laird, Toronto lawyer and Ontario party president in 1977.	Ontario	$300,750	$78,433	$12,394	$106,311	$485,494
Maurice **Lamontagne** b. September 7, 1917; app. April 6, 1967; ret. September 7, 1992. Ottawa economist; advisor in the St. Laurent administration; economic advisor to Opposition leader Mike Pearson in 1958; MP in 1963; Secretary of State, 1964; resigned in 1965 after so-called furniture scandal; director of Canadian Corporate Management Co. Ltd. (a Walter Gordon company), Canadian General Electric Co. Ltd., and Constellation Life Assurance Co.	Quebec	$300,750	$724,026	$43,146	$370,093	$1,394,869

416

Daniel Lang b. June 13, 1919; app. February 14, 1964; ret. June 13, 1994. Toronto lawyer; wartime naval officer; Forest Hill Village councillor; law partner of Roland Michener; Liberal fundraiser; prominent member of Cell 13, group dedicated to rebuilding Liberal Party after 1957 and 1958 débâcles.	Ontario	$348,850	$883,610	$52,774	$403,341	$1,635,801
Léopold Langlois b. October 2, 1913; app. July 8, 1966; ret. October 2, 1988. Quebec City lawyer; wartime naval officer; MP, 1945–57; director of Canadian Foundation Co. Ltd. and a related construction company, A. Janin & Co. Ltd., and of Montreal Life Insurance Co.; deputy government leader in the Senate, 1974–79.	Quebec	$324,450	$430,523	$29,411	$252,284	$1,007,257
Louise Marguerite Renaude **Lapointe** b. January 3, 1912; app. November 10, 1971; ret. January 3, 1987. Former journalist (*La Presse* and *Le Soleil*); served on Canadian delegation to UN; Speaker of the Senate, 1974–79.	Quebec	$312,750	$323,106	$17,803	$152,707	$788,563
Fernand **Leblanc** b. July 1, 1917; app. March 28, 1979; ret. July 1, 1992. Montreal chartered accountant; married a senator's daughter; Montreal-Mercier Liberal worker; elected in a by-election; MP from 1964 to 1979.	Quebec	$26,175	$708,532	$22,604	$193,889	$928,596

LIBERAL SENATORS: TABLE OF REMUNERATION

	Province or territory represented	1. Accumulated Remuneration as of Dec. 31, 1979*	2. Expected Future Remuneration to Date of Retirement†	3. Yearly Pension at 75‡	4. Actual Value of Pension at Retirement§	5. Total Value of Senatorship at Retirement ‖
Derek Lewis b. November 28, 1924; app. March 23, 1978; ret. November 28, 1999. St. John's lawyer; Secretary of the Liberal Federation of Canada, 1970–75; the main Liberal fundraiser in Newfoundland.	Newfoundland	$56,900	$1,516,383	$61,010	$523,334	$2,096,617
Paul Henry Lucier b. July 30, 1930; app. October 23, 1975; ret. July 30, 2005. Whitehorse businessman (from La Salle, a Windsor suburb), alderman, and mayor; member, National Advisory Council on Fitness and Amateur Sport.	Yukon	$133,200	$2,474,519	$103,235	$885,532	$3,493,251
Jean Marchand b. December 20, 1918; app. December 9, 1976; ret. December 20, 1993. Labour organizer; member of Royal Commission on Bilingualism and Biculturalism until 1965 when he took a seat in the Commons as one of the Three Wise Men from Quebec; held various portfolios before quitting to run (unsuccessfully) in Quebec provincial election of Nov. 15, 1976; named to Senate the next month.	Quebec	$101,450	$838,138	$32,058	$274,989	$1,214,577

418

Charles McElman b. June 18, 1920; app. February 24, 1966; ret. June 18, 1995. Liberal careerist who became secretary of the N.B. Liquor Control Board in 1946 after serving five years in RCAF; private secretary to Premier J. B. McNair; executive secretary to N.B. Liberal Association and executive assistant to Premier Louis Robichaud.	New Brunswick	$318,250	$984,187	$52,076	$446,699	$1,749,136
Fred McGrand b. July 5, 1895; app. July 28, 1955; life appointment. Country doctor who served seventeen years in the N.B. Legislature (Speaker for five years, Minister of Health for eight); active on Senate committees in his mid-eighties.	New Brunswick	$438,700	$247,047	——	——	$685,747
George McIlraith b. July 29, 1908; app. April 27, 1972; ret. July 29, 1983. Ottawa lawyer; MP for Ottawa West, 1940–72; parliamentary assistant to C. D. Howe, 1945–52; various ministries, 1963–72.	Ontario	$219,950	$145,824	$10,487	$89,952	$455,726
Gildas Molgat b. January 25, 1927; app. October 7, 1970; ret. January 25, 2002. Manitoba MLA (1953–70) for his home riding of Ste. Rose in the Dauphin Lake area (now lives in Winnipeg); provincial Liberal leader, 1961–68; director, Border Chemical Co. Ltd.; director of small family firm selling farm implements.	Manitoba	$249,500	$1,838,242	$81,394	$698,178	$2,785,920

LIBERAL SENATORS: TABLE OF REMUNERATION

	Province or territory represented	1. Accumulated Remuneration as of Dec. 31, 1979*	2. Expected Future Remuneration to Date of Retirement†	3. Yearly Pension at 75‡	4. Actual Value of Pension at Retirement§	5. Total Value of Senatorship at Retirement ‖
Joan Neiman b. September 9, 1920; app. September 1, 1972; ret. September 9, 1995. Wartime officer in WRCNS and Brampton lawyer; candidate in Ontario provincial elections, 1963 and 1967; wife of Clem Neiman, Ontario campaign chairman in 1968 and 1972 federal elections; director of Security Trust Co.	Ontario	$212,550	$1,007,458	$48,692	$432,503	$1,652,511
Margaret Norrie b. October 16, 1905; app. April 27, 1972; ret. October 16, 1980. Truro farmer; former university teacher; Liberal candidate in N.S. election of 1956; mother-in-law of Wallace McCain, president of McCain Foods Ltd., Florenceville, N.B.	Nova Scotia	$219,950	$29,269	$6,536	$58,057	$307,276
H. A. (Bud) Olson b. October 6, 1925; app. April 5, 1977; ret. October 6, 2000. Operates farm supply business at Medicine Hat and farm at Iddesleigh, near the Red Deer River; elected Social Credit MP in 1957, 1962, 1963, and 1965; switched to Liberals in 1967 and named Minister of Agriculture in 1968; defeated in 1972.	Alberta	$92,200	$1,638,439	$70,070	$601,044	$2,331,683

420

Name / Biography	Province					

Norman Paterson
b. August 3, 1883; app. February 9, 1940; still life appointment.
An Ottawa man for many years, but still Laird of the Lakehead (president of N. M. Paterson & Sons Ltd., grain merchants and Great Lakes shipowners — his sons Donald and John run the family business in Winnipeg and Thunder Bay respectively); joint dean of the Senate (with Salter Hayden).

Ontario $526,200 $115,076 — $641,276

Raymond Perrault
b. February 6, 1926; app. October 1, 1973; ret. February 6, 2001.
Onetime PR man; B.C. Liberal leader, 1959–68; MLA, 1960–68; MP, 1968 (defeated NDP leader Tommy Douglas) to 1972 (beaten by NDPer); senator, 1973; government leader in Senate and member of Trudeau cabinet, 1974–79; Opposition leader in Senate, 1979; renamed government leader in Senate, 1980, and appointed B.C. representative in Trudeau cabinet (the Liberals having won no B.C. seats).

British Columbia $287,825 $1,688,181 $76,242 $653,992 $2,629,998

William Petten
b. January 28, 1923; app. April 8, 1968; ret. January 28, 1998.
St. John's businessman and son of Senator Ray Petten, from Kelligrews, on Conception Bay, who became a broker in St. John's and joined the Senate in 1949, a few months after Newfoundland entered Confederation. Ray Petten died in 1961. William Petten is a director of Fishermen's Union Trading Co. and became government whip in the Senate.

Newfoundland $287,000 $1,277,030 $62,129 $532,927 $2,096,957

421

LIBERAL SENATORS: TABLE OF REMUNERATION

	Province or territory represented	1. Accumulated Remuneration as of Dec. 31, 1979*	2. Expected Future Remuner- ation to Date of Retirement†	3. Yearly Pension at 75‡	4. Actual Value of Pension at Retirement§	5. Total Value of Senatorship at Retirement ‖
Maurice Riel b. April 3, 1922; app. October 1, 1973; ret. April 3, 1997. Montreal lawyer (member of Stikeman, Elliott, Tamaki, Mercier & Robb, John Turner's old firm); Liberal fundraiser; director of a number of companies, including Royal Trust, Canadian Provident insurance companies, Canadian Liquid Air Ltd., and PPG Industries Canada Ltd. Former director of such government-related agencies as the Bank of Canada and the old Industrial Development Bank, and the government-supported Panarctic Oils Ltd.	Quebec	$188,750	$1,179,697	$55,273	$474,123	$1,842,570
Daniel Riley b. May 11, 1916; app. December 21, 1973; ret. May 11, 1991. Saint John lawyer; MP for Saint John–Albert, 1949–53; defeated 1953 and 1957; switched to provincial Legislature in 1963 and became important minister in Louis Robichaud's administration; left Legislature in 1967; chairman, N.B. Board of Commissioners of Public Utilities and N.B. Motor Carrier Board, 1967–74.	New Brunswick	$183,250	$610,007	$27,160	$232,971	$1,026,228

Pietro Rizzuto b. March 18, 1934; app. December 23, 1976; ret. March 18, 2009. Road-paving contractor (Corival Inc. and related companies) in Montreal suburb of Laval; first Italian-born senator; left Sicily at twenty, started as a labourer and became a millionaire in Canada; active in Italian-Canadian groups; member, Quebec Road Builders and Heavy Construction Association.	Quebec	$99,000	$3,312,888	$132,014	$1,132,392	$4,544,280
Louis Robichaud b. October 21, 1925; app. December 21, 1973; ret. October 21, 2000. Lawyer from Richibucto; MLA from 1952 to 1971; Premier (first Acadian to be elected to the office), 1960–70; chairman, Canadian section, International Joint Commission, 1971–73.	New Brunswick	$183,250	$1,644,371	$74,739	$641,092	$2,468,713
Yvette Rousseau b. February 18, 1917; app. March 28, 1979; ret. February 18, 1992. Former president of the Advisory Council on the Status of Women (succeeded by Doris Anderson, defeated Liberal candidate in Eglinton in 1978 by-election); mother of eight; former teacher; former textile worker in Sherbrooke; union organizer; vice-president of Confederation of National Trade Unions.	Quebec	$26,175	$678,163	$21,442	$190,456	$894,794

LIBERAL SENATORS: TABLE OF REMUNERATION

	Province or territory represented	1. Accumulated Remuneration as of Dec. 31, 1979*	2. Expected Future Remuneration to Date of Retirement†	3. Yearly Pension at 75‡	4. Actual Value of Pension at Retirement§	5. Total Value of Senatorship at Retirement ‖
Frederick Rowe b. September 28, 1912; app. December 9, 1971; ret. September 28, 1987. St. John's educator; school inspector; deputy minister of public welfare, 1949–52; won seat in Legislature in 1952 and held several portfolios and deputy-premiership under Joey Smallwood before elevation to Senate in 1971; his son Bill became Liberal leader in Newfoundland 1977 to 1979.	Newfoundland	$229,050	$366,827	$19,523	$167,463	$763,340
Donald Smith b. July 7, 1905; app. July 28, 1955; ret. July 7, 1980. Dentist from Liverpool, on the South Shore; member of town council; elected MP, 1949; riding vanished in redistribution of 1953; named to Senate two years later.	Nova Scotia	$438,700	$18,936	$20,467	$156,423	$614,059
Herbert Sparrow b. January 4, 1930; app. February 12, 1968; ret. January 4, 2005. Businessman-farmer; owner of a Kentucky Fried Chicken franchise in North Battleford (where he was an alderman, 1957–65); unsuccessful provincial candidate in 1964 and 1967; past president, Saskatchewan Liberal Association; president, The Ranch House Ltd., Sparrow Enterprises Ltd., Prairie	Saskatchewan	$288,875	$2,360,768	$99,331	$852,037	$3,501,680

Name	Province				
Richard Stanbury b. May 2, 1923; app. February 15, 1968; ret. May 2, 1998. Toronto lawyer; partner in Cassels, Brock; son of Western Ontario judge; president, Toronto and District Liberal Association, 1961–64; chairman, policy committee, Liberal Federation of Canada, 1965–68; president, Liberal Federation of Canada, 1968–73; director, Beneficial Finance Co. of Canada, Rogers Telecommunications Ltd.; brother of Robert Stanbury, MP for York-Scarborough, 1965–77.	Ontario	$288,875	$1,309,579	$63,246	$542,511	$2,140,965
David Steuart b. January 26, 1916; app. December 9, 1976; ret. January 26, 1991. Former leader of Saskatchewan Liberals, 1971–76; mayor of Prince Albert, 1954–58; was owner of Prince Albert appliance store (Steuart Electric); MLA from 1962 to 1976; held four portfolios in government of Ross Thatcher.	Saskatchewan	$101,450	$593,840	$21,858	$187,498	$882,788
Norbert Theriault b. February 16, 1921; app. March 28, 1979; ret. February 16, 1996. Member of N.B. Legislature from 1960 to 1979; held two portfolios (Municipal Affairs, Health and Welfare) between 1965 and 1970; father of nine; a general merchant at Baie Ste. Anne; president, Theriault Bros. Ltd.; president, Miramichi Commercial Fishermen's Association.	New Brunswick	$26,175	$1,053,904	$36,797	$315,635	$1,395,714

425

LIBERAL SENATORS: TABLE OF REMUNERATION

	Province or territory represented	1. Accumulated Remuneration as of Dec. 31, 1979*	2. Expected Future Remuneration to Date of Retirement†	3. Yearly Pension at 75‡	4. Actual Value of Pension at Retirement§	5. Total Value of Senatorship at Retirement ‖
Andrew Thompson b. December 14, 1924; app. April 6, 1967; ret. December 14, 1999. Social worker; special assistant to Lester Pearson when Liberals were in opposition; elected to Ontario Legislature in 1963; provincial Liberal leader from September 1964 to November 1966; stepped down without having led the Liberals into an election; director of Canadian Food Products Ltd. and Del Zotto Enterprises Ltd.	Ontario	$300,750	$1,522,392	$70,551	$605,175	$2,428,317
George van Roggen b. July 22, 1921; app. November 4, 1971; ret. July 22, 1996. Vancouver lawyer; a director of Weyerhaeuser Canada Ltd. and chairman of Senate standing committee on foreign affairs; married former Diana Whittall, ex-wife of George (Buzz) Beurling, the wartime fighter ace; practised law in the Yukon before return to Vancouver; his father, also a lawyer, was Dutch consul-general in B.C.	British Columbia	$230,850	$1,100,578	$55,432	$475,483	$1,806,911

Guy **Williams** b. October 7, 1906; app. December 9, 1971; ret. October 7, 1981. Native leader; born at Indian village near present town of Kitimat; president, Native Brotherhood of B.C., for fourteen years; active in fishermen's co-operative movement.	British Columbia	$229,050	$67,634	$8,103	$69,510	$366,194
Dalia **Wood** b. August 21, 1924; app. March 28, 1979; ret. August 21, 1999. Montreal businesswoman; head of the Liberal association in Pierre Trudeau's riding of Mount Royal and Trudeau's campaign manager; a former provincial chairman of the Liberals. A predecessor in the riding post, Montreal lawyer John Ewasew, was named to the Senate in 1976; he died fifteen months later, in March 1978, at 56.	Quebec	$26,175	$1,479,119	$56,352	$500,540	$2,005,834

Not included in this list are figures for living Liberal senators who resigned or retired before December 31, 1979, such as John Nichol, Paul Martin, John Aird, and Eugene Forsey. Hartland Molson, who lists himself as an Independent, and Donald Cameron, who is listed as an Independent Liberal, are also excluded, as are Edward Lawson, who gives no affiliation for himself in the *Parliamentary Guide*, Hamilton McDonald and Sarto Fournier, who died in 1980, and Harry Hays and John Connolly, who died in 1982.

Sources: *Senate and House of Commons Act.* R.S., c. 249, s. 1, Chapter S–8, amended 1974–75–76, c. 99, s. 1, and *Members of Parliament Retiring Allowances Act.* R.S., c. 329, s. 1, amended 1974–75, c. 81, ss. 83 to 94, Pierre G. Normandin, ed., *The Canadian Parliamentary Guide, 1979.*

*Accumulated remuneration, calculated from the day of appointment of each senator till December 31, 1979, includes the sessional indemnity, the standard free-tax allowance, and the additional pay received for holding the posts of Leader of the Government in the Senate, Leader of the Opposition in the Senate, Speaker of the Senate, or Deputy Leader of the Government in the Senate. These are aggregate figures which total the actual amounts received at the time. Accumulated remuneration does not include any estimate for the value of free travel, the senators' office and secretarial costs, or other perquisites of office. The calculations were made using information on salary levels supplied by the administrative office of the Senate.

†Expected future remuneration to retirement has been calculated from January 1, 1980, assuming the 7 per cent annual increase of the present indemnity and allowance as stipulated in the current legislation. This estimate does not include any additional pay received for holding extra posts in the Senate after December 31, 1979, or any normal perquisites such as free travel allowances, secretarial costs, or office expenses. For senators whose appointment is for life, length of tenure has been calculated using the complete expectation of life on GAM71 mortality tables. The calculations have been made by B. J. Vincent Co. Ltd., Actuarial and Employee Benefit Plan Consultants, with data supplied by the administrative office of the Senate.

‡The yearly pension at 75 for senators appointed before June 2, 1965, is $2/3$ of final sessional indemnity. For senators appointed after June 1, 1965, it is 3 per cent for each year of credited service (maximum 25 years) of final six-year average sessional indemnity. This greatly favours the younger senators, who can look forward to many more years before retirement, and explains the relatively small pensions that older senators with shorter tenures in office will receive. Final sessional indemnity has been calculated on the basis of the assumptions explained above. These figures will therefore understate the actual pensions received by senators who hold extra paid posts in their last years in office.

§Actual value of pension at retirement is the actuarially calculated amount it would cost each senator upon retirement at 75 to fund an annuity in a private-sector pension plan equal in value to the pension benefits he or she will receive given the present legislation and the life expectancy indicated by GAM71 mortality tables on the assumption used by pension planners that pension funds earn 6 per cent over the long term. The calculations have been made by B. J. Vincent Co. Ltd., Actuarial and Employee Benefit Plan Consultants, using data supplied by the administrative office of the Senate. Senators holding appointments for life do not have a Senate pension plan.

‖Total value of senatorship at retirement is the sum of columns 1, 2, and 4. This represents the approximate financial return to each individual for his or her position as senator at the time of retirement or — for life appointees — at the time of death.

LIST OF INTERVIEWS

GRITS is the product of close to twenty years spent observing, inter-viewing, and writing about Canadian politics. Many people saw me specifically in connection with this book between September 1977 and January 1982; others were interviewed for research on another project begun in 1973 involving government elites and never completed but added to and used here instead; and many more supplied material for related articles which were published in 1975 and 1976 in the *Globe and Mail*, and in 1976, 1977, 1978, and 1980 in *Saturday Night*, material which appears in *Grits* in different form. In addition, dozens of Liberals at party conventions, campaign workers and candidates from all three parties on the hustings, journalists in buses and airplanes and at political meetings, political scientists and historians in libraries and common rooms, talked to me about the party in passing and enriched my understanding of its role in Canadian life. Nearly a dozen people, mostly public servants, asked for anonymity before consenting to be interviewed and their names are not listed below or used in the text. The following were good enough to answer specific questions, often at great length. Some of them saw me on several occasions, a few as often as a dozen times. To all of them I am very grateful.

Hon. Douglas Abbott
Hon. John Aird
David Anderson
Doris McCubbin Anderson
Hon. Ron Atkey
Hon. Lloyd Axworthy
Thomas Axworthy
John Baldwin
Jean Barbeau
Hon. David Barrett
Leroy Barry
William Bennett
Lise Bissonnette
Ann Brennan
Robert Bryce
Garry Carl
Pat Carney

John Carson
F. S. Chalmers
Egan Chambers
Marie Choquette
Wallace Clement
Marshall Cohen
Hon. John Connolly
Ramsay Cook
George Cooper
James Coutts
Donald Creighton
David Crombie
Marshall Crowe
Joseph Cruden
Hon. Barney Danson
Dorothy Petrie Davey
Grace Curtis Davey

Hon. Keith Davey
George Davidson
Louis Desrochers
John Deutsch
Hon. C. M. Drury
Gordon Dryden
Claude Dupras
Gordon Edick
Marc Eliesen
Tex Enemark
John Robert Evans
Roy Faibish
Gordon Fairweather
George Ferguson
Harry S. Ferns
Douglas Fisher
Brian Flemming
Alastair Fraser
Claude Frenette
Hon. Royce Frith
Douglas Fullerton
Mimi Fullerton
Gordon Gibson
Hon. Alastair Gillespie
Hon. John Godfrey
Gerald Godsoe
Martin Goldfarb
Ralph Goodale
Jerry Goodis
Allan Gotlieb
Harold Gordon
Hon. Walter Gordon
Hon. Heward Grafftey
Jerry Grafstein
Allan Gregg
Hon. Alvin Hamilton
Michael Hatfield
Hon. Richard Hatfield
Hon. Harry Hays
Michael Hicks
William Hood

Alison Grant Ignatieff
George Ignatieff
Mel Jack
Pauline Jewett
A. W. Johnson
Serge Joyal
Naim Kattan
Hon. Eric Kierans
Bud Kinney
Stanley Knowles
Hon. Marc Lalonde
Hon. Judy LaMarsh
William Lee
Hon. Merv Leitch
Douglas LePan
Hon. René Lévesque
David Lewis
Hon. Peter Lougheed
Hon. Douglas McArthur
Michael McCabe
Fred McCain
Alexa McDonagh
David C. McDonald
Hon. Donald S. Macdonald
J. A. McDougald
Hon. Patrick McGeer
Hon. Bryce Mackasey
Arch MacKenzie
Maxwell Mackenzie
Paul Maddox
Paul Manning
Hon. Jean Marchand
Lorna Marsden
David Matas
Bruce Matthews
Tony Merchant
Patrice Merrin
Brian Mulroney
Hon. Lowell Murray
Hon. John Nichol
Robert Nixon

Richard O'Hagan
Hon. Grattan O'Leary
Bernard Ostry
Sylvia Ostry
Hon. André Ouellet
James Palmer
Hon. Wilson Parasiuk
John Payne
Hon. Jean-Luc Pepin
George Perdicaris
David Peterson
Heather Peterson
James Peterson
Hon. Lazarus Phillips
Hon. J. W. Pickersgill
Jean Pigott
Hon. Yvon Pinard
Grace MacDougall Pitfield
Michael Pitfield
Paul Plante
Wynne Plumptre
Simon Reisman
Hon. James Richardson
A. E. Ritchie
Ed Roberts
Hon. John Roberts
Gerry Robinson
Kathryn Robinson
Michel Rochon

Abraham Rotstein
Edward Rubin
Annette Saint-Denis
Hon. Jeanne Sauvé
Hon. Maurice Sauvé
Branny Schepanovich
Gordon Sedgwick
James Service
T. K. Shoyama
David Smith
Stuart Smith
Hon. Sidney Spivak
Graham Spry
Hon. Davey Steuart
Ian Stewart
John Swift
Nick Taylor
Ethel Teitelbaum
Dale Thomson
Rt. Hon. Pierre Elliott Trudeau
Hon. John Turner
Janny Vincent
David Walker
Michael Webb
William Wilder
Frank Withers
Hon. Dahlia Wood
Charles Woodsworth

NOTES

Names and dates of statements quoted in the text are listed below. When a quotation is not followed by the speaker's name in the text it's because anonymity was requested, occasionally for whole interviews, more often just for certain statements.

Relevant books and articles are cited here in short form; full listings are in the Bibliography.

Page	*Line*	FOREWORD

ix   8   "Since 1921, the Liberals had been out of office federally in Canada for only two protracted periods . . .": In 1926, the Conservatives under Arthur Meighen were briefly in office from June 28 to September 25.

ix   16   "Provincially . . . when the 1970s began, six out of the ten provinces had boasted Liberal administrations.": In October 1970, the four Atlantic provinces, Quebec, and Saskatchewan were all Liberal. By October 1971, the governments in New Brunswick, Saskatchewan, and Newfoundland had been defeated, and the trend continued. During the 1979 federal campaign, the Liberals in P.E.I. called an election and were defeated, leaving the party without a single provincial administration.

PART 1: KEITH DAVEY AND THE POLITICS OF JOY

3   1   "Keith Davey was restless in the Senate chamber . . .": The material in this section is derived from several interviews with Senator Davey, particularly on August 15, 1977, July 19, 1978, June 4, 1979, and February 20, 1980.

7   22   "Davey had been born in Toronto in 1926 . . .": Material on Senator Davey's childhood and young manhood is derived from interviews with Senator Davey himself, and with Grace Curtis Davey, September 1, 1977, James Service, August 26, 1977, and Gordon Dryden September 13, 1977.

8   3   ". . . he quickly landed a job . . . at the Toronto *Star* . . . under . . . Joseph ('Holy Joe') Atkinson . . .": For the relationship between Atkinson and King see *The Mackenzie King Record*.

9   28   "Veterans swarmed the campus . . .": For a description of the university's mood in the late 1940s see "Alma Mater Sleeps Around" by James Eayrs in *Greenpeace and Her Enemies*.

10   18   "I never thought of Davey as having formulated any political ideas . . .": Douglas Fisher to the author, November 23, 1979.

12	11	"It was a popular triumph . . .": House of Commons standings after the election of 1957 were: Progressive Conservatives 112, Liberals 105, CCF 25, Social Credit 19, Others 4. In 1958 they were: Progressive Conservatives 208, Liberals 48, CCF 8, Others 1. For a brilliant analysis of the meaning of those results, see *The Canadian General Election of 1957* by John Meisel.
12	32	"In its initial stage, the group's chief organizer . . .": Material on Cell 13 is from interviews with Gordon Dryden, September 13, 1977, and October 9, 1977, James Service, August 26, 1977, Keith Davey, as mentioned above, Royce Frith, August 19, 1977, Gordon Edick, August 17, 1977, Hon. Walter Gordon, August 22, 1977. Another description of its beginnings is included in *The L-Shaped Party* by Joseph Wearing.
13	34	"Their immediate concern was that . . . Louis St. Laurent . . .": After he announced his retirement later that year, the former prime minister recovered his health and practised law in Quebec City for several years.
14	6	"Jack Pickersgill, the Minister of Citizenship and Immigration . . .": As an assistant to two prime ministers, Mackenzie King and Louis St. Laurent, Pickersgill was the most important backstage figure in Ottawa in the 1940s and early 1950s. Later, as MP for Bonavista-Twillingate, he became one of St. Laurent's key ministers, then a highly effective member of the Liberal Opposition during the Diefenbaker era, a cabinet minister again under Pearson, chairman of the Canadian Transport Commission, author and editor of books on his Liberal mentors, literary executor of their estates, and general all-round keeper of the Liberal myth.
15	11	"It included several lawyers . . .": For a discussion of what happened to individual members of the Cell 13 group in the twenty years after its formation, see Part 6.
16	37	"If they had been asked . . . to analyse their ideology . . .": For a discussion of Liberal ideology, see *Political Parties and Ideologies in Canada* by William Christian and Colin Campbell, and "Conservatism, Liberalism and Socialism in Canada: An Interpretation" by Gad Horowitz.
17	28	"In the early 1950s the Liberals had been in possession of a larger war chest . . .": For a discussion of Liberal fund-raising in the King–St. Laurent period, see *The Government Party* by Reginald Whitaker, the most important book on the Liberal past and a superb study of the King–St. Laurent era.
18	24	Frith quote: Senator Royce Frith to the author, August 19, 1977.
18	30	". . . the Liberals held only three of the ten provincial governments before the 1957 federal defeat.": The Liberals had been turned out of office in New Brunswick and British Columbia in 1952 and Nova Scotia in 1956. They had not held power in Saskatchewan or Quebec since 1944 or Ontario since 1943. In Alberta they had not formed a government since losing power in 1921. In 1957 they still held Newfoundland, Prince Edward

Island, and Manitoba, but they were to lose Manitoba in 1958 and P.E.I. in 1959.

20   1   "At the time of the Liberal disaster in 1957, Walter Gordon was . . .": The material on Walter Gordon is taken from many interviews with him, notably on August 22, 1977; from conversations with Keith Davey, Royce Frith, and Gordon Dryden, cited above; from his biography by Denis Smith, *Gentle Patriot: A Political Biography of Walter Gordon*, and his autobiography, *A Political Memoir*, McClelland and Stewart, 1977; and from Lester Pearson's three-volume autobiography published by the University of Toronto Press, among other sources.

21   16   "Harry Gordon had been a partner in Clarkson's . . .": For further material on Clarkson, Gordon, see "Finishing School for the Upper Class" by Barbara Moon in the *Globe Magazine*, May 1, 1965, and *The Story of the Firm*, by A. J. Little.

22   33   ". . . the group of mostly upper-middle-class intellectuals who banded together in the League for Social Reconstruction . . .": For a discussion of the LSR and its influence on Canadian life, see *The League for Social Reconstruction* by Michiel Horn and *Hammer the Golden Day* by Hugh Keenleyside, which describes the reactions of his colleagues in External Affairs to the league.

25   21   Ignatieff quote. Alison Grant Ignatieff to the author, January 22, 1982.

27   1   Rotstein quote. Abraham Rotstein to the author, April 11, 1977.

30   1   "In his time, Lester Pearson was a man admired by almost everyone who knew him.": The material on Lester Pearson, his life and career, is distilled from dozens of conversations and interviews with his colleagues and friends over many years, from a reading of his three-volume autobiography, Walter Gordon's autobiography, and Hugh Keenleyside's autobiography, and from the author's own close observation of him during the period that he was Leader of the Opposition and Prime Minister of Canada.

30   13   ". . . Pearson was the *beau idéal* of the old Ottawa establishment . . .": For a further discussion of that establishment, see Part 4.

30   32   Ferns quote. Harry S. Ferns to the author, August 20, 1973.

32   24   Ritchie quote. From Charles Ritchie, *The Siren Years*, page 187.

37   24   Davey quote. Keith Davey to the author, August 15, 1977.

39   13   Connolly quote. Senator John Connolly to the author, October 27, 1977.

39   19   "He [Davey] had a talent for mobilizing and motivating people . . .": Material on Keith Davey and the organization of the Liberal Party in the 1960s is taken from many interviews with Davey, already cited, with Gordon, Frith, Jerry Grafstein, and other Liberals involved at the time, and from the author's own observations of the period.

43   4   "When John Diefenbaker was able to hang on to power . . .": Party standings in the House of Commons after the 1962 elec-

tion were: Progressive Conservatives 116, Liberals 99, Social Credit 30, NDP 19, Others 1.

43   20   "After the 1963 election, when the Liberals attained a minority . . .": Party standings in the House of Commons after the 1963 general election were: Liberals 129, Progressive Conservatives 95, NDP 17, Social Credit 24.

45   7   Pickersgill quote. Jack Pickersgill to the author, November 13, 1981.

46   5   Maryon Pearson quote. Keith Davey to the author, August 15, 1977.

48   27   "On election night, November 8 . . .": Party standings in 1965: Liberals 131, Progressive Conservatives 97, NDP 21, Ralliement des Créditistes 9, Social Credit 5, Others 2.

PART 2: PIERRE TRUDEAU AND THE POLITICS OF PASSION

55   28   Manning quote. Paul Manning to the author, November 19, 1978.

56   1   "Many months before . . . Richard O'Hagan . . . had convened a meeting . . .": This lunch took place on November 28, 1977.

59   1   "Laurier was the silver-tongued orator . . . [who] . . . praised all things British as beautiful . . .": Significantly, when Laurier had to abandon his pro-British stance during the conscription crisis of the First World War, he not only knew he would never again win an election in Canada — which was not surprising, since he was well into his seventies — he also expressed doubts that any French Canadian should ever try to be prime minister again. On the day after his defeat in the bitter election of 1917 in Winnipeg, the usually Liberal *Free Press*, which had opposed him, published a picture of Laurier with the pious caption, "Swept Aside by Patriotic Canada". See *Laurier, a Study in Canadian Politics*, by J. W. Dafoe.

59   5   "St. Laurent was Uncle Louis . . .": St. Laurent's image was so comforting, English Canadian Liberals liked to stress that he wasn't really very French at all. The Winnipeg *Free Press* expressed this opinion cogently in an editorial written during a warm-up visit to western Canada just before the election campaign of 1949: "In Mr. St. Laurent, the Canadian who is half Irish, speaks English with no trace of French . . . and might have been brought up in Halifax, Winnipeg or Victoria." See *Louis St. Laurent, Canadian* by Dale Thomson, page 266.

59   13   "In English-Canada . . . the intellectuals and the two old parties had tended towards mutual distrust.": In his introduction to *The Vertical Mosaic* by John Porter, John Meisel suggests that scholars in Canada have traditionally thought that to be engagé is to be corrupted. In *The League for Social Reconstruction*, Michiel Horn describes the involvement of intellectuals in the LSR and the CCF, and refers to the Waffle movement in the NDP

in the 1970s as their only other significant involvement. Canadian intellectuals in the late 1920s and 1930s who couldn't find jobs in the universities went into the federal public service, as described in Part 4.

60   15   ". . . [Trudeau] remained in the country outside Quebec . . . 'un inconnu très connu'.": The phrase "the well-known stranger", applied to Georges Pompidou, the premier of France in the 1960s, was used first to describe Trudeau in the Toronto *Globe and Mail*, April 23, 1968, by Keith Spicer, a political scientist who was later the first federal Commissioner of Official Languages. It's also used in *The Maple Leaf Forever* by Ramsay Cook.

62   1   "When Trudeau first became a celebrity . . . a myth was made about his past life . . .": That Trudeau's life is a superb subject has long been acknowledged in Canadian journalistic, literary, and academic circles. During the week after he won the election of 1980, the author and a political scientist then in a government job were talking about Trudeau and saying that his biography — the real biography, the one that could be attempted when he was out of office, when his papers were available and his friends and enemies were no longer too frightened of his wrath to talk — could be a great work in the hands of the right writer. Who could do it, they wondered? Someone who knew Canadian history intimately, and had studied political theory, who spoke and wrote both French and English, who was conversant with Freud, Jung, R. D. Laing, Max Weber, Elia Kedouri, Montesquieu, Lord Acton, Ivor Jennings, someone who understood both the Montreal and Ottawa milieus and their complexities. The list of necessary qualifications for the ideal biographer went on until we were roaring with laughter. Clearly, no one less than a new Erik Erikson would do. In the meantime, there have been many studies exploring Trudeau's profundities and inconsistencies from various angles: two of the best early ones, *Journey to Power* by Don Peacock and *Mandate '68* by Martin Sullivan, were published the year of his leadership race; *Shrug* by Walter Stewart, the first critical examination, came out in 1971; *Trudeau* by George Radwanski is a book by a thoughtful admirer taking a coolly rational overview of Trudeau's life and work; *Northern Magus* by Richard Gwyn puts forward the arresting notion that Trudeau is a magician with a special bond with Canadians. A long *New Yorker* profile "Prime Minister/Premier Ministre", by Edith Iglauer in the July 5, 1969, issue, is still the best, most balanced description of his life before he became prime minister, a source from which all other writers draw. The best analyses of his ideas are in *The Maple Leaf Forever* by Ramsay Cook and in Cook's introduction to *Approaches to Politics* by Trudeau, as well as a paper by Reginald Whitaker in the *Canadian Journal of Political and Social Theory*, Winter 1980. In French, there are two minor

books, *Le Phénomène Trudeau* by Jean Pellerin, an old colleague from *Cité libre*, and *Les Crises de Pierre Elliott Trudeau*
by Claude Savoie, an FLQ sympathizer. The account of Trudeau's
life and ideas here is drawn from all these sources, and from
extensive conversations and interviews over many years with
several dozen of Trudeau's friends and close colleagues, as well
as with Trudeau himself.

62   24   ". . . [Trudeau] did make it clear to the newspaperman George
Radwanski, in . . . a series of . . . interviews . . .": These interviews resulted in *Trudeau*, a biography by George Radwanski,
a valuable source for Trudeau's view of his own life.

65   10   Pitfield quotes. Grace Pitfield to the author, October 26, 1974.

65   19   "They heard . . . that she had married a Frenchman.": In English Canada, certainly until the 1960s and in small communities
long after that, French Canadians were usually called "the
French", or "the Frenchmen", or "the frogs", just as English
Canadians in Quebec were called "les anglais", or "maudits
anglais". The words "anglophone" and "francophone" were
officialese, invented in Ottawa in the 1960s.

66   9   "According to Roddy Choquette . . . Charlie Trudeau was paid
a million dollars . . .": From an interview with Choquette by
Robert McKenzie, published in the *Toronto Star*, April 8, 1968.

66   18   ". . . [Charlie Trudeau] was *bleu* . . . backing Camillien Houde
. . .": Charlie Trudeau's relationship to Maurice Duplessis, who
preceded Houde as Conservative leader before founding the
Union Nationale, is less clear. They were classmates at law
school and Grace Pitfield remembered Charlie Trudeau coming
to see her husband, Ward Pitfield, some time in the 1930s,
possibly for the purpose of raising money for Duplessis in the
early days of his career when he was cast as a political reformer.

67   38   Choquette quote. Roddy Choquette to Robert McKenzie,
Toronto Star, April 8, 1968.

69   16   "If it's the adolescent's job to forge himself an identity . . .":
In his book *Identity, Youth and Crisis*, Erik Erikson describes
the adolescent identity crisis as occurring "in that period of the
life cycle when each youth must forge for himself some central
perspective and direction — must detect some meaningful
resemblance between what he has come to see in himself and
what his sharpened awareness tells him others judge and expect
him to be. . . . Some young individuals [resolve this crisis]
through participation in ideological movements passionately
concerned with religion and politics, nature or art. Still others
. . . through what appears to be a prolonged adolescence, eventually contribute an original bit to an emerging style of life: the
very danger which they have sensed [that of having their identity submerged by some stronger person's] has forced them to
mobilize capacities to see and say, to dream and plan, to design
and construct in new ways." Some intrepid doctoral student
will no doubt yield to the temptation to apply this analysis to

Trudeau's long search for a theory about his society and a métier through which to prove the theory.

70 35 "... [fellow campers] were astonished by [Trudeau's] penchant for quoting Baudelaire ...": Trudeau was also partial to quoting Plato and Marcus Aurelius, as was fitting for a man with a classical education. After he married Margaret Trudeau, he took to referring to lines from a poem called "Desiderata", written by an attorney from Terre Haute, Indiana, named Max Elormann, whose treacly sentiments ("No doubt the universe is unfolding as it should" et alia) were much beloved of the middle-class adolescents of the 1960s counter-culture who did drugs and bought posters on which the whole of the work was inscribed; he never quoted William Blake as far as anybody could remember, though Margaret Trudeau said she admired that mystic greatly, especially his *Songs of Innocence*.

73 19 Lemelin quote. Roger Lemelin to the author, as quoted in *Maclean's* magazine, "Our heroes on the eastern front", August 1971.

75 5 "It was just after the Liberals' triumphant victory in the election of 1949.": In 1949, the Liberals won 190 of the 264 seats, the most triumphant election in the long history of Liberal triumphs.

75 17 "The Ottawa of Louis St. Laurent was ...": For a description of that Ottawa and of St. Laurent himself, see *My Years With St. Laurent* by Jack Pickersgill and *Louis St. Laurent* by Dale Thomson, both of whom worked with St. Laurent closely during his years in office.

79 13 Trudeau quote. From a speech to the Ontario Liberals' policy conference, October 2, 1976, transcribed by the Prime Minister's Office.

79 28 Trudeau quote. Pierre Trudeau to David Frost, on "Frost Over Canada", program broadcast by CTV, February 23, 1982. For a lucid account of personalism see *Emmanuel Mounier and the New Catholic Left* by John Hellman, a book that has a brief description of the involvement with personalism of Trudeau and Pelletier.

80 35 "The magazine was published irregularly over the next decade ...": Eighty-eight issues of *Cité libre* were published between June 1950 and July 1966, twice a year through 1954, four times in 1955, once in 1956, thrice in 1957, four times in 1958, and once in 1959. A "Nouvelle Série" began in January 1960 and the magazine was published regularly ten times a year after that.

82 15 "People who took the trouble to read ... [Trudeau's] body of work ...": For analyses of that work, see *The Maple Leaf Forever* by Ramsay Cook and "Reason, Passion and Interest: Pierre Trudeau's Eternal Liberal Triangle" by Reginald Whitaker, in *Canadian Journal of Political and Social Theory*, Winter 1980.

87 3 Bruneau quote. Nina Bruneau to Sylvia Fraser, "The Private

Trudeau'' in the *Star Weekly*, June 29, 1968.

87   12   Cook quote. From *The Maple Leaf Forever* by Ramsay Cook, page 41.

88   10   ''Their original disgust for the Liberals had been due to the . . . nature of the party's Quebec wing in the heyday of Mackenzie King . . .'': For descriptions of the Quebec wing of the Liberal Party in the King–St. Laurent era, see *The Government Party* by Reg Whitaker and *A Party Politician: The Memoirs of Chubby Power*, which were sensitively edited by Norman Ward.

91   15   ''Lesage was quickly able to capitalize on Lapalme's efforts . . .'': I am indebted to Maurice Sauvé for much of this material on the reforms of the Liberal Party under Lesage.

92   23   ''In December 1962, during the Diefenbaker minority . . . Lamontagne wrote for Pearson a strong speech . . .'': This speech and the difficulties he had with Pearson over a Quebec policy are described by Lamontagne in *Lester Pearson and the Dream of Unity*, by Peter Stursberg, a valuable oral history of the period.

92   30   Trudeau quote. Pierre Elliott Trudeau to the author, September 22, 1968.

93   24   Trudeau quote. From ''New Treason of the Intellectuals'' in *Cité libre*, April 1962. Translation taken from *Federalism and the French Canadians*, a collection of Trudeau's essays.

94   13   Trudeau quote. *Cité libre*, April 1963.

95   16   Trudeau quote. From ''Pelletier et Trudeau S'expliquent'' by Pierre Trudeau and Gérard Pelletier in *Cité libre*, October 1965.

95   26   Lévesque quote. René Lévesque to the author, October 21, 1981.

97   8   ''Marchand had never forgotten . . .'': Jean Marchand to the author, June 6, 1978.

98   31   Robertson quote. George Ignatieff to the author, March 19, 1978.

100   22   Trudeau quote. Pierre Elliott Trudeau to the author, September 22, 1978.

100   36   ''. . . a complex arrangement was worked out with . . . Lazarus Phillips . . .'': This arrangement was described to the author by Lazarus Phillips, June 8, 1978.

103   20   Davey quote. Keith Davey to the author, July 9, 1974.

103   30   O'Hagan quote. Richard O'Hagan to the author, February 23, 1979.

112   27   Marchand quote. Walter Gordon to the author, August 22, 1977.

113   6   Trudeau quote. Pierre Elliott Trudeau to the author, September 22, 1978.

113   15   Gordon quote. Walter Gordon to the author, August 22, 1977.

113   26   Alex Pelletier quote. Alex Pelletier to Sylvia Fraser, in the *Star Weekly*, June 29, 1968.

113   36   Carole Corbeil quote. In ''Don't Say It in English'', the *Globe and Mail*, March 29, 1980.

116   20   Walker quote. Frank Walker to the author, April 5, 1968.

117   9   Davey quote. Keith Davey to the author, July 9, 1974.

120   1   ''Within a few months of Trudeau's twin triumphs in 1968 . . .'':

Party standings in the House of Commons after the June 1968 federal election were: Liberals 155, Progressive Conservatives 72, NDP 22, Social Credit 14, and Independent 1.

120 34 Trudeau quote. Pierre Elliott Trudeau to the author, September 22, 1978.

122 6 "Above all, he encouraged the exercise in 'participatory democracy' . . .'': See Stephen Clarkson's chapter "Democracy in the Liberal Party'' in the fourth edition of Hugh G. Thorburn's *Party Politics in Canada*, the precursor of a book that will analyse the rise and fall of the participatory movement within the Liberal Party.

123 6 Trudeau quote. Pierre Elliott Trudeau to the author, September 22, 1978.

126 14 "He was unimpressed when . . . political scientists began to write that he had created a presidential office . . .'': See "Participatory Autocracy'' by Stephen Clarkson in *Canadian Forum,* December 1968, and "President and Parliament: The Transformation of Parliamentary Government in Canada'' by Denis Smith in *Apex of Power,* edited by Thomas Hockin.

127 2 Pickersgill quote. J. W. Pickersgill to the author, November 13, 1981.

127 13 Gordon quote. Walter Gordon to the author, April 12, 1977.

130 29 " 'If you had any sense you'd know it's horse shit . . .' '': I am indebted to Stephen Clarkson for this story; he heard it from an Ontario Liberal campaign worker in October 1972.

131 26 Trudeau quote. Pierre Elliott Trudeau to the author, June 1970.

PART 3: JAMES COUTTS AND THE POLITICS OF MANIPULATION

137 1 "The twenty-sixth of March . . . was not the kind of day James Coutts . . . enjoyed.'': Biographical material in this section is from several interviews with James Coutts, principally on July 9, 1974, June 28, 1977, September 10, 1977, and November 22, 1979, and from other interviews with many people over several years.

142 5 Davey quote. Keith Davey to the author, February 1963.

144 16 Canada Consulting quote. From a brochure printed and distributed by the Canada Consulting Group in 1970.

146 1 Coutts quote. James Coutts to the author, July 9, 1974.

146 16 ". . . Trudeau was returned shakily to office [in October 1972] . . .'': House of Commons party standings after the election of 1972 were: Liberals 109, Conservatives 107, NDP 31, Social Credit 15, Independent 2.

147 1 "Within hours . . . Jerry Grafstein and Gordon Dryden were on the phone to each other . . .'': The material on the Toronto group and the election of 1974 in this section is from interviews

with Grafstein (July 12, 1974) and Dryden (Sept. 13, 1977) and with Keith Davey (July 9, 1974), Dorothy Petrie (July 18, 1974), Eddie Rubin (June 28, 1974), Jerry Goodis (July 5, 1974), and James Coutts (July 9, 1974).

147   28   "Many such meetings were held over the next few weeks with a dozen people . . .": Kaplan, Roberts, and O'Connell were defeated Toronto MPs, Upper, Yankou, and Petrie were experienced Liberal activists; Abbott, Coutts's old friend from Calgary who by now had left an executive job at Brascan to operate a furniture-stripping business in Oakville, Ontario, was thinking of running in the next election; Kathy Robinson was a law student; and Floyd was a young aide to Robert Nixon, the Ontario Liberal leader.

149   25   "The Torontonians were furious . . .": The encounter between the Toronto Liberals and Pierre Trudeau was described to the author by Jerry Grafstein (July 12, 1974) and Keith Davey (July 9, 1974) and expanded on later in a conversation with Anthony Abbott (October 1, 1974).

150   9   Marchand quote. Jean Marchand to the author, June 6, 1978.

157   23   Callwood quotes. From "Margaret's First Hurrah" by June Callwood in *Maclean's* magazine, August 1974.

158   16   "On July 8, the party won a majority . . .": Party standings after the federal election of July 1974 were Liberals 141, Progressive Conservatives 95, NDP 16, Social Credit 11, Independent 1.

161   14   Edick quote. Gordon Edick to the author, August 17, 1977.

161   17   "To counteract Trudeau's tendency to treat party affairs . . . mechanically . . .": See "The Big Red Machine Is the Davey-mobile" by Christina Newman in the *Globe and Mail,* July 7, 1975.

162   35   "When the job of principal secretary . . . fell open . . . Davey . . . advised Trudeau to hire Jim Coutts . . .": The material in this section is from several interviews with Keith Davey (notably September 15, 1975, and November 4, 1976) and James Coutts (notably October 28, 1975, November 18, 1975, and September 10, 1977).

163   27   "The job of chief aide to Liberal prime ministers of Canada was a role that had been played by many men . . .": The way they played the role has been described in *The Things That Are Caesar's* by Arnold Heeney and *My Years With Louis St. Laurent* by J. W. Pickersgill.

165   35   Coutts quotes. James Coutts to the author, September 10, 1977.

167   7   "Coutts . . . carefully set about putting together his own team in the PMO . . .": Material in this section is from interviews with James Coutts (September 10, 1977), Brian Flemming (June 30, 1977, October 28, 1977), Tom Axworthy (February 23, 1978, November 9, 1978), Michel Rochon (June 28, 1977).

167   34   Axworthy quote. Tom Axworthy to the author, February 23, 1978.

PART 4: MICHAEL PITFIELD AND THE POLITICS OF
MISMANAGEMENT

179	4	"Pitfield was born in 1937 . . .": Biographical details are from several interviews with Michael Pitfield (on April 18, 1974; June 26, 1974; December 3, 1974 — by telephone while he was teaching at Harvard; February 23, 1979); with Grace Pitfield (October 26, 1974); and with Grattan O'Leary (April 17, 1974).
182	11	Pitfield quote. Michael Pitfield to the author, circa March 1960.
183	33	Samples quote. McCartney Samples to the author, circa May 1964.
191	15	"The original Ottawa mandarins — as members of the group that was dominant in the federal public service during those forty years came to be called . . .": The material on the Canadian public service in the period from the late 1920s to the late 1960s is drawn from scores of interviews conducted over a period of seventeen years by the author which resulted in several articles on this subject in *Maclean's, Saturday Night,* and the *Globe and Mail* and the chapter "Present at the Creation: C.D.'s Boys" in *The Canadian Establishment* by Peter C. Newman. Interviews particularly valuable for use here were conducted with John Baldwin, William Bennett, Robert Bryce, John Carson, Marshall Crowe, George Davidson, John Deutsch, George Ferguson, Douglas Fullerton, Allan Gotlieb, Alvin Hamilton, George Ignatieff, A. W. Johnson, William Lee, Douglas LePan, Michael McCabe, Maxwell Mackenzie, Bernard Ostry, Sylvia Ostry, Wynne Plumptre, Simon Reisman, and A. E. Ritchie. Books that touch on the subject are *The Things That Are Caesar's* by Arnold Heeney, *Hammer the Golden Day* by Hugh Keenleyside, *The Siren Years* and *Diplomatic Passport* by Charles Ritchie, *My Years With Louis St. Laurent* by J. W. Pickersgill, Douglas LePan's superb essay "Portrait of Norman Robertson" in *International Perspectives*, July/August 1978, and the book about Robertson by J. L. Granatstein, *A Man of Influence*. Professor Granatstein's eagerly awaited book on the mandarins, *The Ottawa Men*, was not available at the time of writing.
191	24	Connolly quote. John Connolly to the author, October 27, 1977.
192	16	"[King's] first step towards realizing this goal was to hire . . . O. D. Skelton . . .": King hired Skelton in part because he mistrusted an exceptionally able External Affairs officer named Loring Christie who had served under Robert Borden and Arthur Meighen, the Conservative prime ministers. Eventually King grew to respect Christie and much later appointed him Canadian minister to Washington. See *William Lyon Mackenzie King: A Political Biography* by MacGregor Dawson.
194	4	"The last of the 'great men' mandarins . . . was A. W. (Al) Johnson . . .": Johnson was part of what was called the Saskatchewan mafia, a group of public servants who had worked for the Saskatchewan government during the period when the CCF

was in power there, and who came to Ottawa in the 1960s after Ross Thatcher, the Liberal leader in Saskatchewan, was elected premier. They included, besides Johnson, T. K. Shoyama, Donald Tansley, Arthur Wakabayashi, and William Haney.

196   3   ". . . George Davidson . . . sent Lester Pearson a one-line note . . .": O. J. Firestone to the author, December 31, 1967.

197   7   Sharp quote. Simon Reisman to the author, June 24, 1974. Reisman, of course, took the job in the Department of Finance, and in the end he was worth a good deal more to the Department of Finance than $2400 a year. In 1970, he became its deputy, when salaries for that job were in the $50,000-a-year range. He took early retirement in 1975 at the age of fifty-five, with an annual pension of $30,000 indexed to the cost of living, to found a consulting business with another ex-deputy minister, James Grandy, who retired at the same time. Reisman and Grandy turned their knowledge of the government gargantua to such advantage for companies like Lockheed that the Prime Minister was compelled by Opposition protests belatedly to extend conflict-of-interest rules to cover retired senior civil servants.

198   18   Ritchie quote. From *The Siren Years* by Charles Ritchie, page 180.

200   27   Deutsch quote. John Deutsch to the author, December 11, 1973.

202   35   Reisman quote. Simon Reisman to the author, June 24, 1974.

204   30   Hamilton quote. Alvin Hamilton to the author, November 1975.

205   23   "Robertson . . . responded in horror . . . it was unthinkable . . .": Marshall Crowe to the author, April 23, 1974.

209   1   "Pitfield formally took part in the process of reforming the public service . . .": For articles on this reformation by some of the principals involved, see: A. W. Johnson, "Management Theory and Cabinet Government" in *Canadian Public Administration (CPA)* and "The Treasury Board of Canada and the Machinery of Government in the 1970's" in the *Canadian Journal of Political Science*; an article by Marc Lalonde, "The Changing Role of the Prime Minister's Office", in *CPA* in 1971; one by Michael Pitfield, "The Shape of Government in the 1980s: Techniques and Instruments for Policy Formulation at the Federal Level", in *CPA* in 1976; and an earlier article by Gordon Robertson, "The Changing Role of the Privy Council Office", in *CPA* of 1971. For another view of the way the rational-planning system worked, see Colin Campbell and George Szablowski's *The Super-Bureaucrats*.

210   26   "Bob Bryce . . . was not sure whether Maurice Lamontagne . . .": Robert Bryce in an interview with the author, November 21, 1981.

213   19   "This was a typical statement of the generally acrimonious attitude to Pitfield . . .": Most public servants interviewed for this section asked for anonymity; their numbers were many, their analysis of political-bureaucratic relationships frequently brilliant.

216	36	"These people also apparently had to be housed in expensive office towers . . .": For a description of the new generation of public servants of the 1970s, see *Nowhere to Go?* by Nichole Morgan, a study published by the Institute for Research on Public Policy.
219	27	Reisman quote. T. K. Shoyama to the author, November 22, 1979.
222	30	". . . Treasury Board which had been split off from the department and was now a central agency on its own . . .": For an explanation of the evolution and function of central agencies, see *The Super-Bureaucrats: Structure and Behaviour in Central Agencies*, by Colin Campbell and George J. Szablowski.
223	24	Reisman quote. Simon Reisman to the author, October 29, 1975.
224	10	"Jack Austin . . . had begun convening regular meetings of a group of economists . . .": Members of the Professional Economists Group, Office of the Prime Minister, who were popularly known as the "group of seven", were: Albert Breton and Thomas Wilson of the Institute for Policy Analysis, University of Toronto; Carl Beigie of the C. D. Howe Research Institute; Ben Gestrin of the Canadian Imperial Bank of Commerce; John Helliwell of the University of British Columbia; and Grant Reuber of the University of Western Ontario.
234	6	". . . economic officials . . . produced *The Way Ahead* . . .", in October 1976, a working paper based on the Utopian (Pitfieldian) hope of generating public discussion on what to do when controls were taken off.

PART 5: JOHN TURNER, MARC LALONDE, AND
THE CRISIS OF LIBERALISM

242	14	"Turner had grown up in the old Liberal establishment . . .": Biographical material in this section is from many interviews over several years with John Turner particularly those conducted on February 12, 1971, July 9, 1974, November 10, 1976, January 24, 1978, and May 8, 1979.
242	31	Turner quote. John Turner to the author, February 12, 1971.
243	5	Turner quotes. John Turner to the author, February 12, 1971.
243	28	Turner quote. For this quotation I am indebted to Ron Haggart and Val Sears, journalists who were students at UBC at the same time as John Turner.
245	32	Davey quote. Keith Davey to the author, February 20, 1971.
250	1	"As the crisis of Liberalism deepened . . . thoughtful Grits . . . began to reflect on Liberal history . . .": Apart from *The Government Party* by Reg. Whitaker, *The L-Shaped Party* by Joseph Wearing, and Peter Regenstreif's unpublished thesis, which have to do mainly with the organization of the Liberal Party, there is very little literature that has a direct bearing on the party's history other than the glimpses contained in the biographies of the

various Liberal leaders from Alexander Mackenzie to Louis St. Laurent, which are listed in the Bibliography and have been drawn on heavily for this section. I am also indebted to J. W. Pickersgill for a discussion of the party's history and for his book on Liberalism.

251   20   "Gradually . . . they drew together and began to use the word liberal as a synonym for reform.": Even so eminent a historian of the period as J. M. S. Careless is reluctant to specify a date when the word Liberal was first used to describe the party. Reformist was the predominant word in the early period of the party's beginnings before Confederation, although *libéral* was somewhat more common in French Canada. By the late 1870s it was the accepted word in English Canada, too; the change-over seemed to come in 1872 when the Quebec and Ontario reformers first united in the House of Commons under a single leader.

251   33   Dryden quote. Gordon Dryden to the author, September 13, 1977.

252   5   "Laurier proselytized that these goals could be reached . . .": Laurier's great speech on Liberalism was made at the Club Canadien in Quebec City in 1877. In it he based his definition of liberalism on the English model of religious toleration, gradual reform, and the freedom of the individual as the corner-stones of the philosophy. It was a speech much admired by Pierre Trudeau, as he said in an interview with the author on September 21, 1978.

254   31   "The elder Kings were model parents for a political leader.": For psychological insights into King's childhood I am indebted to *Knight of the Holy Spirit*, a fascinating study of Mackenzie King by Joy Esberey.

256   34   Pickersgill quote. J. W. Pickersgill to Peter C. Newman, circa 1967, from an undated transcribed interview in the author's possession.

258   13   "The business communities in both that city and Montreal . . .": For a thorough analysis of the relationship of business with the Liberal Party see *The Government Party: Organizing and Financing the Liberal Party of Canada 1930–58* by Reginald Whitaker.

259   24   "In brief, King dealt with Canada as though it were . . . a 'consociational democracy' . . .": For a discussion of consociationalism, see S. J. R. Noel's essay "Consociational Democracy and Canadian Federalism".

260   11   "How much of [King's] success was due to luck and how much to cunning will probably always be debated in Canada.": There are some signs of revisionism on Mackenzie King in the 1980s. C. P. Stacey, the dean of Canadian historians, speaks of him rather more favourably than he ever has before in the second volume of his *Canada and the Age of Conflict*, and H. S. Ferns, in a review of Joy Esberey's book on King, *Knight of the Holy*

Spirit, in *The Times Literary Supplement*, June 12, 1981, paid tribute to his acumen as an observer of social reality. Both historians had previously been tellingly critical of King, Stacey in *A Very Double Life* and Ferns in the book he co-authored with Bernard Ostry, *The Age of Mackenzie King*.

261   9   Griffin quote. A. G. S. Griffin in a letter to Peter C. Newman, January 9, 1973.

262   22   King quote. From *William Lyon Mackenzie King* by MacGregor Dawson, page 318.

262   29   "No one ever wrote King's political maxims down in a little red book . . .": Jack Pickersgill came close to contriving a "Sayings of Chairman King" in his short book *The Liberal Party*, published in 1962, which outlined the basic principles of Canadian Liberalism for the benefit of those striving to be elected that year. It was even bound in an orangey-red.

264   2   Pitfield quote. Michael Pitfield to the author, April 18, 1974.

264   18   "Western discontents with the federal government . . .": I am indebted to several Westerners for analyses of the response in the West to the Liberals' policies of the 1960s and 1970s, particularly Patrick McGeer (November 16, 1978), Tex Enemark (November 20, 1978), Gordon Gibson (November 17, 1978), and Nick Taylor (April 30, 1979). For a comprehensive analysis of the Liberals' situation in the region, see *Prairie Liberalism* and *The Regional Decline of a National Party*, both by David Smith.

265   25   Thatcher quote. Keith Davey to the author, July 9, 1974.

267   7   Granatstein quote. From *Mackenzie King: His Life and World* by J. L. Granatstein, p. 103.

267   22   "Walter Gordon's father . . . switched parties . . . in 1962.": Walter Gordon to the author, July 19, 1980.

267   38   McDougald quotes. Mr. and Mrs. J. A. McDougald to the author, June 9, 1974.

269   11   "In 1969, Edgar Benson . . . disturbed businessmen . . . with his White Paper on tax reforms . . .": The saga of federal tax reform had started in 1962 when John Diefenbaker appointed Kenneth Carter to head a royal commission on this question. The Carter Report, tabled in 1967, proposed a radical restructuring of the tax system with the prime objective being equity for all taxpayers: individuals and corporations, rich and poor, should bear an equitable share of the national tax burden. The Carter philosophy of a "buck is a buck" — however the buck was obtained — led to such proposed innovations as taxing all capital gains, taxing bequests and gifts in the same way as other income, and abolishing the mining industry's lavishly preferential treatment. *Proposals for Tax Reform*, the White Paper that Edgar Benson tabled in November 1969, went beyond these proposals to add a large tax increase. The White Paper proposals advocated a Robin Hood increase of the tax burden on the better-off individual taxpayers so as to lighten the load on the poorer:

three million would have to pay more tax enabling three million to pay less and 750,000 to escape paying any income tax. However, businessmen were going to suffer — by limitations on allowable expense account deductions (no conventions, no entertainment), by tax on all capital gains at full personal tax rates, by the withdrawal of give-away concessions to the mining industry, and by elimination of the favourable tax treatment of small corporations. The threatened closing of some loopholes and the more rigorous fiscal handling of small businesses managed — along with the tougher approach to middle and upper income tax brackets — to spark a revival of small businessmen as an angry, vocal, and ultimately powerful pressure group. Their organization of effective lobbying was helped by financial contributions from larger firms. The participation of business spokesmen in parliamentary committee hearings, through the media, and via informal channels was so effective that Bill C-259, which the Minister of Finance finally introduced on June 18, 1971, was no longer a proposal for a transformation of the tax system but merely a series of reforms to adjust the present one. The Act to amend the Income Tax Act which came into effect on January 1, 1972, did introduce a capital gains tax but only on fifty per cent of realized gains; tax rates on the higher income brackets were increased, but not drastically, while new tax exemptions were introduced (child-care expenses) and other deductions increased (RRSP contributions); businessmen's exemptions were tightened, depletion allowances reduced, small-business taxes increased, but all less dramatically than the White Paper had proposed. In sum, business critics, who had claimed the White Paper's suggested changes would retard economic growth, felt the new Act's impact on the economy would be neutral. Beyond this, in contrast to the original goal of increasing taxes on gifts and bequests, estate and gift taxes were removed, resulting in additional tax relief for wealthy individuals. The total size of this unanticipated tax windfall for the wealthy is estimated to have been $4.5 billion (in 1971 dollars). Carter's Report and Benson's White Paper had indeed been neutered. I am indebted to Professor John Bossons for access to his research and verification of many of these points.

270	25	Ross quote. Grattan O'Leary to the author, September 30, 1974.
272	3	". . . Marc Lalonde was a little boy on Ile Perrot . . .": Biographical material in this section from an interview with Marc Lalonde by the author and Stephen Clarkson, April 11, 1979, and several other interviews and conversations over a period of twenty years.
276	31	Lalonde quote. Marc Lalonde to the author, April 21, 1978.
277	7	Underhill quote. See *In Search of Canadian Liberalism* by Frank Underhill, page 218.
277	23	". . . the Manifesto of 1964, which [Lalonde] signed along with Trudeau and five others.": The five others were Albert

		Breton, Raymond Breton, Claude Bruneau, Yvon Gauthier, and Maurice Pinard.
279	2	Lalonde quote. Marc Lalonde in a discussion at the Liberal Party Policy Workshop, Toronto, March 25, 1977.
279	14	"As soon as [Lalonde] took up the role of principal secretary . . .": For Lalonde's view of that role, see "The Changing Role of the Prime Minister's Office", *Canadian Public Administration*, Vol. 14, No. 4, Winter 1971.
280	3	"Lalonde immediately fired off a stiff note to the writer . . . ": This exchange and the one that follows took place between Marc Lalonde and the author in September and October 1968.
282	3	"The events that followed — which came to be called the October Crisis . . .": The Byzantine complexities of that period are described at length in *Rumours of War* by Ron Haggart and Aubrey Golden and in the *Canadian Annual Review* for 1970, which contains an authoritative reconstruction of the crisis by John Saywell. Later, the findings of a three-year inquiry into the October Crisis, undertaken for the government of Quebec by Jean-François Duchaine, a lawyer, exonerated the Trudeauites of René Lévesque's charge that the federal government had exploited the crisis deliberately to discredit separatism. Ottawa, the report said, had acted on the basis of urgent requests from the Montreal Legal Department and the Quebec Provincial Police to the Quebec government of Robert Bourassa, who relayed them to Ottawa. The McDonald Commission, which investigated the role of the RCMP's Security Service in the October Crisis for the federal government, found that although the Security Service had been providing the federal government with intelligence on subversive organizations within Quebec, including the FLQ, it was not asked at the time of the crisis for its judgment whether a state of "apprehended insurrection" existed in the province. A month later, in November, Commissioner Higgitt was asked whether the War Measures Act needed to be continued and advised the government that, as far as the RCMP was concerned, special emergency powers were not needed. The Security Service continued its counter-espionage work against what it saw as the forces of subversion regardless of the government's formal emergency legislation. For these insights into the commission's findings, I am indebted to Professor Peter Russell, who acted as its research director.
283	25	Lalonde quotes. Marc Lalonde to Peter C. Newman and the author, October 23, 1970.
284	35	Anderson quote. David Anderson to the author, October 24, 1970.
285	13	Turner quote. John Turner to the author, February 12, 1971.
285	38	Davey quote. Keith Davey to the author, February 20, 1971.
287	11	"Jean Marchand . . . didn't agree.": Marchand's views on the Quebec Leader's role were given in an interview with the author, June 6, 1978.

287   25   "... there were ... expectations that he would be able to continue the reforms of the Quebec wing ... begun in the Pearson era.": For discussions of those reforms I am indebted particularly to Maurice Sauvé, John Payne, and Claude Frenette.

292   33   Lalonde quotes. Marc Lalonde to the author, April 21, 1978.

293   26   Pinard quotes. Yvon Pinard to the author, June 6, 1978.

294   22   Joyal quote. Serge Joyal to the author, April 21, 1978.

294   30   "Joyal remained scornful of 'Lalonde's chapel' ...": Joyal ran for mayor against Jean Drapeau in the Montreal municipal elections of 1978 and was defeated. He then returned to federal politics, running in the new riding of Maisonneuve-Hochelaga in 1979.

294   38   Lalonde quote. Marc Lalonde to the author and Stephen Clarkson, April 11, 1979.

295   21   Ouellet quote. Brian Mulroney to the author, April 18, 1978.

295   29   Lalonde quote. Lowell Murray to the author, November 26, 1977.

296   15   "The Liberals twice tried to neutralize Heward Grafftey ...": Described to the author by Heward Grafftey, June 5, 1978.

297   4   Mulroney quote. Brian Mulroney to the author, April 18, 1978.

299   19   "By 1979, nearly a quarter of the officer-category jobs were held by francophones.": Figures from the Commissioner of Official Languages, Annual Report, 1979, and the Public Service Commission of Canada, Annual Report, 1979.

300   6   "It was a minor revolution." And some felt it was basically misguided. The objective of the Official Languages Act of 1969 — and of the Trudeauites' bilingualism policy which it reflected — had been to ensure, as Pierre Trudeau said, "that both French- and English-speaking Canadians should be able to feel at home in all parts of this country, and that their rights as members of our major language groups should be respected by the federal government." But after a decade, the government's programs to carry out these objectives had engendered broad scepticism. Before Keith Spicer retired from his job as the country's first Commissioner of Official Languages in 1976, he had written in his fifth annual report that the language training program for civil servants should be phased out: after all the money spent on immersing them in the waters of francophonia, only eleven per cent of the anglophones in the federal civil service had attained a sufficiently high level of French to be able to use it effectively in their working lives. Spicer thought that it would take far longer than originally anticipated to produce a bilingual public service and that government funds should be spent instead on educating the young. Despite his clear misgivings, Spicer was completely in favour of the principle of making the federal public service bilingual. But other influential voices were raised against the idea itself in both English Canada and French Canada. Apart from the public scorn of the Parti Québécois, and the obstinate pressure of the Bourassa and Lévesque governments to make

French the sole official language of Quebec, such prominent Québécois social scientists as Hubert Guindon considered that Ottawa's obsession with coast-to-coast bilingualism in federal government service had completely missed the mark as a way to deal with Quebec's needs for cultural survival within its own borders.

301   2   Lalonde quote. Marc Lalonde to the author and Stephen Clarkson, April 11, 1979.

301   34   Victor-Lévy Beaulieu quote. From "Separation is a family fight" in the *Toronto Star*, January 5, 1978.

305   35   Davey quote. Keith Davey to the author, June 4, 1979.

310   19   "In 1979, Turner was already a member of nine corporate boards . . .": They included: Canadian Fund, Inc., Canadian Investment Fund (U.S.), Canadian Pacific Limited, Crédit Foncier Franco-Canadian, Crown Life Insurance, MacMillan Bloedel, Marathon Realty, Sandoz (Canada), and Wander Limited. In 1980, he added three more important board appointments to his credit: Bechtel Canada Limited, Massey-Ferguson Limited, and the Seagram Company Limited which gave him access to the biggest of the big-businessmen, Conrad Black of the Argus Corporation and the Bronfman family at Seagrams. In addition he sat on several non-corporate boards, notably the board of York University, where such businessmen as Roy Bennett of Ford, Fredrik S. Eaton of Eaton's, Sonja Bata of the shoe company, Allen T. Lambert of the T-D Bank, and Michael Koerner congregated. He was also connected with dozens of other corporate elite networks through his close friends Simon Reisman, who had been his deputy minister in the finance department and was now a consultant to business with his own Ottawa firm, and William Macdonald, another partner in McMillan, Binch, and a corporation tax expert.

314   24   "'Without us,' one forthright senator told an inquiring scholar . . .": This quotation and much useful documentation of the Senate's makeup and activities can be found in Colin Campbell's *The Canadian Senate*.

314   30   ". . . despite the full-time services of consultants and lobbyists hired to press their companies' cases . . .": In the late 1970s the Canadian Federation of Independent Business (which claimed to have reduced the annual tax burden on small business by more than $1 billion through its lobbying), the Canadian Manufacturers' Association, the Canadian Chamber of Commerce, and the Business Council on National Issues had combined staffs of 250 and spent over $10 million each year expressing the views of small, medium, and big business to ministers, policy-makers in the bureaucracies, and regulatory agencies, to Members of Parliament, the media, and the public. Observers estimated that another $100 million is spent by special-interest groups (like the Canadian Association of Broadcasters) or through individual lobbyists and consulting

firms like Reisman and Grandy Limited or Public Affairs International, the one headed by the two former deputy ministers, the other staffed by former executive assistants to Liberal cabinet ministers.

316   17   "[Wilder] believed the majority of the cabinet was in favour of his application.": On the pipeline decision Trudeau did overrule the views of the majority of his cabinet ministers. He preferred the advice of Marshall Crowe, who had been a senior policy adviser in his office, before moving on to head up first the Canada Development Corporation and then the National Energy Board, the government regulating agency responsible. Crowe was a tough, clever Westerner with thirty years' experience in government and business. Wilder's consortium included several giant international oil companies, among them Exxon and Shell, and Crowe saw its proposal's feasibility as suspect on many grounds, including projected costs and projected gas yields. Ironically, during the NEB hearings on the pipeline application, Crowe was challenged by several public interest groups as to his impartiality in the matter of the Mackenzie Pipeline on the basis that he had served as chairman of the Canada Development Corporation when it belonged to the Wilder consortium. Hearings had to be suspended for months while the case was reviewed in the Supreme Court of Canada. Eventually Crowe's role as chairman was disallowed for the course of the hearings, even though Bora Laskin, the Chief Justice, said there wasn't a shred of a suggestion that Crowe was biased. The suggestion that Crowe might be pro-Wilder was a joke in the oil-and-gas industry for months, since he was widely known for his resolutely unbiased High Mandarin attitudes. Shortly after taking part in the final decision on the Mackenzie Pipeline, Crowe left the government service to set up his own consulting firm.

317   3   Coutts quote. Jim Coutts to the author, June 28, 1977.

319   10   Flemming quote. Brian Flemming to the author and Stephen Clarkson in a long-distance telephone interview, July 22, 1979.

PART 6: THE POWER MACHINE AND
THE POLITICS OF DESPERATION

325   16   Coutts and Davey quote. Keith Davey to the author, June 4, 1979.

325   25   "They knew they were living in an era of leadership politics, at the pinnacle of . . . one of the most leader-dominated parties in the democratic world.": For a discussion of prime-ministerial power in Canada, see *Apex of Power: The Prime Minister and Political Leadership in Canada*, Second Edition, by Thomas Hockin.

326   1   Coutts quote. Tom Axworthy to the author, November 8, 1978.

326	13	Axworthy quote. Tom Axworthy to the author, November 8, 1978.

326 13 Axworthy quote. Tom Axworthy to the author, November 8, 1978.

327 27 Trudeau quote. Pierre Elliott Trudeau to Stephen Clarkson, February 23, 1979.

328 31 "Joan Patteson, the bank manager's wife . . . remembered . . .": Story told to the author by F. A. McGregor, King's former private secretary, circa November 1963. In *My Years With Louis St. Laurent*, Jack Pickersgill describes talking to Mackenzie King on the telephone the day before the 1949 election and taking Mr. St. Laurent to have tea with him a few days afterwards.

332 6 Gobeil quote. In "I Look Back and We Are Singing" by Madeleine Gobeil in the *Globe and Mail*, October 13, 1975.

334 4 Cook quote. Ramsay Cook in a letter to the author, March 27, 1981.

335 33 Trudeau quotes. Pierre Elliott Trudeau to the author, September 28, 1978.

336 29 "In the period just before the 1973 party convention . . . Gordon Dryden . . . had realized . . .": Story told to the author by Gordon Dryden, September 13, 1977.

338 26 Trudeau quote. Witnessed by the author, November 28, 1977.

339 10 O'Hagan quote. Richard O'Hagan to the author, May 12, 1979.

340 1 Davey quote. Keith Davey to the author, October 27, 1977.

341 28 Trudeau quote. In *Cité libre*, April 1963.

343 26 "[Lalonde] was the key figure in managing the largest bloc of sure Liberal votes in the country . . .": The Liberals had won a substantial majority in Quebec in every federal election since Wilfrid Laurier had first consolidated the vote there in 1896 with three notable exceptions: in 1911, when Laurier had suffered serious losses in his home province over his Imperial Naval Bill; in 1930, when Mackenzie King was buffeted in Quebec as elsewhere by the onset of the Depression; and in 1958, when John Diefenbaker, aided by Maurice Duplessis's electoral machine, had swept Quebec along with the rest of the country. In the election of 1921, Mackenzie King had won all 64 seats in Quebec.

344 11 "On paper [the Liberal Party] had been democratized.": For a discussion of changes in the power of the extra-parliamentary Liberal Party, see *The L-Shaped Party*.

344 27 ". . . the party was in essential ways no more powerful than it had been under King and St. Laurent. In fact, some political scientists argued that it was slightly less so . . .": Stephen Clarkson has suggested this in his chapter in Howard Penniman's *Canada at the Polls: The General Elections of 1979 and 1980*, a thesis that will be developed further in his future book on participatory democracy in the Liberal Party.

345 14 Grattan O'Leary quote. For this and many other perceptions of the nature of political power, I am greatly indebted to the late Senator Grattan O'Leary, who talked to me at length on three occasions in 1974, April 17, June 26, and July 9, describing his Ottawa experiences of more than sixty years.

345 34 "It had been repeatedly charged that Trudeau had wilfully 'presidentialized' the prime-ministership . . .": After the publication of Thomas Hockin's *Apex of Power*, these charges were repeated often by Conservative MPs. Their views were confirmed in November 1979 when Trudeau, in an exchange with students at the University of Montreal during his period as Opposition leader, was reported to have said in the Montreal *Gazette*, ". . . a presidential system of government like that of France might be best for Canada. . . . I can say that now, but if I had said it before resigning, people would say, 'Oh, now he wants to be President Trudeau. . . .'" Sinclair Stevens, Conservative member for York-Peel, had this statement read into the minutes of the House of Commons Standing Committee on Miscellaneous Estimates on November 4, 1980, when Trudeau was once again prime minister. Trudeau, who was appearing before the committee at the time, did not deny having made the remarks.

346 29 "Davey, by contrast, no longer saw Trudeau alone on a regular basis . . .": Keith Davey to author, June 4, 1979.

347 25 "Coutts had let the senior bureaucrats know immediately on his arrival in Ottawa . . .": On his response to the bureaucracy and its relationship with the party in power, Coutts had very definite ideas, which grew out of a report he had prepared for the Privy Council Office as a management consultant under contract in the early 1970s. It was described to the author in an interview on September 10, 1977.

349 4 Robertson quote. Repeated to the author by Sylvia Ostry, May 13, 1979.

349 30 Coutts quote to Eugene Forsey. Exchange described in "Eugene Forsey: unrevised, unrepentant, and now retired", by Jeffrey Simpson, in the *Globe and Mail*, May 30, 1979.

350 9 "They thought he had made the PMO into 'a walled-off Cathay . . .'": This quote on Cathay was read to the author, by an employee of the PMO who asked to be anonymous, as having been made by Richard Whalen, an aide to Richard Nixon when he was president of the United States, as a description of the White House that was analogous to the PMO's ambiance in 1978 and 1979.

351 1 Coutts quote. James Coutts to the author, September 10, 1977.

351 3 ". . . he had put together a team of Liberal professionals uncannily like the new frontiersmen Bobby Kennedy had recruited . . .": The literature on the Kennedys is vast and much of it was familiar reading to Keith Davey, Jim Coutts, Tom Axworthy, Colin Kenny, et alia. Of particular interest in this connection is "All the Bright Young Men", by Ward S. Just in *The Reporter*, August 16, 1962, and *The Making of the President, 1960* by Theodore White.

351 36 "Axworthy was Coutts's resident expert on Liberal history . . .": See "Innovation and the Political Party" by Thomas Axworthy. Unpublished M.A. thesis, Queen's University, 1972.

352	32	". . . an intensive study of the Kennedys' campaigning style as described in a book by their chief advance man, Jerry Bruno . . .": See *The Advance Man* by Jerry Bruno and Jeff Greenfield.
353	8	Conservative joke. Walter Baker, Progressive Conservative member for Grenville-Carleton quoted in "Ottawa Notebook", the *Globe and Mail*, January 22, 1979.
354	17	"Now [Davey] said he saw the party's role 'realistically' . . .": Keith Davey to the author, August 15, 1977.
357	18	". . . the whole question of appointments continued to make Davey uncomfortable . . .": The circumstances surrounding Davey's appointment to the Senate were described to the author by Walter L. Gordon, August 22, 1977, and Keith Davey, October 21, 1977. At the time Davey was appointed, nine other senators were named by Pearson, all of whom, with the exception of Norman MacKenzie, the president of the University of British Columbia from 1944 to 1962, were boisterously Liberal, a circumstance that caused considerable adverse comment from the Opposition and in the press, since Pearson was supposed to be practising "the new politics". For the changes that Pearson attempted to make in the distribution of patronage, see *The L-Shaped Party* by Joseph Wearing.
358	25	"There were something in excess of three hundred and fifty full-time appointments . . .": For information on the nature and the number of appointments available to the federal party in power, I am indebted to Jean Pigott, a former MP, who was made Senior Adviser for Human Resources in the Progressive Conservative government of Joe Clark, and who allowed me access to the lists of jobs she had compiled from material available in the Privy Council Office records when the Conservatives assumed office in 1979. Mrs. Pigott also discussed these lists at length on November 23, 1979.
361	33	Mulroney quote. Brian Mulroney to the author, April 10, 1979.
362	24	Mackasey quote. Lorna Marsden to the author, May 3, 1979.
364	28	Exchange between student and Trudeau. As reported in "PM Hustles For Support On Prairies", by Wayne Cheveldayoff, in the *Globe and Mail*, March 16, 1979. Exchange between Davey and Coutts. Keith Davey to the author, June 4, 1979.
365	6	Davey-Coutts exchange. Keith Davey to the author, June 4, 1979.
365	14	"Robinson was considered to be a factotum — as were the three other national directors who had succeeded Davey: Allan O'Brien, Torrance Wylie, and Blair Williams . . .": Allan O'Brien was national director from 1966 to 1969, Torrance Wylie from 1969 to 1972, Blair Williams from 1973 to 1975, and Gerry Robinson from 1975 to the autumn of 1978. For a brief period, Gordon Gibson replaced Robinson, having been appointed by Pierre Trudeau in December 1978, without consultation with either Coutts or Davey. Gibson was replaced as soon as the 1979 campaign began when he returned to British

Columbia to stand as a candidate in North Vancouver-Burnaby by Gordon Ashworth.

366   33   Davey quote. Keith Davey to the author, July 19, 1978.

368   4   "Goldfarb made the major part of his income . . .": Martin Goldfarb to the author, April 17, 1979.

370   15   ". . . the party elite, though that was a word they themselves would never use.": The dominance in most political parties by a small group has been described frequently by political theorists, notably in *Political Parties: Their Organization and Activity in the Modern State* by Maurice Duverger and *Political Parties: A Sociological Study of the Oligarchical Tendencies of Modern Democracy* by Robert Michels.

370   23   Davey quote. Keith Davey to the author, August 15, 1977.

370   30   "To win a majority of the available parliamentary seats in English Canada . . .": Colin Kenny to Stephen Clarkson, July 13, 1979.

371   23   Fullerton quote. Mimi Fullerton to the author October 17, 1977.

371   30   Smith quote. David Smith to the author, August 26, 1977.

372   3   Grafstein quoting William Shakespeare, *Henry V*, Act III. Jerry Grafstein to the author, June 5, 1979.

374   7   McDougald quote. J. A. McDougald to the author, June 9, 1974.

374   17   Grant quotes. Alison Grant Ignatieff to the author, January 22, 1982.

375   5   Vincent Massey quote. See *The Young Vincent Massey* by Claude Bissell, page 234.

377   36   Grafstein quote. Jerry Grafstein to the author, August 26, 1977.

380   16   Parasiuk quote. Wilson Parasiuk to the author, April 26, 1979.

380   34   Pickersgill quote. Jack Pickersgill to the author, November 13, 1981.

381   25   Munro and Hellyer quotes. Overheard by the author, April 17, 1982.

382   1   Sauvé quote. Jeanne Sauvé to the author, April 12, 1979.

382   24   Axworthy quote. Tom Axworthy to the author, October 26, 1977.

382   29   "These ideas also derived from Mackenzie King and his espousal of the Christian idealism of the early twentieth century . . .": I am indebted to David Biron, who is writing his doctoral thesis on this subject, for extending my perception of this aspect of King's early intellectual influence.

382   38   Trudeau quote. Speech delivered to the Liberal Party of Canada Convention, February 24, 1978, and transcribed by the Prime Minister's Office. Authorship by Coutts and Axworthy, described by Tom Axworthy to the author, February 24, 1978.

383   27   "[Careless] . . . once remarked that more than a century after 1867 . . .": Maurice Careless to David Trick, March 25, 1981.

384   1   Gregg quotes. Allan Gregg to the author, March 4, 1980.

385   22   Murray quotes. Lowell Murray to the author, November 9, 1978, and July 23, 1979.

387   29   Axworthy quote. Lloyd Axworthy to the author, July 18, 1979.

BIBLIOGRAPHY

The observer of the Liberal Party of Canada has two main sources of printed information apart from what is reported and analysed in the daily and monthly press. Biographies and memoirs of the chief protagonists give one impression of the human reality in the political game. The works of Canadian social scientists — historians and political scientists, economists and sociologists — present the same raw material in more theoretical and systematic frameworks. What follows is a list of books and articles in both categories that have been helpful in the research for this book.

Sheila McLeod Arnopoulos and Dominique Clift, *The English Fact in Quebec*. McGill-Queen's University Press, 1980.

Tom Axworthy, "Innovation and the Party System: An Examination of the Career of Walter L. Gordon and the Liberal Party". Unpublished M.A. thesis. Queen's University, 1970.

J. M. Beck, *Pendulum of Power: Canada's Federal Elections*. Prentice-Hall of Canada, 1968.

Carl Berger, *The Writing of Canadian History. Aspects of English-Canadian Historical Writing: 1900 to 1970*. Oxford University Press, 1976.

André Bernard, *What Does Quebec Want?* James Lorimer, 1978.

Michael Bliss, *A Canadian Millionaire: The Life and Times of Sir Joseph Flavelle, Bart. 1858–1939*. Macmillan of Canada, 1978.

John Bossons, "An Economic Overview of the Tax Reform Legislation", *Proceedings of the Twenty-third Tax Conference*. Canadian Tax Foundation, 1972, pp. 54–5.

Robert Bothwell and William Kilbourn, *C. D. Howe: A Biography*. McClelland and Stewart, 1979.

Ed Broadbent, *The Liberal Rip-Off: Trudeauism vs. The Politics of Equality*. New Press, 1971.

R. B. Byers and John Saywell, eds., *Canadian Annual Review of Politics and Public Affairs, 1978*. University of Toronto Press, 1980.

Dalton Camp, *Gentlemen, Players and Politicians*. McClelland and Stewart, 1970.

—, *Points of Departure*. Deneau and Greenberg, 1979.

Colin Campbell, *The Canadian Senate: A Lobby from Within*. Macmillan of Canada, 1978.

— and George J. Szablowski, *The Super-Bureaucrats: Structure and Behaviour in Central Agencies*. Macmillan of Canada, 1979.

J. M. S. Careless, *Brown of The Globe*. Vol. I: *The Voice of Upper Canada, 1818–1859*. Macmillan of Canada, 1959.

D. Owen Carrigan, *Canadian Party Platforms, 1867–1968*. Copp Clark, 1968.

W. Christian and C. Campbell, *Political Parties and Ideologies in Canada*. McGraw-Hill Ryerson, 1974.

Harold D. Clarke, Jane Jenson, Lawrence LeDuc, and Jon H. Pammett, *Political Choice in Canada*. McGraw-Hill Ryerson, 1979.

Stephen Clarkson, *City Lib: Parties and Reform*. Hakkert, 1972.

—, "Pierre Trudeau and the Liberal Party: The Jockey and the Horse", in Howard R. Penniman, ed., *Canada at the Polls: The General Election of 1974*. American Enterprise Institute, 1975.

—, "The Defeat of the Government, the Decline of the Liberal Party, and the (Temporary) Fall of Pierre Trudeau", in Howard R. Penniman, ed., *Canada at the Polls, 1979 and 1980: A Study of the General Elections*. American Enterprise Institute, 1981.

Wallace Clement, *The Canadian Corporate Elite: An Analysis of Economic Power*. McClelland and Stewart, 1975.

Paul-André Comeau, "La transformation du parti libéral québécois", *The Journal of Liberal Thought*, Vol. 2, No. 2, Spring 1966.

Ramsay Cook, *Canada and the French-Canadian Question*. Macmillan of Canada, 1966.

—, *The Maple Leaf Forever: Essays on Nationalism and Politics in Canada*. Macmillan of Canada, 1971.

John C. Courtney, ed., *Voting in Canada*. Prentice-Hall, 1967.

—, *The Selection of National Party Leaders in Canada*. Macmillan of Canada, 1973.

Donald Creighton, *John A. Macdonald: The Young Politician*. Macmillan of Canada, 1952.

————, *John A. Macdonald: The Old Chieftain*. Macmillan of Canada, 1955.

————, *Canada's First Century (1867–1967)*. Macmillan of Canada, 1970.

Richard H. S. Crossman, *The Myths of Cabinet Government*. Harvard University Press, 1972.

J. W. Dafoe, *Laurier: A Study in Canadian Politics*. Reprinted by McClelland and Stewart, 1963.

R. MacGregor Dawson, *William Lyon Mackenzie King: A Political Biography*. Vol. I: *1874–1923*. University of Toronto Press, 1958.

Peter Desbarats, *The State of Quebec: A Journalist's View of the Quiet Revolution*. McClelland and Stewart, 1965.

Arthur W. Donner and Douglas D. Peters, *The Monetarist Counter-Revolution: A Critique of Canadian Monetary Policy (1975–1979)*. James Lorimer, 1979.

Pierre Dupont, *How Lévesque Won: The Story of the P.Q.'s Stunning Election Victory*. James Lorimer, 1977.

Maurice Duverger, *Political Parties: Their Organization and Activity in the Modern State*. Methuen, 1954.

James Eayrs, *Greenpeace and Her Enemies*. Anansi, 1972.

F. C. Engelmann and M. A. Schwartz, *Political Parties and the Canadian Social Structure*. Prentice-Hall, 1967.

Joy E. Esberey, *Knight of the Holy Spirit: A Study of William Lyon Mackenzie King*. University of Toronto Press, 1980.

H. S. Ferns and B. Ostry, *The Age of Mackenzie King: The Rise of the Leader*. William Heinemann, 1955.

Frederick J. Fletcher, "The Mass Media in the 1974 Canadian Election", in Howard R. Penniman, ed., *Canada at the Polls: The General Election of 1974*. American Enterprise Institute, 1975.

Paul Fox, ed., *Politics: Canada*, 3rd ed. McGraw-Hill Ryerson, 1970.

Blair Fraser, *The Search for Identity: Canada, 1945–1967*. Doubleday Canada, 1967.

Richard French, *How Ottawa Decides: Planning and Industrial Policy-Making (1968–1980)*. James Lorimer, 1980.

G. P. deT. Glazebrook, *A History of Canadian Political Thought*. McClelland and Stewart, 1966.

Walter L. Gordon, *A Choice for Canada: Independence or Colonial Status*. McClelland and Stewart, 1966.

————, *Storm Signals: New Economic Policies for Canada*. McClelland and Stewart, 1975.

————, *A Political Memoir*. McClelland and Stewart, 1977.

Government of Canada, *Final Report of the Royal Commission on Canada's Economic Prospects* (The Gordon Report). Ottawa, 1958.

J. L. Granatstein. *The Politics of Survival: The Conservative Party of Canada, 1939–1945*. University of Toronto Press, 1967.

————, *Canada's War: The Politics of the Mackenzie King Government, 1939–1945*. Oxford, 1975.

————, *Mackenzie King: His Life and World*. McGraw-Hill Ryerson, 1977.

Dennis Guest, *The Emergence of Social Security in Canada*. University of British Columbia Press, 1980.

Hubert Guindon, "Two Cultures: An Essay on Nationalism, Class and Ethnic Tension in Contemporary Canada", in Orest M. Kruhlak et al., eds., *The Canadian Political Process: A Reader*. Holt, Rinehart & Winston, 1970.

————, "The Modernization of Quebec and the Legitimacy of the Canadian State", in Daniel Glenday et al., eds., *Modernization and the Canadian State*, Macmillan of Canada, 1978.

Richard Gwyn, *Smallwood: The Unlikely Revolutionary*, rev. ed. McClelland and Stewart, 1972.

————, edited by Sandra Gwyn, *The Northern Magus: Pierre Trudeau and Canadians*. McClelland and Stewart, 1980.

Ron Haggart and Aubrey E. Golden, *Rumours of War*. New Press, 1971.

John D. Harbron, *This Is Trudeau*. Longmans Canada, 1968.

Douglas Hartle, *The Expenditure Budget Process in the Government of Canada*. Canadian Tax Foundation, 1978.

Arnold Heeney, *The Things That Are Caesar's: Memoirs of a Canadian Public Servant*. University of Toronto Press, 1972.

John Hellman, *Emmanuel Mounier and the New Catholic Left, 1930–1950*. University of Toronto Press, 1981.

Thomas A. Hockin, ed., *Apex of Power: The Prime Minister and Political Leadership in Canada*, 2nd ed. Prentice-Hall of Canada, 1977.

J. E. Hodgetts, "The Civil Service and Policy Formation", *Canadian Journal of Economics and Political Science*, Vol. 23, No. 4, November 1957.

————, *The Canadian Public Service: A Physiology of Government (1867-1970)*. University of Toronto Press, 1973.

John W. Holmes, *The Shaping of Peace: Canada and the Search for World Order*. Vol. I: *1943-1957*. University of Toronto Press, 1979.

Michiel Horn, *The League for Social Reconstruction*. University of Toronto Press, 1980.

Gad Horowitz, "Conservatism, Liberalism, and Socialism in Canada: An Interpretation", *Canadian Journal of Economics and Political Science*, Vol. 32, No. 2, 1966.

David L. Humphreys. *Joe Clark: A Portrait*. Deneau and Greenberg, 1978.

Bruce Hutchison, *The Incredible Canadian. A Candid Portrait of Mackenzie King: His Works, His Times, and His Nation*. Longmans, Green, 1952.

————, *Mr. Prime Minister, 1867-1964*. Longmans Canada, 1964.

————, *The Far Side of the Street*. Macmillan of Canada, 1976.

A. W. Johnson, "Management Theory and Cabinet Government", *Canadian Public Administration*, Vol. 14, 1971.

————, "The Treasury Board of Canada and the Machinery of Government of the 1970's", *Canadian Journal of Political Science*, Vol. 4, 1971.

Hugh Keenleyside, *Hammer the Golden Day*. McClelland and Stewart, 1981.

Marc Lalonde, "The Changing Role of the Prime Minister's Office", *Canadian Public Administration*, Vol. 14, No. 4, Winter 1971.

Judy LaMarsh, *Memoirs of a Bird in a Gilded Cage*. McClelland and Stewart, 1969.

Allen Thomas Lambert, *Report of the Royal Commission on Financial Management and Accountability*. Canadian Government Publishing Centre, 1979.

Brian Land, *Eglinton: The Election Study of a Federal Constituency.* Peter Martin Associates, 1965.

James Laxer and Robert Laxer, *The Liberal Idea of Canada.* James Lorimer, 1977

Lawrence LeDuc, Jr., "The Leadership Selection Process in Canadian Political Parties: A Case Study". Ph.D. thesis. University of Michigan, 1970.

A. J. Little, *The Story of The Firm, 1864–1964: Clarkson, Gordon & Co.* University of Toronto Press, 1964.

Donald C. MacDonald, ed., *Government and Politics of Ontario.* Macmillan of Canada, 1975.

Jim McDonald and Jack MacDonald, eds., *The Canadian Voter's Guidebook.* Fitzhenry and Whiteside, 1972.

F. A. McGregor, *The Fall & Rise of Mackenzie King: 1911–1919.* Macmillan of Canada, 1962.

Neil McKenty, *Mitch Hepburn.* McClelland and Stewart, 1967.

John T. McLeod, "Party Structure and Party Reform", in Abraham Rotstein, ed., *Prospect of Change: Proposals for Canada's Future.* McGraw-Hill, 1965.

John McMenemy and Conrad Winn, *Political Parties in Canada.* McGraw-Hill Ryerson, 1976.

Kenneth D. McRae, ed., *Consociational Democracy: Political Accommodation in Segmented Societies.* McClelland and Stewart, 1974.

Edward McWhinney, *Quebec and the Constitution (1960–1978).* University of Toronto Press, 1979.

Jonathan Manthorpe, *The Power and the Tories: Ontario Politics, 1943 to the Present.* Macmillan of Canada, 1974.

Lorna R. Marsden and Edward B. Harvey, *Fragile Federation: Social Change in Canada.* McGraw-Hill Ryerson, 1979.

Vincent Massey, *What's Past Is Prologue.* Macmillan of Canada, 1963.

John Meisel, *The Canadian General Election of 1957.* University of Toronto Press, 1962.

————, ed., *Papers on the 1962 Election.* University of Toronto Press, 1964.

————, *Working Papers on Canadian Politics.* McGill-Queen's University Press, 1972.

Robert Michels, *Political Parties: A Sociological Study of the Oligarchical Tendencies of Modern Democracy.* Dover, 1959.

Henry Milner, *Politics in the New Quebec.* McClelland and Stewart, 1978.

Denis Monière, *Le Développement des idéologies au Québec: Des origines à nos jours.* Editions Québec/Amérique, 1977.

John A. Munro and Alex I. Inglis, eds., *Mike: The Memoirs of the Right Honourable Lester B. Pearson.* Vol. II: *1948–1957* and Vol. III: *1957–1968.* University of Toronto Press, 1973 and 1975.

H. Blair Neatby, *William Lyon Mackenzie King.* Vol. II: *1924–1932.* University of Toronto Press, 1963.

————, *Laurier and a Liberal Quebec: A Study in Political Management.* McClelland and Stewart, 1973.

Peter C. Newman, *Renegade in Power: The Diefenbaker Years.* McClelland and Stewart, 1963.

————, *The Distemper of Our Times.* McClelland and Stewart, 1968.

————, *The Canadian Establishment.* McClelland and Stewart, 1975.

S. J. R. Noel, "Consociational Democracy and Canadian Federalism", *Canadian Journal of Political Science*, Vol. IV, No. 1, 1971.

————, "Leadership and Clientelism", in David J. Bellamy et al., eds., *The Provincial Political System: Comparative Essays.* Methuen, 1976.

————, "Political Parties and Elite Accommodation: Interpretations of Canadian Federalism", in J. Peter Meekison, ed., *Canadian Federalism, Myth or Reality.* Methuen, 1977.

Grattan O'Leary, *Recollections of People, Press and Politics.* Macmillan of Canada, 1977.

Dennis Olsen, *The State Elite.* McClelland and Stewart, 1950.

Khayyam Z. Paltiel and Jean Brown Van Loon, "Financing the Liberal Party, 1961–1965", in Committee on Election Expenses, *Studies in Canadian Party Finance.* Queen's Printer, 1966.

Khayyam Zev Paltiel, *Political Party Financing in Canada.* McGraw-Hill, 1970.

Donald Peacock, *Journey to Power: The Story of a Canadian Election.* The Ryerson Press, 1968.

Lester B. Pearson, *Mike: The Memoirs of the Right Honourable Lester B. Pearson.* Vol. I: *1897–1948.* University of Toronto Press, 1972.

Jean Pellerin, *Le phénomène Trudeau.* Editions Seghers, 1972.

Gérard Pelletier, *The October Crisis.* McClelland and Stewart, 1971.

George C. Perlin, *The Tory Syndrome: Leadership Politics in the Progressive Conservative Party.* McGill-Queen's University Press, 1980.

J. W. Pickersgill, ed., *The Mackenzie King Record.* Vol. I: *1939–1944.* University of Toronto Press, 1960.

————, *The Liberal Party.* McClelland and Stewart, 1962.

———— and D. F. Forster, eds., *The Mackenzie King Record.* Vol. II: *1944–1945,* Vol. III: *1945–1946,* Vol. IV: *1947–1948.* University of Toronto Press, 1968, 1970, and 1970.

————, *My Years with Louis St. Laurent: A Political Memoir.* University of Toronto Press, 1975.

Michael Pitfield, "The Shape of Government in the 1980s: Techniques and Instruments for Policy Formulation at the Federal Level", *Canadian Public Administration,* Vol. 19, 1976.

John Porter, *The Vertical Mosaic: An Analysis of Social Class and Power in Canada.* University of Toronto Press, 1965.

Dale Posgate and Kenneth McRoberts, *Quebec: Social Change and Political Crisis,* 2nd ed. McClelland and Stewart, 1980.

Robert Presthus, *Elite Accommodation in Canadian Politics.* Macmillan of Canada, 1973.

Herbert F. Quinn, *The Union Nationale: A Study in Quebec Nationalism.* University of Toronto Press, 1963.

George Radwanski, *Trudeau.* Macmillan of Canada, 1978.

Peter Regenstreif, "The Liberal Party of Canada: A Political Analysis". Unpublished Ph.D. Thesis. Cornell University, 1963.

————, *The Diefenbaker Interlude. Parties and Voting in Canada: An Interpretation.* Longmans, 1965.

John Richards and Larry Pratt, *Prairie Capitalism: Power and Influence in the New West.* McClelland and Stewart, 1979.

Charles Ritchie, *The Siren Years.* Macmillan of Canada, 1973.

Gordon Robertson, "The Changing Role of the Privy Council Office", *Canadian Public Administration,* Vol. 14, 1971.

Claude Savoie, *Les Crises de Pierre Elliott Trudeau.* Guérin, 1979.

John T. Saywell, ed., *The Canadian Annual Review for 1960 . . . 1970.* University of Toronto Press, 1961 . . . 1971.

———, ed., *Canadian Annual Review of Politics and Public Affairs, 1971 . . . 1977.* University of Toronto Press, 1972 . . . 1978.

———, *The Rise of the Parti Québécois, 1967–76.* University of Toronto Press, 1977.

Joseph Schull, *Laurier: The First Canadian.* Macmillan of Canada, 1965.

———, *Edward Blake: The Man of the Other Way (1833–1881).* Macmillan of Canada, 1975.

———, *Edward Blake: Leader and Exile (1891–1912).* Macmillan of Canada, 1976.

———, *The Great Scot: A Biography of Donald Gordon.* McGill-Queen's University Press, 1979.

Jeffrey Simpson, *Discipline of Power: The Conservative Interlude and the Liberal Restoration.* Personal Library, 1980.

Oscar Douglas Skelton, *Life and Letters of Sir Wilfrid Laurier.* Vol. I: *1841–1896.* Oxford University Press, 1921. Reprinted by McClelland and Stewart, 1965.

Richard Simeon, *Federal-Provincial Diplomacy: The Making of Recent Policy in Canada.* University of Toronto Press, 1972.

D. V. Smiley, *Canada in Question: Federalism in the Seventies.* McGraw-Hill Ryerson, 1972.

David E. Smith, *Prairie Liberalism: The Liberal Party in Saskatchewan (1905–1971).* University of Toronto Press, 1975.

———, *The Regional Decline of a National Party: Liberals on the Prairies.* University of Toronto Press, 1981.

Denis Smith, *Gentle Patriot: A Political Biography of Walter Gordon.* Hurtig, 1973.

C. P. Stacey, *A Very Double Life: The Private World of Mackenzie King.* Macmillan of Canada, 1976.

Richard J. Stanbury, *Liberal Party of Canada: An Interpretation.* Mimeo. Ottawa, June 15, 1969.

Douglas Steubing with John Marshall and Gary Oakes, *Trudeau: A Man for Tomorrow.* Clarke, Irwin, 1968.

Geoffrey Stevens, *Stanfield.* McClelland and Stewart, 1975.

Walter Stewart, *Shrug: Trudeau in Power*. New Press, 1971.

_____, *Divide and Con: Canadian Politics at Work*. New Press, 1973.

Peter Stursberg, *Lester Pearson and the Dream of Unity*. Doubleday Canada, 1978.

L. G. Thomas, *The Liberal Party in Alberta: A History of Politics in the Province of Alberta, 1905–1921*. University of Toronto Press, 1959.

Dale C. Thomson, *Alexander Mackenzie: Clear Grit*. Macmillan of Canada, 1960.

_____, *Louis St. Laurent: Canadian*. Macmillan of Canada, 1967.

Hugh G. Thorburn, ed., *Party Politics in Canada*, 4th ed. Prentice-Hall of Canada, 1978.

Bruce Thordarson, *Trudeau and Foreign Policy: A Study in Decision-Making*. Oxford University Press, 1972.

Lionel Tiger, *Men in Groups*. Thomas Nelson & Sons, Ltd., 1969.

Warner Troyer, *200 Days: Joe Clark in Power*. Personal Library, 1980.

Pierre Elliott Trudeau, *Federalism and the French Canadians*. Macmillan of Canada, 1968.

_____, *Approaches to Politics*, trans. I. M. Owen. Oxford University Press, 1970.

_____, *Conversations with Canadians*. University of Toronto Press, 1972.

_____, ed., *The Asbestos Strike*, trans. James Boake. James, Lewis and Samuel, 1974.

Frank H. Underhill, *In Search of Canadian Liberalism*. Macmillan of Canada, 1961.

Pierre Vallières, *The Assassination of Pierre Laporte: Behind the October '70 Scenario*. James Lorimer, 1977.

Norman Ward, "The Liberals in Convention", *Queen's Quarterly*, Vol. 65, No. 1, 1958.

_____, ed., *A Party Politician: The Memoirs of Chubby Power*. Macmillan of Canada, 1966.

Joseph Wearing, *The L-Shaped Party: The Liberal Party of Canada 1958–1980*. McGraw-Hill Ryerson, 1980.

INDEX

Page numbers for Notes are in italics.

97, 281, 288. *See also* Marchand, Jean;
Pelletier, Gérard; Trudeau, Pierre Elliott
Tolmie, Ross, 193
Toronto Daily Star, 35, 258. See also *Star*
(Toronto); *Toronto Star*
Toronto Star, 48, 111, 145, 283, 316, 317,
319, 333. See also *Star* (Toronto);
Toronto Daily Star
Toronto *Telegram*, 8, 56, 62
Towers, Graham, 76, 193, 195, 205
Town, Harold, 116
Tremblay, René, 94
Trick, David, *456*
Trotter, James, 15, 373
Trudeau, Charles, 67, 85, 329
Trudeau, Charles-Emile (Charlie), 63,
65–8, 70, 159, *438*
Trudeau, Grace (Elliott), 65, 66–7, 68,
70, 84–5, 329
Trudeau, Margaret (Sinclair), 54, 56, 132,
133, 138, 156, 157–8, 162, 170, 173,
188, 311, 328, 332, 335, 387, 389, *439*
Trudeau, Pierre Elliott
—and English Canada, 53, 56, 78, 116,
125, 149–50, 155–6, 170–2, 234, 271,
278, 304, 305–6, 309, 325, 333, 337,
386
—federalism and national unity, 57, 60,
62, 78, 83, 93, 94, 116, 172–3, 271,
277, 280, 302, 304–6, 320, 340, 341,
342, 385. *See also* Quebec federalists;
Quebec separatism
—interviewed, *439, 440, 441, 446, 453,
454*
—in Ottawa (before 1968), 59, 75–8, 101,
103–4, 105–6, 186, 245, 247
—relations with media, 56–8, 60–1, 116,
123, 154, 162, 168, 169, 171, 172, 173,
279–80, 325, 327, 339–40, 346, *436*
—studies of, *437–8*
—writings by, *439, 440*
BACKGROUND AND PERSONALITY:
—accused of homosexuality, 113–14
—arrogance, 131, 133–4, 156, 171, 236,
302, 309, 325, 327, 328, 355–6, 364,
387, 389
—childhood and education, 63–75, 278,
438–9
—eccentricities ("style"), 55, 58, 60,
69–70, 73, 74, 86, 106, 113
—elitism, 117, 133, 159, 162, 174, 345
—"Frenchness" of, 53, 58–61, 62–3,
68–70, 78, 133, 156, 234, 299, 385
—as intellectual, 55, 58, 59–61, 72–5,
82, 84, 103, 105, 116, 126, 133, 151,

156, 189, 309, 311, 329, 330, 333–4,
348, 364, *439*
—marriage and children, 54, 156, 157,
170, 173, 174, 300, 318, 328, 329,
330, 332, 333, 335, 339, 387, *439*.
See also Trudeau, Margaret (Sinclair)
—"myth" surrounding, 60, 62, 68,
71–2, 73, 78, 84, 85–6, 106, 107, 116,
173, *437*
—as "outsider", 53, 55, 58–61, 87, 311,
325, *437*
—philosophical and religious beliefs, 59,
68, 72, 79–80, 82–3, 115, 227, *439*
—self-discipline, 69–70, 71–2, 74, 84,
106, 133
—shyness, 85–6, 102, 103, 117, 125,
132
—social life, 60, 85–7, 103, 113–14,
132–3, 188–9, 330–3
—wealth, 70, 73–4, 85, 171, 278, 311,
387
AND LIBERAL PARTY:
—criticizes Pearson, 94, 104, 149, 341
—and English-Canadian Liberals, 53–5,
58, 102, 109–10, 117, 125, 148, 150,
158, 161, 172, 230, 241, 309, 320–1,
326, 333, 336, 347, 385, *442*
—joins party (1965), 55, 87, 88, 95–6,
100, 149, 278
—leadership campaign (1968), 106–10,
112–16, 186, 278, 280, 288
—and party politics, ix–x, 53, 105,
117–19, 120–3, 125–6, 129–30,
151–60, 162, 172, 241, 271, 318–19,
335–41, 347, 354–5, 364
—and Quebec Liberals, 53, 102, 104,
115, 154–5, 158, 167–8, 277–8,
287–9, 301–2, 325. *See also* Quebec
federalists
AS PRIME MINISTER:
—accused of sellout, 133, 187, 281, 301,
333
—cabinets, 54, 121, 150, 170, 172, 299
—constitutional reform, 54, 107, 133,
189, 209, 303, 304, 320, 327, 389
—economic policy, 169, 171, 222,
226–38, 269, 311–13, *447–8*
—New Year's Eve interview (1975), 169,
233, 312
—in October Crisis. *See* October Crisis
—and Pitfield. *See* Pitfield, Michael, and
Trudeau
—policies, 112, 133–4, 152, 155, 209,
210, 214, 222, 327, 341. *See also*
Trudeau: constitutional reform;